Chicago's
Most Wanted

Chicago's
Most Wanted

The Top 10 Book of Murderous Mobsters, Midway Monsters, and Windy City Oddities

Laura Enright

Potomac Books, Inc.
Washington, D.C.

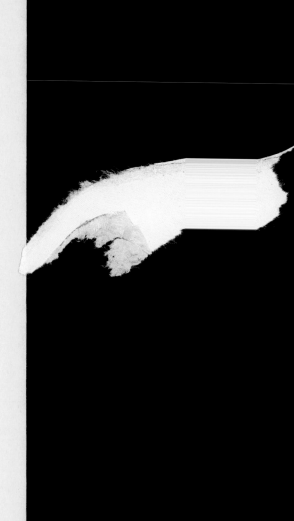

Published in the United States by Potomac Books, Inc.
(formerly Brassey's, Inc.).

Library of Congress Cataloging-in-Publication Data

Enright, Laura, 1964–
    Chicago's most wanted : the top 10 book of
murderous mobsters, midway monsters, and windy
city oddities / Laura Enright.
        p. cm.—(Most wanted)
    Includes bibliographical references and index.
    ISBN 1-57488-785-8 (pbk. : alk. paper)
    1. City and town life—Illinois—Chicago—
Miscellanea.   2. Legends—Illinois—Chicago.
    3. Chicago (Ill.)—History—Miscellanea.
    4. Chicago (Ill.)—Biography—Miscellanea.
    5. Chicago (Ill.)—Social life and customs—
Miscellanea.   I. Title.   II. Series.
F548.36.E57 2005
977.3'1104'0922—dc22   2004027615
                (alk. paper)

Printed in Canada on acid-free paper that
meets the American National Standards
Institute Z39-48 Standard.

Potomac Books, Inc.
22841 Quicksilver Drive
Dulles, Virginia 20166

First Edition

10 9 8 7 6 5 4 3 2 1

Contents

Illustrations

Acknowledgments

I owe a huge debt of thanks to the ever-patient Don Jacobs and the folks at Potomac Books who gave me this chance and helped me along. And to Stu Shea who hooked me up with Potomac Books, as well as Diana Bucko who helped me with all the nitty gritty. And to my friends at the Park Ridge Library.

I'd also like to thank Eric McCreary for being the greatest nephew an aunt could ask for.

Introduction

Chicago is a city that, when told it couldn't do something, went ahead and did it anyway. One of the most beautiful and powerful cities in the world was built on a swamp but never succumbed to it. In its early years, it was the fastest-growing city in the world, the prodigy of the Midwest outdoing its sibling cities, some of them even older than Chicago. Far from a toddling town, it was, and is, a charging town, meeting challenges head-on, losing big and winning bigger. It drew to it and eventually began to breed inspired thinkers whose inventions, innovations, and philosophies helped it plow forward against all odds. What one comes away with when reading about Chicago is its sense of duality: State Street finesse bleeding into Stockyard brutality. Its remarkable elegance always seems overshadowed by a raw unpredictability. Chicago's a stout being, strong and determined with a touch of stubbornness but just as much charm, humor, and honesty. Chicago approaches challenges like grand adventures, either winning the day or, as in the case of her sports teams, shrugging and saying, "Well, there's always next year."

The choices I've made in the following lists don't necessarily have statistical backup. My goal was to dig up some

hidden historical gems to go along with the better-known aspects of the city in hopes of inspiring the reader to dig further. The biography of Chicago is rich with fascinating
places, people, and events, and I've touched on only a small
number.

Titans of the Town

C hicago rose to unexpected prominence in a relatively short period of time. Four main industries helped this along: The grain, lumber, meatpacking, and mail-order trades. Many of the following people found themselves in the right place at the right time and through determination and hard work, founded empires. The curious thing about these early titans is how, once they gained their fortunes, they became very paternalistic to the city that had been so lucrative for them. Some practiced a form of tough love that didn't sit well with the recipients.

1. KING OF CHICAGO

He was a dour workaholic who was born in 1834 in Massachusetts and grew to become one of the richest men in the world. Leaving the family farm at age seventeen, Marshall Field worked for twelve hours a day, six days a week for five years as a clerk in a dry goods store in Pittsville, Massachusetts. When he came to Chicago in 1856 he found a quagmire downtown that kept women from shopping. As a salesman for Cooly Wadsworth he was so well liked by his bosses they lent him money to buy a junior partnership in the business. Five years later, he was doing business with Levi Leiter and Potter Palmer, who served as the perfect mentors. Remembering his first observation of the town,

Field worked at creating an environment for the female shopper. When Palmer retired in 1868, he helped Field and Leiter open a store of their own on State Street. It was a huge, opulent affair of white marble that sold the finest and often exotic goods. Field had learned much from his time with Palmer. The clerks would be well groomed, respectful, and attentive. When Field, Leiter and Company opened on October 12, 1868, a huge crowd of people waited outside. The night of October 8, 1871, Field and his employees spent hours removing as much stock as possible before the Chicago Fire forced them to evacuate the store. Two weeks later, he was back in business in an abandoned horse barn on the South Side while a new store was built on Market and Madison. A second grand opening was held for the new Field, Leiter and Company on April 25, 1872, but sales were low. It lacked the glamour of the first store. Purchasing parcels of land on State Street, he relocated the store back to the site of its former success in a building even grander than the first. In the meantime, he amassed a real-estate fortune that would eventually be worth $23 million.

He also invested in the coal, iron, and steel industries. In 1880, he bought out Leiter and a year later, the name of the largest retail store in the world was changed to Marshall Field and Company. It stretched from State Street to Wabash Avenue. It had a medical dispensary and post office, and when Field discovered that women were leaving the store for lunch, he added a tearoom that would expand to an entire floor of fancy restaurants. Later would come a nursery, writing rooms, a library, and even meeting rooms for civic organizations. Occasionally a charitable man, he donated money to the University of Chicago, and founded The Field Museum with a $1 million grant. But he was also a stern and fiercely antilabor man, who fired any employee fraternizing with a labor union. He had a rigid code of conduct for his employees, expecting them to refrain from drink or gambling even on personal time. By 1895, he was one of the richest men in the country. In 1906, however, perhaps worn out from a life of hard work and little else, Marshall Field fell victim to pneumonia and died. A bell rang through State Street announcing the news. Most of his $120 million fortune went to his grandchildren. Control of the company went to John G. Shedd, who had risen in the ranks of the company to become president. The Field name moved on from retail to making a mark in publishing, the arts, and charitable works. In honor of Marshall Field, on the day of his funeral in 1906 all the stores on State Street closed. It's very likely he would have suggested they stay open.

2. THE MERCHANT PRINCE

After conquering the merchant trade, Potter Palmer began a second successful career in real estate. Potter was born in New York in 1826, descended from Quakers. A few states away, Chicago was little more than a frontier town. The two would form a symbiotic relationship. After a stint at a general store when he was eighteen, Potter opened his own store, then shifted his territory from New York to Chicago, opening a dry goods store in 1852. Located on Lake Street, P. Palmer and Company prospered and in 1856 he promoted his assistant, Marshall Field, to head salesman. The key to Palmer's merchant success, one that Field and his partner Levi Leiter continued to follow, was an unwavering show of respect for the customer, especially women customers. Prior to Palmer, the filthy conditions of the muddy streets kept women from downtown. They were also discouraged from doing business unescorted.

Palmer had a goal. He foresaw clean sidewalks, spacious stores with magnificent show windows, and women feeling relaxed enough to browse around within. He schmoozed with them, remembering their tastes, insisting that his staff show the same courtesy. The customer was always right. He sold exotic merchandise, pleasing to the eye, and was the first merchant in the city to advertise in newspapers. He ran sale days, and issued receipts with purchase so that, should consumers decide they didn't want the item, they could return it.

To compete, the other merchants in town had to follow suit. Palmer also delivered goods to the home, free of charge. As his status as a merchant grew, he began to buy up real estate, especially on State Street, which he dreamed of making a strip of commerce for the city. In 1868, the building known as "Palmer's Palace" was built. Located at the corner of State and Washington Streets, the store was six stories high, with marble facing and Corinthian columns, and had been built to house the business of his former partners, Marshall Field and Levi Leiter. The year before, at the suggestion of his doctors, Palmer had left the merchant trade to retire and take it easy. A multimillionaire, he vacationed in Europe for a year, and then returned in 1868 to a life of socializing at parties and the racetrack or White Stocking baseball games (a team he backed financially). When he decided to build the new store, he talked his old partners, Field and Leiter, into relocating there. Palmer went on to his next project, the magnificent Palmer House hotel located on State and Quincy, which opened on September 26, 1870. Recently married to twenty-one-year-old socialite Bertha Honoré, he built the eight-story, 225-room hotel as a wedding gift to her. It was said to be the only fireproof hotel in America. A year later, it would fail the test. Both the grand Field, Leiter and Company building and the Palmer House were destroyed in the fire of 1871. This was barely a hiccup to the likes of Field or Potter.

The second Palmer House was even more elegant than the first. It was the first hotel equipped with elevators, electricity, and telephones, and boasted, once again, that it was fireproof. While the fathers of Chicago business flocked to Prairie Avenue, Palmer chose an overgrown portion of Lake Shore Drive to build his castlelike mansion. Gothic in structure, it would cost over $1 million and would host some of the city's most memorable balls and parties, overseen by Bertha Honoré Palmer, who had become Chicago's hostess. His real-estate instincts were as sharp as his instincts for retail. The land he bought on State Street became a major financial district, and remains so even today. His move to Lake Shore

Drive inspired others in the elite to follow suit, creating what is now known as the Gold Coast. Unfortunately, the castle that started it all is no more. Potter's mansion was demolished in 1950 and replaced by a high-rise apartment building. Palmer himself enjoyed the rest of his days having left an imprint on the city. He died in May 1902, a few weeks shy of his seventy-sixth birthday.

3. THE REAPER KING

Cyrus McCormick helped revolutionize not only farming, but the business of farming. Prior to McCormick's horse-drawn reaper, farming was often done at a loss. Wheat, a major cash crop, often rotted in the fields because only a two-to-three-day window existed for harvesting it with the farmer's slow tools. McCormick's mechanical reaper could cut and harvest at least one-and-a-half acres of wheat per hour. Born in 1809 in Rockbridge County, Virginia, McCormick's inventor father inspired him with his ideas, one of them being a reaper. Where his father failed, Cyrus succeeded. Receiving a patent in 1834, several years of improvements and patent battles (Abraham Lincoln providing representation for one of the trials) followed before McCormick began looking for locations for his manufacturing plant. Forming a partnership with businessman Charles M. Gray in 1847, he built a factory on the north branch of the Chicago River and started McCormick Reaper Works. Since the $120 cost made it a huge investment and farmers didn't have money until after the harvest, McCormick pioneered a staple of American business: credit. With a $30 down payment, a farmer could purchase a reaper and pay the rest after the harvest. Thanks to the railroad, the bulk of the machines could be easily transported to the farms, illustrating a symbiotic business condition leading to the success of Chicago. By 1900, 214,000 reapers were produced annually. McCormick also tried his hand at the publishing industry by starting the *Chicago Times*, and was an outspoken opponent to the Civil War, standing behind Northerners sympathetic to the Southern cause. With no other interests or hobbies, he was at work by dawn and rarely out of the office before midnight. He expected a similar work ethic from his employees, but unlike his contemporaries, suffered the union of iron molders in his company because he recognized the value of skilled labor. Cyrus McCormick Sr. died in 1884, at the age of seventy-five, the words "work, work" the last he spoke.

4. IT'S IN THE MAIL

Montgomery Ward was responsible for starting one of the chief businesses that helped build Chicago: mail order. He was born in Chatham, New York, in 1844 and found his way to Chicago after working at various dry goods firms in St. Louis, Missouri, and St. Joseph, Missouri. Gaining a deeper understanding of retail as a clerk at Field, Palmer and Leiter, his years as a traveling salesman helped spark an idea. Traveling salesmen bought goods from farmers cheap, and then took them to the cities to be sold for a much higher profit. In reverse, they brought goods to the farmers from the city, purchased cheap, but sold to the farmers for highly inflated prices. Ward found his niche by doing away with the salesman. By purchasing goods in bulk, he could pass the savings on to the farmers by selling to them directly from a catalog. His first mail-order dry goods business was originally to open in late 1871, but the Chicago Fire destroyed his stock. Investing another $2,400, though, Ward plowed ahead anyway, and within two years issued his first catalog, one sheet of paper with 163 items on it. It was a resounding success. His low prices did cause speculation from the *Chicago Tribune* that some sort of fraud was involved, but farmers ignored the paper's warnings thanks in large part to Ward's revolutionary unconditional money-back guarantee. The catalog went from eight pages in 1874 to seventy-two pages in 1875, and by the end of the 1880s it was a whopping 540 pages. Twenty-four thousand items were advertised and the company employed 300 clerks to fill the orders of the $1 million annual business. By World War I, Montgomery Ward

had become an American institution. Ward was also something of an ecological philanthropist. Having purchased
property on Michigan Avenue, he was concerned to see the
dumping that went on in Grant Park, where there were also
squatters' shacks, railroad sheds, and freight cars stored. He
began a one-man campaign to make sure the lakefront went
to parks rather than development and he took his battle to
court. It was not a decision appreciated by everyone—even
some of the poor people that he was fighting for—but he continued and prevailed. In 1897, the Supreme Court decided
that, with the exception of the Art Institute, no building was
allowed on the strip of property between Michigan Avenue
and the lake. It was a victory that would benefit Chicagoans
for generations to come. Ward died of pneumonia in 1913
and was buried in Rosehill Cemetery to join other Chicago
titans. After his death, Ward's widow presented Northwestern
University with $9 million to create a medical and dental
school. Sadly, Montgomery Ward's empire did not dominate
for long. Not long after his arrival, Richard Sears came to
town and outplayed him at his own game. Montgomery Ward
tried to compete with the large department stores but got
into the game late, opening retail outlets in small cities at
first and waiting until much later to enter the major cities.
Ward's State Street store didn't open until 1957. Eventually,
Montgomery Ward went out of business.

5. IT'S IN THE MAIL II

Richard Sears was a natural salesman, a master of marketing, able to convince customers to buy items that they didn't
need or particularly want. Richard Sears was born in 1863 in
Minnesota and went from farmboy to station agent on the
Minneapolis and St. Louis railway. Offered the chance to sell
watches that had been left by salesmen at the station, he
unloaded them quickly at a bargain rate. Inspired, he moved
on in 1886 to build his own store, R.W. Sears Watch Company in Minneapolis. Setting up headquarters in Chicago a
year later, when Alvah Roebuck answered an ad for a watch

repairer, the partnership was born. Interestingly enough, Sears wearied of the business and sold his interest to Roebuck, moving to Iowa to work in banking, but retail was in his blood, and he returned to Chicago in 1892, joining Roebuck in another mail-order business. The Sears, Roebuck and Company catalog grew faster even than that of its competitor Montgomery Ward by playing on the rural sense of inferiority, offering farmers the chance to own goods that city folks had. They also offered unbeatable prices. In 1893, the 196-page catalog sold everything from clothes, to saddles, to food and drugs, to refrigerators and farm equipment. Sears even sold ready-to-assemble houses. In 1900, the catalog swelled to 1,100 pages. Lacking Sears's enthusiasm for this sort of crazed success, Roebuck sold out to Sears in 1897 and left a very wealthy man. A clothing supplier for Sears, Julius Rosenwald, bought shares and became vice president. In 1906, Sears and his 9,000 employees moved into a forty-acre building on Chicago's West Side, which contained its own printing plant to produce the catalog, dining halls, and even landscaped parks. He'd created the largest retail business in the world. He even took Ward's return policy one better by offering a "send no money" policy. Richard Sears decided to retire in 1909 because of a dispute with Rosenwald over offering discounts and promoting popular items to encourage sales, though the parting was on a friendly note. The mogul retired to his Wisconsin farm and left behind an estate worth $25 million after his death on September 28, 1914. He also left behind a name synonymous with retail, still going strong, though perhaps slightly shaky, well over a century after its creation.

6. CHILLY RETURNS

Born in 1839, Gustavas Swift was brought up on a New England farm, his first foray into business selling dressed beef from a wagon. Having gone in on a butcher shop with his brother in 1859, by 1872 he'd formed a partnership with James A. Hathaway and together they expanded their cattle business to Albany and Buffalo. Success, however, lay in Chicago, the capital of the railroad industry, and he arrived in 1875 turning to the meatpacking trade. A great deal of money could be saved on freight costs if sides of beef could be shipped instead of live cattle. In an effort to capitalize on these savings, Swift invented the refrigerated railway car, which would revolutionize not only the meatpacking industry, but food shipping as a whole. The refrigerated car threatened eastern butchers who had the market cornered on meat. "No Impure Chicago Beef Sold Here!" read signs in butcher shop windows. To counteract the boycott, Swift gave wholesalers the chance to buy a minority interest in his business if they distributed his beef. If any resisted, he simply built his own establishments, with storage facilities and professionally trained staff. The lower prices convinced Americans to buy his meat. A frugal perfectionist, Swift believed he had a right to conduct business in his own fashion. He was uncompromising with unions and unafraid to hire from as far away as New York to break strikes. As time went by, his business grew to packinghouses in Kansas City, Omaha, and St. Louis, and offices in Britain and the Far East. By 1903, over 20,000 people were employed by Swift and Company and the corporation amassed sales of $200 million. Swift himself passed away that year at age sixty-three, leaving behind an empire that would go on for decades to come.

7. EVERYTHING BUT THE SQUEAL

Philip Armour once estimated that he lost $10.21 per steer on the beef he sold, yet earned a profit of $10.80 on the by-products of that steer that butchers had always tossed away. Hide, hooves, bones, and grease could be transformed into glue, soap, buttons, and even margarine. Intestines could be cleaned for sausage casings. Low-quality meat could be canned for new products such as pork and beans. The digestive aid pepsin could be made from the inner lining of the hog's stomach. That's why it was once said that at the stockyards, they used everything but the squeal. Born in 1832 in New York, Armour arrived in Chicago the same year as Swift after forays as a prospector and soap maker. He turned to selling hides in St. Paul, Minnesota, but took advantage of the Civil War to enter a partnership with packer John Plankinton to supply fresh meat for the war. In 1875, he came to Chicago, where he amassed several million dollars in the pork market. By 1892, he had offices in Chicago, Omaha, and Kansas City, and diversified into manufacturing toiletries, medicines, and hospital accessories. A workaholic, his one big passion was the challenge of building a fortune in a town like Chicago. In 1893, Armour was the second-richest man in town. As ruthless as he could be with the workers, he was surprisingly charitable with children. At the mission founded by an endowment of his late brother, Joseph, he would hand out gold and silver dollars to the children he spoke to. The nondenominational Armour Mission was run very much like Hull House, with a kindergarten, a library, and a free medical dispensary. Later he would establish the Armour Institute, which would become the Illinois Institute of Technology, and provided tuition for students, regardless of race, who were unable to afford the $60 a year. While the institute was a male school, he established a high-school-level academy for young women, and a library for poor neighborhoods. There was hope with children, Armour believed. With adults, he was much more cynical. They were beyond reform. He was every bit as vehement against labor unions as his fellow meatpackers and hired strikebreakers at his plant. After the third one, he demanded that his workers sign agreements not to join a union. While playing outside with his grandchildren one winter, Armour caught a cold that turned into pneumonia. He died in January of 1901 at the age of sixty-eight.

8. THE ROAD TO HELL

In Graceland Cemetery, there stands a huge Corinthian column erected as a monument to one of the biggest names in

Chicago history. Beneath this monument, buried in a pit of reinforced concrete bolted together with steel rails, George M. Pullman sleeps in a lead-lined casket. The security is due to the fact that the name of Pullman had become so hated in labor circles that it was feared his body would be desecrated by the very people he had tried to help. He was born in New York in 1831, and dropped out of school at fourteen, taking a job as a clerk in a general store. Possessing an aptitude for carpentry, he apprenticed as a cabinetmaker for his older brother. In the early 1850s, while barely into his twenties, he developed a way to raise buildings so that foundations could be placed under them. He was an answer to the prayers of Chicago's city fathers; so in 1855, Pullman moved to Chicago and began raising the buildings to help with its sewage problems.

With the fortune from that endeavor, he moved on to designing the Pullman sleeper car, a train car with luxurious appointments that would revolutionize train travel. As they were larger than most railroad cars, railroad bridges and station platforms had to be enlarged to accommodate them. Once the railroads were convinced that the Pullman cars would be a valuable addition to their lines, they turned out to be a huge success for both Pullman and Chicago. Beginning in 1867, his Pullman Palace Car Company became one of the city's major employers, and eventually he had plants in other major cities. Flush with success, in 1880 Pullman tried his hand at social engineering, establishing Pullman, Illinois, on the shore of Lake Calumet, ten miles south of Chicago. In Pullman's mind, it wasn't the unfair labor practices of industrialists such as himself that were upsetting the workers of the city. It was the slums they lived in. Serene surroundings, he theorized, would create a serene and content workforce. Pullman's employees were actually paid better wages than many and he relied on a skilled workforce, believing in keeping them contented and loyal to the company. Pullman created for his workers a beautiful town, exquisitely landscaped, with stores, parks, free kindergarten, and schools and a library housing a thousand books (though few citizens could afford to use it, since it charged an annual fee of $3 for adults, $1 for children). It was close to a utopia, but it was shrewd business as well. Pullman didn't build this city to help his workers as much as to get more work out of them. The 12,600 workers and their families who lived there relinquished a lot of control of their lives to do so. They swore never to drink, even on personal time, and were subject to periodic house checks by Pullman supervisors to make sure they were following all the rules. Denied permits for public speaking, union organizers were kept out of town. Utilities were bought from Pullman, and the company store (with profits to go to Pullman) was where citizens shopped. Rents were set high enough to guarantee a 6-percent return on his investment in the town. For a while, it seemed a small price to pay.

The trouble began in 1893, when the Depression caused Pullman's business to slow. Pullman had guaranteed investors a certain percentage of return on their investments. In order to fulfill this, Pullman cut wages, working hours, and eventually jobs, but expenses in the town of Pullman never lowered. Once living charges were taken from their checks, many workers found themselves taking home pennies every week. Some took home nothing. Pleas for relief brought little sympathy from Pullman; so in 1894, in one of the ugliest disputes in labor history, workers went out on strike. Eugene Debs convinced the railway union to strike in sympathy with the workers, and soon the strike became a national issue as the railroads ground to a halt. In response to this national emergency, President Grover Cleveland sent federal troops to put down the strike, and by July it was over, the plant reopening in early August. Pullman never made one concession to the people he was squeezing so hard. But the victory was a cold one for Pullman who began to see, far too late, the bad blood his actions had wrought. He died in 1897 of heart failure, his health weakened by events of the previous four years. Under the cloak of night, and heavy security, Pullman's casket was placed in Graceland Cemetery, and it took graveyard workers two days to fill in the grave.

9. HIS BOLOGNA HAS A FIRST NAME

That yellow package of hot dogs in the grocer's meat section has a lot of history behind it. This Bavarian-born butcher has a name that's as recognizable as his product. Born in 1859, Oscar Mayer made plans to move to America with cousins in 1873, living with and working for them when they landed in Detroit. They moved to Chicago in 1876. At the age of seventeen, Mayer apprenticed at the Armour Meatpacking Company, and then moved on to Kohlhammers meat market. It was here that he learned the customer service side of the meat business. In 1883, Mayer and his brothers, Gottfried and Max, who'd joined him in Chicago, rented a butcher shop in a German neighborhood on the North Side and opened Oscar Mayer and Brothers Company. Having suggested in a letter home a few years earlier that Gottfried learn the art of sausage making, Mayer's company was able to specialize in homemade sausages and wieners. Though Gottfried managed the production department and Max ran bookkeeping, eventually the name was changed to Oscar Mayer and Company, and he went from storefront butcher to relying on wagon salesmen to help peddle his product through the city and suburbs. By 1900, the company employed forty-three workers. While this wasn't the phenomenal growth shown by the Swift and Armour companies, Mayer seems to have beaten them on one crucial front: marketing. Swift and Armour are known brands, but neither has the name recognition of Oscar Mayer. In 1929, his became the first company to achieve this, thanks in part to the fact that in each package, every fourth wiener was wrapped in a yellow paper ring carrying the Oscar Mayer name as well as a U.S. government inspector stamp. His name became synonymous with a safe product. Little Oscar and the wienermobile debuted in 1936. A little person wearing an oversized chef's hat would tour the country in a specialized vehicle shaped like a hot dog in a bun. With the advent of TV, commercials for the company were backed by memorable theme songs such as "I Wish I Were an Oscar Mayer Wiener" or "My Bologna Has a First Name." With marketing tools such as this, the Oscar Mayer name became emblazoned on the American psyche. He also came up with new product ideas such as packages of sliced bacon, which appeared in 1921. While the company moved its headquarters to Madison, Wisconsin, in 1919, Mayer kept his Chicago plant at 1241 N. Sedgewick Street and Mayer himself remained in Chicago until his death in 1955 at the age of ninety-five.

10. JUST AROUND THE CORNER

Born in 1873, Charles Walgreen was the son of Swedish immigrants. In 1887, the family moved from Rio, Illinois, to Dixon, Illinois, where Charles eventually spent a year at Dixon Business College before finding a bookkeeping job in the town's largest store. From there he did piecework at a shoe factory, became a $4-a-week apprentice at a neighborhood drugstore, then finally decided to head to Chicago. After a series of jobs in North and South Side pharmacies, Walgreen passed the Illinois State Board of Pharmacy in 1897, and then headed off to Cuba to handle the pharmaceutical detail in the Spanish American War. In 1901, he borrowed money from his father and purchased a store, turning it into the typical neighborhood pharmacy. Realizing he needed to offer more than just the usual perfumes, pills, and tonics, he started taking a customer's order over the phone, a nearby assistant wrapping the goods up as Walgreen spoke, and a delivery person leaving before the customer hung up. The increase in business as a result of that practice taught Walgreen that it wasn't only the quality of the goods, but the quality of the customer service that attracts business. Opening his second store in 1909, Walgreen added a soda fountain. In winter, however, the business dropped, so he began selling sandwiches, hot meals, and desserts to make up the difference. By 1916, along with his first two stores, there were stores in Joliet, Illinois, in Indiana, and in Wisconsin. In 1927 came the opening of the first New York Walgreen's and by the time he retired in 1934, there were 500 stores to the Walgreen name. Sadly, Charles Walgreen had little time to enjoy the fruits of his labor. In December of 1939, Walgreen lost his battle with cancer at the age of sixty-six. What started out as a little local pharmacy selling tooth powder and toiletries has become the largest drug store chain in the United States.

The Mayors

To be mayor of Chicago takes pioneer determination to ride herd on a city that always seems to be up to something. Successful mayors learned how to finesse an incredibly diverse city so that everyone felt taken care of. They weren't afraid to get their hands dirty or to be politically bloodied in a fight. Some were crooked, some merely cunning. Some were colorful, and others downright crazy. Some attempted reform during periods when reform wasn't taken too kindly. And one, firmly holding the reins of the powerful Democratic Machine, used a combination of conciliation, charm, and plain old Irish stubbornness to build a dynasty that lasted two decades. We'll start with him.

1. RICHARD J. DALEY: SIX TERMS 1955–1976

"The Machine" was actually assembled well before Richard J. Daley took office, but he used it to his full advantage. A native of the fiercely Irish community of Bridgeport, Daley was born in 1902, son of working-class parents. He worked his way up the political ranks until becoming chairman of the Cook County Democratic Party (CCDP) in 1953. In 1955, Daly pushed himself as the CCDP mayoral candidate (over then-mayor Martin Kennelly) and won the election, retaining his position as CCDP chief while also serving as mayor to keep tight control on the city's political system. Like Anton

Cermak before him, who felt that successfully running Chicago meant getting the rulers of all the wards to pull together, Daley believed that a smooth-running Machine needed a strong mayor to guide it. He would be that mayor. Daley was a builder, providing jobs through projects like O'Hare Airport, the Sears Tower, and McCormick Place. Roads were paved, expressways built, and new Loop parking garages added. Yet, Daley the wheeler-dealer was unequipped for the uncompromising activism of the 1960s and '70s. Instead of facing the issue of racial discrimination straight, Daley offered housing-starved African Americans the Robert Taylor Homes, an ambitious, if misguided, housing project meant to appease yet segregate African Americans. Unprepared for the vehemence of antiwar protesters during the 1968 Democratic Convention, Daley denied the protesters a parade permit, then sent thousands of policemen to deal with them as they marched toward the convention center. Despite an inability to change, Daley remained mayor until his fatal heart attack in 1976. Richard J. Daley's funeral seemed like that afforded a national leader. It was attended by government figures, mayors and leaders from other cities, and thousands of Chicagoans who lined up to pay their respects. It's hard to imagine what might have been if he had been able to finish just one more term, but for many he will always be "Hizzoner, Da Mayor."

2. RICHARD M. DALEY: FOUR TERMS 1989–PRESENT

For Richard M., the Daley name was both a blessing and a curse. Those who loved the old man turned hopeful eyes to the son, while there were those who feared that Caesar's heir was coming to collect the crown. In his years as mayor of Chicago, however, Richard M. Daley seems to have laid to rest the notion that he may try to resurrect the Machine. He's reached out as the city's manager. There was no mudslinging in his 1989 campaign against incumbent Eugene Sawyer, simply a promise of strong leadership. Without the Machine to guarantee him votes, Daley needed to rely on the good will of the people. As mayor, he's eliminated the patronage job system leaned on so heavily by former mayors. He's balanced the budget by trimming the fat off City Hall. He's also taken a more progressive course in his administration, approving city benefits to homosexual couples who live together, backing a neighborhood restoration program that enables the neighborhoods to exhibit civic pride without sacrificing ethnicity, and spearheading a community policing program that's become a national model. He's racked up a number of awards and headed the U.S. Conference of Mayors in 1996. He occasionally shows the stubborn resolve that kept his father in office, but in this postindustrial Chicago, "livability" has become a key concern, and Richard M. has responded to that in a way that his father quite possibly never could.

3.   ANTON J. CERMAK: ONE TERM 1931–1933

Anton J. Cermak's rise to power revealed a man much more politically savvy than his early days of brawling and boozing would have indicated. Known as Tough Tony, Cermak's large family came to America from Bohemia and worked the mines in the tough town of Braidwood, sixty miles southwest of Chicago. He worked jobs no one else wanted, eventually starting his own business hauling and selling kindling, and began his political career as a precinct captain moving up to the Illinois state legislature. In 1918, dissatisfaction with the Bohemian faction of the city led him into the arms of the Roger Sullivan Machine. This outsider in the Irish Machine would refine and redefine machine politics for decades to come after a power struggle within the organization helped Cermak take charge of it. In the 1931 race for City Hall, Mayor Big Bill Thompson played on Cermak's humble beginnings, calling his challenger "Pushcart Tony" and "Bohunk," but Cermak won the day by courting votes in every section of town. Then Tough Tony surprised everyone by fine-tuning City Hall as well as himself. Believing that there was enough to go around for everyone, Cermak took the smaller machines and created the Machine, which embraced the city's ethnic diversity while encouraging all wards to work together. And he would hold the reins. Anton Cermak never got to see the fruits of his mayoral labor. In 1933, while sitting next to President Franklin Roosevelt during a Miami visit, Cermak was hit by a bullet meant for the president. He died from complications shortly after. His innovative idea, however, lived on and helped pull Chicago politics out of the ward battles it was mired in, making the system much more sophisticated, if equally open to corruption.

4. HAROLD WASHINGTON: TWO TERMS 1983–1987

Chicago's first black mayor was a complicated man. The irony of his 1972 conviction for failing to file four years of income tax returns is that Washington's birthday was April 15. Born in 1922, Washington put his enthusiasm into everything he did. He showed great promise in school, served as a staff sergeant in the Pacific, and upon returning to Chicago, became the first black president of the Roosevelt University student council before graduating with honors. Serving five terms in the Illinois House of Representatives, he sponsored bills for fair employment practices, low-cost housing, and the rights of women, the elderly, and the handicapped. His first run for mayor in 1976 stalled due to a lack of funds, but in 1982, he cut short his second term in Congress to make another attempt at City Hall. His campaign against incumbent Jane Byrne and Richard M. Daley was a difficult one and race figured prominently. When he took office in 1983, Mayor Washington was up against a City Council majority trying to freeze him out. If asked, the council would swear that race was not an issue, but for the first time in its history, blacks had reached the highest tiers of city government and this must have rankled with some of the old-timers in the council. Washington's record was spotty, but he was an eloquent man and his enthusiasm for the city and her people was obvious. An African American mayor leading Chicago's St. Patrick's Day parade was, in itself, a positive symbol that times were changing. Washington was reelected in 1987 and by this time, the City Council was more cooperative. Sadly, however, on November 25, 1987, Washington was found slumped over his desk in his fifth-floor office of City Hall having suffered a fatal heart attack. Like Daley before him, he'd spent his final years serving the city he loved.

5.   JAYNE BYRNE: ONE TERM 1979–1983

Chicago's first female mayor holds the distinction of breaking the powerful Machine, though she had few political distinctions before that. Born in 1934, she came from the rich Northwest Side neighborhood of Sauganash. After meeting Richard J. Daley through her family, she held a variety of positions until she was sent in to clean up the Department of Weights and Measures in 1968. Understanding the value of the press, thanks partly to her reporter husband, Jay McMullen, she used them as much as they used her. When she was fired by Daley's successor, Michael Bilandic, over her attempt to better regulate cab companies, the battle was on. In her campaign against Bilandic, she referred to the mayor and his loyal alderman as "a cabal of evil men." Bilandic's downfall was the blizzard of 1978–1979. Byrne jumped on every misstep made by City Hall and the storm won the day for her. Once elected mayor in 1979, she beat both Bilandic and the Machine, but what Byrne didn't realize was that she yearned to hold the reins as much as mayors of the past. Her administration was fraught with City Council battles and many of the reforms she promised were never delivered. One of the promises she reneged on led to the city's first strike by the fire department. Yet one more distinction.

6.   WILLIAM B. OGDEN: ONE TERM 1837–1838

When William B. Ogden first set foot in Chicago what he saw was a swampy mess. It was 1835 and he'd come to Chicago to look over real estate bought by relatives. At first put off by the muddy village, he changed his tune when a few land-speculating deals began to pay off. Like so many of the visionaries of the time, Ogden was able to look past Chicago's roughness and see its potential. He built the city's first railroad (now known as the Chicago and Northwestern) and helped create the Illinois and Michigan Canal. Both helped to make Chicago a center for commerce in the Midwest. Giving Cyrus McCormick $25,000 enabled the inventor to build his reaper works in Chicago and change the business of agriculture forever. Ogden built the first drawbridge over the Chicago River, became the first president of the now-prestigious Rush Medical College, and even started the brewing industry. And on May 2, 1837, he became Chicago's first mayor. His term only lasted a year, but his efforts helped get the infant city up on her feet and toddling toward the future.

7.   CARTER HARRISON I: FIVE TERMS 1879–1887 & 1893
CARTER HARRISON II: FIVE TERMS 1897–1905 & 1911–1915

Another father-and-son act, the Harrisons held pretty much the same views and enjoyed long mayoral terms because of them. "You can't make people moral by ordinance, and it's no use trying." This philosophy helped keep Carter Harrison I in office for five terms. A suave Yale graduate from Kentucky, he came to Chicago in 1855 and was elected mayor in 1879. With the voting power split between the wealthy businessmen and the ethnic working class, Harrison's charisma appealed to both sides. Above all, he believed that every citizen had a right to make and spend money as desired. Harrison told the vice merchants to keep it out of the public's eyes, and no one need be wiser. And while Chicago became known as the "most open city" in the nation, ethnic tensions lessened and businesses of all stripes thrived. Sadly, Carter Harrison I, while still in office, was murdered in his home by Patrick Prendergast, an unstable fanatic. Like his old man, Carter Harrison II wasn't interested in legislating morality. Instead, he devoted his energies to civic reforms like cleaner water and better sewage, the nitty-gritty workings that make life more comfortable for everyone. Power resided with the aldermen. Decades before mayor-driven machines, the wards came first, the city second. To develop a coalition with the aldermen, Harrison the younger often had to look the other way on certain activities, something he was willing to do to get his reforms passed. He convinced railroad companies to elevate the tracks over the streets to cut down on pedestrian deaths. His parks commission built playgrounds in the inner cities. And with the support of the morally questionable Coughlin and Kenna of the First Ward, he kept ruthless millionaire Charles Tyson Yerkes from gaining a monopoly over Chicago's electric streetcar business.

8. WILLIAM E. DEVER: ONE TERM 1923–1927

What most Chicago mayors understood was that this was a very wet town. Talk of restricting booze usually sent rumbles through the city where the Volstead Act was pretty much ignored. Gangsters made millions off the booze-starved populace, and crime flourished. There's something noble, then, about William E. Dever's attempts to enforce the unpopular law. It made him a one-term mayor, but in a time when lesser mayors were selling their allegiance to the mob to ensure an eternal place in City Hall, Dever stuck to his guns. Born in 1862, Dever was elected mayor in 1923 after Big Bill Thompson had used up his chances. Well bred and urbane, Dever promised reforms and made a sincere effort to carry his promises through, cleaning up the mess left to him by the previous administration. A former judge, Dever was not a fan of Prohibition, but it was the law, and he would see that law carried out. So successful was he, that national journalists billed Chicago as the driest city in America. His efforts even managed to chase Al Capone to Cicero to set up shop. Unfortunately, Dever had to spend so much energy on upholding the Volstead Act that he was unable to concentrate on other reforms. And while Chicago might have been dry, this state of affairs was hardly a voluntary thing. When Big Bill Thompson staged a comeback in 1927, the city welcomed him with open arms. In so doing, the city may have thrown out of office the most honest mayor in Chicago history.

9. WILLIAM HALE "BIG BILL" THOMPSON: THREE TERMS 1915–1923 & 1927–1931

"The worst you can say about him is that he's stupid." That statement was actually made about Big Bill by one of his sponsors. Low on ambition in most things, he ran for alderman in 1900 because he made a $50 bet in a poker game that he would. Poorly educated, his major claim to local fame was as captain of the Chicago Athletic Club's water polo team. His campaign promise to clean up Chicago in 1915 didn't last long. In fact, by his last election, supporters celebrated his victory by gathering on a floating speakeasy in Belmont Harbor, which became so overcrowded it sank. His became one of the most corrupt administrations in Chicago history and, once this corruption caught up with him, he was voted out of office. His excursion to hunt exotic fish in the South Seas was notable for the fact that his party never left the Mississippi River. A reform-weary Chicago did bring him back for one more term, but he ended up having a breakdown in midterm and became even more ineffectual than he was before. Big Bill died in 1944. Figuring his estate at only $150,000, people were surprised to find that the cash, stocks, bonds, and gold certificates from past graft in his safety deposit boxes brought the estate up to $2,103,024. This estate was hotly contested by his wife, Maysie, and mistress Ethabelle, who settled for $250,000. It would seem he was more ambitious than people thought.

10. "LONG" JOHN WENTWORTH: TWO TERMS 1857–1861

At six feet six inches tall, "Long" John Wentworth was one of the crazy ones. A burly, blustery mayor whose ego outweighed his 300-pound frame, when asked once how it felt to sit next to the Prince of Wales during the future monarch's visit to the city, Wentworth replied, "I was not sitting beside the Prince. He sat beside me." He came to Chicago in 1836 at the age of twenty-one. Eleven years after a hitch in Congress, he was elected mayor of Chicago in 1857. His appetite was immense. He ate thirty dishes in one sitting, all on the table at once, with between a pint and a quart of brandy every day. His appetite for control was just as strong. A hands-on mayor, it wasn't unusual for him to sit in on some police raids himself. He instituted chain gangs in the city. Tired of bumping his head on low-hanging signs, he organized a posse of vaguely drunk police and express-wagon drivers to drive around and take down every low-hanging sign. In a snit after locals convinced the state legislature to create a police commissioner board to take control of local police, Wentworth assembled the entire force in his office and fired them (a few days later, the police board began to rehire the police). Then there was the Sands, an infamous red-light district, that the reform-minded Wentworth and a mob of thirty policemen and hundreds of citizens tore down one night when most of the neighborhood was off watching a dogfight on the other side of town. He died on October 16, 1888, and was buried beneath a sixty-five-foot tombstone in a huge burial plot that he bought so that, "if I get tired of lying on my back, I will have room to turn over and kick."

Architecture

1. **THE PRAIRIE STYLE**

The father of the prairie style, Frank Lloyd Wright was born in Wisconsin in 1867, studied engineering at the University of Wisconsin, and found his way to Chicago hoping to make a bold statement for a solely American style of architecture. Apprenticing with Louis Sullivan, he opened his own firm in Oak Park and worked on designs that were organic: The colors, the style, the materials all complemented nature without subduing it. While he could be arrogant and controlling, designing even down to the decorative pieces, and often the cost of his designs reflected that arrogance, he almost always left the client satisfied. His minimalist style was perfect for his design of the Imperial Hotel in Tokyo. Completed in 1922, it was the only major building that survived the large earthquake the following year. In the 1930s, Wright formed the Taliesin Fellowship in Spring Green, Wisconsin. Later, Taliesin West would be established in Arizona. The fellowship gave young architects a chance to live, work, and learn with Wright. Wright considered modern cities congested and dirty, so he designed to reflect a quiet, meditative approach to the modern dwelling. His design for "Falling Water" is a perfect marriage of a building with its surroundings. Built above a small waterfall in Pennsylvania, it flows itself, snug in the rocks surrounding it. Terraces jut out over the falls, trying to touch the branches of the surrounding trees. Wright's celebrity rose thanks in part to the new medium of television, as his opinionated demeanor was perfect for talk shows. He went from being the brash upstart in the beginning of his career to being the elder statesman toward the end. In 1959, Wright died in Arizona at the age of ninety-one. His work continues to be an inspiration to architects around the world.

2. THE BUNGALOW BELT

"Bungla" was a type of housing built for British subjects living in India. It became one of the most popular building

Author's Collection

A row of bungalows in a Chicago neighborhood. These compact houses designed for the middle class became predominant in Chicago's newly constructed neighborhoods of the first half of the twentieth century. Today, one-third of all single-family homes in the city of Chicago are bungalows.

styles in the Chicago neighborhoods during the early twentieth century. The twentieth century saw a tremendous growth spurt in Chicago's neighborhoods. Strides in the mass-transit system made living in the city no longer quite as necessary. Low-cost housing was needed and these little gems, set in suburbs newly incorporated by Chicago, were just the answer. They were solid, rectangular, one-and-a-half story, single-family homes built from similar plans, yet designed to fit the individual as well. The bungalow was a middle-class answer to the stuffy Victorian mansions popular at the time. One-third of all Chicago single-family homes are bungalows. Built between 1910 and 1940, they were also the first to incorporate central heating, electricity, and modern plumbing. Entrances faced the front, garages were built in the back, and cars gained access through public alleys, which also took garbage pickup from the street and hid it in the alleyway. Lined up side by side, they were separated by gangways five to fifteen feet, but the uniformity of the style, and the fact that fences were rarely installed in the front of the house, lent a closeness to the neighborhood. Built with solid brick construction, the bungalows were sturdy and well insulated, and new construction on bungalows offered a boom in business to local brick makers. The year 2000 saw the launch of the city's Bungalow Initiative, intent on preserving the Bungalow Belt. The initiative pays tribute to the importance of the bungalow in modern architecture, and offers incentives for improvement and modernization to individual houses. The bungalow is a form of architecture unique to Chicago, and the city is finally recognizing that.

3. STEEL AND GLASS

Ludwig Mies van der Rohe was Europe's premier architect in the 1930s. He was born in Germany in 1886 and became an architectural draftsman. By the age of twenty-four he started his own practice, enthusiastic about the architectural possibilities of glass. By 1927, he, along with Walter Gropius and Peter Behrens, designed a housing estate that stunned the establishment with its audacious reliance on low, boxlike structures. His design for the German Pavilion at the Barcelona International Exposition, completed in 1929, was considered a work of art. A year later, he became the director of the Bauhaus but the Nazis were rising to power, and he was unable to continue under the Nazi regime. He closed the school in 1938 and answered an invitation from John A. Holabird to become the director of the architecture school at Armour Institute of Technology in Chicago. Like other architects, he hoped to steer Chicago away from its reliance on the old classical themes of stone-and-brick structures with heavy ornamentation, and bring it toward what he considered would be the clean design of the twentieth century. Steel and glass would be his tools and the future would be streamlined. There were those who criticized his work for its coldness. According to critics, Mies inspired a legacy of soulless steel-and-glass cages, and it's true that many of the designs inspired by his philosophy would turn out to be just that. Yet he also designed the twin apartment buildings at 860–880 North Lake Shore Drive, among the first glass-and-steel high-rises in the world. Mies worked for the International Institute of Technology until 1958 when he retired from his post. Mies van der Rohe continued designing until his death in 1969 from cancer of the esophagus.

4. THE PLANNER

In 1909, Daniel Burnham published the Plan of Chicago. He envisioned a utopian future for Chicago, full of, among other things, a lakefront that would blossom with parks and recreation. That vision was perhaps inspired by his plans for the White City. Born in New York in 1846, his family moved to Chicago in 1855. As a youth, he'd gone from a job as a salesman at a mercantile house to an apprentice draftsman with the office of Loring and Jenny, two of the most notable architects in Chicago. After a brief stint in Nevada, he was back in Chicago resuming his architectural career under Peter Wright, then joining John Wellborn Root in 1873 in a successful eighteen-year partnership. They designed office buildings, railroad stations, hotels, and churches. The Montauk Building, the Rookery, and the Monadnock Building were three of their most famous creations. Burnham's strength, however, was in administration, and his position as director of works for the World's Columbian Exposition of 1893 seemed tailor-made for him. Thanks to Burnham's influence, some of the greatest names in architecture, landscaping, and art came together to create a background for what would be the most popular world's fair ever. Sadly, in 1891, John Root died unexpectedly. Had he lived, the fair might have taken on a more modern look, which would have pleased Louis Sullivan, who criticized Burnham for relying too much on an imitation of the neoclassical style. But Burnham's vision of a white, clean city in a classical, Grecian style would prove to be popular with the crowds who attended. Perhaps most importantly, it would show what could be done, not only with park and lakefront land, but also with the city itself.

Burnham drew up a plan that would encourage the beautification of public spaces along with making the Chicago River a focal point downtown. Eventually, the plan was accepted by Mayor Fred Busse in 1910, and Charles H. Wacker, a wealthy brewer, became chairman of the Chicago Plan committee, made up of civic and business leaders. Not everyone was a fan of the plan. Montgomery Ward fought against public building on lakefront property downtown, and many property owners objected to the idea of street-widening plans that would cut into their front yards. Burnham's plan, however, gave Chicago a blueprint to work with and over the next several decades, the plan would inspire public works projects in the city. Burnham went on to create plans for Washington, D.C., Cleveland, San Francisco, and Manila. Three years after his great plan of 1909, he sailed with his wife to Europe and while in Germany, succumbed to complications from food poisoning and colitis.

5. **FROM THE BATTLEFIELD**

Born in 1844, Dankmar Adler was originally from Germany, but when he was ten his widowed father took him to Detroit. He received private drawing instruction and eventually apprenticed to a well-known architect before father and son moved to Chicago in 1861. Sharing his father's abolitionist beliefs, Adler enlisted in the Illinois Light Artillery. Despite his lack of formal education, Adler was well read on the latest scientific principles, and he took the opportunity during the war to learn a great deal about engineering. Techniques used on the field began finding their way into modern architecture. After the war, he formed a partnership with Edward Burling and the fire of 1871 kept them busy. Adler's most famous pairing, however, was with Louis Sullivan, who started as an employee in the firm Adler started after leaving his partnership with Burling in 1879. Adler had the flair for engineering, Sullivan for design. Together they made an impression on the city. The Auditorium Building is the jewel in their career and they made a reputation for theater design.

Along with a building known as the Schiller Building, the firm designed the Chicago Stock Exchange in 1893, which would eventually be demolished. On this building, to solve the problem of support in the uncertain Chicago soil, Adler developed the "Chicago caisson." Deep in the ground were wells, lined with waterproof wood sheeting and steel rings to avoid water seepage and collapse. Once deep enough, the wells were filled with cement to make solid concrete supports. The Chicago Stock Exchange would utilize the first caisson foundation in Chicago. The strength of this support opened the way for skyscrapers to go higher. The partnership of Adler and Sullivan was like oil and water, however. The tailored Sullivan was haughty and clipped in his dealings with the draftsmen. Adler, on the other hand, was friendly and paternal. This could be one reason why the partnership, successful as it was, eventually split. Like Burnham and Root, the talents particular to Adler and Sullivan worked

wonders when they worked. Unlike Burnham and Root, however, the team never became true friends. The breakup
would come in 1895 as Sullivan went his own way. Adler
would continue on his own way as well, writing articles on
architecture. He died in 1900, at the young age of fifty-six.

6. CHICAGO RIVIERA

They wanted the Chicago Cubs, but settled on a hotel instead. And what a hotel it was. Located on the lakefront at
Sheridan near Foster, the Edgewater Beach Hotel was the
hot spot of the upper crust in the 1920s, '30s, and '40s.
When John T. Connery bought the vacant property on Sheridan, he turned to Ben Marshall, of Marshall and Fox, to
design a hotel. What Marshall designed was a luxurious
Spanish-style hotel located on the lake. Thanks to its Mal-
tese Cross form, most of the rooms had a view of Lake Michigan. In 1916, the 400-room pink resort opened. Six years
later, a second 600-room unit had to be built to accommodate the overload of guests wanting to stay at the resort.
Movie stars, sports stars, big names of the big bands all
chose the Edgewater Beach when they came to town. Wed-
dings were held there as well as proms and dances. Radio
and television shows were broadcast from there. The hotel
boasted its own radio station (home of WGN radio for many
years), print shop, a state-of-the-art film studio, chocolatier,
and not only a heliport but also a seaplane for those just jet-
ting in from the coast. The Edgewater Beach Hotel was like
having a piece of the French Riviera or Monaco in Chicago's
own backyard. It spoke to the glamour of the early part of
the century. But glamour eventually fades, as did the popularity of Edgewater. When Lake Shore Drive was extended
past the hotel, the hotel's prized position on the lakefront was
gone. The original owners had sold their stock in the hotel
by the late 1940s, and other entertainments like television
competed for the hotel's interest. Eventually, in 1967, the
great resort was demolished.

7. **THE FATHER OF THE SKYSCRAPER**

His utilization of steel frame construction for his Home Insurance Building paved the way for taller buildings in Chicago. Born in Massachusetts in 1832, William Le Baron Jenny attended engineering school in France where he learned the fundamentals of metal construction. Back in the States, he joined the Union Army in 1861 as an assistant in the engineering department and rose quickly through the ranks. By the time he was discharged in 1866, he held the rank of major. Jenny's work stressed practicality over embellishment, which was just fine with real-estate developers interested in saving money, and Jenny's innovative "bridge frame construction" helped cut down on costly construction time. Chicago's roughness attracted many architects and Jenny was no exception. At the right time, Jenny was also able to see the potential and take advantage of the new technology still in the development stage, and both Chicago and architecture benefited from it. The steel-frame construction he introduced opened the city up to bigger and better buildings and was soon adopted in cities across the country. Jenny entered into several partnerships during his career, and even though he accepted a brief appointment as professor of architecture at the University of Michigan in 1876, he continued to work from his office in Chicago. He was a learned man, and his knowledge of history, science, and art brought him acclaim from editors and university administrators. He was appointed to the commission of architects for the 1893 World's Columbian Expo. He also served as president of the Illinois chapter of the American Institute of Architects. In 1905, after a long career of helping the city grow, he retired to California, where he died two years later. He now resides in Graceland Cemetery, resting among his fellow architects.

8. **CENTURY OF PROGRESS**

Louis Skidmore was named as chief designer of the 1933 Century of Progress Exposition. Fair organizers were devoted to making it a technological wonder. The firm Skidmore, Owings and Merrill (SOM), established in 1936 (Skidmore and Nathaniel Owings were joined by John Merrill in 1939), would be the firm behind some of Chicago's most important buildings, incorporating the futuristic concept of the 1933 Expo. The Inland Steel Building, completed in 1958, became their first building of merit. At nineteen stories, it also became the second major new building completed in downtown since the Depression. It was the first skyscraper constructed using external supports and a flat, thin, steel-and-glass curtain wall. It was also the first major high-rise with underground parking. Part of SOM's strength was the architects in the firm. Like the later John Hancock Tower and the Sears Tower, Inland Steel was designed by Bruce John Graham who joined SOM in 1951. Another visionary at the firm was the late Fazlur Kahn, one of the foremost structural engineers who partnered with Graham on the Sears Tower and John Hancock Tower. It was the late Myron Goldsmith, joining the firm in the late 1940s, who came up with the steel-and-concrete framing systems that supported the height of the John Hancock Tower. Critics spoke out against what many considered were SOM's cold steel-and-glass boxes. Architecture began to change toward the end of the twentieth century, returning to designs that better related to their surroundings. SOM answered the call with architect Adrian Smith's design for the NBC Building, which seems almost joyous in its return to an art deco style. Thanks to talent such as this, and the firm's willingness to experiment and not be constrained, the Chicago skyline is that much more impressive.

9. SYMBIOSIS

Louis Sullivan felt man's connection to nature should be remembered and honored. His designs were often holistic, philosophical, metaphysical, giving the viewer pause for thought. Born in Massachusetts in 1856, he studied at the Massachusetts Institute of Technology and became heavily influenced by Prof. William R. Ware, who believed that American architecture was relying far too much on the classic styles. Sullivan came to Chicago in 1873 and worked briefly with William Le Baron Jenny's firm before enrolling in the architectural school Ecole des Beaux-arts of Paris. Turned off by the school's reliance on neoclassicism, he toured the great monuments of Italy, and by 1883, he was back in Chicago, joining forces with Dankmar Adler. They went on to design buildings like Holy Trinity Cathedral, the Getty Tomb in Graceland Cemetery, and Carson, Pirie Scott and Company. He had hoped that the Columbian Exposition would showcase the promise of Chicago architecture, but was disgusted to discover the course steered toward the classic style. In 1895, the partnership of Sullivan and Adler dissolved on poor terms and Sullivan found himself heading into rough waters. Thanks to both hard economic times and his own arrogance, he found himself selling off his possessions to pay the bills. By 1910, impoverished and suffering from insomnia, he was still designing buildings but never regained his former status in the architectural world. In 1922, he designed his last project—the Krause Music store facade. In 1924, Louis Sullivan, once one of Chicago's premiere architects, died at age sixty-seven, his last days spent in a low-class Chicago hotel. Despite his inauspicious end, Louis Sullivan remained a driving force in the architectural styles to come. Sullivan's theory that form follows function was the rallying cry behind a new school of architects like Frank Lloyd Wright.

10. **THE ENGINEER**

Half of one of the most influential and important partnerships in Chicago architecture, John Wellborn Root believed that America needed to create its own style, honoring the past but not bound by it. He was born in Georgia in 1850. The family found themselves in England after General William T. Sherman overran their town, and Root studied music and architecture. When he returned to the United States, he earned a civil engineering degree from New York University. He found his way to Chicago in 1871, working as a draftsman for the firm of Carter, Drake and Wright where he met Daniel Burnham. The two went on to start their own firm in 1873. With Burnham's head for administration, and Root's genius for design, theirs became one of the top architectural firms in the city. Their buildings were designed with simplicity and economy in mind, Root believing that commercial structures could be captivating and practical. For the Monadnock Building, developers wanted no surfaces that projected or indented. Root designed a building inspired by the pyramids, sleek in its starkness, the slight sloping at its base not only adding ornamentation, but also helping distribute the weight of the heavy building. Its sixteen stories represented a remarkable feat for its all-masonry construction.

Not stopping there, however, in 1892 the firm went higher, designing the twenty-two-story Masonic Temple which, when it was built, was the tallest building in the world. The Montauk Building provided a foundation problem that couldn't be solved with the Egyptian-inspired base. Root came up with a "floating foundation" that spread a column load safely over a large area of topsoil, stabilizing the building. It was a major innovation in architecture and used by architects for many years after. He wrote many essays regarding the responsibility architects had to create a new American style. Some heeded the call, others didn't. His partner, for example, would turn back to the classic style so favored in Europe to build the White City of the world's fair. In the fall of 1890, Burnham and Root were named supervising architects. With the help of Frederick Law Olmsted and Henry Codman, they began work designing an American Venice located on a sandy swamp in Jackson Park. Sadly, Root would never see his vision become reality. In January of 1891, he died from pneumonia; Daniel Burnham at his bedside.

Politics

1. THE MACHINE

As American as apple pie, the political machine is a product of the marriage between the sort of speedy industrialization and unchecked urban growth that occurred in the late nineteenth and early twentieth centuries. While corrupt, it could also give the normally disenfranchised a level of power, small as it might be. Politicians sold favors for votes and the average citizen sold votes for favors. Chicago, the fastest-growing city in the country for many decades, was ripe for machine politics. Not as successful as Albany, New York, or as corrupt as Boston, Chicago's machine outlasted both with a reputation beyond its borders. It wasn't flashy. It was a workhorse, plodding along, never taking more than it could chew. As the urban infrastructure grew in early twentieth-century Chicago, bringing with it job opportunities, the machine grew stronger. The machine was in place before him, but Mayor Anton Cermak refined it, taking control of the various bosses and leading them in one direction. Richard J. Daley, however, became the embodiment of machine politics. It was his position as mayor and chairman of the Cook County Democratic Party that cemented his power. He was smart enough to finesse the pockets of power in the city, and enjoyed the support of labor by placating the unions. The role as builder he adopted kept the city working, kept the favors flowing. It was the race issue that saw the downfall of the machine. African Americans weren't interested in the status quo. They desired equal opportunity in jobs, housing, and power in government. Daley and the old-time machine politicians were unprepared to deal with this situation brewing. He was still in charge in the end, but the machine was weakening to the point where it wouldn't survive Daley's demise.

2. THE BOMB

In 1886, the eight-hour day was only one of the luxuries denied the average worker. Chicago had been built by the wealthy elite's money but on the backs of the workers, and labor was fighting hard for a rise in basic working conditions. Some even advised anarchy. On May 4, 1886, a rally was held in Haymarket Square in response to a clash the day before between labor and police at the McCormick Reaper Works. The gathering, according to what Mayor Carter Harrison I told Police Inspector John Bonfield, was tame. When the meeting began at 7:30 P.M., it hadn't produced much of a crowd. By nightfall, only about 200 people remained. Leaving earlier, Harrison instructed Bonfield to let the people have their meeting in peace. Bonfield decided otherwise, moving in his 178 policemen and ordering the attendees to disperse. As Samuel Fielden, the speaker, stepped off the wagon, a bomb was thrown from the crowd. One officer was killed instantly by the blast while the others opened fire in the crowd. Fifty-nine policemen were wounded, eight killed, with most of the dead and wounded felled by friendly fire. It's estimated that between four and ten civilians were killed while thirty were wounded. Eight scapegoats were quickly rounded up, among them August Spies, as well as Samuel Fielden whose alibi seemed airtight since he was stepping off the speaker's platform as the bomb was thrown. In this case, thoughts and words, not deeds, were what sent five of the men to the gallows. There were those who begged for clemency for the men, and even some of the business leaders were softening. There was one holdout. The decision on what to do with the men was left in the hands of the biggest name in the city. Marshall Field's reply was simply, "Hang the bastards." Of eight men indicted in the Haymarket Square bombing, one, Louis Lingg, saved his jailers the effort of execution by blowing his face off with a dynamite cartridge that had been smuggled in. Three, Samuel Fielden, August Neebe, and Michael Schwab, obtained commutation of their sentences to life in prison and would later be pardoned. But Spies, George Engel, Adolph Fischer, and Albert Parsons were hanged. To this day, the identity of the bomb thrower remains a mystery, his motives equally so.

3. **THE LEVEE**

The Levee District, part of the First Ward, had more brothels per square mile than any place in the city. It was lorded over by Aldermen "Bathhouse" John Coughlin and Michael "Hinky Dink" Kenna. The quiet, teetotaling Hinky Dink gained his nickname from his diminutive stature. Bathhouse John was the colorful one of the duo, dressing in silk bowlers, colorful frock coats, and gloves. He grew up in an area known as Connelly's Patch. Bath left school at fifteen, working a series of jobs before getting a job in a Turkish bathhouse on Clark Street, rubbing down politicians, merchants, and underworld figures. Opening a few bathhouses himself, he gained the name "Bathhouse" John and in 1892 was elected alderman for the First Ward. When Kenna was elected alderman in 1897, Bathhouse found a partner to rule the First Ward, taking advantage of the protection money that flowed from the Levee. Also from Connelly's Patch, Kenna left school at ten, and became a gopher for the saloonkeepers in the district. He was quiet but aggressive in his business sense, making friends with madams, prostitutes, and anyone who might come in handy. He went from owning his own newsstand in Chicago to becoming a circulation manager on the *Lake*

County Reville in Leadville, Colorado. Back in Chicago, he opened a saloon, working quietly in the back room of politics. Hooking up with Bathhouse John Coughlin was the start of a partnership legendary in Chicago politics. In 1896, Coughlin and Kenna sought to fix the First Ward's lack of finances by holding an extravagant Christmas ball where vice lords and prostitutes mixed openly with police, politicians, and businessmen. From that first ball to the last in 1910, the tradition made its hosts lots of money. The Levee, however, had finally caused enough outrage among the public to shut it down in 1912. In 1923, a law was passed allowing only one alderman per ward. Kenna deferred to Bathhouse and stepped down, but retained his title as Democratic ward committeeman and his influence. As the gangster years came along, Coughlin and Kenna found themselves dancing to the drum of Big Jim Colosimo, Johnny Torrio, and Al Capone. The First Ward had become a darker place than ever before, and was no longer a place for the gentler corruption of Bathhouse and Hinky Dink.

4. THE CONVENTION CAPITAL OF THE WORLD

Okay, we had that little disaster in '68, and that made people think twice in '96, but Chicago has hosted more political conventions than any other city in the United States: twenty-five to be exact. Why? Location, location, location, among other things. Chicago's railroad system reached out in all directions and with the aviation age, Chicago's two airports made it even more convenient. Not to mention the hotels and restaurants. A slight lodging problem plagued the 1860 convention. The young town simply didn't have enough room at the forty-two inns, so conventioneers slept on cots and billiard tables. During 1916, two parties came to town, the Republicans, and an offshoot of the Republican Party that had split off four years before. The Republicans backed Charles Evans Hughes and the Progressives backed Theodore Roosevelt, who had backed Hughes's election as New York governor in 1906. Eventually, Roosevelt withdrew, giving Hughes the backing from both parties, but Hughes lost the presidential election to Democrat Woodrow Wilson. The 1932 Democratic convention in Chicago saw the nomination of Franklin Roosevelt as their candidate while the Republicans chose Herbert Hoover. More important was the vote by the delegates to finally repeal the 18th Amendment. Then there was the 1968 convention fiasco that scared both parties away from the city for twenty-eight years. When the 1996 convention came to Chicago, there was concern that the city might not be able to handle what it had handled so well so often before. The city and the country, however, had changed and while protesters did appear, it was mild in comparison to '68. Bill Clinton was again chosen as the Democratic presidential nominee.

5. **1968**

Peace demonstrators had more than enough points to back up their position without their more militant faction threatening to dump LSD in the water supply, release black widow spiders in the convention hall, or toss Molotov cocktails. But the city had already weathered a few riots that year and Mayor Daley was savvy enough to know that the protesters were out to cause a confrontation. Lyndon Johnson turned to Chicago's mayor in the hope that he'd be in control enough to host an uneventful Democratic convention. That Sunday before the convention, Daley's Chicago looked like a war zone with police-heavy streets and national guardsmen marching around. To those in uniform ordered to protect those streets, the thousands of demonstrators seemed like an invading army. Refused permits to sleep in Lincoln Park, demonstrators gathered anyway, refusing to budge. At curfew, police moved in, releasing gas. This was just the beginning. As the issue of Vietnam was battled over on the convention floor, the war continued on the streets. Wednesday, 15,000 protesters gathered in Grant Park to listen to speeches. A phalanx of police moved in when a teenage boy climbed up a flagpole and lowered the American flag. The

protesters began pelting cops with rocks and various substances (including feces), and the cops started smacking
heads. While cops overreacted, certain elements in the protesters inflamed the already-tense situation with talk of guer-
rilla war tactics. When 7,000 protesters began marching to
the convention hall, police were ordered to clear the streets.
By that time, Daley had assembled 12,000 police, 5,000 national guardsmen, and 6,000 specially trained Army troops.
The actions of Daley's forces were televised nationally as
television news coverage turned from the convention inside
the hall to the Chicago streets outside. When the smoke
cleared, the Democrats went on to lose one of the closest
political matches in presidential history, and many pointed
the finger at Daley. The city would heal from the wound of
1968, Daley would continue to win mayoral elections, but
the times they were a-changin', and Chicago would never be
quite the same again.

6. 1919 RIOTS

Between 1916 and 1919, approximately 50,000 blacks migrated to Chicago from the South to join those already in the
city. Conditions were better in the North, but segregation was
still a condition even in Chicago. A number of riots occurred
for various reasons shortly after the end of World War I. A
recession struck the country in 1919, and soldiers returned
to find that their jobs had been given to European ethnic immigrants or black migrants. When room for housing grew
limited, African Americans were forced out of white neighborhoods with intimidation and violence. On July 27, a
group of black boys were swimming in the "black" section of
Lake Michigan around Twenty-Fifth Street, when they drifted
into the "white" section at Twenty-Ninth Street. A white man
on the beach began throwing rocks at them, one hitting Eugene Williams who slipped unconscious into the water. Horrified, the boys swam back to Twenty-Fifth Street where they
told a black policeman about the incident. At Twenty-Fifth
Street, not only would the white policeman there not arrest

the rock thrower, he wouldn't permit the black officer to arrest him. The boys ran back to Twenty-Fifth Street beach and told a group there who marched back to the Twenty-Ninth Street beach. Before long, bricks and rocks were being thrown and six days of rioting began. White and black mobs roamed the city beating and killing anyone of the "wrong" race. Innocent people were pulled from vehicles and beaten or shot. By the time the national guard was called in, a total of twenty-three blacks and fifteen whites had been killed while 500 citizens had been injured. Arson left more than 3,000 residents without homes. After interviewing 450 witnesses for Eugene Williams's inquest, the Cook County coroner's final report stated that he had been swimming off Twenty-Ninth Street beach when stone throwing between black and white youths kept him from coming ashore. Clinging to a railroad tie, Eugene's strength eventually failed and he drowned. It was, undoubtedly, an attempt by officials not to put a racial face on the incident. They did include one wise suggestion in what was otherwise a half-baked report. They suggested that current economic conditions needed to be carefully considered and solutions found so that such an occurrence would not happen again. Sadly, almost fifty years later, another race riot would erupt due to the fact that those very conditions were never really attended to.

7. **THE BEER RIOTS**

Prohibitions of various sorts have been tried in Chicago. One of the most notorious attempts wasn't so much to control booze, but to control the influence of immigrants, which had grown considerably in the city. The Know Nothings was an ultraconservative, "no foreigners need apply" political party that didn't appreciate the fact that Chicago was the melting pot of the Midwest. In 1858, Dr. Levi Boone, great-grand-nephew of Daniel Boone, was elected mayor and instantly went after the Germans, whom he disliked particularly for their alliance with the Irish in certain political matters. He set up a policy that only natural-born citizens could apply for city jobs. He then hit both ethnic enclaves where it would hurt the most: in the saloons. Back then, saloons were the meeting centers of the neighborhoods. After work, men would hoist a few and discuss the news of the day, which often turned to politics. Boone decided to increase the liquor license fee from $50 to $300 a year. He then enacted an old law that forbade beer sales on Sunday, which was a big day for festivals and gatherings. Sunday was the one day that immigrant German and Irish workers could relax and enjoy themselves, and beer was a large part of the festivities. Defiantly, German beer hall and saloon owners kept their establishments open, refusing to pay the liquor license fee, and approximately 200 Germans were arrested for defiance of the law. On April 21, 1855, a mob of 400 disgruntled German and Irish converged on Courthouse Square, demanding the release of the prisoners and threatening the judge. Afterwards, they marched on Randolph and Clark Streets and disrupted traffic until police were dispatched and chased the mob off to their homes on the North Side. When they returned, they were armed with clubs, swords, axes, and shotguns, and the 400 had swelled to more than a thousand. Two hundred and fifty police were stationed in Courthouse Square, with cannons placed near City Hall. As the mob started onto the Clark Street drawbridge, the mayor shouted for the bridge tender to open the bridge. Using entreaties and threats, though, the mob convinced him to close it again. The riot that consumed Courthouse Square lasted more than an hour, both sides ending up wounded, with one death officially noted. In the end, sixty people were arrested, fourteen tried and two found guilty. As for the Know Nothings . . . they eventually faded. Dr. Boone eased up on his program and beer was again allowed to be sold on Sunday. Boone left office a one-term mayor.

8. JESSE

Criticized for being too militant on certain issues and for involving himself in issues that many felt didn't concern him,

Jesse Jackson's message is sometimes obscured by his methods. However, he has spent most of his life working for human rights. Born in 1941 in South Carolina, after high school he turned down a contract with the Chicago White Sox because a white player's salary was higher than his would be. In 1959, he attended the University of Illinois but again found a need to stand on principle when he turned down an athletic scholarship after being told that a black player would never be a quarterback. Headed in a different direction, Jackson transferred to North Carolina Agriculture and Technical College, and received a bachelor's of arts in sociology before going on to attend the Chicago Theological Seminary where he was ordained a Baptist minister in 1968. A few years *before* that, he was named head of the Chicago branch of the Southern Christian Leadership Conference (SCLC), and then the national branch of Operation Bread Basket (designed to convince businesses to hire and sell to blacks).

Jackson's Chicago Freedom Movement urged integration in schools and housing. He created Operation PUSH (People United to Save Humanity) in 1971 after a disagreement with the people at SCLC and soon went after the big cheese, organizing a group in 1972 to challenge Mayor Richard J. Daley at the Democratic National Convention. Jackson's charisma and intelligence helped him become a national figure but he was also able to organize Chicago's black community like no other before him. In 1984 and 1988, Jackson made runs for the presidency, which, while unsuccessful, still proved that the possibility of a black president seemed more in reach than ever in the nation's 200-plus years. His decisions to intervene in foreign affairs have been controversial, yet in 1991 he helped convince Saddam Hussein to release American hostages after the invasion of Kuwait. In 1994, he was sent to Nigeria by President Clinton as a peace envoy. Moving his Rainbow Coalition to Washington, D.C., Jackson continued to work for social change on a national level. In 1995, his son Jesse Jackson Jr. was elected to the House of Representatives, bringing a Jackson that much closer to the White House.

9. "CHICAGO AIN'T READY FOR REFORM"

These were the words, and perhaps the motto, of Mathias "Paddy" Bauler, alderman for the North Side's Forty-Third Ward for thirty years. Colorful and brash, he learned poker, pinochle, and pool as a young boy in the saloon his parents owned. Born in 1890, he worked behind the bar as soon as he was old enough, and ran his own speakeasy during Prohibition where politicians threw their victory parties. His first run for alderman in 1925 was unsuccessful, but his second attempt in 1933 produced a win. With the repeal of Prohibition, Bauler was able to open a legitimate saloon that same year. His aldermanic philosophy was no nonsense: fix the streets, collect the garbage, and clean the sidewalks. He had very little patience for the reformers he called "political science kids." To him, if something wasn't broken, you didn't fix it. The year he was elected, he had a scuffle with a Chicago policeman whom he shot twice; he later claimed the shooting was self-defense. The charges were dropped, but it was an odd incident for an alderman in his inaugural year. A classic storyteller, he held court at wild parties, traveling the world with his Forty-Fifth Ward pal, Charles Weber, and it didn't seem to matter where they got the money for the trips. But even as Bauler was relaxing in his role as alderman, his style of politics was in its heyday. Like Bathhouse and Hinky Dink, the city was outgrowing him. He reigned as alderman until 1967, and then retired to New Mexico before returning to Chicago in 1976, a year before his death. Paddy Bauler was a character, and while his politics might have been questionable, he sure was fun to watch.

10. KINGMAKER

I'll let you in on a little secret: John F. Kennedy very well could have won the 1960 presidential race without winning Cook County. Oh, it would have been closer than it already was, but the legend is largely apocryphal in keeping with Richard J. Daley's image as "kingmaker." Not that Daley's backing didn't help Kennedy in the long run, and the president turned to him a number of times during his administration for one favor or another. But while the Cook County votes Daley garnered for Kennedy bolstered the candidate's 8,000 margin in Illinois, the real force lay with the media. TV pollsters were declaring Kennedy victorious the night of the election, even though the official count wasn't in till the next day. Before that, Texas had turned for Kennedy. The rest is history. Republicans did charge the Daley administration with voter fraud, and instances like the precinct where fifty-four voters cast eighty-four votes did seem a little shady. But Republicans ultimately backed down, realizing that, should they demand an investigation, their own shady dealings downstate might be uncovered. That's the thing about king-making. Sometimes it all boils down to whose shady dealings end up most successful.

Skyscrapers

The Loop gets its name from the el tracks that travel in a loop around the financial district. Within this small loop a lot of business was conducted—a lot of business requiring a lot of floor space in a small area. With little land available in the early days of that cramped district, Chicago's skyline rose upward out of necessity. That necessity would inspire the construction of taller and taller buildings and because of that, Chicago is home to three of the tallest buildings in the world. Not a bad average for the "second city."

1. HOME INSURANCE BUILDING

The granddaddy of today's skyscrapers was a ten-story building, puny by today's standard but nonetheless an important piece in the evolution of the modern city skyline. When it was built between 1884 and 1885, the Home Insurance Building was remarkable because of its height. Architect William Le Baron Jenny designed his building utilizing breakthroughs in steel construction derived from bridge construction. Prior to this, a building's weight was borne by exterior walls, reducing the amount of windows available. Jenny designed his building so that an internal cage of iron bore the weight. This steel-frame construction opened up design possibilities not only for more and larger windows (a definite plus before electricity) but cleverer designs and ornamentation. And most importantly, Jenny's construction paved the way for taller buildings. It was no longer necessary for a building to be constructed in a "box" shape, and that would be more convenient for the space-constricted Loop. With the advent of hydraulic lifts for elevators and strides in fire-proofing, buildings could stretch higher and higher into the sky, each one a testament to architecture and engineering. Sadly, Jenny's building, which might be given landmark status today, didn't survive the test of time. It was torn down in 1931 to make way for the bigger and the better.

2. JOHN HANCOCK TOWER

From the ninety-fourth floor observatory of the John Hancock building you can see Illinois, Michigan, Indiana, and Wisconsin. This is the building that challenged the world. At one time the tallest in the world, it now comes in fourth, third in Chicago, and at one hundred stories, its height still makes it a popular tourist attraction and an imposing part of the Chicago skyline. Designed by Skidmore, Owings and Merrill, it was built from 1964 to 1969. At 1,105 feet, its unbroken lines are not a straight rectangle, like the Amoco Building, but rather taper down to a wider base. The width at the base is designed to provide maximum floor space for public shopping. There are also twenty stories for offices in the middle, and forty-eight stories of apartments toward the top. Also helping to support the structure in the high winds coming off the lake are the X braces running up the sides. It may no longer reign as the world's tallest, but it still has a distinctive strength to it, and a sturdiness that fits in well with the town.

3. THE SEARS TOWER

Kuala Lumpur, Shmuala Lumpur! That building in Kuala Lumpur may be the tallest in the world, but it's only by a few feet. The Sears Tower remains, in the hearts of all Chicagoans, the mother of all skyscrapers. It remains the tallest in Chicago. In fact, the buildings surrounding it look very much

J.T. Schmidt and Associates, Inc. (Crystal Lake, Ill)

The one-hundred-story John Hancock Tower (center) designed
by Skidmore, Owings and Merrill includes forty-eight
floors of apartments on the upper levels.

like children running around at the feet of this giant. The
John Hancock Tower may have paved the way, but the Sears
Tower pushed the envelope. Designed by Bruce Graham of
Skidmore, Owings and Merrill, the 110-story tower solved
the problem of stability in the windy city by utilizing a "bundle
tube" design. Nine squares, seventy-five-feet-square each, are
anchored in a deep concrete slab below the three sub-base-
ments. Two of the nine tubes stop at the fiftieth floor, two
more stop at the sixty-sixth floor, the next three stop at the
ninetieth floor, and the last stretches up the full 1,454-foot
height. Along with giving it its distinctive form, the tubes
bundled together provide lateral strength. Though the name
remains the Sears Tower, Sears moved its headquarters to
Hoffman Estates in 1992.

4. THE AMOCO BUILDING

Imagine placing a giant white Tetris rectangle in the midst of the city and you have the Amoco Building. At first glance you may simply think, "Why?" But upon studying it you may find it starting to grow on you. There's something clean about its simplicity. Facing Grant Park, the eighty-story Amoco Building rises to 1,136 feet and has no corner offices, the corners being indented. Designed by Edward Durell Stone of the Perkins and Will Partnership, it was built in 1974 and is noted for the uncaring arrogance of its design. It's pretty nervy to completely deplete the Carrara quarry (where Michelangelo got material for his little art projects), but they did, using the marble to completely wrap the outside of the building. Unfortunately, the marble slabs weren't able to withstand the temperature extremes and the thin slabs began to buckle at the southeast corner. Eventually, from 1990 to 1992, the marble was reclad in slabs of speckled North Carolina granite.

5. MARINA CITY

The two towers of Marina City have been compared to corncobs. Built from 1959 to 1967, they were designed for twenty-four-hour urban living, an answer to downtown workers fleeing to the suburbs. What Bertrand Goldberg designed was something totally different than what had gone before. The towers appear every bit as sturdy as other business skyscrapers on the skyline, but the rounded, scalloped shape softens it for daily living, as well as helping ease the problem of wind shear. The concept was simple: Offer Loop workers interested in downtown apartments the luxuries found in a neighborhood. If Austin Powers lived in Chicago, he'd live in Marina City. It is a city within a city. Within the buildings are stores, a restaurant, a fitness center, bank, swimming pool, skating rinks, a theater, a bowling alley, and an office tower. And don't worry about parking. The first half has garage floors. Situated on the river, the pie shape of the apartments

with balconies cantilevering from the perimeter columns offers a lovely view of the city. Goldberg pioneered the use of
concrete core construction. The cost-effective method at-
taches the floors to a central cylinder. Upon their completion,
the towers were the tallest in the world, and while that distinction didn't last long, Marina City, with its futuristic form,
remains a fascinating part of Chicago.

6. THE JEWELER'S BUILDING

This scraper is both good looking and functional. Now
known by the address 35 East Wacker, the building was at
one time the Pure Oil Building, and before that, the Jeweler's
Building. Built between 1924 and 1926, the building is
twenty-four stories high, sheathed in decorative terra-cotta
and based on a fifteenth-century Italian monastery. It was
designed by Frederick J. Thielbar and John Reed Fugard in
association with Giaver and Dinkelberg with the intention of
attracting jewelry designers, wholesalers, and retailers. With
this in mind, developers placed a parking garage in the central core. Jewelers could drive into the building from Lower
Wacker Drive and drive into elevators that would take them
to their office floors where they could park and head off to
their offices. By 1940, however, mechanical failure with the
elevator, as well as larger cars, made the garage obsolete
and the garage was converted to office space.

7. LAKE POINT TOWERS

Designed by John Heinreich and George Schipporeit, Lake
Point Towers was inspired by a 1921 sketch by Mies van der
Rohe (both men were students of Mies van der Rohe). With
its three gently rounded wings and softly mirrored finish, it's
a futuristic yet wonderful complement to the Lake Michigan
shoreline. When it was completed in 1968, it was the tallest
apartment building in the world and was meant to be one of
three towers, but the other two were never built. Instead, it
remains alone, slightly offset from the main clusters of high-

J.T. Schmidt and Associates, Inc. (Crystal Lake, Ill)

The sleek design of Lake Point Towers (center) was
inspired by the work of Mies van der Rohe.
Navy Pier can be seen in the left foreground.

rises, a lone sentinel standing on the shore, looking out over the lake.

8. THE TRIBUNE TOWER

Located on North Michigan Avenue, the Tribune Tower pays a gothic homage to a publishing empire. In 1922, Robert R. McCormick, publisher of the then–*Chicago Daily Tribune*, held an international architectural competition to design the paper's headquarters. The winning design by John Howell and Raymond Hood (who would later build Rockefeller Center in New York) was the sort of fortresslike structure you'd expect to see Batman hanging out in. And in fact, bats can sometimes be seen flying around the tower's lighted spire at night. At the base of the building are pieces of stone that came from other famous buildings like Westminster Abbey, the Coliseum of Rome, the Taj Mahal, and the Great Wall of China. The building was completed in 1925, but was criticized for its gothic look by supporters of the then-emerging Chicago school of architecture, who preached a more practical, less ornamental design of architecture. The gothic style, however, complete with flying buttresses at the crown, still gives it a distinctive power, a sort of conservative power similar to that held by the Tribune Company itself.

9. 333 WACKER DRIVE

Architect William Pedersen, of Kohn, Pedersen, Fox, designed 333 Wacker Drive with a vision of blending it harmoniously with its surroundings. The three-story base of polished granite and Vermont marble raises the office floors above the rear elevated train tracks. But it's the remaining thirty-three stories that make it such a striking edifice. At 850,155 square feet, the building is located where the Chicago River divides into the north and south branches, and its 365 feet of curving green glass facing the river seem to flow as the river flows. The glass picks up the reflection of the water as well as the surrounding buildings, and shimmers when the sun

J.T. Schmidt and Associates, Inc. (Crystal Lake, Ill)

The neo-Gothic Tribune Tower on North Michigan Avenue.

shines upon it, giving it an almost magically prismatic quality and making it a highlight of the riverboat tours

10. IBM BUILDING

This building holds the distinction of being the last office building designed by Ludwig Mies van der Rohe. Located between Wabash and State Streets, it's a fifty-two-story rectangle of brown-tinted glass and steel. Toward the end of his life, Mies van der Rohe worked toward achieving elegance in a simpler design. The streamlined, unadorned design of the IBM Building reflects this philosophy. The building utilizes the sun's reflection off the tinted glass to provide the ornamentation. But while it can appear elegant in its starkness, the building also has a coldness to it. From some angles it resembles the sort of computer chip one might find in an IBM computer.

Disasters

Chicago should have been doomed from the start. Built on marshland on the banks of a river, she's experienced a curious number of disasters involving fire, and she's weathered a number of storms, both natural and political. Yet, she's kept going. Just goes to show that you can't keep a good town down.

1. THE GREAT CHICAGO FIRE

It's now believed that it wasn't a cow, but rather a drunken neighbor breaking into Mrs. O'Leary's barn to purloin a bit of milk for his Irish punch (milk and whiskey), who started the Great Chicago Fire of 1871. In the darkened barn, a match was dropped and the rest is history. The city was still recovering from a severe summer drought, and since September 30, twenty major fires had broken out, four of them multiple alarm. Built primarily of wood, Chicago was also the center of the country's woodworking industry, full of furniture mills and lumberyards. It grew up in a hurry, but the fire department didn't keep pace. Flames broke out in the O'Leary barn at Jefferson and De Koven Streets on October 8 at 8:40 P.M., spreading rapidly in the common alley. Fueled by the wind, the fire swept through the financial districts, incinerating Chicago's premier hotels and museums and burning its way through some of the city's finest homes and mansions, while

Chicago Historical Society

"Chicago in Flames/View from Randolph Street Bridge, No. 1,"
by Werlag and Druck, Wandsbeck, Germany, 1871–1872.
Historians now believe that the infamous Great Chicago Fire
of 1871 was not started by Mrs. O'Leary's cow, as popularly
believed, but by a drunken neighbor.

the oily river clogged with boats gave it plenty to feed off of.
Prisoners in the basement of the courthouse were freed and
told to flee the inferno. Women gave birth in the streets,
some burned to death on the spot, and many residents
jumped into Lake Michigan to escape the fire. Some never
made it out. Around 3 A.M. on October 10, rain finally fell and
doused whatever hot spots remained, but the fire had leveled
a good portion of the city. The exact number of deaths remain uncertain because many who didn't drown were incin-
erated, but it's estimated that 300 people died. Fifteen
thousand buildings were lost, with the damage estimated at
$200 million. The fire bankrupted sixty insurance compa-
nies. Chicago may have been down, but it wasn't out. More
than half of the city was rebuilt within a year, and the fire

actually offered city planners a clean slate to devise an even grander city, paving the way for some of the most notable architecture in the world. Sadly, anti-Irish sentiment (much of it appearing in the *Chicago Tribune*) fueled the myth of the cow and the lantern, and Catherine O'Leary went to her grave years later with the stigma of that night weighing upon her. In 1997, 126 years after the blaze that transformed a city, a resolution passed by the city of Chicago officially exonerated Mrs. O'Leary and her cow. And fittingly, on the spot where the O'Leary homestead once stood, now stands the site of a fire academy.

2. THE *EASTLAND* TRAGEDY

Out of gratitude for the hard work of their 7,000 employees, the Western Electric Company organized a grand picnic to be held in Michigan City, Indiana. Passage across Lake Michigan for employees and their families was arranged on a slender steamship known as the *Eastland*. Once called "the aristocrat of the lakes," she was also a disaster waiting to happen. The ship's construction made her top-heavy when passengers were aboard, and the concrete used to shore up rotting upper decks only added to this. To help improve a slow season, the ship's owners put more lifeboats on board, enabling the city inspector to increase the certificate passenger limit to 2,500, which meant severe overcrowding. At 6:30 A.M. on July 24, 1915, excited passengers began boarding, most preferring the view from the upper decks. As was his custom, Capt. Harry Peterson ordered that both ballast tanks be emptied to straighten the gangplank and make boarding easier. The ship rose but began to list toward the river side (port). Number two ballast tank was filled, but soon the ship listed toward the dock. More adjustments were made, but the list went back to port and continued to grow. Lines holding the *Eastland* to the pier snapped, sending people sliding off the sloping deck as the ship rolled over. The Chicago River became thick with struggling people, with those beneath the water grabbing at the clothes of those on the surface, pulling them under. Flotation devices tossed out by the people on the dock only served to further clog the river. In the meantime, nearby ironworkers grabbed acetylene torches to cut through to the screaming victims trapped in the holds, despite Capt. Peterson's efforts to stop them and save the ship. Recovery lasted for three days, as men in diving suits went down to hunt for survivors in the holds of the ship. A net was stretched across the river to catch the bodies of men, women, and children floating out to the lake. When it was over, 844 bodies were sent to the Second Regiment Illinois National Guard Armory on Carpenter Street for identification. In the July heat they were embalmed on the spot as lines of grieving relatives came in to find their loved ones. Whole families were wiped out. In one church, a funeral mass was held for thirty victims, some of the coffins resting on the front pews. Funeral parlors ran out of hearses so Marshall Field donated some of its delivery trucks to be used for the purpose. When all was said and done, this maritime disaster took more lives than the Great Chicago Fire. There were no icebergs involved. No squalls or legendary gales. Simply the greed of a ship line that went bankrupt shortly after, and the incompetence of a captain who never sailed again.

3. THE UNION STOCKYARD FIRE

Built in 1865, the 450 acres of the revolutionary Union Stockyards helped make Chicago "the hog butcher to the world." Slaughterhouses, barns, offices, and other buildings packed the area, crisscrossed with railroad tracks. One out of every five Chicagoans worked there, but it was a harsh place to work and live. The stench of death permeated the air. Waste from the meatpacking plants traveled to the Chicago River via a waterway nicknamed "Bubbly Creek" because the waste fermenting there percolated. Such conditions inspired Upton Sinclair to write his famous novel, *The Jungle*, which, in turn, inspired President Theodore Roosevelt to back new food safety laws. The stockyards saw a number of fires in its time but the most serious occurred around 4 A.M. on December 22, 1910, when a fire broke out in the basement hide room of the Nelson-Morris number seven plant. By the time five engines and two hook-and-ladder trucks arrived, the fire had already engulfed the basement and first floor of the six-story building, the wooden floor saturated with animal grease fueling the spread. The lack of a sprinkler system made conditions worse while the reserve of saltpeter used to cure hundreds of hogs in the building was also of great concern. The layout of the yards made fighting the fires difficult as structural obstacles limited access to the burning buildings. Portable ladders were needed to climb over the freight cars. The building burned for sixteen hours before the blaze was finally put out. Twenty-six hours more and the fire was officially declared struck out. Four hundred thousand dollars in damages was nothing compared to the toll the fire took in lives. Twenty-one firefighters and three civilians were killed, and fifteen firefighters were injured. An entire hook-and-ladder company had been wiped out. Eventually, the stockyards would be closed down, but not after more years of bloodshed, animal and human.

4. THE CHICAGO FLOOD

No lives were lost in the Chicago Flood of 1992, but the magnitude of the problem caused billions in damage and shut down the Loop. The sharp irony is that it happened in a city known for its great fires. On the morning of April 13, water was discovered flooding into the Merchandise Mart located at the North branch of the Chicago River between Wells and Orleans. Several blocks away another basement began to flood, and by 9:30 A.M., city engineers discovered that a decades-old freight tunnel beneath the river had been punctured by a piling placed around the support structure of a bridge. The leak was filling the forty miles of tunnels leading right into the Loop. Downtown was evacuated while the Army Corp of Engineers worked to create a plug that could withstand the pressure of the water it would need to hold back. As days passed, fish were showing up in the state office building and the city worried over possible disease from the river water seeping in. There was also a concern about water hitting Commonwealth Edison transformers and the damage that could do. Eventually, a successful plug was devised and 131 million gallons of water were drained slowly, to keep the foundations from imploding, and diverted into a deep tunnel project so it wouldn't pollute Lake Michigan before it was sent to a water reclamation plant. The process took a month, crews working in twenty-four-hour shifts. Once the water was out, the cleanup began. Damage exceeded one billion dollars, and while larger companies and businesses were faced with weeks of recovery, many small businesses never reopened. The Chicago Flood is another example of the city winning the battle with nature. This time.

5. THE BLIZZARDS OF '67 & '79

On January 26, 1967, twenty-four inches of snow stopped Chicago in its tracks. After a spate of unseasonably warm temperatures, the first flakes started falling at 5:02 A.M. and continued for twenty-nine hours. Twenty-four million tons of snow made roads impassable. Stranded commuters took refuge in hotels, and even in their cars. O'Hare International Airport was closed for three days. Offices and schools took several days to reopen. Those unprepared for such a bombardment found themselves trudging through the snow dragging sleds and toboggans to do their grocery shopping. Making matters worse were the periodic snowfalls and the bitter cold occurring for days after. So much snow fell that a few train cars of the powder were shipped to Florida to surprise children who'd never seen snow before. Twelve years later, on January 12, 1979, the city was blanketed again, this time by a twenty-inch accumulation that fell on top of the seven- to ten-inch base left over from a New Year's Eve storm. Along with transportation problems, garbage could not be collected and began piling up, attracting an excess of rats. Problems at the cemeteries also delayed burials for several weeks. Probably the most notable thing about the '79 blizzard was that it led to the unseating of a mayor. Mayor Michael J. Bilandic was sharply criticized for City Hall's handling of the blizzard and no one's spears were sharper than those of his opponent, Jayne Byrne. When Election Day rolled around, Chicagoans let their frustration be known and elected Jayne Byrne as Chicago's first woman mayor.

6. THE HEAT WAVE OF '95

From July 12 to July 16, 1995, the city sizzled like never before. One hundred and six degrees Fahrenheit on July 13 set the record for the warmest July temperature ever recorded in the city. In some high-rises it reached 120 degrees. It wasn't just the heat, it was the humidity, with record-high levels both day and night. Pavement buckled, cars broke down in the streets, and power grids failed thanks to record-high electrical usage, leaving residents without electricity for up to two days. One contributing factor to the extreme city heat was "the urban heat island" effect. High concentrations of buildings and asphalt absorb more heat during the day and radiate more heat at night compared to rural areas. By the end, 733 people were dead. Most were elderly and alone, unable to afford air-conditioning or too afraid to open their windows in high crime areas. Many were found only because of the stench of decay. Heat wave–related deaths continued after the city cooled down as patients died in the hospital several weeks later. An inadequate heat wave warning system, as well as inadequate hospital and ambulance facilities, played a part in the deadliest heat wave in the city's history.

7. OUR LADY OF ANGELS

On a cold December 1, 1958, two boys emptying trash in Our Lady of Angels School returned to their second-floor classroom and told their teacher that they smelled smoke in the basement stairwell. So began the drama that unfolded at 2 P.M. that day. The teacher contacted a neighboring teacher, then, per school policy, went to inform the principal before sounding the fire alarm. The principal was substituting in another classroom downstairs, so rather than waste more time, the teacher hurried back to her classroom where the smoke in the hallway was already thick. She and the neighboring teacher evacuated their students, but by the time the first teacher ran back to pull the fire alarm, it was too late. The long corridor of the second floor was already engulfed in flames. Screaming children still trapped on the second floor rushed to classroom windows and began jumping to the pavement twenty-five feet below. After the fire was struck out, the bodies of many who couldn't reach the sills were found piled in front of them. Ninety-two students and three nuns lost their lives in the five-alarm blaze to which sixty fire companies and ambulances responded. Though the cause of the fire was never pinpointed, a number of factors made the situation much worse. Built in 1903, the building contained no sprinkler system. The school was overcrowded with up to sixty children in each of the twenty-four classrooms. The corridors were covered with a combustible rubbery paint, which produced a thick black smoke as it burned. Fire alarms rang only in the building, not at the nearest fire department. The only bright spot in this tragedy is that it inspired an improvement in fire safety laws that helped make schools a lot safer.

8. CRASH OF FLIGHT 191

On May 25, 1979, the most deadly commercial airline crash in U.S. history occurred as American Airlines Flight 191 crashed half a mile from the end of the runway. Taking off from what was then known as Chicago International Airport at O'Hare Field (now known simply as O'Hare Airport), the plane was headed on a nonstop flight from Chicago to Los Angeles with 271 persons on board. Passengers included *Playboy* magazine's managing editor Sheldon Wax and its fiction editor Vicki Haiden. On takeoff the plane reached 400 feet and then lost its portside engine and began to roll sharply to the left. A minute later, it plowed into a field, barely missing the adjacent Des Plaines trailer park. All on board were killed as well as two on the ground, and the flames and smoke from the wreckage reached an altitude higher than even the plane itself was able to attain. Carrying an enormous amount of jet fuel, the plane's wreckage burned so hot that it kept rescue personnel from getting close for a good portion of time.

9. THE LOOP CRASH

The elevated train is a fixture of Chicago. On February 4, 1977, a crash occurred in the Loop the likes of which has never been seen before or since. Switching problems sent Evanston express trains traveling counterclockwise around the outer loop track instead of the inner one. While the problem was eventually corrected, a few Evanston trains were finishing up their runs on the outer track. At the State/Lake station, around 5:25 P.M., one such train was loading up. Behind it, a Ravenswood train waited for the Evanston train to clear the station so it could pull in. Two blocks away, at the Randolph/Wabash station around the bend, an Oak Park–bound Lake-Dan Ryan train finished up its boarding. At 5:27, ignoring the restrictive signal, the motorman pulled out at a speed of less than fifteen miles per hour around the Lake & Wabash curve and collided with the Ravenswood train. Oddly, even after the collision, he began to apply motor power. With the Ravenswood train on an elevated curve, the first three cars were forced upward and outward, crashing to the street 100 feet below. The last four cars stayed on the tracks and held the fourth car, still buckled to it, dangling above the street. One hundred and eighty people were injured, with eleven killed, and rescue efforts continued for two hours to extricate people from the wreckage. Nearby businesses were turned into makeshift infirmaries as the injured were rescued from the trains, and priests administered last rites to those most seriously hurt. It was revealed later that the motorman of the Oak Park–bound train had a poor safety record (including a previous derailment), and he was held responsible for the crash. Nothing since has happened to match this crash. Hopefully, the record won't be broken.

10. **FORT DEARBORN MASSACRE**

We end this chapter at the beginning. The Fort Dearborn Massacre occurred on the cusp of Chicago's birth and illustrates its never-say-die spirit. Built in 1803 on the south bank of the Chicago River, Fort Dearborn was basically an outpost, housing a mere hundred soldiers. There seemed little need for more. Relations between settlers and the local Native Americans, the Potawatomi, were peaceful until the War of 1812. Then British agents began to stir up trouble and arm Midwestern tribes who feared encroachment by white settlers. That same year, a group of British-backed Winnebago Indians attacked a farm four miles south of Fort Dearborn, shooting and scalping two farmhands. A fearful community sought refuge at the fort. Realizing they could never withstand an attack, Fort Dearborn captain, Nathanial Heald, was ordered to evacuate the fort and travel by foot and wagon to the nearest U.S. fort. Members of the pro-American Miami tribe arrived to act as an escort. They made it about a mile and a half away before hostile Native Americans swarmed down upon them. Friendly Potawatomi were able to break into the frenzy and grab several settlers away, but of the ninety-four people attempting to flee, about sixty were killed. The fort was burned to the ground. Yet, as would happen so often in its history, Chicago rose from the ashes four years later as settlers again returned to the area. And in those sixty years, until the city burned down again, Chicago became known as the fastest-rising city in the world.

Feats and Faux Pas

L ike architects, engineers found Chicago a challenging place to put their talents and imaginations to work. The great Ellis Chesbrough helped the town out of a number of jams. But then there were those architectural slipups, whether accidental or planned, that didn't quite work out.

1. THE ILLINOIS-MICHIGAN CANAL

It was the concept of a canal connecting Lake Michigan and the Illinois River that helped make the smelly swamps the Indians called "Chigagou" so appealing. In 1674, when explorer Louis Joliet proposed such a canal, portages to get from the lake to the Illinois River, which was a route to the Mississippi River, were arduous as canoes and heavy cargo had to be carried between the two rivers. It wasn't until 1821, however, that Congress authorized financing for a canal to be built that would connect Lake Michigan with the Illinois River. Once this canal was built, it would connect by water the east with the untamed west, opening up more efficient opportunities for trade. But by 1841, the canal was in financial jeopardy. A panic that hit a year after ground was broken in 1836 stopped federal payments for the project. When work was suspended due to lack of funding in 1841, future mayor William Ogden and fellow canal commissioners worked on ways to finance completion and finally developed a bond and loan program that would do this. But the cost was in more than just money. There was a cost in human lives as well. Irish immigrants, long looked down upon by society, were nonetheless employed to do some of the most brutal labor in any city they landed in. Hired to work on the canal, the Irish worked in a frenzy in the steamy summer months and the frigid winter, often without shovels or tools, digging the ditch by hand, if necessary. For a dollar a day, and enough whiskey to hold them, they labored six days a week, devoting only Sunday to church. Malaria, waterborne diseases, and sheer exhaustion took many Irish lives. The hundred-mile canal, however, was completed in 1848. Sixty feet wide, six feet deep, it ran from Ashland Avenue on the South branch of the Chicago River down into the Illinois River near LaSalle-Peru, Illinois. Along the way, it crossed various aquatic roadblocks as surface streams called for constructing slackwater pools, while differences in water levels in other areas were dealt with by building aqueducts. Canals were cut from the Calumet River, the Des Plaines River, and the Fox River to help feed water into the Illinois-Michigan and keep it open. Along with opening up the West, it helped raise the status of the little settlement of Chicago. Speculators came to town to buy and sell the soon-to-be-valuable land, followed by businessmen who built the industries that would employ the immigrants who would follow after that. The irony of the Illinois-Michigan Canal is that, while it would remain a valuable addition to transportation, by the time it was finally opened, it was already becoming unnecessary. In 1825, the world's first public railway was built. By 1848, Ogden, one of the canal's biggest proponents, would be on to his next venture: bringing the railroad to Chicago. Within a decade, Chicago would be the railroad capital of the world.

2. FLOATING FOUNDATIONS

Chicago's loose, marshy soil proved a major hurdle for early builders of the city. Trying to reach the bedrock between ninety and 150 feet down was next to impossible with the water and the soil that caved in when regular digging equipment was used. Sixty to seventy-five feet of sand and soft clay lay above that bedrock and couldn't support the foundation piles being dug. With the water level of Chicago being only around fifteen feet belowground, it was difficult to construct buildings with two and three levels of basements. To accommodate the number of people utilizing the increasingly busy downtown center known as the Loop, builders had to build up, but the soil left little support for buildings taller than a few stories. An ingenious German immigrant named Frederick H. Baumann devised a way to support masonry buildings up to six stories tall by digging down to a shallow layer of dry clay, and in the building's basement constructing huge stone pyramids that rested on beds of concrete to support the weight of the walls. These broad pyramids allowed the structure to settle evenly. When Burnham and Root designed the ten-story Montauk building, John Root decided to adopt Baumann's pyramid support, but there was one problem. On the heaviest side of the Montauk building was a wall that would hold a high stack of fireproof vaults. Baumann's pyramids would leave little, if any, room for these vaults. Mulling it over, Root came up with a plan of his own. For this side, he laid down a thin base of cement on the level clay, on which he laid a grillwork of steel rails. This was covered with cement to prevent rusting. Repeated enough times, this two-foot-thick raft was then fitted with a cast-iron shoe into which the building's frame columns were placed. Dubbed "floating foundations" by Root, this support turned out to equal the support strength of a seven-foot-high pyramid. While Root's revolutionary support foundation was used on only one side of the Montauk building, later buildings designed by Burnham and Root and other firms would use this method, which turned out to be cheaper than the foundations used before. It was only after the discovery in the 1890s of caisson-created foundations, which were able to reach down to hard rock, that the floating foundation was no longer needed. But it helped lead the way for bigger and better things in Chicago.

3. **THAT FRUSTRATING RIVER**

The Chicago River's potential as a transportation route connecting the eastern part of the country with the rest of the country was instrumental in the city's amazing growth. As Chicago grew, however, it became apparent that this blessing was a double-edged sword. It was, for decades, a wild and untamed creature. In 1849, an ice jam caused the river to rise, which lifted ships into the city. Ice floes remained a problem, causing damage and sometimes loss of life. During the 1871 fire, it was hoped that the river would come to the town's rescue, but it was so polluted that parts of it burst into flame as the fire fed on the surface oil. The pollution in the river, which had been used as the dumping ground for the meatpackers and industrialists, threatened the safety of the Lake Michigan drinking water. After an 1885 cholera epidemic, it was decided that the river needed to be turned. Looking to engineer Ellis Chesbrough, the town deepened a bed in the canal, which, along with pumps at Bridgeport, caused the river to flow back into the bed of the canal.

On July 18, 1871, the town turned out to watch the temporary dam holding back the river torn down. It appeared that nothing happened. The waters remained motionless. Someone suggested throwing straws into the water. The straws floated uncertainly at first before finally beginning to move south. With that, Chicago had the only river in the world that flowed backward. The poor thing always seemed to be in the way, though. In 1928, when downtown Chicago was expanded, $9 million was spent moving the south branch of the river fourteen miles west. But despite all these labors at taming her, it seemed the hardest task of all would be cleaning her. As the town began to wake up to the beauty of the river running through the city, efforts began to scrub the river free of a century of disrespect. In 1970, both the Chicago and Calumet Rivers were discovered to be dirtier than ever. It would take a massive effort to reverse the damage. A huge storm water control project was started to prevent sewage from flooding and heading into the river. Guidelines for riverbank usage were drawn up. A riverwalk plan for the north branch was created. And soon sections of the river were even available for boat tours and canoeing. Still, while the people of Chicago seem to be getting along with its river, the flood of 1992 made the city realize how insistent the river could be when it wanted to be.

4. TUNNELS ALL AROUND

In 1840, at the corner of Lake and Michigan, Chicago's first pumping station was built by the private organization known as the Chicago Hydraulic Company. The station pumped water from 150 feet out in Lake Michigan. When it was discovered that fresher water could be drawn from further out into the lake, the city tried to place an intake crib 600 feet offshore, but efforts were hampered by Michigan's rough waves. The brilliant engineer, Ellis Chesbrough, came to the rescue as he would so often for Chicago. He came up with an idea to construct a water tunnel beneath the lake. At two miles long and dug sixty feet through clay under the lake level, Irish immigrants toiled in sixteen-hour shifts in the claustrophobic conditions, never certain if one wrong strike would cause a rupture and bring the fury of the lake down upon them. During the other eight hours, bricklayers came in to lay the bricks that lined the five-foot diameter tunnel. Completed in 1867, the tunnel led to an intake crib made of timber two miles offshore, while the shore end of the tunnel was connected to a pumping station completed two years later. While this would be the jumping-off point for the major waterworks of the city, Lake Michigan wasn't the only body of water people were burrowing under. In 1867, another engineering project began that would address the problem of the traffic jams on river bridges. With river traffic increasing, drawbridges over the river were raised for longer periods of time. In July of that year, J.K. Lake began construction on the Washington Street traffic tunnel, which, at 1,605 feet, was completed in 1869. That same year, the second tunnel under LaSalle designed by William Bryson was started and, at 1,890 feet long, opened in 1871. In 1901, a series of freight tunnels would begin to worm their way beneath most of the downtown streets. Many were intended to carry the telephone and telegraph cables of the Illinois Telephone and Telegraph Company. When the company ran out of funds in 1903, the Illinois Tunnel Company took over the twenty miles of tunnel and as an organized series of tunnels were built, a new company was formed in 1904. The Chicago Warehouse and Terminal Company constructed tunnels under railroad and private property, connecting shafts and elevators to buildings. This allowed freight haulers to avoid the still-congested Chicago streets. Though it changed hands in 1912, the system continued with about sixty-two miles of tunnels, forty feet beneath Chicago. The tunnels were equipped with track for trolleys and electric locomotives and were in operation until 1959 when their controlling companies, the Chicago Tunnel Company and the Chicago Tunnel Terminal Company, were liquidated. They would be all but forgotten until 1992, when a leak in one of the freight tunnels led to the flooding of the downtown Loop.

5. WHEN IN DOUBT, RAISE THE CITY

In the early days, Chicago was a muddy town. That's not unusual, since the city was built on a marsh. Chicagoans tried not to let the muck deter them from daily life, plowing ahead through the ankle-deep mire or utilizing walkways built of wooden planks that only ended up rotting from the moisture beneath. One tale of the time spoke of a man protruding head and shoulders from the street when a passerby asked if he could lend assistance. The man in the mud replied, "No thanks, I have a fine horse under me." Chicago had a take-it-as-it-comes sort of attitude to inconveniences in the city, but the mud was a serious threat. It was a breeding ground for germs, especially cholera, which broke out periodically and killed many in the city. Ladies avoided certain areas as much as possible because their dresses, dragging in the filth, would pick up the various diseases and bring them home. At last, the Chicago Board of Sewerage Commissions turned to Ellis Chesbrough from Boston to come up with a plan. He recommended a storm sewer system, the first of the kind in the country. Since the city was only three to four feet above the level of Lake Michigan, the first step would be to raise the city. In stepped George Pullman, a man who made a lot of money perfecting a way to raise buildings. His system involved surrounding the building with hundreds of men turning hundreds of jackscrews placed beneath the building at the same time. A signal was given and the men pulled a turn, and then waited for the next signal. It was painstaking, but so smooth that when the Briggs House hotel at Randolph and Wells was raised, the hotel was open for business all the while. Once the building was raised, storm sewers were installed on the streets and streets filled in to the level of the doors. The buildings would be jacked up from four to fifteen feet with suitable foundations placed beneath the buildings. It took almost two decades to finish the job and the project became the talk of the nation.

6. THE DEEP TUNNEL

Chicago has had a battle with pollution since its beginning when settlers to the area noted the stench produced by the swampy river. While reversing the river's flow helped send the city's sewage away from Lake Michigan, the city's freshwater source, if storms were severe enough, the sewage-tainted storm water could still find its way back into the lake. Plus, while the flood of 1992 is still fresh in the minds of Chicagoans, there were two other incidents, 1954 and 1957, when the river actually flooded over and into downtown Chicago. Water, which had so often been a boon to the city's economy, could also be a detriment when not controlled. Along came the Deep Tunnel Project (at the time of this writing, still under construction), said to be the biggest project of its kind ever. At approximately $3.6 billion, it is certainly the largest public works projects in the city's history. One hundred and fifty to 350 miles below the city, 130 miles of tunnels (some thirty-five feet in diameter) will divert storm water overflowing from sewers into huge reservoirs. Upon its completion, the project will be able to hold forty-one billion gallons of water. The project will not only aid Chicago with her storm water, but will help with flood control for fifty-one suburbs in Cook County. The Deep Tunnel Project came in handy during the flood of 1992 when 131 million gallons of water were diverted from the flood tunnels downtown to the project's tunnels to await treatment.

7. A PLANNED COMMUNITY

Once his business and wealth had been established in Chicago, George Pullman decided to tackle the problem of worker apathy. The majority of workers in his factory left work and returned to neighborhoods full of crime, vice, and poverty—if they returned home at all. These neighborhoods also had plenty of saloons to keep a man busy after work. Inspired by a visit to Saltaire, Northern England, where Sir Titus Salt had built his workers a town free of crime, disease, and despair, Pullman returned home intent on doing the same in Chicago. Pullman's idea was the grandest-planned community the country had seen.

Thirty-eight hundred acres of land in Lake Calumet, nine miles south of Chicago, were chosen and work started May 26, 1880. Forty-five million fired clay bricks and sixteen million feet of lumber constructed the buildings designed by noted Chicago architect Solemen S. Beman, while the layout of the park, the arcade, and the open spaces was placed in the hands of landscape architect Nathan F. Barrett. By a lake with an ornamental fountain stood a fancy hotel and a limestone church. The Arcade Building, made of brick and glass, held the town's post office, bank, a library housing six thousand books, theater, and shops. Athletic Island, a man-made island in Lake Calumet, held one of the best sports facilities in the United States, with an ice-skating rink, rowing course, two grandstands, and a cinder track. Pullman even held its own version of the Olympics every Memorial Day, known as the Spring Games. Every residence had indoor toilets, running water, and gas. The paved, tree-lined streets were lit by gaslights and the grounds were meticulously cared for at the cost of the company. This was all paradise to workers used to living in neighborhoods oozing with mud and dirt. Without a case of cholera or typhoid, the town had the lowest death rate of any community its size. There were rules to living in this paradise, however. In trying to better the workers' lives, Pullman attempted to control them like children. The workers could only rent, not own, the houses. The only drinking establishment was in the Florence Hotel (named after Pullman's favorite daughter), which was off-limits to the average worker. The worker who was discovered drinking on or off duty could be fired and evicted. And inspections were conducted regularly to make sure all rules were being followed. Those who could handle the rules found the town a far cry from the slums many had come from. Those who couldn't found it beautiful but constricting. Few felt at home in a town they were unable to voice an opinion on. The inspections left citizens with a constant feeling of scrutiny.

Trouble really began in 1885 when, due to a recession, Pullman issued an across-the-board pay cut. This was a severe blow to the workers who earned slightly better than average, but still low wages. Talk of strike was frowned upon. Anyone talking about it was fired. Then came the panic of 1893, which hit everyone hard, particularly the nation's railroads. As his sleeper car business went down, Pullman was forced to close his Detroit plant and cut wages 25 percent or more. Yet, he still guaranteed a full rate of return to his investors. A cut in pay, then, did not mean a cut in rent. An unskilled worker making an average of $38 per month was still expected to come up with the $14 a month rent. The cost of food in the company stores didn't lower, either. Many workers found themselves with a roof over their heads, but starving. When pressed on these matters by members of the newly formed American Railroad Union, Pullman no longer had the air of the fatherly benefactor but rather of the steely eyed businessman. To him, his worker's utopia was a real-estate venture, one he refused to lose money on. On May 11, 1894, two thousand tradesmen and unskilled workers went on strike to protest the laying off of three members of the arbitration committee who had been assured that there'd be no reprisals by the company. As sympathy for the workers' plight spread to twenty-seven states, and members of the American Railway Union refused to handle any trains that included Pullman cars, President Grover Cleveland dispatched federal troops to Chicago, despite objections from Governor John Altgeld. Violence erupted when the soldiers entered the town, but they were able to quell the riot. A federal report later condemned Pullman for his failure to deal fairly with his workers as well as for rent gouging. Four years later, Pullman died, and the citizens were given permission by federal courts to buy their property. In 1971, the South Pullman District was designated a national landmark.

8. STREETERVILLE

For three decades he was master of all he surveyed. On July 11, 1886, George Wellington Streeter and his wife, Maria, found his homemade steamboat running aground on a sand-bar offshore from what is now Superior Street. He was given permission by the wealthy property owners on shore to stay until his boat was repaired. He ended up staying thirty years. It began slowly. Over time, sand began to fill in between the boat and the shore. Along came contractors in need of a place to dump their debris from construction and Captain Streeter was only too happy to oblige. Before they knew it, the Streeters were smack in the midst of acres of new land. A Civil War veteran, Streeter was a man of many hats—showman, Mississippi steamboat operator, a circus promoter—and he knew an opportunity when he saw one. He claimed the one hundred or so acres of land as his, deciding that it wasn't part of Chicago or Illinois, and declared it the "District of Lake Michigan." From an office in the Tremont Hotel, he sold parcels of the land to interested buyers. One can imagine what the wealthy elite thought when a shanty-town rose up on their doorsteps. As the case went back and forth in the courts, Streeter also stood his ground with a gun since his neighbors staged police raids on the area. In 1918, however, he lost his case. He was evicted from his land for selling liquor on Sundays. Afterward, deputies burned every-thing to the ground. His fate was sealed when the Michigan Avenue Bridge opened in 1920. Suddenly, what had been an eyesore of a landfill was considered prime residential and commercial real estate. Streeter heirs continued the fight till 1940 but to no avail. Chicago has a lot to thank George Streeter for. Were it not for his rundown little steamboat slamming into a simple little sandbar, Streeterville, with the ritzy stores and eateries, and even the Chicago campus of Northwestern University, wouldn't be enjoying the benefits of that landfill today.

9. CAMP DOUGLAS

It was originally built as a Union Army training post. The year was 1861. The Civil War was beginning, and few people fore-saw the horror that it would become. Ultimately, what this camp at Thirty-First Street and Cottage Grove became was one of the cruelest prisoner of war camps ever. Between 1862 and 1865, twenty-six thousand Confederate prisoners were crammed into the temporary wooden barracks to wait out the war. The first prisoners came in the still-frigid month of February. Blankets and sacks with holes in them were ex-changed for the prisoners' clothes, which had been confis-cated to help keep the prisoners from attempting to escape. Punishment was brutal. Beatings were frequent and food was withheld. Some starved to death, others froze to death in tents. The winter of 1864 was particularly bitter and 1,091 prisoners in four months succumbed to it, a record even for Camp Douglas. The camp is gone now. All that remains is a monument erected by Southern veterans. No one is sure how many died at Camp Douglas—the records have been lost. Beneath the monument is a mass grave where the dead were buried toward the end. Estimates are upward of 6,000, and a bronze tablet in the monument is inscribed with the names of some of the soldiers buried there. Others were buried in unmarked paupers' graves in the southeast corner of what would become Lincoln Park. In 1867, those remains were reinterred about five miles from the camp in Oak Woods Cemetery.

10. THE ROBERT TAYLOR HOMES

This was the largest housing project in the country. Completed in 1962, it joined the ranks of Cabrini-Green and Dearborn Homes, along with the Henry Horner Homes, as some of the most depressing and dangerous areas to live in the world. It was the Daley administration's attempt to deal with the issue of housing for African Americans. Rather than open the city up by doing away with restrictive housing laws, the Daley administration decided instead to cram black citizens into boxes. Believe it or not, it was a sincere attempt by Daley to address the issue of housing during the second southern-black migration, but it failed to address the economic and social realities blacks were faced with in the city. Often, families who took the chance to live in the soulless projects never came out of them. They were cities within a city, segregating with kindness. The Robert Taylor Homes, housing around twenty-eight thousand people in its twenty-eight sixteen-story units, were clumped together on islands of concrete and like other housing projects, were infested with drugs and gangs and the hopeless. Decent housing projects could be built. After the first migration, the Ida B. Wells Homes were completed in 1941 and located in the Black Belt. They provided homes for 1,662 families and were a godsend to black families whose spirits were slowly being crushed to death by the lack of decent housing. The first Cabrini Homes, named after Frances Cabrini, were row houses, right next to each other, built in an area that had been cleared out of slums. The structures were built in 1942, fifty-five two- to three-story buildings that were not opulent but, with green lawns around them, resembled more of a neighborhood than future projects. The extension to this project, built in 1959, was the start of what would become Cabrini-Green: Fifteen seven-, ten-, and nineteen-story buildings, followed by the William Green Homes built in 1962, consisting of eight sixteen-story buildings. After the Chicago Housing Authority was taken over by the Department of Housing and Urban Development, an effort was begun to redevelop the whole system, starting with the projects themselves. Demolition began to make way for smaller, mixed-income housing with private-housing vouchers given to the inhabitants to make the transition easier. The concept is to turn projects into communities that can offer hope to the lives of every Chicagoan.

Maritime

Chicago's position near a great lake and a major tributary was a curse to builders due to its soggy soil. But it was a boon to trade as the city's accessibility via water helped spur on its unprecedented growth.

1. CHRISTMAS SHIP

Every year, the Schuenemann brothers brought Christmas trees to Chicago. August and Hermann Schuenemann lived in a small port in Wisconsin. Their German immigrant father was a farmer until a Civil War injury damaged his sight and the brothers were forced to hire out as farmhands. August joined the crew of the locally owned schooner *Ella Doak*, which hauled lumber to Chicago and, finding the water to his liking, bought barges of his own, deciding to take advantage of the Christmas tree market booming in Chicago and Milwaukee. By 1889, younger brother Hermann joined him in the business, and together they bought decrepit old schooners and made them seaworthy. In 1898, though, their schooner, the *S. Thal*, in the freezing cold of a Midwest December, was dashed on the beach of Glencoe. The next morning, residents found wreckage but no bodies. With newborn twin daughters at home, Hermann had decided to skip that run so August went instead and never returned. Carrying on the family business, Hermann bought his own tree farm in Wisconsin and sold the trees retail from the Clark Street Bridge in Chicago. In 1912, Schuenemann rented the forty-four-year-old, 123.5-foot, *Rouse Simmons* for the Christmas tree run, but on November 23, 1912, just off Two Rivers Point, Wisconsin, the *Rouse Simmons* foundered. All eighteen people, including Hermann Schuenemann, were killed. It wasn't completely the end of the tradition of Schuenemann Christmas trees in Chicago. Hermann's widow kept up the family business, but the trees sold at Clark Street Bridge from the deck of a ship didn't arrive in Chicago by ship, but rather by railroad.

2. NAVY PIER

Daniel Burnham's plan of 1909 called for utilizing miles of lakefront property for parks and recreation. Not an easy sell for a town looking for the commercial function in everything. When the Army Corps of Engineers looked at the lakefront, they didn't see pristine parks but rather the potential for docking facilities for maritime traffic. At the time, commercial lake traffic was still a primary way of shipping in Chicago. Reaching a compromise, in 1910, five municipal piers were planned for both commercial and recreational functions, but only one was built. Navy Pier (formerly known as Municipal Pier) was 3,000 feet long, sitting on 20,000 wooden pilings. At the time the largest pier in the country, between 1918 and 1930 it was a vital point for freight and passenger traffic. When the Great Depression hit, business, including shipping, fell off and the rise in trucking made Navy Pier obsolete. During World War II, it became a naval training facility and afterward served as a branch of the University of Illinois until 1965. It wasn't until 1976, though, that its place in the Burnham plan became apparent as it began to host civic and cultural events. In 1989, seeing the pier's worth, a Metropolitan Pier and Exposition Authority was created by the city of Chicago and the state of Illinois and $150 million was committed to help realize its full recreational potential. Now, it regularly hosts cultural events (at 170,000 square feet, Festival Hall is a popular place for expositions and conventions), and is home to museums, shops, a ballroom, restaurant, entertainment and recreational facilities. There's even a skating rink, carousel, and Ferris wheel that's lit up at night.

3. THE WEARIN' OF THE GREEN

St. Patrick's Day is a major holiday in the city of Chicago. Every March 17, streets are blocked off and a grand parade is held not so much to honor St. Patrick as to celebrate the Irish. And every year for decades now, the Chicago River has been dyed green (though, considering how polluted it was for so many years, dyeing it green was unnecessary). The tradition started in 1962, when crews were using a greenish dye to trace the source of pollution entering the river. When Stephen Baily, a labor leader, noticed that the dye had stained the overalls of one of the crew green, he went to his pal, Richard J. Daley, and suggested dyeing the river green to celebrate St. Pat's Day. Daley, who loved the river and liked the idea of incorporating it into one of his favorite days, agreed. The first attempt left the river green for a week. It has since been discovered that forty (down from 100) pounds of vegetable dye is sufficient to produce the desired green for a few hours. So every March 17, the entire city enjoys the wearin' of the green. Even the river.

4. RUDE AWAKENING

At 2:30 A.M., on September 8, 1860, many of the 700 passengers aboard the *Lady Elgin* were fast asleep in their cabins. Twenty minutes later, they were in the cold waters of Lake Michigan, either dead or clinging to wreckage. Fifty-five years before the *Eastland* disaster, the wreck of the *Lady Elgin* seven miles off the coast of Winnetka was the worst disaster in local maritime history. After attending a political rally in Chicago, passengers were returning to Milwaukee aboard the *Lady Elgin* when a storm came up. It might not have been a perilous event to ride out were it not for the schooner *Augusta* coming from the other direction. Troubled by a shifting load and sailing practically on her side, the *Augusta* sailed straight into the *Lady's Elgin's* side, aft of her port paddlewheel. By the time the two ships had disconnected, the *Elgin's* side-wheel and hull planking pulled away, while the *Augusta* had regained her own stability. Unable to see the *Elgin*, the *Augusta* captain assumed she had sailed away and continued, leaving the *Lady Elgin* to founder in the churning waters. The collision knocked out most of the ship's oil lamps, increasing the confusion. The ship was equipped with the required number of lifeboats and jackets, but time was her worst enemy. Shaken from their sleep, the crew was unsuccessful in launching two lifeboats. Cattle in pens belowdecks were driven overboard to lighten the vessel, and cargo was moved to the starboard side in hopes of raising the hole in the ship's side out of the water. A few coal shovelers tried to staunch the flow of the water with a mattress to no avail.

As the ship began to sink and disintegrate, passengers cut off from the life preservers turned to anything they could find that would float. By dawn, survivors clinging to wreckage were washed to shore by the tide, but the undertow forced many of the makeshift rafts into the breakers. Of the 400 on their way to shore, 160 were saved, the rest drowned in the surf. Northwestern University student Edward Spencer is a notable hero of the day, repeatedly running back into the surf to rescue whoever he could. His heroism saved eighteen people, but cost him the use of his legs for the rest of his life. For months, bodies continued to wash up along the shore of Lake Michigan, some so badly decomposed they couldn't be identified. The loss of the passenger list in the wreck meant that an exact figure of the dead couldn't be calculated. Upon returning to port and hearing the news of the *Lady Elgin,* the horrified captain of the *Augusta* immediately claimed that he misjudged the distance due to *Lady Elgin's* incorrect light configuration and that he never realized the extent of the damage. Fearing for his own struggling vessel, he went on to port. The press still vilified him and he was arrested for formal hearings. So hated was the name of the *Augusta* that the ship was quietly renamed the *Colonel Cook* to avoid the possibility of being destroyed. The *Augusta's* captain and crew sailed on another vessel known as the *Mojave*, but, interestingly, the *Mojave* disappeared on the fourth anniversary of the *Lady Elgin* disaster. The theory is that the ship foundered in northern Lake Michigan, and the crew may have been lynched for their part in the *Lady Elgin* wreck four years previously.

5. TIMBER PIRATES

By the 1850s, Chicago was the timber capital of the world. From the vast forests of upper Wisconsin and lower Michigan, the trees were cut and floated down rivers to the lake, where schooners or lumber hookers hauled it to Chicago to be processed and sent west on the railroad lines. As supply dried up, the Chicago and Milwaukee lumber barons turned to federal lands to fill the need. During the winter months, mariners became lumberjacks, poaching trees off federal lands and sending the timber along the same river route back to Chicago. Laws had been passed decades before to protect the Navy's supplies of oak and red cedar, but it wasn't until the big boom of the 1850s that revenue agent Isaac Willard was sent by the General Land Office of the Department of Interior to investigate. The timber pirates had upped the ante from mere poaching to burning government boats and buildings, stealing back seized timber and even murdering an agent in Iowa. The inn where Willard and another agent stayed was set ablaze, though both escaped. The poachers were even brazen enough to chase off Willard's agent after he had prepared a load of seized lumber to be sent back to Chicago for federal auction. Realizing that more power was necessary to back up Willard and his agents, Washington sent in the iron-hulled warship, the *Michigan*, the fastest, most heavily armed vessel prowling the Great Lakes. With the ironside's backing, Willard's raids on poachers became so successful that they almost shut the outlaw industry down. The lumber barons, however, turned to politics to get their way, pressuring Congress to withdraw funding from the agencies established to fight the poaching. The campaign worked, and unimpeded, the poachers continued their work, ultimately depleting the forests by the end of the century.

6. THE MYSTERY IS SOLVED

In 1989, after barge operators on the Sanitary and Ship Canal reported obstructions affecting the run of the canal, investigators found a sunken graveyard lining the bottom of the canal: cars that had been reported stolen and dumped to collect the insurance. When the vehicles were lifted from the water, one of them, a blue Cadillac, contained a body in the trunk. It was the body of Diane Masters, an elected public official of Moraine Valley College and the wife of an attorney. Reported missing in 1983, she'd been bludgeoned and shot, and sunk with her car into the canal. The search for Diane had been intensive, but there had been little evidence to go on. Had this sunken graveyard not been discovered, the case of Diane Masters might still be open. With no evidence directly linking the murder to her husband, Alan Masters, federal prosecutors charged him instead with conspiracy to deny Diane her civil rights by killing her. According to prosecutors, after stopping at a local bar following a Moraine Valley College trustee board meeting, she returned to her Palos Hills home where she and Alan Masters got into an argument. The argument led to violence when he struck Diane, knocking her out. Panicking that he killed her, Masters incorporated the help of friends to take the blue Cadillac, with Diane in the trunk, to the Sanitary and Ship Canal. Shots were fired into the trunk and the car dumped into the canal. Alan and Diane Masters weren't the only prominent names in the case. Alan Masters's "friends" turned out to be former Willow Springs chief of police Michael Corbit and a lieutenant in the Cook County sheriff's office. All three were found guilty and sentenced to the federal penitentiary. After six years, Diane Masters could finally rest in peace.

7. AIR AND WATER SHOW

Every summer for over forty years, U.S. Thunderbirds have migrated to Lake Michigan for the Annual Chicago Air and Water Show, the oldest and largest free admission air and water show of its kind. The headline act of the show, the Air Force's squadron of high-performance aircraft, conducts precision aerial demonstrations over the lake, flying in tight formation to the delight of the spectators below. Other military aircraft are featured as well as civilian air show performers such as Northern Lights Aerobatic team and Red Baron Stearman Squadron. The exhibitions are held along the lakefront, from Fullerton Avenue with North Avenue Beach as the focal point.

8. YOU NEVER KNOW WHAT MIGHT POP UP

Lodner Darvantis Phillips had a dream of traveling beneath the water and built vessels that enabled him to do so. This was a pretty impressive thing for a man who lived in the beginning of the nineteenth century. He was actually able to perfect a craft that enabled his family to take day trips submerged beneath Lake Michigan. Some of his earlier efforts, however, were not quite as seaworthy. One sunk to the bottom of the Chicago River, but was raised twenty years after his death and sold to a William Nissen of Chicago. Phillips went on to invent and receive patents on many innovations that proved useful in future aquatic and submarine research. One of his inventions, a diving suit, was instrumental in helping recover the bodies from the *Eastland* tragedy decades later. Diver William Deneau had the unpleasant duty of recovering bodies in the hull of the capsized *Eastland*. On one of his dives, he came across a submarine resting at the bottom of the river. Called the *Foolkiller*, once it was raised, it was discovered to contain the skeletal remains of a man and a dog. Submarine and skeletal remains were put on exhibit on State Street. It's uncertain who the pilot was, but the theory is that perhaps William Nissen went to take his new sub out for a test run, and never came back.

9. FREAK OCCURRENCES

Ice buildup isn't a threat in the middle of Lake Michigan with a maximum depth of 923 feet, but in the shallow areas, the bays and harbors, and along the shoreline, the ice can form quickly. This is usually more an inconvenience than anything else, sealing off Great Lake ports from commercial shipping. In the early days, ships could be trapped, even sunk, as ice damaged their hulls. In 1873, the *Ironsides* and the *Messenger* were trapped in ice off White Lake. Local ship operators trying for one last cargo before the ice built up risked losing their ships, since many insurance companies wrote policies that expired before winter set in. On March 12, 1849, however, the ice became more than a mere inconvenience. On this day, a dislodged ice jam at the south branch of the Chicago River began moving downriver. The ice slammed into bridges, wharves, steamboats, propeller-powered ships, twenty-four brigs, sloops, and twenty-seven canal boats, sweeping away a number of men in the canal boats as well as two children. One man was even seen several hours later, waving a handkerchief, adrift in a canal boat, but there wasn't a vessel left to reach him. His fate remains uncertain. Many a mariner has tasted the danger of the elements when out in the middle of the lake, but few have had to worry when they were in the safety of port.

10. HOUSEBOATS

The Great Depression took the hopes and dreams of many people, and their homes as well. When foreclosures and evictions skyrocketed, many Chicagoans turned to the river for support, moving onto houseboats until conditions improved and they could afford dry land again. Often built on old barges, houseboats sailed the north branch of the Chicago River, and while many were ramshackle vessels, with tarpaper sides and tiny stovepipes for heat and cooking, some sported occasional homey touches like window curtains and flower boxes. Artists would set up easels along the bank and paint the poignant tableau. Even after the post–World War II economy brought a boom that set the country back on its feet, some people remained on the river well into the 1960s, perhaps finding the currents of the river more to their liking than the hard soil of dry land.

The Reformers

The unbridled economic and population growth made Chicago, by the end of the 1800s, a perfect place for the reformers of the day. Many of the reformers fought to raise the standard of living for all, but especially the most powerless: women and children.

1. TO SAVE A CITY

The queen of social reform in Chicago, Jane Addams's pioneering efforts at Hull House inspired the careers of others. Jane was born in 1860, and her father, a fierce abolitionist and friend of Abraham Lincoln, instilled in her a sense of justice. Among the first generation of women to graduate college, she found little out there save teaching, missionary work, or marriage. Traveling to Europe with her friend, Ellen Gates Starr, she visited Whitechapel's Toynbee Hall, Britain's first university settlement serving the poor, in the heart of London, England, and realized how valuable such an institution would be in the slums of Chicago. In 1889, on the corner of Halsted and Polk Streets, a two-story mansion built three decades before by real-estate developer Charles J. Hull was chosen as the site for Addams and Starr's social experiment. Hull House bettered lives by introducing classes in art, music, and theater. Teaching the importance of personal hygiene and fitness, it offered public baths and a public swimming pool as well as Chicago's first public playground. There was a boys' club, a day nursery, a kindergarten, a coffee-house, a dining room, an employment bureau, and a board-ing club for working girls. Addams and her disciples effected political change as well, and factory inspection laws, model tenement codes, and the first juvenile court in Chicago were some of the results. Addams branched out from her efforts at Hull House, establishing the Women's International League for Peace and Freedom in response to World War I. She wrote books about social reform, received fourteen hon-orary degrees and in 1931 became the first American woman to win a Nobel Peace Prize. Four years later, the hero of social reform in Chicago died of cancer. Thousands filed past her coffin in Hull House saying good-bye.

2. NEVER BACK DOWN

Born in 1862 in Mississippi, into slavery, Ida B. Wells fought to keep her eight siblings together after her parents suc-cumbed to yellow fever when she was sixteen. Not a woman who backed down easily, on a train to Memphis one day Wells refused to leave the front car for the smoker car and was physically forced to move. Sueing the railroad, she won a $500 judgment only to lose it when the railroad appealed. It was a severe lesson in social justice she wouldn't forget. Attending college, she also taught school in Memphis, speak-ing out about the poor quality of black schools. Writing for a church newspaper on the topic of civil rights and unjust laws, she was soon asked to write for other black newspapers. In 1889, as part owner of the Memphis newspaper *Free Speech*, she continued to criticize the state of black schools and lost her teaching job. Her chief crusade became the issue of lynching after three young black businessmen were lynched in Memphis in 1892. After the offices of *Free Speech* were firebombed, Wells's resolve grew stronger. Moving to New York, she became a writer for a black publication, *New York Age,* and lectured throughout the nation and twice in Great Britain on the condition of African Americans. Attending the

1893 World's Columbian Exposition, Ida B. Wells became a vocal critic of how the fair excluded black America, even criticizing Frederick Douglass for agreeing to speak at the fair's "Jubilee Day" (or Colored People's Day) though she quickly changed her mind after hearing the speech. Douglass, Wells, Ferdinand L. Barnett, and I. Garland Penn published a booklet entitled *Why the Coloured American Is Not in the World's Columbian Exposition*. Seeing the state of black Chicagoans, Wells decided to remain and married Barnett. In 1895, Wells published an in-depth study on lynching entitled *A Red Record: Tabulated Statistics and Alleged Causes of Lynching in the United States*. In 1910, she founded the Negro Fellowship League. From 1913 to 1916, she was the first woman in Chicago to be appointed a probation officer of the Chicago Municipal Court. As a champion for social justice, she kept her fight going right up to the end, passing away in 1931 at the age of sixty-eight.

3. **THE SETTLEMENT LADY**

As founder of the University of Chicago Settlement Home, Mary McDowell was called the "Settlement Lady." Her goal was to break down ethnic barriers and help the disenfranchised of the city. Born in Ohio in 1854, she came to Chicago at the age of twenty, becoming an associate of Jane Addams. Addams recommended her to head the University of Chicago Settlement House, which was established in 1894 and grew from one small flat into four more with a kindergarten, classrooms, concerts, and lectures. As with Hull House, immigrants could learn English, take classes in health care, and gain access to public bathhouses as well as attend vocational schools. These were rare opportunities in the rough community. The Back of the Yards neighborhood was surrounded by the slaughter yards, Bubbly Creek, the polluted arms of the Chicago River, and one of the city's municipal dumps. Garbage collected in ditches, and children wore long clothes to prevent being bitten by the mosquitoes that infested the area. Packingtown had the highest tuberculosis rates in the country. McDowell, along with other settlement workers, pressured aldermen to clean up the neighborhoods and was strident about garbage disposal, even taking trips abroad to study foreign methods. In 1923, Mayor William Dever appointed her Public Welfare Commissioner, but Mc-Dowell was equally outspoken on matters concerning women. She was the first president of the National League of Women Voters' committee on International Co-operation to Prevent War. Truly believing all were created equal, she organized the first interracial committee of women after the 1919 riots and later acted as executive of the Chicago branch of the NAACP. Hers was a life committed to justice and helping her fellow citizen. In 1936, Mary McDowell died at the age of eighty-one.

4. HAYMARKET WIDOW

Begging her husband, Albert, to flee to Wisconsin after the Haymarket riot, Lucy Parsons became a Haymarket widow when he surrendered several weeks later. Born in Texas around 1853, little is known about her early background. Possibly a former slave, she was said to be of African American, Indian, and Mexican heritage. The Parsons wed in 1872, and came to Chicago a year later as the city was experiencing the pains of economic and social unrest. Increasingly vocal on social concerns, they drew the ire of a number of officials and influential people. While her husband Albert founded the Trades and Labor Assembly of Chicago and was elected secretary of Chicago's Eight Hour League, Lucy also had her activist passions, calling for the abolition of capitalism, which she felt caused wage workers to be little more than slaves to American businessmen. All must have equal rights no matter the race or gender. Prior to Albert's hanging, Lucy searched the country for supporters, explaining the conditions that led to the riot of over 200 people. Albert was executed anyway, leaving Lucy even more determined that this would never happen again. In 1891, she coedited *Freedom, a Revolutionary Anarchist-Communist Monthly* and published *The Life of Albert R. Parsons, with Brief History of the Labor Movement in America* in 1889. Editing the *Liberator* for a year in 1905, she also helped establish the Industrial Workers of the World and spoke at various forums in the city. During the 1930s, she lectured around the country on fair working conditions. Sadly, Lucy Parsons's life came to a tragic end in 1942, when the wooden stove in her home caught fire and both she and a friend were killed. She was buried in Waldheim Cemetery, next to the grave of her husband and the Haymarket martyrs.

5. **CHICAGO HOSTESS**

Bertha Honoré Palmer captured the heart of the Merchant Prince of Chicago and became the city's hostess to the world, using her influence with the 1893 World's Fair to advance the notion of women's rights. She was born in 1849, the daughter of a Kentucky real-estate developer who moved the family to Chicago in 1855. When Bertha Honoré married Potter Palmer in 1870, she was twenty-one and he was forty-four. An elegant debutante, as well as an outspoken feminist, she was the queen of Chicago society. Potter Palmer built a castle on Lake Shore Drive with a great hall, marble floors, and a grand oak staircase that rose high into an eighty-foot tower. In this mansion, Bertha played hostess to visiting princes, stars of the stage, artists, politicians, and presidents. A believer in equal pay for equal work, she also held meetings for women activists, encouraged female factory workers to reach for more, and even helped millinery workers organize a strike. Through the Chicago Women's Club, she supported the causes of female reformers. And when plans for the 1893 Columbian Exposition were being arranged, she played a key role in the erection of the Women's Building, the exhibit that honored the role of women in history. She sailed for Europe to encourage interest in the women's exhibit and while in Paris went on an art-buying spree. When she came back, she introduced Chicago to the most extensive collection of Impressionist art in the country.

A few years after Potter Palmer died in 1902, Bertha moved to a new estate in Sarasota, Florida, and enjoyed the farming life until her death from cancer in 1918. She was brought back to Chicago to be buried next to her husband in Graceland Cemetery.

6. **A RARE BREED**

Born in Germany in 1847, John Peter Altgeld was the first foreign-born governor of Illinois and the first governor to live in Chicago. He was also one of the most courageous, whose pardoning of the three surviving Haymarket martyrs, if nothing else, earned him a place in history. Studying law in Missouri, three years later he was practicing law in Chicago where he wrote a booklet entitled, "Our Penal Machinery and Its Victims" in which he argued that, rather than rehabilitate prisoners, incarceration only created repeat offenders and that the justice system was geared to favor the rich over the poor. After a five-year term as judge of the superior court of Cook County, Altgeld ran a successful campaign for the governorship. In 1893, as governor, he found himself reviewing the case of the Haymarket Square riot. What Altgeld found was a questionable jury selection, perjured testimony, and a hostile judge. His pardoning of the remaining three men touched off a fury of protest across the country. Accused of encouraging anarchy, his foreign birth was brought into question and he was even burned in effigy. Remaining in office for three years, another incident rocked his career as Pullman employees, backed by the American Railway Union, went on strike. Asked to send in the Illinois militia to break the strike, Altgeld refused. He had used the militia before in contentious strike situations, but only to maintain law and order. Attorney General Richard Olney, a railroad director determined to break the strike by any means necessary, turned to President Grover Cleveland, who ordered federal troops into Chicago. The strike finally ended, but a furious Altgeld spent years speaking out against Cleveland. When it was time for reelection, Altgeld was beaten by Republican

John R. Tanner. In 1902, while delivering a speech in Joliet, Illinois, John Peter Altgeld suffered a cerebral hemorrhage and died the next morning. Curiously, ten years had done much to change the nation's attitude toward this leader and his death was marked publicly as a great loss. And indeed it was. During his term as governor, he began many programs of social reform, including attempts to prohibit child labor, starting factory inspections, and introducing new laws prohibiting discrimination against trade unions. Altgeld was a man who believed in justice and bettering the life of all citizens even when it wasn't politically safe.

7. THE HIPPOCRATIC OATH

On July 9, 1893, performing the first open heart surgery, Daniel Hale Williams saved the life of a young black man who might have been turned away from other hospitals. Williams himself wasn't permitted to work at the city's hospital, so he founded his own, then went on to found the National Medical Association for black physicians in 1895. Born in Pennsylvania in 1858, Williams came to Chicago in 1880 and graduated from the Chicago Medical College. Treating both blacks and whites in his South Side practice, and yearning to take his work further, he convinced Marshall Field, Philip Danforth Armour, and George Pullman to contribute money to the construction of Provident Hospital, the first interracial hospital in the United States, with a predominantly white advisory board, but a mostly black staff and board of trustees. Williams also established the first nursing school in the nation for black women at Provident Hospital. Interestingly, dark-skinned blacks criticized him for the number of light-skinned black employees. His own heritage was a mix of African American, Native American, and white, and few of his critics considered the fact that while he could have passed for white, he didn't, choosing instead to work toward bettering conditions for the black race. After a stint as a surgeon-in-chief of Washington, D.C.'s Freedman's Hospital, where he established another school for black nurses, he returned to Provident and in 1900 also served on the staff of Cook County Hospital until 1906. He moved on to St. Luke's Hospital in 1907 and remained until 1931. Weary of the racial infighting going on at Provident, in 1912 he resigned, continuing his work to encourage blacks in the medical community, and teaching surgery at the black Meharry Medical College in Tennessee for ten days annually until his death in 1931.

8. HAYMARKET MARTYR

On November 11, 1887, Albert Parsons was among four men hanged for the Haymarket Square riot. The Haymarket rally was held to encourage workers to stand up for their rights, a cause Albert Parsons believed in passionately. Born in Alabama in 1848, Albert Parsons served in the Confederate Army at the age of thirteen, but after the war, he grew so ashamed of the cause he'd been fighting for that he campaigned for the rights of freed slaves and even married a former slave, Lucy Gathings. Moving to Chicago in 1872, the couple immersed themselves in labor reform. Albert founded the Trades and Labor Assembly of Chicago in 1878 and was elected secretary of the Chicago Eight Hour League. He was also editor for two of the more radical newspapers of the day—*The Socialist*, and *The Alarm*. On May 4, 1886, a rally was held on Des Plaines Street near Haymarket Square to protest unfair labor practices. What started out as a relatively well-behaved rally turned into a riot when a bomb was thrown into the crowd. A featured speaker that night, by the time the bomb was thrown, Albert and Lucy had moved on to a hall on W. Lake Street. Accused anyway, along with seven other leaders of the rally, Parsons fled to Wisconsin but surrendered on June 21, 1886. In August, a jury found all eight defendants guilty and while originally all eight were sentenced to death, only four would swing for the crime, Parsons among them. The Haymarket martyrs satisfied the urge of the city to blame someone and the urge of the city's business elite to send a message to uppity workers. Thankfully, it was the message of Parsons and his fellow labor reformers that stood the test of time.

9. GIFTS TO THE CITY

Julius Rosenwald believed in giving back to the community and gave over $60 million to various civic causes. He was born in Springfield, Illinois, in 1862, and his father was a top clothing merchant. In 1885, he joined his cousin in a clothing firm in Chicago and they became suppliers to Sears, Roebuck and Company, a new mail-order firm that Rosenwald and his brother-in-law bought stock in. In 1895, Rosenwald became vice president in the company. When Richard Sears retired, he handed the presidency of the company to Rosenwald, who retooled the company, streamlining it and improving the quality of goods and services. He opened retail stores and took the mail-order business national. Concerned about employee working conditions, Rosenwald offered health benefits and paid vacations. Rosenwald's social conscience increased with his wealth. In 1917, he formed the Julius Rosenwald Foundation, which contributed to the building of YMCAs throughout the city. Impressed by the autobiography of Booker T. Washington, Rosenwald believed that Jews and blacks shared a kinship in each race's suffering. He funded the building of over 5,000 public schools for blacks in the Deep South and contributed millions to black universities. He also funded over two dozen residential and recreational centers. Obtaining land on Michigan and Wabash Avenues, he built the Michigan Boulevard Garden Apartments, providing low-income housing for African Americans. Rosenwald also donated $75,000 to build the Chicago Hebrew Institute. He also promoted the idea for the Museum of Science and Industry, purchasing items for some of the exhibits, and donating $5 million. Unfortunately, he didn't live to see it completed. Suffering from bone disease and a weak heart, Rosenwald died in 1932. The Museum of Science and Industry opened in 1945.

10. THE SON-IN-LAW

Born in 1847, Henry Demarest Lloyd was admitted to the New York bar in 1869 and eventually moved on to a career in journalism with the *New York Post*. A local reformer, he fought against the corrupt policies of New York machine "Boss" William Tweed. Arriving in Chicago in 1872, he joined the staff of the *Chicago Tribune*, investigating corruption in business and politics as chief editor. Considered America's first investigative journalist, one of his chief targets was the monopoly of the Standard Oil Company. He married Jessie Bross, daughter of *Tribune* publisher William Bross, and moved to Wilmette, north of Chicago. Lloyd's interest in reform grew beyond the *Tribune* and, in 1885, he left the paper to unsuccessfully pursue a state Senate seat in both 1888 and 1894. He also used the time to write books about labor issues. It was his stand on the Haymarket martyrs, though, that drove a wedge between his father-in-law and himself when he asked Governor John P. Altgeld to grant clemency to the convicted men. For this, William Bross made sure the couple wouldn't inherit *Tribune* stock. This did nothing to quell Lloyd's passion. A strong supporter of ending child labor and of women's suffrage, he also supported Eugene Debs in the 1894 Pullman strike and even opened his home to Debs and other reformers. Lloyd became the Wilmette treasurer in 1886 and served on both the school and village boards. Two more books, *Labour Co-partnership* and *Country Without Strikes*, resulted from studies in England, Ireland, Switzerland, and New Zealand. Three years after his last book, in 1903, Lloyd passed away from pneumonia. At fifty-six, he was fighting to the end, working to encourage public ownership of Chicago's mass-transit system.

The Columbian
Exposition

The 1893 World's Columbian Exposition drew twenty-seven million people to the fair, fourteen million from abroad. It was the greatest tourist attraction in American history. The exposition's white plaster-coated buildings were temporary structures built in the classical Greek and Roman style (which Louis Sullivan considered a step back architecturally). It took two-and-a-half years to turn a swampy Lake Michigan shore into what many considered an American Venice. The lagoons, basins, and interconnected canals, along with the statues, elaborate fountains, and gleaming white buildings, turned it into a magical city within a city known to many as the White City.

1. ALL ROADS LEAD TO CHICAGO

Despite initial scoffing, there were reasons why Chicago ended up hosting the fair. Chief among them were location and locomotion. Chicago was the railroad capital of the country. Easily accessible by water, Chicago had one of the most efficient transportation systems in the country. There were also 2,000 unused acres to serve as a massive canvas for the designers of the fair, and Chicago showed a can-do spirit. Two years after the 1871 fire, Chicago had not only built itself up again but was playing host to the Interstate Industrial Expo. Intended to last four weeks, the expo lasted from September 5 to November 12, attracting 60,000 visitors. Five hundred and eighty businesses exhibited (most of the exhibits from Chicago) and the show was so successful that an annual Chicago Industrial Exposition was held for the next eighteen years. At the time, there were two other major contenders for the 1893 fair: New York and St. Louis. A citizens committee to bring the fair to Chicago was formed and the committee pledged that it would come up with a $10 million financial commitment. This convinced Congress to give the prize to Chicago. And what a prize it turned out to be. The business leaders knew full well how lucrative such an exposition would be for a city. It would bring in masses of people, people willing to spend money. Money spent at their stores, hotels, and restaurants. Plus, if done right, it would increase Chicago's prestige. Chicago might finally graduate in the eyes of the nation from a rowdy cow town to the cultural center of the nation.

2. PICKPOCKET DECREE

Mayor Carter Harrison I ran his office with a light touch. He firmly believed in the adage "live and let live." There was vice in Chicago, especially in that part of town known as the Levee, but for many this vice was part of mere survival. The Columbian Exposition posed a problem, however. People would be coming from all across the world and those visiting the White City might not be so inclined to step out and visit the "black city" (as Chicago was being called because of the industrial soot that darkened everything) if crime frightened them off. This would not please the business leaders who wanted to pull some of the White City spenders into Chicago proper. So, a compromise was set. He couldn't stop pickpockets and petty thieves altogether, but he offered them a deal through crime kingpin Mike McDonald. No one's pocket was to be picked at the entrance of the fair. Any pickpockets who kept their trade to the center of the city would be released immediately if they were arrested during daylight hours. When the sun went down, all deals were off. If a pickpocket was caught at the fair, he could get off the hook by paying the arresting officer a $10 fee. This helped inspire the police to keep their eyes sharp while working the fair. By all accounts, the mayor's crime reduction plan was a success and everyone was happy, especially those dealing in prostitution who saw their business increase during the 183 days of the fair. This proves once again that Chicago truly is the city that works.

3. **THE WONDER OF TWO CONTINENTS**

Organizers planning the 1893 World's Columbian Exposition wanted an attraction that would rival Paris's Eiffel Tower, which had been built for the 1889 Paris Exposition Universelle. A national contest was conducted for "unique" ideas. In stepped George Ferris, a thirty-four-year-old Pittsburgh bridge designer. Initially, his Ferris wheel design was rejected, but, when the enterprising young man came up with well over $350,000 from investors, event planners gave him the go-ahead. It became the hit of the fair, even though the delay in acceptance meant that it was still being constructed well after the start of the fair. For fifty cents a ride, 1.5 million people paid to sit in one of the thirty-six railcar-size cabins capable of holding forty people and climbing up to 264 feet for a breathtaking view of the gleaming rooftops. Nothing like it had ever come before. Days after the fair had officially closed, the wheel still turned to give all who'd been waiting a chance. But the joy it brought others was not to be for the creator. Once it was taken apart, Ferris still squabbled with the fair organizers over the $100,000 in profits. Searching unsuccessfully for another fair sponsor, he moved the wheel to another location in the city, but the crowds mobbing it at the expo were long gone. For a decade, the wheel traveled, but it drew more complaints from neighbors than anything else. It made an appearance at the St. Louis World's Fair in 1904, but was eventually dynamited and sold for scrap. In 1896, thirty-seven-year-old George Ferris died suddenly, never living long enough to see smaller versions of his wheel

Chicago Historical Society

After five decades of incredible growth, the 1893 World's
Columbian Exposition marked Chicago's coming-of-age as an
international metropolis. The most talked about aspect of the fair
was the impressive White City, a massive but temporary collection
of neoclassical buildings and interconnected waterways
constructed on land reclaimed from Lake Michigan.
This photograph shows the Grand Basin of the White City with the
Statue of the Republic in the foreground.

become the cornerstones of carnivals and amusement parks
everywhere.

4. CULINARY DELIGHTS

At the 1893 World's Fair, people could taste cultures they
had never tasted before. Trainloads of fresh produce were
brought in daily. The influx caused the lowest wholesale pro-

duce prices in Chicago's history. Approximately fifty heads of beef were slaughtered daily, and the Wellington Catering Company, owners of fancy restaurants downtown, gained sole rights to supply food for the fair. The lucrative deal gave Wellington the right to demand that all restaurants at the fair obtain their provisions from their nine acres of restaurants, kitchens, and storage warehouses. For those of timid palettes, there were basic American meals of boiled meats, potatoes, breads, and desserts. The Irish Village served potatoes as well as oatmeal, corned beef, and freckle bread washed down by a selection of ales. The Germans had a beer garden to go along with their Wiener schnitzel. For the adventurous, there were exotic dishes from the Orient, or pita bread and zelebria on the Streets of Cairo were they could refresh themselves with the cool fruit drinks or thick spicy coffees of Persia, Algeria, and Tunisia. Many companies used the fair to introduce new products. Fairgoers could stop by the Heinz pickle booth and try a pickle, or visit the Quaker Oats exhibit for a steaming hot oat muffin. Walter Blake Company, the Van Houten and Zoom Company, and the Blooker Dutch Cocoa Company offered tantalizing chocolates, and for added sweetness, six hives of various bee breeds were working like crazy to produce 252 pounds of honey. You could have beef tea in a bouillon cup, along with star hams and condensed meat, all thanks to Armour and Company. And if the trip to the honey hives was too much for you, you could sweeten your tea with the new miracle product saccharin. It was said to be a healthy substitute for sugar. Oh, and let's not forget the new sensation, Cracker Jack. Yes, there were a lot of sights to see at the 1893 exposition and a bounty of tastes to savor as well.

5. PARLIAMENT OF WORLD RELIGIONS

In 1993, Chicago hosted a Parliament of World Religions: nine days of workshops, panels, and seminars that successfully opened the dialogue among all religions. It was held in honor of the 100th anniversary of the first Parliament of

World Religions, which took place during the World's Columbian Exposition. In 1893, the parliament's committee was made of Roman Catholic bishops, Reform Jewish rabbis, and Protestant ministers from a variety of denominations. Held at the Hall of Columbia in the Chicago Art Institute, the concept was to open up dialogue and find a common ground between all the religions of the world. Basically a series of lectures, there were three daily sessions held over seventeen days. For all its organizers' good intentions, the 1893 Parliament placed a slightly higher legitimacy on Western religions, in particular Christianity, as if non-Christian religions had to justify their worth in comparison. There were no official representatives of new religions sprouting up such as Mormonism and Spiritualism and there were no Native American representatives, nor delegates from other nature religions. Still, criticism of religions was prohibited and a level of respect was given to all. Considering the time, the fact that a sense of unity with all religions was attempted is an admirable thing. One hundred years later, it was leaders from non-mainstream religions calling for a new parliament and working to gain the support of Chicago's Judeo/Christian communities. A wider scope of world religions was represented including Islam, New Age, Native American, Goddess Worship, Sikhs, and nature religions. Best of all, all the religious leaders got together to brainstorm for a paper regarding a global ethic that all religions could agree on. A proud legacy to those farsighted thinkers who set the ball rolling more than a hundred years ago.

6. A SUBTLE HINT OF RACISM

The layout on the midway typed as "savage curiosities" the exhibits from Africa, Asia, the Dutch East Indies, and the Middle East, which came off as more anthropological than a celebration of fellow cultures. The cultural slap was not lost on prominent black leaders like Ida B. Wells and Frederick Douglass, who publicly decried that the accomplishments of millions of blacks were all but ignored by organizers choosing instead to represent black America by exhibiting "African savages brought here to act the monkey," as Douglass wrote. Hoping to soften the charges of racism, organizers devised a Colored People's Day (also known as Jubilee Day), held on August 25, but stands giving away watermelons only added insult to injury. Ida B. Wells boycotted the fair, criticizing Frederick Douglass for agreeing to lecture on this day. He was intent on being heard though. At seventy-five years old, the heat bore down upon him, and a gang of whites jeered him, but the former slave gathered his resolve and challenged the American people to live up to the Constitution. "We Negroes love our country. We fought for it. We ask only that we be treated as well as those who fought against it." It was a poignant and powerful speech that caused Ida B. Wells to immediately apologize to Douglass after reading about it the next day. With Chicago newspaper editor Ferdinand L. Barnett, and other prominent black leaders, Wells and Douglass issued a pamphlet detailing the plight of the Negro in post-Reconstruction America, and criticized the fair-organizers. True, a few African Americans served at fair-sponsored events and others exhibited (among them, a student from Iowa named George Washington Carver). But the ethnic makeup of the fair contrasted sharply with the ethnic makeup of the world.

7. **SCORES OF ATTRACTIONS**

The exhibits at the fair could be wondrous. Japan constructed a 40,000-square-foot building and garden complex and the Ho-o-den, a Japanese palace, located on Wooded Island. Hawaii supplied a replica of a huge volcano for the midway and for a few cents you could see private shows such as dancing girls and snake charmers in the Algerian and Tunisian village, Egyptian swordsmen fighting duels on the Streets of Cairo, and acrobats and musicians in the Chinese Village. Along with the human menagerie, there was Hagenback's Zoological Arena: a menagerie of lions, tigers, and bears performing tricks in a huge arena modeled after the Coliseum in Rome. Thomas Edison's kinetoscope, the mother of the movie camera, debuted in the Electricity Building, where another Edison creation, an eighty-two-foot tower, strung with 18,000 lamps, stunned fairgoers from the Midwest and underdeveloped parts of the world, who saw electrical light for the first time there. The electric light illuminated the grounds at night, adding to the magic. The Woman's Building—designed, decorated, and managed by women—was dedicated to women, showing their accomplishments in science, health care, literature, philanthropy, and more. The Horticulture Building had some of the oddest attractions including Los Angeles' thirty-five-foot tower of 14,000 oranges. The tower, with an eagle at the top, was replenished by fresh fruit every three to four weeks. Oranges played a part, along with lemons and grapefruit, in the construction of the Liberty Bell sent by San Diego and shown in the Agricultural Building. The Manufacturers and Liberal Arts Building held Johann Sebastian Bach's clavichord, Amadeus Mozart's spinet, and Ludwig van Beethoven's grand piano. Charles Yerkes donated his $500,000 telescope, which at sixty-five feet in length and weighing seventy tons, was the largest telescope in the world.

8. LITTLE EGYPT

She was the scandal of the midway. In 1893, corsets were tight, ankles covered, and midriffs—well, people weren't really even sure what a midriff was. Until Little Egypt. Sol Bloom, a twenty-one-year-old Polish-Jewish immigrant, was an impresario who knew how to sell. Under Bloom's guidance, the midway became the world's first sideshow. Having a passion for the Middle Eastern world, he placed the Algerian Village, the Streets of Cairo, and other such displays in areas of prominence on the midway, accenting this with North African females skilled in the art of the "belly dance." The most famous of these dancers was Little Egypt who, by today's standards, would be considered rather flabby, but who amazed the crowds with her talented abs. Dressed in veils, Little Egypt gyrated her bare midriff before the crowds, performing a dance that would later be dubbed the "Hootchi Kootchi." Scores of imitators performed under the name of Little Egypt to the point where the average fairgoer could never really be sure if they were seeing the real thing. Some historians argue that Little Egypt actually appeared many years later at Coney Island, but there are written accounts of a performer with such a name at the Columbian Exposition. Back then, exposing that much skin was unheard of amongst the good, Christian folk who strolled through the fair. In fact, revivalist Dwight Moody (namesake of Chicago's Moody Bible Institute) set up tent tabernacles across Jackson Park hoping to draw the decent folk away from the immorality of the midway. It didn't really work. While tens of thousands visited the tabernacles, the midway remained a vibrant part of the fair and even inspired midways of future carnivals and amusement parks like Coney Island and Chicago's now-long-gone Riverview.

9. A SAD END

To Carter Harrison I, the lowliest prostitute was just as important as a Marshall Field. He was able to communicate with every level of society and believed that everyone had a right to a piece of the pie. That made for a dark day, and a very sad end to the fair, when Mayor Carter Harrison was assassinated. Two days before the closing, he spoke to a group of mayors on "All Cities Day." Later that day, he was shot in his own home by a disgruntled madman who had been turned down for a job at City Hall. The most popular fair in history would have to be officially closed, and great ceremonies had been planned to do so, but the city's heart wasn't in it. Events scheduled for the closing were canceled and at the end of the final day, with flags at half-mast, the World's Columbian Exposition ended with a cannon salute and the orchestra playing Beethoven's Funeral March. The pageantry was saved for the funeral of the fallen leader. Two hundred mourners paid their respects in a City Hall draped with black crepe. The next day, tens of thousands followed the funeral cortege to Graceland Cemetery. Militia followed the hearse, and behind them rode the elite of Chicago. Behind them walked the high officials of the city, and behind them walked the rest of the city. Representatives of every ethnic enclave attended, plus firemen, police, civic employees, and leaders of labor unions. That was the legacy of Harrison. The love of the entire city followed that hearse regardless of class or background. Lining the street were spectators waiting for hours to catch a glimpse of the procession. Some lowered their hats. Some fainted in grief. Some burst through the police barricades and rushed to the funeral carriage just to touch it or kiss it. And when the casket was finally lowered into the crypt, the hearts of the city lowered with it. In one act of crazed violence, the glamour and fantasy of the White City was over, leaving Chicago with the cold reality of a violently restless world and great men gone too soon.

10. FIRE IN THE WHITE CITY

After the 1893 World's Fair, the White City was pretty much left abandoned and neglected by a town uncertain what to do with the once-magnificent buildings. After the expo had closed, coal dust settled on them while groups of homeless men settled in the Court of Honor. In January 1894, fire blazed through a number of buildings, leading the city to decide, months later, to hire a salvage company. On July 5, 1894, however, before the company could set to work tearing down what remained and cleaning up, arsonists set another fire that took care of the job. Chicagoans hurried to the tops of skyscrapers to watch the spectacle, remembering, perhaps, another fire that destroyed a city. But, like that fire, this one offered an opportunity for a fresh start for Jackson Park. Already, Daniel Burnham had begun formulating his plan for both the park and the city itself, which would be finished more than a decade later as his Chicago Plan of 1909. The plan was the first complete effort to find order in Chicago's untamed development. Support for the plan came from the community as early as the mid-1890s and the possibilities of what could be done with the lakefront ignited an interest among many sectors of the city. What remained long after the expo was closed and the White City was destroyed was the sense of hope that had permeated the fair: a feeling that a utopia could be found even in the midst of a major metropolis. It is a dream that has eluded humanity from the beginning but one that all cities continue to chase.

Inventions and Innovators

Chicago seems to attract lively, creative minds in every field, and many discoveries were made here. Some would lead to the betterment of humankind. One could lead to its destruction. Some just added a little happiness to our lives.

1. OH HAPPY DAY

One of the most uplifting musical styles came from the personal agony of one man. During the Roaring Twenties, Thomas Dorsey was one of the most popular blues pianists of all time. Born in Atlanta in 1899, his popularity came early, in his teens, after he moved to Chicago. Copies of his blues song, "It's Tight Like That," sold millions. In 1932, however, Dorsey's wife and baby died, leaving him devastated. Unable to return to his old life of blues, he went in another direction, writing songs of faith, hope, and inspiration. By incorporating blues elements with religious music, the music remained sacred yet accessible outside the church. The death of Thomas Dorsey's family led to the birth of gospel music, and his first song was written a month after the loss. "Take My Hand, Precious Lord," would become one of the most popular gospel songs ever. Dubious churchgoers were at first put off by the seemingly disrespectfully upbeat music originally known as "Dorsey's." As the years went by, though, he won over skeptics with such songs as "Today," "Search Me, Lord," and "Peace in the Valley." In the 1930s, Dorsey created the National Convention of Gospel Choirs and Choruses, then went on to start the first gospel publishing company and eventually started the first commercial gospel concerts. The South Side became the gospel music capital. Other stars would follow in his wake, including Roberta Martin and Mahalia Jackson, who he trained, and the Dorsey style inspired The Edwin Hawkins Singers who in 1969 had a pop hit with "Oh Happy Day." Gospel music has become an international industry and every summer Chicago hosts Gospel Fest in Grant Park. Thomas Dorsey illustrates that, even in the darkest of times, a light can be seen if we take the hand offered us.

2. A CITY WITH HEART

In 1913, Dr. Daniel Hale Williams was the only black surgeon among the charter members of the American College of Surgeons. On July 9, 1893, he was the first doctor daring enough to attempt open heart surgery. He had little choice. James Cornish, a young black man wounded in a bar fight, was rushed to the South Side's Provident Hospital with a knife wound in his chest. Provident was first in race relations, opening the city's first interracial hospital in 1891, but a heart operation such as what Williams was about to attempt was unprecedented. There were no X-rays, antibiotics, anesthesia, or anything to make such dangerous and invasive surgery safer. Cornish's chances were slim either way with a severed artery and an inch-long gash in the pericardium, the sac surrounding the heart. Both had to be closed immediately or he'd bleed to death on the table. Using catgut, Dr. Williams carefully sutured the wounds and closed the chest back up. Cornish was discharged fifty-one days later. There have been other medical firsts here. The first diagnosis of a heart attack occurred in Chicago in 1912, and 1922 saw the first use of an incubator. Cook County saw the establishment of the world's first blood bank in 1937. And in 1989, doctors at the University of Chicago performed the first successful liver transplant from a living donor. But it was the bravery of one doctor well over a hundred years ago that pioneered the operation that saves so many lives today.

3. **THE SECRET BENEATH THE BLEACHERS**

On December 2, 1942, beneath the stands of the University of Chicago's Stagg Field, a monster was born. In an effort to beat the Nazis to it, the U.S. government had turned to Nobel Prize winner Enrico Fermi and a team of forty-three physicists to create the first nuclear reactor. Proving a nuclear chain reaction could be turned on and off, it would be a major step in the construction of an atomic bomb. Under the guise of a project for the University of Chicago's new metallurgical lab, Chicago Pile No. 1, as it was called, was constructed out of materials that were hardly state of the art. Layers of solid graphite bricks held spheres of deadly uranium compound in place. These in turn were held together by a wooden frame. Should the reactor run out of control, three physicists had the dangerous job of standing by the top of the pile and pouring a cadmium mixture over the pile in the hope of cooling it. A control rod, withdrawn from the reactor a few inches at a time, indicated on a measuring device that the pile had gone critical. Figuratively speaking, the reaction had caught fire and the genie was out of the bottle. The team's work in nuclear reaction would lead to the bombs that destroyed Hiroshima and Nagasaki and to the Cold War, which in itself led to future discoveries in the nuclear world. Not all were used for destruction. Medical science has benefited greatly from that first reaction. Sadly, Enrico Fermi had only twelve years to see what would come next, as cancer took his life in 1954. As time went on, his work would lead to cancer treatments that would help prolong the lives of others. In the 1960s, the Fermilab, named in his honor, was built in the Chicago area.

4. BEFORE THE WRIGHT BROTHERS

You've heard of Wilbur and Orville Wright, but have you ever heard of Octave Chanute? He designed the Union Stockyards and made a fortune building railroads. But his passion was flying machines. He began collecting information on flying machines in the 1850s, and had even organized an international aviation conference in conjunction with the 1893 World's Columbian Exposition. A year later, he published a compilation of aviation information that became possibly the most influential book on aviation of his time. Prior to becoming Gary, Indiana, sandy Miller Beach was the perfect setting for experimental flight. Chanute and his assistant, Augustus Herring, would take a glider, note the distance flown, and then go home to make improvements. One of the most successful contraptions they produced was a truss arrangement similar to that of railroad bridges. This glider flew 360 feet in one glide. In the 1900s, after reading Chanute's book, Wilbur Wright wrote the inventor hoping to gain advice on his own flying contraptions. Through the correspondence that followed, Chanute encouraged Wilbur to keep trying, and grateful for his help, the Wrights invited Chanute to Kitty Hawk, North Carolina, to witness what they hoped would be their first successful flight. Cold weather forced him off Kitty Hawk though, so he returned to Chicago, arriving on December 17, 1903. Upon his return, he received the telegram sent by the Wrights' sister Katharine. Very simply, but joyously, it read "The boys have done it." It would only be a matter of time before manned flight was commonplace.

5. THE REFRIGERATED CAR

Seeing the possibilities for profit in the meatpacking industry, Gustavus Swift set about revolutionizing it. The shipment of cattle in slatted railroad cars to Chicago, before being shipped from Chicago to slaughterhouses in other parts of the country, was tremendously wasteful. Swift calculated that for every healthy steer that arrived in Chicago, only 40 percent were edible. The answer was to slaughter in Chicago and ship the edible parts for sale nationally, but the technology didn't exist. Most refrigerated cars stored the ice in with the meat, which risked discoloring the meat and making it unsalable. Refrigerated transport was also difficult in summer since re-icing crews had to open the doors frequently, which raised the temperature and risked the meat. The public didn't trust shipped beef either, and Eastern butchers saw the meatpacking industry as putting them out of business. Despite Eastern protest and lack of funds, Swift hired Boston engineer Andrew S. Chase to invent a state-of-the-art refrigerator car. Chase placed the ice in ceiling bins rather than in the car itself. This gave workers the chance to re-ice by opening the roof, not the main doors. Air passing through bunkers positioned at the top of the car cooled, dropped to the floor, and forced warmer, lighter air out through ventilators. This plan took the Chicago meat industry from the local market to the national, and eventually to the international as the innovation was applied to refrigerated ships. The advent of the new refrigerated cars wasn't without initial setbacks. Railroads balked at the idea of building the cars. They made a good deal of money off shipping livestock. They set high rates for chilled beef, sometimes three times higher than those for livestock. Undeterred, Swift made a deal with the Grand Trunk, a young railroad that didn't have their resources as firmly rooted in the livestock trade. Once the hurdles had been overcome, the industry saw what Swift had known: that even more profit could be made from the meatpacking industry. And just as the emergence of the railroad helped make Chicago a major transportation hub in the nation, the refrigerated car helped make Chicago the center of meatpacking for the world.

6. MORE CHEESE, PLEASE

There was a time when the average American wasn't a huge fan of American cheese. Made in huge chunks, lacking any sort of uniformity, most cheeses didn't last long. Enter

James L. Kraft, a Chicagoan by way of Buffalo, New York, by way of Ontario, Canada, where he was born in 1874. He tried a number of ventures and fell in with the Buffalo Cheese Company in 1903. Phased out by his partners, he found himself heading to Chicago with $65, two rolls and coffee, and a bag of oats for his horse named Paddy. Having invested in fifty pounds of cheese, he began to sell cheese from the back of a wagon and ended up $3,000 in debt that first year. He developed a good rapport with grocers in town and when he began to package the cheese in individual portions, wrapped in tinfoil packages or placed in glass jars, he saw an upturn in sales. By 1907, convincing his brothers to join, he began J. L. Kraft and Brothers and imported old-world cheeses to sell to the immigrant neighborhoods hungry for a taste of home. In 1916, he patented a way to pasteurize processed cheese to increase shelf life. During World War I, the unspoilable bricks of cheese were the perfect food to send the boys overseas and the government ordered six million tons of it. In 1924, setting up a test kitchen, the company went on to bigger things. By the time Kraft died in 1953, at the age of seventy-eight, the Kraft Foods Company owned more than fifty subsidiaries across the world and diversified the products to include Miracle Whip, macaroni and cheese dinner, and Parkay Margarine, as well as caramels and ice-cream toppings. Not exactly hard cheese.

7. SIMPLE AS 1, 2, 3

On display at the Smithsonian Institution in Washington is a strange little item, a wooden macaroni box with staples, rubber bands, wire string, and meat skewers. Built by Door Eugene Felt in 1885, it was called a comptometer. You may know it better as a calculator. The following year he constructed a metal version of it, and in 1887, he received a patent for it. Two years later, having founded Felt and Tarrant MFG with Robert Tarrant, Felt was granted a patent for the comptograph, a fancy name for the calculator with a printing device. Comptometers were bulky little affairs: a large metal box with nine rows of keys, one for each digit. Zero was represented by the absence of a digit. A lever on the right side cleared the display. As time went by, the comptometer became more sophisticated but still difficult for the average person to use. There was a lot of training that went into being a comptometer operator. The machines themselves could weigh up to twenty-five pounds and go for as high as $400. Technology has come a long way from the comptometers, but that little wooden macaroni box gave us quite a boost.

8. AGAINST THE GRAIN

By 1850, thanks in large part to Cyrus McCormick and his reaper, as well as advances in transportation and storage, Chicago became the grain capital of the world. The Board of Trade had a dilemma: how to streamline the process of selling the grain. Before this revolution, grain was brought to the city by the farmers who lugged it in bags and found potential buyers who examined the grain and bought the grain. The rise in grain volume, as well as an increase in the number of sellers and buyers, made this process impractical. What the Board of Trade decided was to have one central location where farmers could bring their grain. Once there it was inspected, graded by type and quality, and sorted by representatives of the Board of Trade. The grain was then mixed together with grain from other farmers who were all given receipts that indicated their grain's type and grade. In the meantime, the purchaser bought the wheat or corn by grade, sight unseen, and was given receipts redeemable in grain. The process made haggling over the millions of bushels of grain passing through Chicago unnecessary. And what the Board of Trade also created was a new kind of currency. What sprang from this was the futures market where shrewd brokers bought the grain that they brought to market months later. This was the start of the first modern commodity exchange. Grains, and later hogs, were marketed in the way stocks and bonds were exchanged. After 1856, the trading that was done in the streets was now done in the exchange, and after hours, commission agents continued their dealings in the lobbies of hotels.

9. THE KIDS ARE ALRIGHT

On July 1, 1899, the Chicago Juvenile Court opened its doors. Prior to this, the problem of juvenile crime had been dealt with by the same criminal courts trying adults. As social reform gained momentum in the later nineteenth century, it was decided that new concepts of dealing with dependent and delinquent children had to be devised. Two key prompters of this new attitude were the Chicago Women's Club and Jane Addams's Hull House Community, and they couldn't have been more different. The Women's Club was made up of socialites, who reflected the concerns of their class and were generally conservative in their philosophies. Hull House was deep in the immigrant poor communities. Both, however, believed that those who often slipped through the cracks, women and children, needed advocacy. The issue of juvenile crime was unique and needed to be dealt with in a unique way. Members of the club helped establish a Jail School. The schools gave children a chance to learn a trade. But it seemed apparent that the judicial process needed to be changed. In an effort to compel the judiciary process to try the juveniles within twenty-four hours of arrest, it was suggested that separate court sessions be held for the trial of boys. Long captivity in the company of hardened criminals only hardened the children as well. The continuation of separate and speedy trials was contingent upon the good graces of the state's attorney and the judge. In 1895, a law to establish separate courts for juveniles was drafted, but it was considered unconstitutional and set aside. Reformers continued their work in bettering conditions for incarcerated juveniles, but never let the idea of a separate court die. They continued to lobby, using other clubs and the press, encouraging other reformers to get their point across. Members of Hull House appeared in court for the children and even advised the judge on the condition of the child's family life and how the children's future might best be served. As they noticed that the courts seemed more interested in incarceration than rehabilitation, Hull House began to lobby for a more adequate system of justice for juveniles. By 1898, appeals were made to the Bar Association to join the fight and the juvenile court bill was resurrected, and eventually accepted. From this point on, juvenile offenders were no longer viewed as adults but as children in need of guidance and help. Family circumstances and postsentencing were more carefully considered. What was termed the "progressive era" truly became so in the judicial system; eventually, this new method of dealing with the issue of juvenile delinquency spread throughout the United States.

10. THE SPEED OF LIGHT

If it weren't for Albert A. Michelson, not only might Einstein's theory of relativity never have come about, but advances in physics wouldn't have, either. Prussian born in 1852, Michelson's family moved to the United States when he was two. He graduated from the United States Naval Academy in Annapolis in 1873, and taught chemistry and physics there. At the academy, he began to experiment with ways of measuring the speed of light. In 1892, he was appointed head of the physics department at the University of Chicago. His work in measuring the speed of light led him to invent the interferometer in 1880, which measured light rays and distances that were impossible even for the most powerful of telescopes. In 1887, together with colleague Edward W. Morely, Michelson proved that the speed of light is constant by running two beams of light against each other from opposite directions. The partners' work showed an absence of "ether" which, at the time, was believed to be an elastic agent involved with electricity and magnetism. Their findings inspired Albert Einstein's theory of relativity. Twenty years after this groundbreaking experiment, Michelson's work in meteorology and spectroscopy would lead him to become the first American awarded the Nobel Prize for Physics. Along the way, he wrote a number of books explaining his work in measuring light, and when he used his interferometer to measure Betelgeuse in 1920, his work helped his colleagues gain a better knowledge of the size of the universe. While he retired as head of the physics department at the University of Chicago in 1930, he continued his work on calculating precise figures to measure the speed of light. A year later, in California, Albert A. Michelson's own light went out at the age of seventy-eight.

News That's Fit to Print

While the number of mastheads has lessened, Chicago still is a great news town. Some of the biggest names in newsprint graced the newspapers of Chicago first.

1. THE EMPIRE

The staunch Republican leanings of the *Chicago Tribune* have been there since the paper's beginnings when, in 1855, Joseph Medill, editor of the *Cleveland Morning Leader*, and Dr. Charles Ray, who dabbled in newspapers in Galena and Springfield, formed a partnership and bought the struggling eight-year-old paper. Under the crusading influence of these two, the *Tribune* would be a major voice in the antislavery movement, a backer of Abraham Lincoln, and, eventually, a reluctant backer of the Civil War. And yet, while he sided with the workingman on some issues, Medill spoke out against unions and other labor causes. He was also viciously racist and anti-Irish and used his paper to denounce blacks and immigrants whenever he could. A founding member of the Republican Party in Illinois and mayor of Chicago from 1871 to 1873, Medill never shied away from mixing journalism and politics. As mayor, he helped supervise the rebuilding of the city, established the city's first library, and helped keep the city from going bankrupt in his first year as mayor. That philosophy of contradiction would stay with the *Tribune* long after his death in 1899. After his death, the reins passed briefly to his son-in-law, Robert W. Patterson, then to his grandson, Robert McCormick, and then Patterson's son, Joseph Medill Patterson, after the older Patterson's unexpected death. McCormick eventually gained control and ran the paper very much as his grandfather had. In fact, even after McCormick's death in 1953, the paper remained a stodgy bastion of the upper class. In the 1960s, the paper killed stories that might prove embarrassing to politicians or businessmen. They continued to use the word "negro" in stories long after other publications had started using the word "black." When changes came, they came slowly. In 1973, the *Trib* devoted a special supplement to the first of the Watergate tapes, and a year later, their editorials called for Nixon's resignation. In 1979, they became one of the first big-city newspapers to occasionally use color, and the 1980s saw an expansion of the paper's foreign press coverage, with bureaus in Rome, Mexico City, Tokyo, Hong Kong, Nairobi, and Warsaw. By 1985, *Time* magazine designated it as one of the ten best newspapers. Of course, evolution takes time.

2. **CHICAGO'S PAPER**

In 1948, the Field family bought the *Chicago Daily Times*, which had started in 1929, and merged it with *The Chicago Sun,* started in 1941. Unlike the rather elitist *Tribune*, the *Chicago Sun-Times* was considered the blue-collar paper, despite its ownership by the city's first family. A best seller in Chicago, while the *Trib* ruled the suburbs, the *Times* is younger than the *Trib* but carried respected names such as Mike Royko, Roger Ebert, Sidney J. Harris, and Irv Kupcinet, giving the *Trib* a run for its money. Though more liberal, its politics weren't worn as prominently on its sleeve as the politics of the *Tribune*. Marshall Field III and later IV would make an attempt at a balanced news style. Its international news coverage was also superior to the *Trib*'s at a time when the world was changing dramatically. It seemed likely to overtake the *Trib* toward the 1980s, but the Fields surprised the city by selling the paper to tabloid prince Rupert Murdoch in 1983. The decision surprised the writers as well. Mike Royko, a longtime columnist of the *Sun-Times*, defected to his hated rival the *Trib* as did advice columnist Ann Landers. As feared, sensationalism crept into the headlines and stories. Circulation dropped as readers turned to the *Trib* for their news. The *Tribune's* Jewish readership increased as the stalwart *Sun-Times* reader left Murdoch's new style. Eventually, the paper began to get back to its solid news roots. Murdoch finally sold the paper, which is now owned by Hollinger International (though Hollinger is now considering selling it), and the paper still has a fine group of writers. But the slight taste of sensationalism is still apparent in the headlines. It's currently the nation's thirteenth-largest newspaper and still has a long way to go to conquer the mighty *Trib*. But this is Chicago, after all, a place where the underdog sometimes finds his way to the top.

3. THE WRITER'S PAPER

The *Chicago Daily News* was launched in 1875 by Melville E. Stone, who'd done some writing for the *Chicago Tribune* and later became the editor of the *Chicago Inter-Ocean*. After writing in the East for some time, he came back to Chicago and started the *Chicago Daily News* with reporter William E. Dougherty and Percy Meggy. A year later, Dougherty and Meggy's shares were bought out by Victor Lawson who handled the business functions while Stone saw to the editorial aspects. Stone felt news should be impartial, free from the bigotries of the editor, and from Hearst-like yellow journalism. He sought out the finest writers, columnists, and cartoonists and this gave the *Chicago Daily News* a legitimacy among writers that the other newspapers didn't quite possess. When Stone retired as editor in 1888, he sold his interests to Lawson, who helped it become one of the most respected evening newspapers in the United States. The first to utilize newsboys and to run full-page ads in the papers, he was also the first to run a daily newspaper column and was careful in hiring competent reporters, even training foreign correspondents before they took their posts overseas. After Lawson died in 1925, and his successor, Walter Strong, died in 1931, Frank Knox was picked to take over the paper and he carried on the tradition of excellence in journalism. By 1978, the *Daily News* had won fifteen Pulitzer Prizes and helped spawn the careers of newsmen like Ben Hecht and Mike Royko, but it was running out of time. Times had changed, TV was king, and newspapers just weren't as popular as they had been. Many had gone by the wayside prior to the 1970s, and the *Daily News'* circulation figures had dropped dramatically. March 4, 1978, saw the last edition printed, a banner headline bidding "So Long, Chicago."

4. THE VOICE

The first home of the *Defender* was the small kitchen of publisher Robert Abbott's landlord. The first issues were four pages long. As time went on, though, the *Chicago Defender* became one of the most influential newspapers in the black community. Robert Abbott had graduated from Kent College of Law in 1899, the only African American in his class. In Chicago, though, discrimination kept him out of the business of law and turned him instead to publishing. The first issue of the *Defender* appeared in 1905. By 1912, Abbott was selling the paper from newsstands. It began to attract national attention by addressing national issues. His headlines were sensational, his editorial policy militant. He referred to African Americans not as "negroes" or "blacks" but as "The Race," "Race men," and "Race women." Before long, local circulation had sped past other black newspapers in the city. Circulation spread down South, thanks to black Pullman porters and traveling black entertainers who agreed to carry the paper South despite the threat from racist organizations like the Ku Klux Klan. The *Defender* became the first black newspaper to reach over 100,000 in circulation. At its height, it would reach 500,000 a week. And Abbott took full advantage of that, calling for antilynching laws and integrated sports. The *Defender* helped inspire the black migration north by suggesting that what people would find in Chicago was the land of milk and honey. In 1940, Abbot handed control of the *Defender* to his nephew, John H. Sengstacke, who founded and became the first president of what is now known as the National News Publisher Association, and who eventually started other newspapers in other cities.

5. THE COLONEL

When Joseph Patterson left to start the *New York Daily News*, Robert McCormick would take over control of the *Tribune* and keep it on a steady conservative course. Col. Robert McCormick (a rank he acquired during the First World War) came from a privileged pedigree and prep-school education. Reserved and aloof, he graduated from Yale in 1903, and attended Northwestern Law School before being admitted to the bar in 1908. Like his grandfather, he entered politics, becoming a Twenty-First Ward alderman. When it came time to choose between politics and journalism, the paper won out. McCormick never hid his elitist views. Believing in free speech, he was also an isolationist, opposing the United States' entry in both World Wars. A friend of big business, he spoke out against labor unions and saw no reason for the Democratic Party, criticizing Jane Addams's progressive beliefs and President Franklin D. Roosevelt's New Deal policies. He carried with him a surprising amount of clout, visiting the White House during various administrations, and even influencing prime ministers on British policies. McCormick helped the empire grow by buying Canadian mills and forests, shipping companies, radio and television stations, and publishing houses. The Tribune Company has become a major player in the media industry, a legacy McCormick left the city after his death in 1953.

6. EBONY

Publisher John J. Johnson's mission was to show that blacks had normal lives, too. He patterned his weekly magazine

Ebony after magazines like *Life*, the *Saturday Evening Post*, and *Colliers*, glossy magazines that gave the reader a glimpse of celebrity life. But it was a white life. Johnson hoped to present black life in the same way. To show the everyday life of blacks, not just the injustices against the community. To profile successful blacks and middle-class blacks and show them beyond the world of shacks and tenements. With a loan of $500, in 1942 he started a weekly called *Negro Digest*, which proved successful.

Eventually, it became *Ebony* magazine, its circulation growing from 10,000 to 500,000 in the first ten years. Faced with the Jim Crow south, though, Johnson found himself traveling a tough road trying to find distributors and advertisers. He brought along J. Unis Pressley, his circulation manager, whose light skin helped him pass for white. In the South he was able to register at hotels and buy food from restaurants that would then be smuggled back to the group. While there were those early on who criticized the magazine for concentrating only on the positive stories, that very coverage provided a service to the civil rights movement by inspiring its readers to reach for more.

7. SLATS

Mike Royko was for many the voice of Chicago. An award-winning columnist for three of the major players in Chicago newspaper history, for six years his column was the first thing people turned to when they read the *Sun-Times*. But when Rupert Murdoch bought the paper, rather than work for a purveyor of tabloid journalism, Royko went across the street to the newspaper he had sworn he'd never work for, the *Chicago Tribune*. He remained there until his death in 1997, at the age of sixty-five. Born in 1932, Mike Royko had the sort of upbringing that gave him his unique voice and that he would eventually assign to one of his most famous characters, Slats Grobnick. Slats was featured in a number of columns, describing his childhood growing up in an apartment over a tavern in one of Chicago's ethnic neighborhoods. Witty, acerbic, often cynical, many times tender, Royko was a champion of the underdog, speaking out against bigotry and injustice. He was sharp-witted and sharp-tongued, and graft was a favorite target, particularly in the Daley administration, which he delighted in skewering in print whenever he could. In 1971, Royko's exposé of the Daley administration, *Boss*, was printed to wide acclaim. While his columns were collected in a number of books, *Boss* remains his most popular, winning him a Pulitzer Prize in 1972. He began his newspaper career as a columnist for the Glenview Naval Air Base newspaper and later the City News Bureau of Chicago before moving on to the *Chicago Daily News*, the paper where he was most content, starting as a reporter and moving on to columnist. When the *Daily News* closed down in 1978, he brought his column to the *Chicago Sun-Times* before leaving for the *Trib* in 1984. Along the way he won the National Press Club Achievement Award in 1990 and the Damon Runyon Award in 1995. Years after his death, Royko remains one of those silenced voices that people still miss.

8. THE WHITE RABBIT

Playboy was born on the cusp of the country's sexual revolution. Hugh Hefner, an unassuming University of Illinois alum, had an idea to play to the prurient interests of men and create a magazine featuring women in various styles of undress. The first issue, published around December 1, 1953, featured a real coup: a nude calendar photo of a pre-blonde Marilyn Monroe. To Hef, his girls were a "triumph of sexuality." And sometimes, it really was about the articles. Mixed with the cheesecake were fascinating articles and interviews. Early writers to grace the pages were James Baldwin, Ray Bradbury, and P. G. Wodehouse. By 1960, the magazine was generating $3 million in profits. Hefner had become a major player in a world hungry for sophisticated naughtiness. What had been known as the Palmolive Building downtown was purchased by Hefner and became the Playboy Building where he ran his empire, though he was equally comfortable running it from his round bed at the Playboy mansion on the Gold Coast. There were Playboy clubs, TV shows, private jets, and Hollywood projects, all with that familiar rabbit logo. *Playboy* wasn't a hit with everyone. Feminists claimed it demeaned women. And religious leaders . . . well, we all can imagine how they felt about it. But there was something naively nerdy about the nudity of *Playboy* magazine. Later, magazines like *Swank* and *Hustler* would play to the more carnal side of a man's lust. *Playboy* was different. Heavily airbrushed, the models weren't there to be leered at but to be appreciated. It was naughty but in a fun way. A teasing way. *Playboy* was perhaps the first magazine that addressed the concept that women were sexual creatures, too, with sexual appetites of their own. This sort of mentality led to *Playboy's* offshoot, *Playgirl*. Equal opportunity, right?

9. THE NEWS SERVICE

Born in 1889, as a young man Claude Barnett moved from Florida to Illinois and with a degree from Tuskegee Institute, worked in Chicago as a postal clerk and ad salesman. Putting his business skills to use, he established a mail-order business that sold photos of famous black Americans, and later formed the Kashmir Chemical Company. In 1918, selling ads for the *Chicago Defender*, Barnett realized that black editors needed a news service for the African American community. A year later, he persuaded his partners in the cosmetic company to invest in this new venture, the Associated Negro Press (ANP). For $25 a week, a publisher could subscribe to the ANP and receive national news releases specific to the black community. Barnett wrote many of the stories, favoring the success stories of black entertainers, politicians, and athletes. By 1935, the ANP was serving 200 subscribers nationally and after World War II, more than a hundred African newspapers signed up. Barnett and his wife, singer/actress Etta Moten, made many trips to Africa and became experts in the art and culture of the African people. Pressuring the U.S. government to accredit black journalists as war correspondents, he began a mission to point out the injustice of the apartheid condition in America. He wrote of segregation in the armed forces and the negative effect it had on the black soldiers willing to die for their country. He pointed out the plight of the black tenant farmers, and from 1942 to 1953 worked to improve their conditions as a special assistant to the secretary of agriculture. For his efforts in bettering the lives of blacks, in 1949 Tuskegee Institute awarded him an honorary doctorate of humanities while the governments of Haiti and Liberia also bestowed honors upon him. By the 1960s, however, Barnett was in poor health. He had achieved his mission of giving a national voice to the black community where they had none before, and by the end of his career, the mainstream media was at last coming around and reporting more on the black community. Barnett sold the ANP in 1964, and died of a cerebral hemorrhage in 1967. Shortly after, the ANP ceased operation.

10. NEWSPAPER WARS

In 1900, William Randolph Hearst knew he needed the support of certain cities to help William Jennings Bryan win the presidency, so he started a newspaper, the *Chicago American*, which would report heavily on Bryant and his campaign. Introducing sensationalism to Chicago news with five-inch headlines detailing gruesomeness and scandal, Hearst still needed an edge in the paper-heavy town. That edge came from Moses and Max Annenberg, who grew up Jewish and tough in the heavily Irish neighborhood known as The Patch. Moses was known as the schemer, while Max settled problems with force. Every day, at 5 A.M., they hustled *Tribunes*, by hook or by crook, and their success caught the attention of Hearst who, in 1902, hired Max to sell the *Chicago American*, by any means necessary. While Max sent brother Moe to sell subscriptions in the suburbs of Cook County, he recruited a gang to help convince dealers to accept larger quantities of the *Chicago American*. Tough guys like Red and

Dan Connors, "Mossie" Enright (no relation to the author—I think), Joe Kane, Walter Stevens, Tom Looney, and James Ragen knew exactly what was necessary to do the job. In one instance, when Marshall Field decided to stop carrying the *American*, Annenberg, his gang, and a group of sixty delivery drivers and newsboys armed themselves with billyclubs and chains and surrounded Marshall Field's store, chanting ominously "Field's Closed" over and over. The message received, the next day Field began selling the *American* again. When Hearst began selling a morning edition known as the *Examiner*, the *Chicago Tribune* and the *Daily News* stepped up the play. In 1910, Robert McCormick and his cousin Joe Patterson of the *Tribune* gave their editor a budget of $1 million to win the circulation war. Impressed with the Marshall Field's incident, the editor hired the Annenbergs away from Hearst for $20,000. In the meantime, a new gang of toughs were hired to sell the *Chicago American*, among them a fancier of flowers, Dean O'Banion. When the *Tribune* cut the cost of their papers by a cent in 1910 and the public responded favorably, Hearst armed his men with pistols and blackjacks and by 1913, twenty-seven news dealers were gunned down by newspaper gangs. Just another case of fierce business dealings in early Chicago. And ultimately, out of the three stars of this story, it would be the *Chicago Tribune* still standing.

Literary

After the Great Fire of 1871, the British royal family and noted English literary figures sent a donation of 8,000 books to replace those in Chicago's library that they were sure must have been burned in the fire. The only problem was that Chicago didn't have a library. In fact, citizens from the richest to the poorest were so focused on earning money that very little thought had been given to cultural niceties such as libraries. That changed, like so many things, after the Great Fire. Now, Chicago boasts two of the best libraries in the country, as well as a host of literary talent that has sprung up over the centuries.

1. LARGER THAN LIFE

Ernest Hemingway lived the adventurous life he wrote about, but he started out in the serene world of Oak Park, Illinois, in 1899. His physician father took him fishing and hunting in woods near his home. His mother exposed him to the world of concerts, operas, and museums. In high school, he wrote for the school magazine and after graduation got a job with the *Kansas City Star*. Adventuresome, he enlisted in the Army to fight in World War I, but was turned down due to poor vision in one eye. Volunteering to be an ambulance driver with the Red Cross, by 1918 he was shipped off to Europe. While in Italy, on the Italian/Austrian front he was wounded by an Austrian mortar shell. It has been claimed that though severely wounded, he refused help for himself until the other more seriously injured soldiers were cared for, but the accuracy of the claim has been questioned. But his wounds were real and he was presented with the Italian Silver Medal for Valor by the Italian government. Returning to the States, he found that wanderlust set in. He joined the *Toronto Star*, and was sent to Paris as a correspondent. Living the bohemian lifestyle, he met the cream of the Paris art world while writers like Gertrude Stein and Ezra Pound taught him about the value of compression in his writing. Combined with his training as a journalist, this helped forge a stronger writer. Writing about personal experiences, his 1929 *A Farewell to Arms* was inspired by a hospital romance he had with a nurse in Italy during the war. He wrote of his love for bullfighting, big-game hunting, and deep-sea fishing. What followed *A Farewell to Arms* wasn't always embraced by critics, but a safari to Africa in 1935 would inspire two of his most acclaimed short stories, *The Snows of Kilamanjaro* and *The Short Happy Life of Frances Macomber*. In 1940, he won more praise with *For Whom the Bell Tolls*. Covering the Spanish civil war in 1937, the Sino-Japanese war in 1941, and the war in Europe in 1944, he become a larger-than-life figure and in some way lost himself. Married four times, moving from Key West to Cuba back to the United States, it seemed writing was becoming more difficult. In 1952, his book *The Old Man and the Sea* was a huge success, but two years later, an airplane crash while visiting Africa left him with such severe injuries that he was unable to personally accept the Nobel Prize presented to him for the novel. Health problems from the crash caused severe depression, which affected his writing. In 1960, drinking heavily, he moved to Ketchum, Idaho, seeking the wide-open spaces of his youth. The shock treatments he sought for his depression had the side effect of memory loss, which also greatly affected his writing. Finally, despondent over being unable to tell his stories, he killed himself with a shotgun, leaving behind a huge record of a full life.

2. LEGAL EAGLE

Despite having sold 25 million copies of his novels worldwide, despite a slew of writing awards and the practical assurance of a spot on the national best-seller list, Scott Turow still seems content with pursuing his legal career. Born in Chicago in 1949, he graduated from Amherst College in 1970, attended Stanford University Creative Writing Center for two years, then went on to teach creative writing at Stanford until 1975 when he entered Harvard Law School. Graduating in 1978, he went on to become an assistant United States attorney in Chicago. His first novel, *Presumed Innocent*, was published in 1987 and became a hit motion picture starring Harrison Ford. He followed that up with *The Burden of Proof*—which became an ABC-TV miniseries—and *Pleading Guilty*. He continues to serve in a number of organizations, practices law, mostly pro bono, and has managed to juggle the two careers expertly. He was appointed to the chair of the Illinois State Appellate Defenders Commission, one of fourteen appointed by former Illinois governor George Ryan in 2000, to consider reforming the capital punishment system. He served on the U.S. Senate Nomination Commission for Northern District of Illinois, and acted as a special prosecutor in the investigation of police corruption in Oak Park, Illinois. And perhaps most notably and pro bono, he successfully convinced the Appellate Court to reconsider the murder conviction of Alejandro Hernandez, a codefendant in the Cruz-Hernandez murder trials. After spending twelve years in jail, Hernandez was freed in 1995 after the acquittal of his codefendant Rolando Cruz.

3. THE CHRONICLER

Into his nineties, Pulitzer Prize winner Studs Terkel remains a unique and powerful presence in the Chicago literary world. *Giants of Jazz* was published in 1956 and played on his affinity for the music. Ten years later came his second powerful book called *Division Street: America*, a book of oral history interviews. He has the ability to translate an experience onto the printed page and weave the reader into it. Terkel was born in New York in 1912. His family moved to Chicago where his mother ran a boardinghouse; no doubt the interaction with the boarders helped hone his talent for telling a story. After graduating law school in 1934, journalism was just one of many careers he found his way into. He's been a civil service employee, a stage, radio, and movie actor, a playwright, a jazz columnist, a disc jockey, film narrator, and sportscaster. He was even in the Air Force briefly. Interviewer and social commentator seems to be his strong suit, though. In his broadcasting career that has spanned forty years, he's interviewed thousands of people, celebrities, and the average Joe. After *Division Street*, he would write other interview-books-turned-national-best-sellers about the Depression, World War II, race relations, working, and aging. The year 2001 saw the publication of *Will the Circle Be Unbroken: Reflections on Death, Rebirth and Hunger for a Faith*. Not an unusual subject considering his age.

4. **OZ**

The Emerald City in the *Wizard of Oz* was possibly inspired by the White City of the 1893 World's Fair. Published in 1900, after L. Frank Baum himself had been living in Chicago for a decade, Dorothy from *The Wonderful Wizard of Oz* was first introduced in Baum's *Mother Goose in Prose* based on stories he told his children. Born in New York in 1856, Baum joined the *New York World* as a reporter in 1873 and later founded *New Era* weekly in Pennsylvania. As the decade wore on, he would dabble in opera, and playwriting, and return to his family's oil business before arriving in Chicago. Desiring to create modern fairy tales less chilling than the Brothers Grimm, his first taste of fame came from publishing *Mother Goose in Prose*. Teaming with illustrator William Wallace Denslow, they created *Father Goose, His Book* which became the year's best-selling book and led to *The Wonderful Wizard of Oz*. Published at his own expense, the book sold 90,000 copies in the first two years, spawning a sequel, *The Marvelous Land of Oz*, and enabling Baum to move to California where he wrote Oz sequels and other children's books under his own and various pen names. Ahead of his time when it came to producing children's entertainment, which at the time wasn't at all profitable, Baum and his business associates produced stage shows and movies based on the Oz books and fairy tales. The continued success of the Oz books enabled him to write one a year, until his death in 1919, twenty years before the most famous adaptation of his Oz story would be created. In 1976, a park in Lincoln Park was named Oz Park to commemorate Baum's creation. Greeting visitors is a statue of the Tin Man as they follow the yellow brick road inside.

5. THE DIARY

He was born in Chicago in 1905 to Jewish-immigrant parents, yet growing up on the dividing line between his Jewish neighborhood and an Italian neighborhood, Meyer Levin felt it safer to hide his Jewish roots. While his first story, published at age fifteen in the magazine *Ten Story Book*, told the story of a boy trying to hide his heritage from his gentile girlfriend, his first two books, *Reporter* and *Frankie and Johnny*, avoided Jewish themes. Early short stories would explore themes like the division between the old- and new-world Jews, but it wasn't until 1931 that he brought his roots into his novel writing. A war correspondent during World War II, Levin began appreciating the Jewish spirit and later novels incorporated this insight. Involved with smuggling Jewish emigrants to Palestine to escape persecution, he witnessed the cruelties of the time. The touching *Diary of Anne Frank*, which he discovered in Germany in 1954, only emphasized this. Translating the diary into English, Levin worked out a deal with Otto Frank—Anne's father, to write a play based on it. Upon completion, however, he was told by Broadway producers that it wasn't good enough, and they hired two others to write. Their version, according to Levin in a lawsuit, was almost identical. Levin would ultimately be awarded $50,000 in damages, but another lawsuit would follow, this time over 1956's *Compulsion*, the fictionalized version of the Leopold and Loeb murder case. In 1964, Leopold unsuccessfully sued Levin, Simon & Schuster, and pretty much anyone involved with the book and the subsequent movie, charging invasion of privacy. Levin went on to pen more best sellers including his last, in 1981, *The Architect*, loosely based on Frank Lloyd Wright. He died that same year in Jerusalem at the age of seventy-five.

6. **THE UNDERDOG**

He wrote about the prey and the predators of Chicago. Nelson Algren was born in Michigan in 1909 and raised on the South Side and later the Northwest Side of Chicago. He obtained a degree in journalism, then fell into depression and became an itinerant worker, riding the rails from town to town and soaking up the details of the life. After *Story* magazine picked up his first story, "So Help Me," he received a contract from Vanguard Press and took to the road again, hanging out with the underbelly of society, recording the experience. From all this came his first novel, *Somebody in Boots*. His second book, *Never Come Moving*, which cast a critical eye toward the Polish-American slums, was hailed as brilliant by some. American Poles, however, branded it offensive, and the Chicago Public Library banned it after pressure from the Polish Roman Catholic Union. In the 1950s, *The Man with the Golden Arm* won the first National Book Award for Fiction, but it was also the peak of Algren's career. Six years later, *A Walk on the Wild Side* was considered clichéd, readers viewing society's outcasts as more inconvenient than interesting. Turning to writer's conferences and lecturing in the 1960s, in 1973 Algren published a collection of short pieces, *The Last Carousel*. Ten years later, his novel, *The Devil's Stockings,* was published two years after his death. Nelson Algren died in New York in 1981, months after election into the American Academy and Institute of Arts and Letters. He influenced a host of writers in Chicago, including Mike Royko, but, sadly, Algren was also underappreciated by his hometown. In the 1970s, *Chicago* magazine held a writer's symposium and invited writers like Jean Shepherd, Arthur C. Clarke, and John Updike. But nowhere on the list was the city's native son.

7. THE POET

Summing up Chicago in a single poem, he dubbed Chicago "City of Big Shoulders" and "Hogbutcher to the World." Carl Sandburg's poetry spoke to critics and the public alike. Named Illinois poet laureate in 1962, he was much more. Born in Illinois in 1878, his first job was as a milk wagon driver at age fourteen. Later jobs included potato digger, window washer, and porter at a barbershop. In 1898, he enlisted in the Illinois Volunteers to fight in the Spanish-American War. Turning to writing, he became a correspondent for a newspaper in Galesburg, and printed his first book of poetry. Dropping out of college in 1902, he found himself in a series of jobs in Milwaukee before moving back to Chicago where he worked as a reporter for the *Chicago World*, and by 1917 was on the staff of the *Chicago Daily News*. His flair for getting to the heart of a story, was apparent in his analysis of the 1919 race riots, "The Chicago Race Riots." He also wrote a popular Pulitzer Prize–winning six-volume biography of Abraham Lincoln in 1939 entitled *Abraham Lincoln: The War Years*. Poetry remained his constant, though. After his work was published in *Poetry* magazine, his fame took off, and he began publishing volumes of poetry that were accessible, flowing with touches of history and stories of American life. He collected American folk songs, wrote children's books as well as an epic novel, *Remembrance Rock,* that starts with the landing at Plymouth Rock and goes through World War II, which showed that, even late in life, he was adventuresome in his writing. In 1951, he won a second Pulitzer for his volume of complete poems.

8. **TARZAN**

Chicago is a long way from the steamy jungles of Africa, but this is exactly where Tarzan was born, in the fertile mind of Edgar Rice Burroughs, who left us with one of the most enduring characters in literature. Born in Chicago in 1875, Burroughs grew up on the West Side. He graduated from a Michigan military academy, then fell into a series of rugged jobs out west before returning to Chicago. In 1912, *All-Story* magazine published "Tarzan of the Apes," a novel he'd started writing in 1911, and after publication it was a huge success, leading to the first Tarzan movie filmed six years later. Also in 1912, *The Mucker* was published. Set in Chicago, it told the story of Billy Lynne, a street kid living by his wits. For Burroughs, writing was meat and potatoes. With a family to support, he didn't finesse his craft, something he came under fire for from a few critics. Rarely were his novels outlined or proofread and generally they took one to three months to complete. Along with the Tarzan novels, he wrote science fiction serials like the Martian Series, the Venus Series and the Pellucidar Series. Some of his last work was conducted during World War II as a war correspondent stationed in the Marshall Islands for the *Los Angeles Times*. He died in 1950, in California, at the age of seventy-five. Decades before, having moved to California after his writing success began, Burroughs began to develop real estate. The community, located in the San Fernando Valley grew to the point where it was time to choose a name for the area. In honor of Burroughs, they decided to call the town Tarzana.

9. **THE PROFESSOR**

The first African American to receive a Pulitzer Prize—for her 1950 poetry collection *Annie Allen*—also received two Guggenheim Fellowships, fifty honorary doctorates from various universities, and served as poetry consultant to the Library of Congress. Rather impressive for a shy little girl from Chicago. Born in 1917 in Kansas, Gwendolyn Brooks's family moved to Chicago when she was four. Her talent for poetry was encouraged, but her strict parents denied her the chance to play with other children in the neighborhood. Growing up reserved, she put her passion into reading and writing. A poem entitled "Eventide" appeared in the magazine *American Childhood* when she was a teen, and after graduating from junior college in 1936, her poems were picked up by the *Chicago Defender,* leading to her first book of poems, *A Street in Bronzeville*, published in 1945. While her work spoke to the soul in everyone, she was especially able to speak to the situation particular to her people as she did in "The Ballad of Emmett Till." Her work was made stronger by an ability to present a message without shoving it down the reader's throat. In 1953, her first novel, *Maud Martha*, was published, and she followed that up with *The Bean Eaters* in 1960 and 1963's *Selected Poems*, which led to her first teaching job at Columbia College. Her next major collection, *In the Mecca,* published in 1968, revealed that her style had become more free verse. That same year she was named Illinois Poet Laureate, and in 1976 became the first African American to receive an American Academy of Arts and Letters Award. She spent ten years as a professor of English at Chicago State University before passing away in 2000 at the age of eighty-three.

10. THE FRONT PAGE

Born in New York in 1893, and dying in New York in 1964, Ben Hecht nonetheless drew his inspiration from Chicago and wove that experience into plays, books, and movies. When he was six, his family moved to Chicago and stayed briefly before winding up in Racine, Wisconsin, in 1903. Once out of high school, he got a job on the *Chicago Daily Journal*, one of many papers in town. Known as a picture chaser, he was ordered to get pictures of big names down on their luck by whatever means necessary. Posing as a gas-meter reader, crawling through open windows, or climbing up fire escapes, his determination so impressed the editors that they put him to work chasing stories and he soon became an ace reporter. In 1914, Hecht joined the staff of the *Chicago Daily News* and, having found his voice, became known for his quick wit and sharp observations. Along with Maxwell Bodenheim, he founded the Player's Workshop, and in 1923 began publishing *The Chicago Literary Times*. The satirical biweekly paper skewered anyone who seemed worthy of skewering, be they politicians, artists, writers, or society names. Eventually, he began writing screenplays, his credits including some of the most famous movies of all time like 1939's *Wuthering Heights*, 1946's *Notorious*, and 1957's *A Farewell to Arms*. *The Front Page* became his best known work. Coauthored with Charles MacArthur in 1928, it was inevitable that Hecht would write a play set in the fast-paced world of a Chicago newspaper. The Cary Grant and Rosaline Russell movie *His Girl Friday* remains one of the classic adaptations of this play. He continued to write into the 1950s, including his autobiography, *Child of the Century*, notable for its 950 pages of memories.

The Roaring Twenties

The whole country was jumping during this decade, but the party in Chicago seemed to be the rowdiest.

1. **THE VOLSTEAD ACT**

This wildly misguided attempt to better the lives of Americans by controlling them had been threatening Chicago and America for decades. After World War I broke out, Congress passed a few measures prohibiting the sale of alcohol and seeing their chance, the "drys," as they were known, tacked their cause onto the cause of patriotism. Breweries were owned primarily by Germans, our enemy in the war, and the valuable grain used to create liquor would be put to better use feeding the soldiers overseas. It wasn't long before the Eighteenth Amendment was ratified and the Volstead Act (named after House Judiciary Committee Chairman Andrew J. Volstead of Minnesota) was passed into law. What was thought to be best for the health of the average American, however, turned out to be a windfall for organized crime. Prohibition went into effect at midnight January 17, 1920, and gang-controlled speakeasies replaced liquor stores, saloons, breweries, and distilleries. Al Capone became master of this game and blood would spill in the streets of Chicago, as gangs of bootleggers both large and small would battle to be the sole supplier to public demand. William Dever tried to counter that sort of corruption. Mayor from 1923 to '27, he became known as the mayor who would clean up Chicago. Speakeasies were shut down, and Al Capone moved his operation to the town of Cicero. When, in a fit of sober rage, Chicago reelected Big Bill Thompson back into office, speakeasies rose again. Organized crime wasn't the only monster lurking in the shadows of the Eighteenth Amendment. Those who couldn't afford the speakeasies turned to whatever recourse they could find. Any liquid containing more than half of 1 percent of alcohol was considered intoxicating and unlawful. Breweries were allowed to brew near-beer, but the alcohol that was deleted was collected and sold illegally. Liquor was smuggled across the border from Canada and Mexico. Since it was legal for drugstores to sell alcohol for prescriptions, doctors made a sideline of handing out thousands of prescriptions. And then there was bathtub gin, a popular and dangerous substitute for the real thing. Home stills began producing hooch from any ingredients available, including the alcohol used in manufacturing. Substances like denatured alcohol that were unfit to drink caused people literally to drink themselves blind, since often the rotgut caused blindness, paralysis, internal bleeding, and even death as vital organs were terminally affected by the poison. The Volstead Act led to a wild, decade-long ride, making millionaires out of some, taking the lives of others.

2. ELLIOT NESS/*THE UNTOUCHABLES*

The battle between Elliot Ness and Al Capone is a legend, fueled by the exaggerations of a man frustrated by the hand history had dealt him. That's not to say that Elliot Ness wasn't heroic, or to say that he didn't play a role in Capone's downfall. Elliot Ness was the first "untouchable." The moniker sprang from a newspaper account claiming that Ness and his men were above bribery. Ness had studied law and criminology at the University of Chicago and was working for U.S. attorney general for Northern Illinois George Johnson when he was chosen to head up the newly formed prohibition offices in Chicago. His main qualification was honesty. In the graft-ridden town of Chicago, that was hard to find. Ness put together a team of equally incorruptible "untouchables," and they began going after bootleggers, raiding breweries and warehouses, making arrests, and seizing hundreds of thousands of dollars of equipment. To gain the trust of the public, Ness relied on the glamour of publicity. Scenes of daring nighttime raids in newsreels and glaring headlines in papers made the Prohibition agent as exciting as the gangster. Capone was slippery, though. Either there was no evidence to tie him to the booze, or Capone was able to bribe or intimidate his way out of any prosecution. Things changed in 1929. The St. Valentine's Day massacre had been the slap in the face that opened the public's eyes to just how brutal the world of the gangster was. The stock market crash embittered the public even more. Gangsters were no longer looked on as romantic, but rather as cruel and vicious and living the easy life while people went jobless, homeless, and starving.

Unfortunately for Ness, the nation was tiring of Prohibition as well, and the Depression affected the budget for the Prohibition program. He continued to go after Capone but to little avail. It would be Attorney General George Johnson who would bring Capone down, by a ledger seized from his headquarters after a tip from a tax investigator. Indicted on tax evasion, he was also fighting indictment on 5,000 counts of violating the Volstead Act, which Ness had gladly testified to. Caught between a tiger and a cliff, in a secret deal with Johnson, Capone agreed to plead guilty to tax evasion and serve two and a half years in exchange for the other charges being dropped. To Ness's disgust, the deal was struck. To Capone's shock, when the case came before a judge, the deal was thrown out and Capone was ordered to stand trial for tax evasion. Ness and his hard-won bootlegging evidence were kicked to the curb. Capone was sent to prison for eleven years. Ness would have been a footnote in history. By

1957, he'd become a failed businessman and a drunk. He began working on his memoirs hoping not only for money to support his family, but for a little recognition. A reporter from New York helped get him a publishing deal, and in April 1957, he was staring at an advance check and the final version of the book. A month later, fate dealt Ness another blow. He was dead, felled by a heart attack before ever seeing the success his book would become. The book was, in large part, an invention. Buried within the myth was the actual story of Ness and his untouchables, but the public loved the myth. Gangsters were larger than life and so should the people who fought them be. Inspired by the book, the television show *The Untouchables* added further to the myth, as did the movie, and before long, Ness was the hero he had tried so hard to be. In some way, this is fitting, even if his efforts were simply a source of irritation to Capone. Elliot Ness and his men were truly untouchable during a time when many men's morals could easily be bought. That's not a bad legacy to leave behind.

3.   **BEAT THE PRESS**

Journalism could be a dangerous occupation during the heyday of the gangster. Just ask Jake Lingle. A beat reporter, he made about $65 a week, yet had $1,400 in pocket the day he died. Straddling both sides of the law, he found his sources in speakeasies, among cops and robbers, and couldn't be picky about where a story came from. There was also talk that he played the middleman for certain elements seeking favors from either police or Al Capone. This could be the reason that Big Al presented Lingle with a diamond-studded belt buckle. Somewhere along the line, though, he crossed someone. On June 9, 1930, heading off to what he felt would be a pleasant day betting at the Washington Park racetrack, Lingle was in a crowd of pedestrians underneath the Michigan Avenue bridge in the Illinois Central Station. Stepping from the crowd, a man shot him in the head, standing over the body only long enough to drop a .38 caliber revolver before running off. Six hundred and sixty-four men were rounded up, but none seemed to fit the description of the tall blond man that witnesses gave police. It wasn't until January 1931 that police arrested St. Louis gunman Leo V. Brothers. Fourteen witnesses were called. Half pointed him out. Half disagreed. Nevertheless, Brothers was convicted, yet served only eight years of a short fourteen-year sentence. It was never discovered why Brothers killed Lingle, if in fact he did kill him. He never said a word about it after.

4. THE CHICAGO THEATER

The stage theater and movie palace of movie palaces, the Chicago Theater opened on October 26, 1921, the flagship of the movie empire of Barney Balaban and Sam Katz.

Stars like Jack Benny, Frank Sinatra, Bob Hope, and the Marx Brothers graced the stage. The gorgeous madam had a staircase modeled after the grand staircase of the Paris Opera. The lobby was five stories high, the auditorium seven, and crystal chandeliers accented the ceiling. A Wurlitzer pipe organ resided in the orchestra pit, capable of fitting fifty musicians. The marquee featured a sculpted mini-replica of France's Arc de Triomphe. Buster Keaton provided live entertainment that opening night and afterward the audience enjoyed a viewing of A Sign on the Door, starring Norma Talmadge. As the decades wore on, and television brought entertainment home, the great movie palaces and theaters of the city began to suffer. By the 1970s, the Chicago Theater was little more than a third-rate movie house bought out by the Plitt theater chain. By 1985, it was decided that it would be more cost effective to simply close the place down. Enter the Chicago Theater Restoration Associates, a group of business people and citizens interested in restoring the theater to its former greatness. Purchasing the palace from Plitt for $25 million, they set to work. By 1986, the great lady was up and running again, Frank Sinatra booked as the opening act. Later it would play host to the Andrew Lloyd Weber smash Joseph and the Amazing Technicolor Dream-

coat and has since become an all-purpose venue for comics, musicians, and even magicians.

5. **THE TOMMY GUN**

Light, concealable, quick, and extremely effective in sending a message, the tommy gun became a symbol of the Roaring Twenties. The Thompson submachine gun was named after its inventor, General John T. Thompson, who created a compact machine gun during World War I that a single soldier could use. Unfortunately, he created a weapon that would be used in the war of organized crime. Gangsters used that power not only to kill their enemies but to send a scare into anyone nearby. It's said that the gun found its way to Chicago in a weapons purchase Dean O'Banion conducted in Denver, Colorado. Another legend has it that "Polack" Joe Saltis and Frank McErlane demonstrated for Chicago the tommy gun's potential when they went after South Sider Spike O'Donnell, who'd been muscling in on their territory. As he stood at Sixty-Third and Western, O'Donnell heard his name shouted out from a car and ducked to the ground in time to avoid the hail of bullets that took out the windows in the drugstore behind him. At first, it was thought that the rapid fire and large amounts of bullets were shot from a repeating rifle. It was only after McErlane's hit on Ralph Sheldon's gang headquarters that police realized what weapon was being used. General Thompson, unfortunately, had to read in the New York papers that the gun he had designed was becoming a symbol of gang violence. In April of 1926, William McSwiggin, assistant state's attorney for Illinois, was gunned down during a Capone raid on rival James Doherty. With the murder weapon in police custody (the killers had dumped it after the crime), Marcellus Thompson, a relative of the general, helped Chicago police track the killers down by using the serial numbers on the gun. Through these numbers, they were able to track down the gun dealer who pointed them in the direction of the group of men who bought the gun the previous February. Scarface was one of those men. By that time, though, the genie was out of the bottle.

6. JOHNNY WEISSMULLER

The 1920s didn't belong exclusively to the gangster. In 1983, Johnny Weissmuler was inducted into the U.S. Olympic Hall of Fame and for good reason. He set records in swimming at the 1924 Olympics in Paris and the 1928 games in Amsterdam. Over thirty years later, the Associated Press named him the greatest swimmer of the first half of the twentieth century. Weissmuller was born in Pennsylvania in 1904, but the family moved to the North Side of Chicago. He began swimming as a therapy to help strengthen muscles attacked by polio at age nine, and at fifteen he was scouted by Bill Bachrach, the swimming coach at the Illinois Athletic Club. In 1921, Weissmuller won both the 50-yard and the 220-yard national championships. When he reached the Olympics he truly shone, setting world records in the 100-yard and 400-meter freestyle events in 1924, and in 1928 winning the 100-meter race. When he retired from swimming in 1929, he held every world freestyle record and had won five Olympic gold medals. His athletic abilities helped him on the path to his new and better-known career as Tarzan the Ape Man. Spotted working out at the pool of the Hollywood Athletic Club, he was tapped as the perfect man for the role; Weissmuller's Tarzan was the most popular, leading to twelve more films during a seventeen-year period. The last of the series was 1948's *Tarzan and the Mermaids*. His next project, still set in a jungle, was the Jungle Jim series, which was released during the '50s and '60s before moving to television in 1958. In the '70s, Weissmuller suffered a number of strokes and became an invalid in 1979. In 1984, he died in Mexico at the age of seventy-nine.

7. BEAT THE PRESS II

Robert St. John was a lot more fortunate than Jake Lingle. He was a little more honest, too. St. John crossed Capone, yet walked away to tell the tale. After Mayor William Dever started cleaning up Chicago, Al Capone moved his operation to the nearby town of Cicero. Hardly clean when he got there, the 150 gambling joints and 123 saloons the Torrio/Capone mob had control of made it that much dirtier. Twenty-one-year-old Robert St. John, editor of the *Cicero Tribune*, made it his mission to expose the connection between town leaders and the mob. He even reported on the brothel run by Capone's brother, Ralph. Scarface was not happy. As St. John headed to his office one morning, a black car drove up and four men, Ralph Capone included, began beating him with blackjacks and billy clubs and a nasty little homemade weapon consisting of a cake of soap in a woolen sock. St. John was hospitalized with severe injuries. Upon his release, when he went to pay his bill, he was told that Al Capone had taken care of everything. Worse yet, shortly after Capone bought controlling interest in the *Cicero Tribune*. Still, while St. John may have lost his job, at least he didn't lose his life.

8. **THE MERCHANDISE MART**

Completed in 1929, this testament to retail soon became a white elephant for Marshall Field when the stock market crashed that very same year. When it opened, it was the biggest building in the world, only to be surpassed later by the Pentagon when that was completed. It had 4 million square feet and sat on a five-acre site near the north and south junction of the Chicago River. Designed by Graham, Anderson, Probst and White, the Merchandise Mart was built in an attempt to consolidate the company's wholesale operations. It was also planned to rent space to other distributors. This massive structure, framed in steel and sheathed in a buff Bedford limestone, was among the first structures to take advantage of Chicago's air rights policy, being built over the North Western Train tracks. The Great Depression, however, hit everyone hard, and the Field company was no exception. They weathered the storm for fifteen years before finally selling the mart to Joseph Kennedy in 1945 for $13 million, less than half of what it cost to build. It turned out to be a wise investment. It now houses mostly interior design showrooms, which are open only to professionals.

9. CLARENCE DARROW

Darrow handled the defense for two of the most sensational cases of the 1920s, taking each case primarily to prove a point. When he defended Leopold and Loeb he didn't deny their guilt. He questioned, instead, the death penalty hanging over their heads. Adamantly opposed to capital punishment, in a two-day, twelve-hour closing statement, he convinced the judge that the defendants should be spared the death penalty. It was a testament to the talent of this famous jurist. In 1893, he had unsuccessfully tried to stop the execution of Patrick Prendergast, the assassin of Carter Harrison I.

Born in Ohio in 1857, the son of an abolitionist, he was eventually admitted to the Ohio bar in 1878. For the next several decades, he dedicated his life to fighting for freedom of speech and the rights of the underdog. He battled capital punishment and Prohibition. He came to Chicago in 1888, and became a friend of judge and former governor John Peter Altgeld. He found himself defending labor leaders and acquiring a level of celebrity, standing up for the powerless and disenfranchised. Faithfully agnostic, he was also a believer in free speech, which was one reason he agreed to defend John T. Scopes in the famous 1925 "Scopes Monkey Trial." Scopes was a schoolteacher accused of breaking a recently passed Tennessee law banning the teaching of evolution in public schools. People tuned into WGN, fascinated to hear the great orator square off against former presidential candidate and fundamentalist Christian, William Jennings Bryan. The case would be dismissed on a technicality, yet was a fascinating bit of theater that mesmerized the nation and led to the successful play and movie *Inherit the Wind.* Along with his legal work, Darrow penned novels and essays and his autobiography in 1932. He died in Chicago six years later at the age of eighty and his ashes were spread in the Jackson Park lagoon.

10. IT WAS FUN WHILE IT LASTED

The day the stock market crashed became known as "Black Tuesday." The 1920s had been a decade of rowdiness and excess and it seemed as if the bill was finally coming due. The construction on the Merchandise Mart the year after the crash helped employ 5,700, but thousands of others went without work, without shelter, without food. In 1929, there were 3,100 foreclosures. By 1931, 1,500 people slept below the Michigan Avenue bridge. By 1933, there were 15,200. Shantytowns were constructed of cardboard and scrap lumber, and hundreds slept in the parks, scouring garbage dumps for food. By the early 1930s, the country was growing weary of the Volstead Act. As the drys had done so successfully more than a decade earlier, the wets began supporting politicians who supported a repeal of the Eighteenth Amendment. In the midst of the Depression, the wets argued that enforcement of this questionable law was eating away at government revenue better spent on feeding the poor. Bringing back booze would bring back the revenue from taxes on that booze, create jobs, and open the markets to farm goods. In 1933, the country rejoiced as the Eighteenth Amendment was repealed. Chicago gangsters found themselves scattering to find a replacement for the lucrative business, and while organized crime ultimately survived the transition, it never had the intensity or influence that it had during those heady days of Prohibition. The 1930s would see another mayor assassinated, and the grand poobah of gangsters die a pathetic death. The good times were over and it was once again time to start from scratch. It would be a difficult decade but World War II was coming, and with its carnage there would come a new prosperity. Once again, Chicago would rise from the ashes.

Jazz

Termed the only purely American form of music, when New Orleans–style jazz hit Chicago, a new style of jazz was born. Chicago became the jazz capital of the world (*The Chicago Defender* was the first to term the new style "jass") and while jazz itself changed and evolved over time, Chicago remains a vibrant jazz city.

1. THE KING

One of the founding fathers of American music, King Oliver, brought New Orleans to Chicago, sowing the seeds for what would become known as Chicago jazz. As a young man, Joe Oliver upstaged everyone with his cornet playing and became Joe "King" Oliver when he joined the 1917 jazz musician migration to Chicago. Born in New Orleans in 1885, he played in a variety of bands before forming the Creole Jazz Band in 1920. The band really gelled when Oliver sent for Louis Armstrong to join up as the second cornet in 1922, and soon they were playing one-night stands across the Midwest. A year later they were in the studio, recording their first record, which would be followed by others on various labels. The Creole Jazz Band was a tremendous influence on the careers of many jazz musicians, black and white, and though fronted by Oliver, it was a true ensemble. In 1927, Joe Oliver and his band performed a successful run at the Savoy Ballroom in New York and while the group disbanded shortly after, Oliver remained in New York, recording with other orchestras before returning to Chicago in 1928. His last known recordings were in 1931. He retired from music in 1937 when he moved to Savannah, Georgia, and died a year later of cerebral hemorrhage at the age of fifty-two.

2. SATCHMO

If King Oliver brought New Orleans–style jazz to Chicago, Louis Armstrong sent it in a whole new direction. Malleable enough to change with the times, his improvisational playing breathed life into Chicago jazz. Born Louis Daniel Armstrong in New Orleans in 1901, at thirteen he learned to play at a reform school. Armstrong worked a number of day jobs, listening to bands at clubs at night. King Oliver gave him his first real cornet and showed what could be done with it. In 1922, he was playing in dive bars and aboard the excursion steamer *Dixie Belle* in St. Louis when a telegram from Oliver brought Satchmo to Chicago, where he became an instant sensation. His toothy smile, warm voice, and bubbly playing reaching impossibly high notes, radiated good times. His stay with Oliver, however, was short lived. Lil Hardin, King Oliver's piano player and later Armstrong's wife, coaxed him to leave Oliver's band and he reluctantly did so, joining Fletcher Henderson's Orchestra in New York in 1924. Later he returned to Chicago, where he switched from cornet to trumpet with the Erskine Tate Orchestra. Before long, he was recording with his own band, the Hot Five, which later became the Hot Seven. A pioneer of scat singing, in the 1930s he went from national to international stardom, becoming the ambassador of jazz, touring Europe and headlining at the London Palladium in 1932. In fact, it was a British reporter, hearing a mispronunciation of Armstrong's boyhood nickname "Satchelmouth," who came up with the new version, "Satchmo." Over the years, with jazz changing from Dixieland to swing to bebop, his popularity waned only slightly, thanks in large part to his personality and infectious enthusiasm. He remained popular worldwide, even touring Africa, Asia, and South America late in his life. His 1963 hit version of "Hello Dolly" even managed to knock The Beatles out of the number one spot on the charts. In 1968 his tenderly optimistic "What a Wonderful World" became a number one hit as well. But the old heart was slowing down. He was hospitalized a number of times but continued to play live and record. In 1971, the man many considered the greatest jazz musician of all time died in his New York home.

3. DIG THAT CRAZY RHYTHM

Benny Goodman's favorite drummer, Buddy Rich, considered him the beginning and end of jazz drummers. Born in Chicago in 1909, Gene Krupa bought his first set of drums at age eleven because they were the cheapest instrument in the Brown Music Company catalog. Attending Bowen High School, he hooked up with a group of musicians known as the "Austin High Gang" (a group of jazz musicians who went to Austin High School and were inspired by King Oliver and Louis Armstrong) and established an exciting style unlike drummers of the past. Prior to Krupa's frenetic style, drummers pretty much just kept time. Krupa played with attitude, hair flying, beat strong, his revolutionary solos instrumental in the creation of tunable tom-toms and inspiring the modern hi-hat cymbal, which allowed the drummer easier access to it with his sticks. It was the tom-toms that made Chicago based OKeh Records' Tommy Rockwell nervous that Krupa's drumming would knock the needle off the wax. Along with Frank Teschemacher, Jimmy McPartland, Bud Freeman, Joe Sullivan, Jim Lannigan, and Eddie Condon, Krupa recorded "Liza," "Nobody's Sweetheart," "China Boy," and "Sugar"—highly energetic swing tunes. Moving to New York in 1929, Krupa found himself playing alongside Benny Goodman and Glenn Miller in the pit band of a new George Gershwin play. After recording sessions with Hoagy Carmichael, he found his way into Benny Goodman's group and in 1936, when Goodman pianist Teddy Wilson and vibraphone player Lionel Hampton joined him at Chicago's Congress Hotel, they became what is considered the first racially integrated group to play a downtown hotel. Inspired, Krupa formed his own band in 1938 along with singer Anita O'Day and Roy Eldridge, and the band's popularity soared until a questionable arrest in San Quentin for contributing to the delinquency of a minor. According to reports, Krupa sent his young valet to get his marijuana cigarettes. Defenders insist that crooked cops set up Krupa because he refused to pay them off. After ninety days in jail, Krupa came out to a soured reputation and waning popularity. Krupa rejoined Goodman's band and later had a number of bands throughout the fifties, performing renowned drum battles with Buddy Rich at Norman Granz's "Jazz at the Philharmonic" concerts. Though a heart attack stalled him, he played on into the 1970s until leukemia and emphysema led to a fatal heart attack in 1973 at the age of sixty-four.

4. THE KING OF SWING

Benny Goodman didn't invent swing, but he helped make it one of the most popular forms of music ever. Goodman was born in 1909 and grew up in Chicago's famed Maxwell Street area. His music lessons came from a synagogue near his home, and later he would join the Hull House band, playing John Philip Sousa marches on his clarinet. Asked to join the "Austin High Gang" even though he attended Harrison High, he played high schools and colleges, then nightclubs such as the Green Mill, all before he was fourteen. Dropping out of school, Goodman pursued a career in jazz, playing in the orchestra of the Midway Gardens. After joining bandleader Ben Pollack in California, Goodman returned to Chicago the following year a featured soloist for Pollack's band. In 1934, he put together a huge dance orchestra, and the Goodman Band debuted at Roosevelt Hotel in New York the following year. The audience loved it, but club managers were skittish. This was a new sound: towering rhythms, urgent beats. This was swing and the kids loved it, leading Goodman to a successful six-month radio show on NBC called "Let's Dance." Playing at the East Coast's Palomar Ballroom on August 21, 1935, they gave birth to the swing era with sensational shows. A jump and jive later, the Benny Goodman Orchestra was playing Carnegie Hall in January 1938. Goodman, who could be moody, self-absorbed, and a perfectionist, was also considered to be the first white musician to utilize black talent. Lionel Hampton and Teddy Wilson played with Goodman, as did other jazz greats like Gene Krupa, Harry James, and Peggy Lee. The end of World War II, however, saw a change in musical tastes that led to hard times for swing and Goodman. People were turning to solo acts, rather than the big bands, while hard-core jazz aficionados were developing an interest in the more intimate bebop appearing in nightclubs. Goodman put together a variety of bands and played through the next few decades, including a 1962 tour of the Soviet Union. While the styles changed over the years, there was still a place for his swing, and he played it until he died of a heart attack in 1986.

5. PIANO MAN

Earl Hines, born in 1903 in Pennsylvania, made the piano an integral part of a jazz combo. His dad played trumpet; his mom, the pipe organ. Classically trained on piano, Hines originally started out on trumpet, which could be one reason why he was known for playing the piano like a trumpet with frequent use of single-note phrases. Quitting high school, he became the accompanist to singer Lois Deppe, who took Hines with her when she moved to Chicago. He played a number of clubs before landing a job with the Carrol Dickerson Orchestra, the band's star a young New Orleans jazzman named Louis Armstrong. When Dickerson himself left the band in 1926, Armstrong took over and began to play the new style of jumping jazz known as Chicago-style jazz. In 1927, renamed Louis Armstrong's Hot Five, they recorded several classic jazz records. Hines formed his own band that played for over a decade at the Grand Terrace ballroom. Nationwide tours and radio brought the band fame, and Hines's intimacy with his piano fit in well with the intimate, increasingly popular styles of Charlie Parker, Dizzie Gillespie, and Sarah Vaughan, whose careers he helped launch. In the early 1960s, however, he'd pretty much been forgotten until he staged a comeback in 1964, performing a series of concerts in New York. The solo recitals, the first time he played solo in his career, were able to revive his career, and he played with his own small band until his death in 1983.

6. **A MAN APART**

With a diamond in his tooth to match those on his vests, Jelly Roll Morton was the first to write out his compositions, his music specifically geared to the three-minute length of 78 rpm records. He inspired the great Duke Ellington and was considered the first great jazz piano player and composer. But Jelly Roll Morton also had a boastful arrogance that stuck in people's minds. Born Ferdinand LeMenth, Morton played piano in the white whorehouses of New Orlean's Storyville district. Proficient on a number of instruments from harmonica to guitar, it was piano that would bring him fame. Passionate about jazz, he rarely associated with his fellow jazzmen and moved around, making money gambling, sharking, and pimping. He was also a vaudeville comedian. Arriving in Chicago in 1922 when jazz was in full swing, his piano solos recorded for the Gennett label in 1923 and 1924 showcase the style of hot blues that influenced a number of musicians at the time. Forming the Red Hot Peppers, he never achieved the fame as a bandleader that King Oliver or Benny Goodman later would, but recordings show his ability to achieve harmony between innovation and composition. In 1928, he left for New York, but the small jazz ensembles were losing their appeal to big bands. Hot was out. Swing was in. By the 1930s, even the diamond in his front tooth was gone. Leaving his wife, he moved to Washington, where he basically worked for food, then to California in 1940, asthmatic and with circulatory problems, writing sad letters home with money enclosed whenever he could afford it. By 1941, he was dead, right before the Dixieland revival that might have resurrected his career. In interviews for a Library of Congress project, he claimed to be the creator of jazz. It seems unlikely. But there's no doubt that Jelly Roll Morton helped to make it a legitimate art form.

7. **MR. SMOOTH**

Named *Esquire* magazine's top jazz pianist in 1946, if Nat "King" Cole hadn't taken the path of a singer, he might have been one of the greatest jazz pianists ever. Either way, the world benefited. Born in Alabama in 1919, the family moved to Chicago when Nat was four years old. In high school, he played piano and even organized a fourteen-piece band. Some nights he would listen to his brother Eddie's combo play at the Green Terrace nightclub. The great names of jazz played there as well and before long, Eddie and Nat were in a band together, Eddie Cole's Solid Swingers, which recorded a few tracks for the Decca label. Landing in Los Angeles in 1937, he found himself playing beer joints and gaining a following. When Johnny Mercer, an executive for Capitol, heard the now Nat King Cole Trio play, they were signed to the label. Cole's voice, which had always been a part of the band, became more prominent with swinging hits like "Straighten Up and Fly Right," and "It's Only a Paper Moon." It was a song known as "The Christmas Song" though, that set him on a new path in 1946. Originally recorded with the Trio, Capitol asked him to re-record it with strings, and that version became a classic. Cole's voice was stirring a sensation, but as famous as Cole was becoming he couldn't escape the reality of the times. When the Coles moved into a restricted area of Los Angeles, they were subjected to a number of racist acts. Successful in a number of mediums, Cole played W.C. Handy in *The St. Louis Blues*, and portrayed himself in *The Nat King Cole Story*. He was the first African American to have his own regular radio program and the first to cross over into the pop charts. In 1957, he became the first black performer to have his own TV show. Its over-sixty-week run might have been longer were it not for the timidness of the sponsors who feared southern backlash. Even at his most popular he moonlighted, playing the jazz piano in public and on record with the jazz greats of the time. The 1960s began with more best sellers, including forays into country-and-westerns albums. But in November 1964, while he was filming *Cat Ballou*, touring in *The Sights and Sounds in 1964*, and planning to record an album, Cole's weight loss became noticeable. On December 7, Cole was diagnosed with lung cancer. On February 15, 1965, that great voice was silenced. Nat King Cole's elegance could be heard in both his singing and his piano playing.

8. WAILIN' SAX

A pioneer in the Chicago style of jazz, Bud Freeman helped bring the saxophone to a prominent position in the jazz band. Born in Chicago in 1906, he grew up on Chicago's far west side and was among the first of the great jazzmen to belong to the Austin High Gang in Austin High School. Freeman learned his saxophone from fellow Austin High member Dick McPartland's dad. His professional debut was in a Wisconsin roadhouse in 1924, but back in Chicago, the gang strengthened their chops by playing at parties and dances. By the end of 1927, Freeman was in the studio with his gang Frank Teschemacher, Dick McPartland, Eddie Condon, Jim Lannigan, Joe Sullivan, and Gene Krupa, recording such Chicago jazz classics as "Sugar," "China Boy," and "Nobody's Sweetheart Now." Freeman's style brought a classical sensibility to the sound evolving into swing. Gigging around with various bands and moving to New York in 1928, he eventually formed his own Windy City Five and a year later he was with the Dorsey brothers before joining fellow Chicagoan Benny Goodman's band. He considered it one of the biggest mistakes of his life. It was a contentious relationship, Goodman being a controlling man, difficult to work with.

Freeman's stay lasted a year. After a stint in the Army, he bounced from one band to another, sometimes forming his own, for the next few decades, touring the United States, Canada, and Europe. He lived in London for the last half of the 1970s, but the 1980 Chicago Jazz Festival brought him home again and he decided to stay. He died eleven years later at the age of eighty-five.

9. SPACE IS THE PLACE

Even the very early Dixieland and swing styles had a certain abandon to them, with the listener never really sure where the musicians planned to take them next. The otherworldly Sun Ra took that abandon to an ethereal level with albums like *Space Is the Place*, *Cosmic Tones for Mental Therapy*, and *Strange Celestial Road*, underscoring his extraterrestrial aura. He claimed to be from outer space, but in reality was born Herman Blount in Alabama in 1914. After playing piano in high school jazz bands and recording as Herman "Sonny" Blount, he made his way to Chicago, playing piano in the Fletcher Henderson Orchestra and arranging music for strip-tease shows at the popular Club Lisa. In the early '50s, he worked at clubs backing Red Saunders and Sonny Stitt, and even toured with B.B. King. But by 1952, having gone through a sort of spiritual crisis, Herman Blount legally changed his name to Le Sony's Ra, and eventually became known as Sun Ra. The Sun Ra Arkestra, a trio led by Sun Ra and featuring Richard Evans and Robert Barry in 1953, would later include John Gilmore, Charles Davis, Marshall Allen, Pat Patrick, Art Hoyle, Julian Driester, and James Scale. Originally they called themselves Myth Science or Solar Arkestra. *Jazzly Sun Ra—Sun Song*, their first album, was recorded in 1956 but, mistrustful of record companies, most of his albums were put out by the Saturn label, run by Alton Abrahams and distributed in editions of only hundreds. A number featured hand-painted covers. While John Coltrane has been considered an innovator in avant-garde jazz,

Sun Ra had begun his experimental journey early in the 1950s.

Even in his early big band work, Sun Ra used exotic instruments such as tympani, bells, and flutes. In 1957, he used the electric piano. In 1963, he used the clavoline, and in 1969, the Moog synthesizer, as well as celesta, organ, and harpsichord. The transition in his work came in Chicago in the '50s, what many consider his golden age. His trippy-sounding piano never overpowers the whole of the piece. A prolific artist, he did the bulk of the writing and arranging himself and even scored the music for the documentary *The City of Jazz* in 1955. Any money made in gigging went into the Saturn label and between 1961 and 1965 they recorded ten albums in New York. Arkestra's performance style began to evolve, along with the music, incorporating dance dress and lighting to enhance the effect. The music grew more adventurous, utilizing soul and African styles as the band became a more intimate bebop ensemble. With Philadelphia as their base, they toured throughout the 1970s (even playing in front of the Pyramids) and well into the 1980s, his love for the music keeping Sun Ra playing even while wheelchair-bound. Sun Ra died in 1992, leaving behind a large catalogue of work, though sadly, much of it is out of print.

10. **MELANGE**

Flavoring their avant-garde sound with many styles, including rock and gospel, the performance of the Art Ensemble of Chicago is theatrical. Faces painted with African symbols and wearing African robes, they incorporate a variety of instruments like log drums and gongs. Founded in 1967 by saxophonist Roscoe Mitchell (who plays a number of wind instruments), bassist Malachi Favors, trumpeter Lester Bowie, Joseph Jarman, and Philip Wilson, they soon became one of the most popular groups in jazz. In 1969, percussionist Famoudou Don Moye joined the band after Philip Wilson left to join the Butterfield Blues Band. That same year the group went to Paris for eighteen months, recording twelve albums and gaining an international reputation. Their openness to new experiences and willingness to improvise, as well as each member's solo projects, have kept the group fresh. The late Lester Bowie, who died in 1999, was well known for his other group Brass Fantasy, and he composed the theme music for the *Cosby Show*. Don Moye has recorded with Brass Fantasy and others. Malachi Favors, fluent on bass as well as banjo, zither, harmonica, melodica, and gong, made a name playing bebop and hard bop. Roscoe Mitchell has recorded both solo and ensemble. His style of improvisation can be heard on his 1966 *Sound* album where silence becomes one of the instruments. Roscoe Mitchell and Malachi Favors are also founding members of the Association for the Advancement of Creative Musicians (AACM), the not-for-profit organization, chartered by the state of Illinois and supported with grants from private organizations, that helps promote the creative development of musicians. Made up of musicians and composers committed to allowing others to showcase their work, the AACM offers grants and commissions as well as concerts, both national and international. Though not officially disbanded, the Art Ensemble of Chicago rarely plays in Chicago anymore, its members focusing on solo efforts. Lester Bowie passed away in 1999. Roscoe Mitchell has suffered health problems but remains a teacher. Their involvement in the AACM, however, made them a driving force in the advancement of jazz.

Blues

Chicago is a blues town. Inspired by the sounds coming up from the Mississippi Delta, the style became meatier, eventually transforming into Chicago Blues, a style that became an inspiration all its own.

1. MUDDY WATERS

When he came to Chicago in 1943, McKinley Morgan brought with him the Delta blues and his nickname, Muddy Waters. Before long, his music gave birth to the Chicago Blues. Born the son of sharecroppers in 1913, Muddy Waters got his nickname because he liked to fish in a muddy creek. Learning harmonica as a young teen, guitar soon followed and eventually he led a band that played the Mississippi Delta clubs. He even recorded for folk archivists as part of a Library of Congress project. Once in Chicago, Waters worked days at a paper mill's receiving docks and played nights in South Side clubs and parties. Delta blues had a slow, low rhythm that complemented the depth of Waters's vocal style. The amplification of an electric guitar was necessary for the dance halls and clubs he was appearing in, and it was this amplification that created the Chicago Blues. The unique Waters sound appealed to future rockers like the Rolling Stones and Eric Clapton when Waters toured England in 1950. The Rolling Stones even named their band after his song "Rollin' Stone." After cutting several singles for the Chess Brothers in 1946, it wasn't until 1948 that his music began selling. Waters's first single for Chess, "Rollin' Stone," became a huge hit. His 1950s blues classics "She Moves Me," "I'm Your Hoochie Coochie Man," and "Got My Mojo Working" are among his songs that have been recorded by rock groups. Waters was also instrumental in the careers of greats like Junior Wells, Buddy Guy, Howlin' Wolf, and rocker Chuck Berry. Once rockers took an interest in his work in the 1960s, his music opened up to a wider audience. The Rolling Stones supplied a little payback when they asked him to open for them at some of their concerts, and *London Muddy Waters Sessions* was a result of some of the sessions he recorded with rock musicians during the late 1960s. In 1971, he received his first Grammy for his album *They Call Me Muddy Waters* and won several more through the seventies. His last public performance was at a 1982 Eric Clapton concert. Less than a year later his sixty-eight-year-old heart that had given such passion to the blues gave out. In 1987, the inspiration he gave to rock music was finally acknowledged when he was inducted into the Rock and Roll Hall of Fame.

2. THE QUEEN

The Queen of the Blues was not to be trifled with, belting out tunes at a time when the blues was primarily a man's game. Koko Taylor came to Chicago from Memphis with her husband, Pops Taylor, a few dollars in their pockets and big plans in mind. It was the famous Chess Records that brought her to the public, though she'd been singing for some time, starting with gospel back in her hometown. Influenced by B.B. King, Big Mama Thornton, and Howlin' Wolf, she turned her sights to the blues, and was discovered by Willie Dixon in 1962, who became her mentor, her business partner, and her lifelong friend. Her first single, "I Got What it Takes," was an anthem about her strength of resolve and talent. The 1966 hit, "Wang Dang Doodle," written and produced by

Dixon, hit number four on the Billboard R&B charts and established her as Queen of the Blues. It was also Chess Records' last big hit. With the death of Chess, Taylor was left looking for a new home. After the rise of the civil rights movement, blacks were turning away from the sharecropper blues of old and turning toward a different style of R&B as well as soul. But this was a woman who'd picked cotton in the South, and mopped floors on Chicago's North Shore to help support her family. She had a deep feisty growl to her voice and a feisty spirit as well, and this little hiccup in her career was hardly going to get her down. Enter Bruce Iglauer and Alligator Records. Iglauer was doing his best to rejuvenate the blues in Chicago and eventually decided to sign Taylor in 1975. Her first album for Alligator, *I Got What it Takes* was a hit and nominated for a Grammy. It would be nine years before she finally won a Grammy, but along the way she won twenty W.C. Handy awards, more than any other female singer, and was the first woman inducted into the Blues Hall of Fame.

3. **"BIG" BILL**

Born William Lee Conley in 1893, founding father Bill Broonzy created a style completely his own. He came up from Mississippi by way of Arkansas, bringing with him a rich culture of black spirituals and folk songs that he meshed with country and urban blues creating his rhythmic, guitar-driven sound that made him one of the premier blues artists during the 1930s. In his teens, Broonzy entertained at local picnics using the skill on the fiddle he learned from relatives. Starting in 1912, he was an itinerate preacher in Arkansas for five years, spent a year in the Army, then headed to Chicago after his discharge. In 1920, he came to town and learned to play the guitar from "Papa" Charlie Jackson. During the day he worked as a Pullman porter, and later cook, molder, and a janitor at Hull House. By night, he performed at house parties and recorded, using an updated version of the ragtime style he'd learned from Jackson. He began to develop his own sound, which, by the '30s, began to mature, sowing the seeds for the electric sounds of Muddy Waters with his occasional use of the electric guitar. It was the unfortunate death of a fellow musician that offered Broonzy his big break in 1938, when the murder of country bluesman Robert Johnson upset the plans of John Hammond, who had planned a Carnegie Hall concert that would showcase the varieties of black music. Broonzy was given the opportunity to replace Johnson and introduce his own music to a massive New York audience. Part of Broonzy's talent was his ability to adapt to changing musical styles. The 1950s saw a change in the sound of blues, thanks in part to bluesmen like him. In his last years, just as he had when he trained with the ragtime of Papa Charlie, and honing his own sound with barrelhouse swing in the '30s, Broonzy geared his next recordings more to the folk crowd. He performed at folk festivals across the United States and recorded with notable folk and blues names as well as touring Europe, where he was a huge success. The British saw in Broonzy the roots of the American rock and roll they were growing to love. Cancer caught up with Big Bill in August of 1958 and after his death, memorial concerts dedicated to Broonzy were performed featuring the new generation of masters like Muddy Waters.

4. WHITE BLUES

With his innovative mixing of blues, folk, rock, and jazz, Paul Butterfield became one of the most notable blues artists to come out of Chicago. Born in 1942, he sang in the church choir and studied the classical flute. Self-taught on harmonica, he found himself sitting in at South Side clubs with Muddy Waters, Buddy Guy, Magic Sam, and other famous bluesmen. While attending the University of Chicago in 1964, he formed the Paul Butterfield Blues Band with Elvin Bishop and Mike Bloomfield on guitar and Butterfield on harmonica. The self-titled album, *Butterfield Blues Band*, gained favorable reviews and a respectable following, and in 1965, they were the first electric band to play the Newport Folk

Festival in Newport, Rhode Island, backing Bob Dylan's experiment in electric folk. While purists booed, the event inspired other folk artists to work electric, bringing folk music to a whole new audience. Considered one of the first white men to play with the passion of the great black performers, Butterfield's take on the blues brought a larger white audience to the blues. His *East-West* album of 1966 showcased Butterfield's openness to all styles of music. Mike Bloomfield's interest in Ravi Shankar flavors the music and the instrumental title track has hints of psychedelia and reggae mixing with the blues, jazz, and rock. After Bloomfield went to start his own band, Butterfield eventually found himself playing with a number of different lineups as the 1970s progressed and his creative differences with producers, and his record company Elektra led to inconsistent albums. Unfortunately, as he struggled to find success by assembling other groups, health problems and years of drinking and a heroin addiction (which he may have acquired as a result of trying to ease the symptoms of peritonitis) took a toll physically and financially. In 1986, his album *Legendary Paul Butterfield Rides Again* would be his last. On May 4, 1987, an accidental overdose took his life on the verge of forty-five. Paul Butterfield did a lot of living in those forty-five years and inspired a generation to experiment to find its muse.

5. SONNY BOY

There were actually two Sonny Boy Williamsons. Sonny Boy II, Rice Miller, happened to be a little older, but ended up taking the moniker as a tribute to John Lee "Sonny Boy" Williamson who was tragically murdered on his way home from a gig. John Lee left the world having taken the harmonica from a backup blues instrument to a dynamic part of the blues sound. Born in 1914 in Jackson, Tennessee, it would take him twenty years to reach Chicago, but by then he had already made a name for himself as a harmonica player and session musician. As a boy, he taught himself how to play the harmonica, developing a solo style that would remain his chief trademark. A speech impediment led to a singing style particular to him as well. The late 1920s and early '30s found him roaming around Tennessee and Arkansas with greats like Sleepy John Sets and Big Joe Williams. When he hit Chicago in 1934, his first recordings reflected the country blues style picked up on his travels through the South. As time went on, he refined his style to fit the more urban blues of the men he was playing with. By 1939, he was the guy called when a harmonica player was needed, and several of his recordings have become blues standards. On the night of June 1, 1948, walking home from a gig at the Plantation Club, Williamson was mugged and left with a fractured skull. He died in Michael Reece Hospital. Williamson was taken from the world of blues at the height of his career, but he left it with a richer sound that would inspire future stars.

6. **MOANIN' AT MIDNIGHT**

Born Chester Arthur Burnett in 1910, Howlin' Wolf was a name better suited to his wild, whooping vocal style. Growing up in the Mississippi Delta region with its rich musical legacy, he hooked up with Charley Patton who showed him the basics of the Delta blues style. Burnett took the guitar his father gave him and honed his skills at weekend fish fries. After the family moved to Arkansas in 1933, Burnett learned to play harmonica from Sonny Boy Williamson and became a showman, falling to his knees or lying on his back howling out the lyrics. It was a Memphis radio station that gave him a break in the 1940s when KWEM gave him a weekly show to showcase his talents. His first record, made in Memphis, was released by Chess Records and sold 60,000 copies. The record of "How Many More Years" and "Moanin' at Midnight" led to a war between Chess and rival label RPM for Wolf with Chess victorious, bringing Wolf to Chicago in 1952. Wolf's recording sales reached their height in 1956 but he remained with Chess, joining the Chess blues revival tour through Europe in the 1960s. He also joined the Rolling Stones, who recorded some of his songs, as a warmup act. This six foot, six inch, 300 pounder left quite an impact on the audiences of Europe as he wailed on the harmonica and wailed out with that frenzied voice. Even kidney problems couldn't keep him from performing in the last years of his life, though the need for a dialysis machine kept him in cities offering that procedure. Howlin' Wolf died in 1976, having influenced countless blues and rock artists that came after, and leaving behind a power-packed body of work featuring that wild falsetto howl that made him unmistakably Howlin' Wolf.

7. **THE CONTEST**

In 1958, Buddy Guy won a "Battle of the Blues" contest held at a Chicago club, which led to a record contract. Quite a feat for a guy who started out gigging to overcome serious stage fright. Born in Louisiana in 1936, he played the clubs of Baton Rouge, developing a blistering guitar style that caught the attention of established musicians such as Muddy Waters, Magic Sam, and Otis Rush. Arriving in Chicago in 1957, he gained work as a sideman in local bands, but it was his victory at the "Battle of the Blues" that led to a contract with a subsidiary of Cobra Records known as Artistic. He recorded two songs produced by Willie Dixon, "Sit and Cry" and "This Is the End," but when Artistic filed bankruptcy Guy found himself out in the cold. Chess Records came to the rescue, signing him in 1960 as a session musician backing Howlin' Wolf, Muddy Waters, Willie Dixon, and others. His 1962 song, "Stone Crazy," rose up the R&B charts hitting number fifteen and helping him to become a major player on the Chicago blues scene. Jimi Hendrix and Eric Clapton cited him as an influence on their work. In 1967, Guy left Chess for Vanguard Records, and his collaborations with Junior Wells in the early 1970s, thanks partly to their backing by famous rock musicians like Bill Wyman, helped increase his influence among white blues and rock fans. Crossing over to the Silverstone label, his 1991 album *Damn Right, I've Got the Blues* garnered him a Grammy, as did his 1993 follow-up, *Feels Like Rain*, and his 1994 album *Slippin' In*. Buddy's been instrumental in keeping the Chicago Blues scene alive, buying the Checkerboard Lounge on the South Side in 1972, and opening Buddy Guys' Legends. The two clubs feature noted blues acts, as well as giving new acts the chance to shine as Buddy did in that 1958 "Battle of the Blues."

8. **BIG DADDY**

The Kinsey Report is considered one of the most contemporary of blues bands, but its musical history goes back decades, to the birth of its namesake Lester "Big Daddy" Kinsey in 1927. Today he's a blues legend, known for his harmonica and slide guitar. But at the age of six, he was using his guitar to play gospel music in his hometown of Pleasant Grove, Michigan. His father, who became pastor of Chase Street Church of God in Christ when the family moved to Gary, Indiana, in 1944, wasn't happy when his son turned to the blues, but it was marriage two years later that convinced Kinsey to put his music aside to raise a family. Three sons came into the family. Ralph Kinsey was born in 1952, Donald Kinsey in 1953, and Kenneth Kinsey in 1963. Little did he know at the time, but he'd helped to create his future band. Donald started playing guitar at the age of four and brother Ralph started on the drums at age six. By their early teens, Donald and Ralph were able to join Big Daddy in a group whose name went from Big Daddy Kinsey and His Fabulous Sons to Big Daddy Kinsey and the Kinsey Report. Lester Kinsey was proficient in several styles of blues, his best being Chicago Blues and later Modern Electric Blues. His slide guitar work and harp playing was the heart of Daddy Kinsey and the Kinsey Report. During the 1970s and '80s, they played clubs and lounges around the area. Guitarist Donald Kinsey left briefly to tour and record with reggae star Bob Marley and was in Kingston, Jamaica, when there was an assassination attempt on the singer's life. Eventually, Donald found his way back home to the family and the band became simply

The Kinsey Report in 1984. In 1985, they signed with Alligator Records. With the release of their album *Bad Situation* the Kinseys went on a world tour. In 1988, Big Daddy let the boys go solo, and they released *Edge of the City* with three W.C. Handy Award nominations coming their way. The band remains a powerful force on the Chicago Blues scene. Big Daddy, who left the band to his sons, succumbed to prostate cancer on April 3, 2001. He was seventy-five.

9. CHESS RECORDS

On June 7, 1990, the building at 2120 South Michigan was dedicated as a Chicago landmark. Formerly Chess Studios, the notes of blues history echoed within it. This was where the greats went to lay down their tracks. Muddy Waters, Howlin' Wolf, Sonny Boy Williamson I, Buddy Guy, even the Rolling Stones paid homage to their heroes, recording in the studios in 1964. And it was all started thanks to two Polish Jewish brothers named Phil and Leonard Chess. Born in Poland, they came to Chicago with their family in 1928 where their father started the Chess and Sons Junk Shop, giving the brothers an early taste of a family business. The business the brothers gravitated to, however, was the nightclub business, and inspired by the artists they booked in the clubs they owned on the South Side, the brothers decided to get into the record business. Originally a two-man operation, they divided their time between the clubs and their fledgling recording label. Purchasing the Aristocrat label, they utilized much of what was in the Aristocrat vault before acquiring new acts of their own. Aristocrat released a variety of music in blues, jazz, and even polka, with Leonard traveling around town, Detroit, and the southern states to push the records in stores. As the label grew, they decided to sell their Macomba Lounge and, in 1950, Aristocrat became Chess Records, the first release under the new name being "My Foolish Heart" by Gene Ammons. That, along with Muddy Waters's "Rollin' Stone," brought great success to the label. Of course, not every decision was a sound one. In 1950, while in Memphis,

Leonard was approached by record producer Sam Phillips to sign a then-unknown singer from Tupelo, Mississippi. Unimpressed with what he heard, he turned the offer down. The singer went on to become the King of rock and roll, Elvis Presley. But Chess had a stable of talent gaining national commercial success. Having moved up from garage status, the label operated from a number of small buildings on the South Side until, finally, the Chess brothers converted a two-story building at 2120 S. Michigan Avenue into a proper record company complete with studios, offices, and its own shipping department. Along with blues singers, Chess released the works of jazz artists, gospel, doo-wop, and rock and roll. Bo Diddley helped pave the way for the rock set, and Chuck Berry classics like "Johnny B. Goode" and "Rock 'n Roll Music" were recorded at Chess. Sadly, as the financial potential from rock and roll coaxed larger labels like Capitol and Atlantic to sign acts, smaller labels didn't have the resources to compete. An offshoot called the Cadet Concept label was Chess' attempt in the late 1960s to tap into that large rock audience, but it met with limited success. In 1969, the years caught up to Leonard Chess and he suffered a fatal heart attack. Phil, deciding to retire to Arizona, sold the company to General Recorded Tape, a California firm that relocated it to New York. From there, the catalog went from Sugar Hill Records to MCA, which, in 1986, reissued a good portion of the Chess product. The Chess brothers helped bring Chicago Blues to national prominence and their legacy lasts in the music produced in their studios.

10. MAXWELL STREET

Searching for fellow bandmate Matt "Guitar" Murphy, the Blues Brothers trek on down to a Maxwell Street diner he may be working in. On the way, they watch John Lee Hooker playing live for the shoppers on the street. This section of *The Blues Brothers* movie provides a glimpse of the great Maxwell Street in the 1980s and what it might have been like in its heyday. The thing about Maxwell Street was that it really didn't change over the decades, until September 1994, when it was demolished to make way for development by the University of Chicago. Among those who supported the creation of a historic district for Maxwell Street were such notable musicians as B.B. King, Buddy Guy, and Bo Diddley. That's because for decades, Maxwell Street was synonymous with music, particularly the blues. In 1910, what are known as "pushcart businesses" began making their way onto Maxwell Street, a mixed residential and commercial section of Chicago. The Maxwell Street Market reflected the changing times of a city adapting economically and ethnically to the environment around it. It became a vital main shopping source for the community where items unavailable anywhere else could be found. For the next several decades, thousands of residents visited the bazaarlike atmosphere where vendors offered special deals on wares, curbside restaurants cooked delicious food novelties, and musicians played wherever they could find a corner. Many of the blues greats would play, and shoppers could hear this music for free. In deference to the historical significance of the old Maxwell Street, the city of Chicago and the university created an alternate site for the market on Canal Street and Roosevelt Road, but the new site is hampered by being farther from public transportation than the original. The city also increased vendor fees for the diminished space five-thousandfold, leaving out in the cold many new immigrants who were the sort of people able to get a spot on the old Maxwell Street.

Chicago Rocks

Chicago has its blues. Chicago has its jazz. But Chicago also has its rock and it remains a ripe source of up-and-coming bands. Here are a few that made it.

1. DISARMED

Leaving at the top of their form, Smashing Pumpkins had a decade-long run as one of the most influential alternative bands. Their music defied definition. It wasn't straight-out metal, nor was it grunge, but it certainly wasn't pure pop. In 1987, Billy Corgan, the son of an R&B musician, and James Iha, fresh from a band called Snake Train, discovered they had similar tastes and formed a band. Joined by the classically trained D'Arcy Wretzky from Michigan, when they shopped their demo around, Metro managers told them that they could become a support band at the club when they found a drummer. Enter James Chamberlain, the son of another R&B musician. Before long they were Metro's main support act, and their successful album, *Gish*, led to an eighteen-month tour. Their fame was rising, but the angst that made their songs so popular was wearing on them all. Corgan in particular considered splitting up then. As if to exorcise his demons, he went alone into the studio and recorded *Siamese Dream,* which would reach number four in 1993 and, ultimately, go double platinum with songs like

"Disarm" and "Today" leading to another round of tours. Their next album, 1995's *Mellon Collie and the Infinite Sadness,* proved their most successful. Then came July 12, 1996: While in New York to play Madison Square Garden, drummer Jimmy Chamberlain and tour keyboardist Jonathan Melvoin overdosed on heroin. Melvoin died, Chamberlain was fired, and the Pumpkins went on. Eventually, a clean Chamberlain was reinstated, but the four founding members decided to end the ride after their 1998 tour, leaving the music world stunned. It was the right decision for the Pumpkins, though, and most importantly they went out on top.

2. **BO KNOWS**

Legendary in R&B circles, his signature beat, chunky and pumping, played out on his custom-made rectangular guitar, proved an inspiration to countless rockers. He was born Ellas Bates in Mississippi in 1928, and moved with his mother's cousin's family to Chicago. At the Ebenezer Missionary Baptist Church he learned to play trumpet and violin and even composed two concertos for violin, but it was the guitar that caught his fancy. As a teen, fascinated by the Baptists' rhythms, he adapted his style of violin-plucking to the guitar and formed the group the Hipsters, which evolved into the Langley Avenue Jive Cats. After graduation, he continued playing locally with his group and took his act to Chess, which helped him re-record the two songs on his demo. "Bo Diddley"/"I'm a Man" on Checker Records (a subsidiary of Chess) became an instant rhythm-and-blues hit in 1954. Other songs followed, like "Bo Diddley's A Gunslinger," "Diddley Daddy," and "Bo's a Lumberjack," as well as "Pretty Thing" and "Hey Good Lookin'." By 1963, his music had hit the UK where it inspired artists like the Animals and the Kinks. Elvis Presley, the Rolling Stones, and Buddy Holly acknowledged the debt their sound owed Diddley and he's remained in action through the decades, inspiring bands like ZZ Top, Prince, and The Clash, with whom he toured in 1979. Inducted into the Rock and Roll Hall of Fame in 1987, in

1996 he received a Lifetime Achievement Award from the Rhythm 'n' Blues Foundation and two years later received a Lifetime Achievement Award at the Grammy Awards ceremony.

3. BIG BAND ROCK

Chicago's sound was a swinging blend of guitar, percussion, and horns diving in for punctuation that led to twenty top-ten singles, twelve top-ten albums, five of them reaching number one, and more than 120 million records sold. The Beatles song, "Got to Get You into My Life," proved horns and rock could work together, and Walter Parazaider, a fan of big bands, decided to form a band around horns. Along with Parazaider, Terry Kath, Danny Seraphine, Lee Loughnane, James Pankow, Robert Lamm, and Peter Cetera played local clubs as The Big Thing. Changing their name to Chicago Transit Authority, they headed west to Los Angeles, continuing the constant gigging. Once signed to CBS Records, their first album, self-titled *Chicago Transit Authority*, was an unusual opener for a new band. It was a double album. Songs like "Does Anybody Really Know What Time It Is?" and "Questions 67 and 68," however, proved perfect for the new FM rock stations and college stations. Reaching number seventeen on the charts, it stayed on the charts for 148 weeks even without a hit single. Shortening their name to Chicago, the band's signature became albums titled with only a number. *Chicago II* went to number four on the charts with the single "Make Me Smile" reaching the top ten. *Chicago III*, another double album, went to number two. Later would come "Color My World," "Saturday in the Park," and "Just You and Me." By *Chicago XI* they had more hits and awards, yet more tension than ever before. Hits such as "If You Leave Me Now" were becoming more popular, with their sound becoming more adult contemporary than originally desired. Then, in 1978, the group suffered a stunning loss. Singer and guitarist Terry Kath accidentally shot himself. The death of Kath set Chicago onto a slightly new path, yet through the '80s and '90s, despite personnel changes, they continued releasing hits, remaining a force on radio as well as popular on the tour circuit.

4. DADDY'S ALL RIGHT

A workhorse among Chicago bands, their hit "Surrender" was an anthem of the late 1970s. Started by Rockford, Illinois, natives guitarist Rick Nielsen, collector of novelty guitars, and bassist Tom Petersson in 1973, they were joined by drummer Bun E. Carlos and singer Robin Zander three years later and were a smash hit—in Japan. Playing wherever they could, they opened for the Kinks, Journey, and Kiss and eventually signed with Epic Records. Their first two albums had little impact on the United States, but went gold in Japan, so the group toured Japan and produced the legendary *Live at Budokan* in 1979, a Framptonesque stroke of luck that became a hit in America. After the successful re-releases of their first few albums they headed into the 1980s with a platinum-selling album, *One on One,* which included the hit single "I Want You." The next six years were uncertain after Zander left for a while, but in 1988, with Zander back on board, their album *Lap of Luxury* went platinum. "The Flame" and their cover of "Don't Be Cruel" proved highly successful as well. The band has never been able to hold onto superstardom, but their bar band sound has been inspirational to many up-and-coming performers including Billy Corgan of Smashing Pumpkins.

5. PLAYIN' OUR SONG

Turned down for the WGN-TV variety show *All Time Hits* because they didn't appear British enough, in 1965 Carl Giammarese, Nick Fortune, Jon Jon Poulos, Dennis Tufano, and Dennis Miccole dubbed themselves The Buckinghams, in honor of Buckingham Fountain, and the British-sounding name helped them pass their second audition with WGN. They appeared each week for almost seventeen weeks. While songs they covered on their contract with Chicago's USA Records—like James Brown's "I'll Go Crazy," The

Beatles' "I Call Your Name," and the Hollies' "I've Been Wrong Before"—were successful locally, it was a song by Jim Holvay that brought them national fame. "Kind of a Drag" toppled the Monkees' "I'm a Believer" out of the number one position. Signing with Columbia Records, another Holvay song, coauthored with G. Beisbier, "Don't You Care" rode the charts to number six. The Buckinghams appeared on the *Ed Sullivan Show*, *American Bandstand*, and *The Smothers Brothers Show* among others, and in 1967, they had a number eleven hit with "Susan" and a number twelve with "Hey Baby (They're Playin' Our Song)." *Billboard Magazine* even voted them the Most Listened to Band of 1967. By 1968, though, their album, *In One Ear and Out the Other,* didn't produce one hit. Disbanding in 1969, Giammarese and Tufano worked as a duo for a while before ending that. They faded into obscurity, Jon Jon Poulos dying of a drug overdose in 1980. Then, in 1985, the "Happy Together Tour" resurrected The Buckinghams' name. Featuring The Turtles, The Grass Roots, Gary Lewis, and The Buckinghams, it was one of the year's top-ten-grossing tours. Since then, The Buckinghams have continued to play similar '60s revival concerts, a popular draw for those craving a little bit of nostalgia.

6. PLYMOUTH ROCK

Possessing the pop sensibilities of the Beatles and rawness of the Rolling Stones, six young men—Patrick McBride, Raymond Graffia, Gerald Van Kollenberg, Walter Kemp, Craig Kemp, and James Chitkowski—called themselves The Patsmen, an homage to St. Patrick High School. It was the summer of 1964 and the Patsmen were playing local dances when they decided on a name change. Since the British called America "the new colony" and there were six members in the band, The Patsmen became The New Colony Six. Their local following grew, but they felt a move to California would help them gain national fame. The house they moved to in California had revolutionary rivals Paul Revere and the Raiders who, like the New Colony Six, wore colonial outfits, but the Raiders went on to fame while the Six couldn't get a nibble. So, back in Chicago, they started a record label with their first release on Centaur Record Corporation, "I Confess," now considered a garage band masterpiece. The next single, "At the River's Edge/I Lie Awake" reached number 111 on *Billboard*. Singles rose up the charts as they revealed an interesting array of styles and inspirations, from the garage sound to harmonious power pop, to psychedelic. Joining Chicago-based Mercury Records in 1967, their romantic "I Will Always Think About You" hit number twenty-two nationally (becoming a number one local hit) and offered their first taste of national fame. "Things I'd Like to Say" reached number thirteen on *Cash Box* but the band was no longer the same, affected by changes and departures. Signing with Chicago-based Sunlight Records, future singles landed lower on the charts. After Ronnie Rice left in 1972, the New Colony Six primarily played live for the next two years before calling it quits. Since the mid-1990s, though, spurred on by a successful reunion concert at Chicago's Park West, members of the New Colony Six have re-formed to take advantage of the various revival tours going on.

7.   FRIENDLY STRANGERS

It's made for speeding down Lake Shore Drive in summer, windows rolled down, wind whipping in your hair, the radio cranked with the meaty horns on "Vehicle" trumpeting like a charge. A rock and roll classic, the fastest-breaking single in Warner Brothers history, "Vehicle" hit number one in *Cash Box* and number two in *Billboard*. Grade school friends Jim Peterik, Larry Millas, Bob Bergland, Mike Borch, Chuck Soumar, Ray Harr, and John Larson formed The Ides of March in high school, lifting the name from Shakespeare's play *Julius Caesar*. A local favorite, they played clubs, sock hops, and basketball games, before becoming the only American band at the time to gain a contract from London Parrot Records. In 1966, their first single, "You Wouldn't Listen" rose to number forty-two on Billboard, and the band spent their summer weekends touring America and Canada. In 1970, they signed with Warner Brothers Records and released "Vehicle," then opened for Led Zeppelin, Jimi Hendrix, The Grateful Dead, and others. The following year, their follow-up "L.A. Goodbye" held at number one for five weeks. By 1973, with fifteen singles and four albums under their belt, the band went into semiretirement. Peterik cofounded the group Survivor and cowrote one of the group's biggest hits, "Eye of the Tiger," the theme song for *Rocky III*. The Ides of March re-formed in 1990 to perform at Berwyn's Summerfaire. The response was so positive that they've been touring ever since.

8. THE HEART OF THE ISSUE

The music of this power pop trio was catchy but edgy, lead singer Jim Ellison's delivery on songs like "Valerie Loves Me" uncertainly strong. Guitarist Jim Ellison met bassist Ted Ansani at Columbia College, and later drummer Mike Zelenko joined the group. Material Issue was unapologetically pop at a time when experimental and dark was vogue. They played any club they could, and as their music found its way on radio, their tours grew outward. Signing a deal with Mercury Records, they became the first Chicago act in a long time to break nationally, eventually finding their way onto *Billboard's* 200. As bouncy as their songs were, as dreamy as they seemed on the surface, they were more intense (ultimately foreshadowing) than anyone might suspect. The aura, however, was always pop—the life of a rock star, glamorized, energetic, and fun. Material Issue didn't shove their intensity down anyone's throat. While Jim Ellison's suicide on June 21, 1996, was stunning, the clues were there. Like other rockers dead before their time for whatever reason, Ellison's death leaves you wondering what might have been for Material Issue.

9. RADIO WARS

A generation of Chicagoans will always remember two stations as the leaders in rock radio. Before WLUP, before

WCKG, Chicagoans tuned into WLS or WCFL, both on AM, for the latest in rock and roll. WLS even had a weekly survey that gave local acts like The Buckinghams and the Ides of March quite a kick when they made it. But these stations had a long history. WLS, originally WES, standing for World's Economy Store, came into being in 1924, as a way for Sears to reach and strengthen the relationship with their rural customers. Later, the call letters would be changed to reflect the World's Largest Store. At the same time, the Chicago Federation of Labor (CFL) hoped to reach both farmers and union workers via the increasingly popular medium of radio. They applied for permission to broadcast in 1926, but the Department of Commerce promptly turned them down. Undeterred, CFL went ahead and built a station anyway. In the 1960s, both stations dropped the farm and labor formats for contemporary ones. The rock war was on; both stations stealing listeners and disc jockeys. Terming itself the "Rock of Chicago," WLS outlasted WCFL but only by a decade. They even started simulcasting on FM and presented major rock acts like the Rolling Stones' *Tattoo You* in 1981, and The Police at Comiskey Park in 1983. But the clock was ticking. Major competition had sprung up in the form of WLUP, WCKG, and WXRT. Eventually, WLS-AM turned to talk radio, and the Rock of Chicago disappeared.

10.   THE NIGHT CHICAGO DIED

The band that gave us "Billy Don't Be a Hero" also presented perhaps the only rock song about the gangster days of Chicago. Ignoring the fact that, if Daddy was a cop on the East Side of Chicago, it would mean he'd be patrolling in Lake Michigan, this guilty pleasure recorded by Paper Lace managed to become a U.S. hit. Paper Lace was a British pop band made up of Cliff Fish, Chris Morris, Carlos Santana, Michael Vaughan, and Philip Wright. Formed in 1969, they won the 1974 ITV talent contest, Opportunity Knocks, and were signed to the Bus Stop label formed by songwriters and producers Mitch Murray and Peter Callender. Murray and

Callender's "Billy Don't Be a Hero" stayed three weeks at number one on the British chart in 1974, followed by "Chicago," which reached number three. In the United States, it wasn't their version of "Billy," but Bo Donaldson and the Heywoods' version, that reached number one. Still, in August, Paper Lace found their own way to the top when "Chicago" reached number one on the U.S. charts. As for the battle between the mob and the cops where "about a hundred cops were dead," it never happened. Capone was too careful a crook to kill cops en masse, especially when most of them were likely on his payroll.

The Sox

T he history of the Chicago White Sox is almost as old as baseball itself. The team has seen a lot over the century. If only it could see another World Series.

1. **THE SOX**

The White Stockings was the original name for the club that eventually became the Chicago Cubs. In 1900, when Charles Comiskey brought his minor league St. Paul franchise to town, he took the discarded name. To save space in their columns, sportswriters referred to them as the White "Sox" and the meatier moniker, better suited for this hardworking crew from the South Side, stuck. On April 24, 1901, the Sox beat the Cleveland Indians to win the first official American League game ever played. Like the Cubs, out of the gate they were killers, even beating their North Side rivals in the first ever subway series in 1906. Sure they suffered a number of forgettable seasons. In 1917, however, they turned it around and easily won the World Series against the New York Giants. Evolving into a dream team in 1919, they were poised to do it again. Then the "Black Sox" scandal hit, dashing the hopes for a championship and tarnishing the team for years to come. The 1950s saw a more aggressive style of play, and from 1951 to 1962 the Sox led the American League (AL) in stolen bases. It seemed that every so often they'd get a taste of that long-ago magic. They lost the 1959 World Series to the Los Angeles Dodgers. In 1983, they won the division by twenty games, but lost to the Orioles in the playoffs. In 1993, the Blue Jays beat them out for the AL championship. From 1996 to 1999, they finished each season second in the AL Central division. This is a hardworking team. The desire, and usually the talent, is there. Only time will tell if the twenty-first century will see another World Series win for the White Sox.

2. **THE BLACK SOX**

A disappointed young fan telling Shoeless Joe Jackson, "Say it ain't so, Joe," while probably fictional, sums up the heartbreak of the city. Despite personality clashes, despite Charles Comiskey's legendary stinginess, the 1919 Sox had gelled as a team and ruled whatever field they played on. The 1917 series win fresh in their minds, Chicagoans wanted that high again. Money, however, became an issue. In the 1917 season, Charles Comiskey promised his team a bonus if they won the pennant. The bonus they received was a case of cheap champagne. That was the sort of guy they were playing for. A few players on the team were able to negotiate large salaries, which helped fuel the infighting and jealousy among the players. Still, the pride in their performance that season spurred the team on to the playoffs. That's when the gamblers started sniffing around. Gambling and sports go hand in hand, and the bad element was ripe in the early years of the game even as far back as the mid-1850s. It was alleged that, while Charles Comiskey posted signs banning betting in the park, first baseman Andrew "Chick" Gandil supplemented his income by giving inside tips to a small-time gambler, Joseph Sullivan. In fact, it seems that Gandil was the instigator of the Black Sox scandal. Heading toward retirement and hoping for one last big score to see him off, Gandil made the proposition to Sullivan that for $100,000, he and some of his teammates would throw the series. Along with Gandil, seven others were eventually accused of being in on the fix: Pitchers Eddie Cicotte and Claude "Lefty" Williams, infielders Fred McMullin and Charles "Swede" Risberg, outfielder Oscar "Happy" Felsch, Buck Weaver, and "Shoeless" Joe Jackson. There is debate, however, over whether or not Jackson and Weaver were actually involved. Weaver attended a few meetings of the plotters, but refused to be a part of it. According to Jackson, he was approached by Gandil but refused. It's believed that Gandil then lied to the gamblers about Jackson's involvement to convince them that all was well with the scheme. The Sox were favored to win the 1919 series against the Cincinnati Reds, but rumors of the fix began to grow. The Sox lost the first two games and some of the players began to grow suspicious. After the second game, the players involved in the fix received only a portion of the payoff, so they began to reconsider throwing the game. When Chicago won the third game, the gamblers refused to pay up. Sullivan gathered the $20,000 expected before the fourth game and those still willing to see the scheme through did so, Cicotte especially making several errors, which helped lead to a Reds 2–0 victory. Game five slipped from Chicago's hands with a score of 5–0.

When the gamblers missed another payment, though, the players decided that it was pointless to keep losing. If they won the series they would definitely collect $5,000 each. The sixth and seventh games went to Chicago. Unfortunately, Arnold Rothstein, one of the group of gamblers fronting the money, threatened the safety of Williams and his wife if Chicago won the series. Chicago lost the final game 10–5. *Chicago Herald and Examiner* sportswriter, Hugh Fullerton, knew something wasn't right. This team was too good to go down that easily. He suggested in his columns that a fix had been in and that club owners needed to attend to the problem of gambling in baseball. Concerned by the negative publicity this would bring to the game, Comiskey brought about an investigation. In September of 1920, a grand jury was convened, and the eight White Sox players, as well as the consortium of gamblers including Joe Sullivan and Arnold Rothstein, were indicted. In June of 1921, a monthlong trial led to acquittals of all defendants based on a lack of evidence. Nevertheless, the damage had been done. Newly appointed independent baseball commissioner Judge Kenesaw Mountain Landis immediately banned all eight players from the game. Even Jackson and Weaver, who insisted they never agreed to throw a game were, in Landis's eyes, equally guilty by virtue of their silence. Jackson, Cicotte, and Risberg continued to play on semipro teams whenever they could. Jackson, who eventually owned a liquor store, was inducted into the Cleveland Baseball Hall of Fame in 1951, a few months before he died. The others all went into various businesses and careers, none ever being reinstated in the major leagues. It's hard to excuse those players who took part in the Black Sox scandal, but it does seem ironic that Charles Comiskey, the one who helped bring it about by his financial pettiness and lack of respect for his players, was inducted into the Baseball Hall of Fame.

3. THE GREAT SHOWMAN

Mobbed by fans wherever he went, Bill Veeck was known as a storyteller, with a laid-back style of humor, down to earth, yet surprisingly philosophical and well read. Some felt his gimmicks were low class and demeaned the game, but wisecracking Bill Veeck believed that the fan came to the game to be entertained and if the playing couldn't provide entertainment, maybe other things could. Bill was born in Hinsdale, Illinois, in 1915. His father, William Veeck Sr., was a Chicago sportswriter and later president of the Chicago Cubs. After his father's death in 1933, Bill went to work for the Cubs organization. In 1941, he and a friend, Charlie Grimm, bought the Milwaukee Brewers, transforming them from a Cub farm team at the basement of the American Association to the winners of three AA pennants. Selling his interest in the Brewers, he turned his talents to the Cleveland Indians, buying into that club in 1946. After Cleveland won the 1948 World Series, Veeck bought the St. Louis Browns in 1951. It was in 1959 that he bought the Chicago White Sox. A maverick, Veeck dared to try new things to improve the game and bring in the fans. In 1947, hate letters streamed in after he signed Larry Doby, the American League's first black player, for the Cleveland Indians.

Unfazed, in 1948 Veeck signed Satchel Paige to pitch for the Indians, and Veeck got the last laugh when the team won the 1948 Series. Best known for the promotions, in 1951 when Veeck signed three-foot-seven Eddie Gaedel and sent him to pinch hit in the second game of a doubleheader, the fans ate it up. Not as easily amused, the president of the American League scolded Veeck and barred Gaedel from baseball. Veeck called the move an act of discrimination against little people. His most famous addition to Comiskey Park came in 1959 with a scoreboard that exploded every time a Sox player hit a home run. Under doctor's orders, he gave up baseball and moved to Maryland in 1961 to take it easy, but in 1975, he was back in Chicago, trying to buy the White Sox to prevent a rumored move to Toronto or Seattle. The American League, apparently not wanting Veeck and his stunts tainting the game of baseball again, turned down his bid, but thanks to Detroit Tigers owner John Fretzer, who convinced the league that it was only fair to give Veeck a shot, Bill was given another chance and became owner of the Sox again. Veeck eventually sold the team in 1981 to current owners, Jerry Reisndorf and Eddie Einhorn, in large part due to the difficulty of obtaining quality players. After players could be free agents, the financially strapped White Sox were priced out of the market. Baseball was now a business, the love of the game taking a backseat, and Veeck couldn't play that style of game. When Einhorn questioned Veeck's management ability, he refused to return to Comiskey Park, spotted instead at the home of Sox rivals the Chicago Cubs. In January 1986, Veeck died at the age of seventy-one. Eight hundred family, friends, and fans attended his memorial service.

4. DISCO DEMOLITION

Steve Dahl had his reasons to hate disco. One of them was that the radio station his morning show was on, WDAI, had become Disco DAI, which didn't leave much room for his show. Steve bounced back with a gig at competitor WLUP, and Jeff Schwartz, a sales manager at "The Loop," along with Mike Veeck, director of promotions for the Sox (and Bill's son), put together a promotion to blow up disco records at Comiskey Park (fans could get into the park for ninety-eight cents if they brought a disco record). Who better to lead the charge than Dahl? Bill Veeck, owner of the White Sox and one of the last great sports showmen, was fine with the idea. The ballclub wasn't exactly drawing people to the stadium with their playing. And so it began—July 12, 1979, a night that will live in infamy in the annals of sports. After the first game of a doubleheader, wearing an Army helmet and green fatigues, Dahl was wheeled out to the field where the pyrotechnics awaited. A roar went up from the stands. What the promoters had banked on was that the crowd was there to have a little mindless fun. What they forgot to consider was the "moron factor." According to this principle, the likelihood of a person turning into a moron increases if A) he's in a crowd, B) he's at a sporting event, C) there are cameras around, and D) all of the above. The "moron factor" causes a person to carry situations to idiotic extremes. Fans who riot after their teams win championships provide a perfect example of the "moron factor." That night, the moron factor ruled. Seventy-five thousand people were in the ballpark while about 15,000 were hanging around outside the park, burning effigies of John Travolta and chanting "Disco sucks!" As Dahl lit the first bomb and put it in the dumpster filled with disco records, several thousand fans burst onto the field and tore up the pitcher's mound. A bonfire was started in center field and sections of the bullpen were torn down, while some fans threw firecrackers of their own. A half hour later, the riot squad arrived, but the damage had been done.

It has been suggested that there was a racist undertone to the night, disco being big at the time in the black and gay communities, and the majority of disco demolitioners that night being young, white males. That seems to read more into the incident than it warrants. A number of the Beavises and Buttheads there that night attended simply to see things blow up. Those who truly disliked disco did so because at its best it was barely listenable and at its worst it was largely a vacuous soundtrack to a blow-dried culture that seemed to be crowding out everything else. Looking at it in terms of race assigns it a little more sociopolitical significance than it deserves.

5. US/CELLULAR FIELD?

When it was decided that Comiskey would feel the blow of a wrecking ball so that a grander stadium could be built across the street, fans were outraged. The old Comiskey had been standing since 1910 after Sox owner Charles Comiskey commissioned Zachary Taylor Davies to design a new park for his team. Costing somewhere in the ballpark of $750,000 when built, Comiskey Park was considered the "Baseball Palace of the World" and was the fifth baseball facility in the nation to be constructed of concrete and steel. In 1926, Comiskey spent $1 million to double-deck the stands all around. Lights were installed in 1939, and Bill Veeck's exploding scoreboard was installed in 1959. The year 1980 saw the addition of skyboxes, giving the rich a chance to enjoy the game without suffering near the unwashed masses. The old park saw four World Series (the Cubs played their 1918 championship there) and the first All-Star Game. On September 30, 1990, a crowd of 42,849 watched the last game to be played in the park, as the White Sox defeated the Seattle Mariners 2–1. It was in 1988 that the go-ahead was given for a new Comiskey Park to be built across from the old one. At a cost of $119 million, the new structure, designed by Rick de Flon, was ready in time for the 1991 season. It was a functional piece of work, with 118 luxury suites, a stadium club, numerous concession stands, souvenir shops, and a museum. Now, it has a new name. In a deal worked out with US/Cellular One, the White Sox will receive $68 million over twenty-three years, to change the name of Comiskey Park to "US/Cellular Field," a cold, clumsy name that would have Charles Comiskey shaking his head, until he received the first check.

6. THE OLD ROMAN

At $50 a month, Charles Comiskey started in the minor leagues, playing for the Dubuque Rabbits as a nineteen-year-old pitcher. He supported himself in the off-season by selling newspapers and candy at the railroad station. In 1877, $50 a month was a pretty fair wage. When he started playing it was for the love of the game, and that was half the compensation. He was a man of contradictions, though. Revered by some, despised by others, Charles Comiskey deserved both sentiments. Nicknamed "the Old Roman" because of his Romanesque profile, he rose to power with hard work and ingenuity. He stayed at the top, however, on the backs of his players. Born in August 1859, the son of an Irish Chicago alderman for the Seventh Ward, it's said that he was the first player to play off the bag when he moved to first base after his pitching arm started giving out. He moved up to pro ball with the St. Louis Browns in 1882 and played six years, five of them as a player-manager. During this time the team won four pennants. Along with Ban Johnson, who took over the young Western League, he purchased the Sioux City franchise, shifting them to St. Paul and then to Chicago in 1906 where they became the Chicago White Sox. The only player to own a baseball club, he built Comiskey Park, the first symmetrical stadium, in 1910 and even introduced night games to America. In 1913, Comiskey introduced baseball to the world by arranging a series of exhibition games in Japan, Australia, Ceylon, Egypt, Italy, France, and England. In consideration of World War I, Comiskey donated 10 percent of the team's gross receipts one season to the American Red Cross. Revolutionary in some respects, he could be surprisingly backward as well. He fought against the idea of blacks playing in the major leagues. He provided the press with free meals after every game, but paid most of his players the lowest possible salaries on contracts that forbade them from moving to another team without the owner's permission. Protesting Comiskey's decision to charge the team to launder their uniforms, the players wore the same unwashed uniforms for several weeks before Comiskey merely took the uniforms from the clubhouse and fined the team. It was this refusal to compromise that led to the Black Sox scandal of 1919 when Comiskey forgot an important fact: It was the player on the field who won the game. Curiously, he paid the attorney fees for the eight players tried in the scandal, yet he also publicly supported baseball commissioner Judge Kenasaw Mountain Landis's decision to ban the eight from baseball for life. Ultimately, the 1919 scandal revealed Charles Comiskey's questionable financial dealings and stingy treatment of his club. Sick at heart, Comiskey became reclusive, spending the remainder of his days at his summer home in Eagle River, Wisconsin, where he eventually died in 1931 at the age of seventy-two.

7. THE END OF THE WORLD

In 1959, through a roller-coaster season, the Sox's standing depended on the performance of other teams. Still, this was a magical ballclub with guys like Nellie Fox (the first Sox player to be named MVP) and Jim Landis (who played several games with a severely injured leg before finally having no choice but to go to the hospital). The front office was a little shaky. Charles Comiskey's granddaughter, Dorothy Comiskey Rigney, had sold 54 percent of her shares to Bill Veeck, and Charles Comiskey II lost controlling interest on the deal. While in litigation, both Veeck and Comiskey tried to keep the court battle from influencing the players. Unlike his grandfather, Charles II was well liked by the ball club, and he in turn liked the club. The awful 1958 season had prompted Comiskey to cut the team's pay by 10 percent, promising they'd be rewarded if their performance improved in 1959. Unlike Grandpa, he made good on his word. The team's record hardly left room for hope but as 1959 wore on, the hopes of the city rose. By the time they reached the playoffs, they seemed unstoppable. On September 22, 1959, the Sox trounced the Cleveland Indians to become the AL champions, the news hitting Chicago at 9:43 P.M. Approximately 20,000 people celebrated in the Loop. Thousands more met the team at Midway. Others fled to bomb shelters. Why? Because Fire Commissioner Robert Quinn, an intense Sox fan, announced the victory by ordering the city's air-raid sirens turned on. Unwitting citizens succumbed to Cold War panic and ran for shelters. That night, Sox fan Mayor Daley took the outrage of citizens in stride, stating that the sirens had been sounded in accordance with the City Council proclamation that bells should ring, whistles blow, and bands play. The World Series was played against the Los Angeles Dodgers, and the Sox got off to an incredible start with an 11–0 win. It would be the biggest win of a six-game series where they won only two games. By game six, the Los Angeles Dodgers' 9–3 win dashed the hopes of the Windy City, and the bells and whistles fell silent.

8. THE FIRST ALL-STAR GAME

In 1933, the city of Chicago was playing host to the Century of Progress World's Fair. Mayor Edward J. Kelly decided a sports event should coincide with the fair to boost attendance affected by the Depression. Arch Ward, sports editor of the *Tribune*, proposed a baseball game that would match the best players of both the American and National Leagues. Ward chose the managers. Connie Mack of the Philadelphia Athletics would manage the American League team, and John McGraw of the New York Giants would be the manager of the National League team. The players themselves were chosen by ballot conducted by fifty-five national newspapers. On July 6, 1933, the first All-Star Game was played in Comiskey Park to a crowd of 47,595. The first All-Star home run belonged to the "Bambino" Babe Ruth, whose two-run smash led the American League to a 4–2 victory. The success of that first game led baseball commissioner Kenasaw Mountain Landis to decide that the All-Star Game should become an annual event. Since then, the All-Star Game has become one of baseball's major events. Three games have been held at Wrigley and three at Comiskey, where the fiftieth anniversary game was played to an American League 13–3 victory. Arch Ward, who had bet his salary that the All-Star Game would be a success, was one of the most influential sports editors of the century. He died on July 9, 1955, and was buried on the morning of the twenty-second All-Star Game. The All-Star Game's Most Valuable Player Award is named in honor of his memory.

9. **THE CUBAN COMET**

Minnie Minoso was another one of those super players who occasionally found their way into Chicago. Born Saturino Orestes Arrieta Armor Minoso in Havana, Cuba, in 1922, his speed would help him become known as the "Cuban Comet." In 1951, '52, and '53, he led the league in stolen bases and tied for the lead in steals in '56. He debuted with the Cleveland Indians in 1949, but was traded to the White Sox in 1951, starting his Sox career off auspiciously by homering off Vic Raschi in the first inning of his first game. He finished his rookie year as the AL leader in triples, with a batting average of .326, second only to Philadelphia's Ferris Fains who hit .341. Minnie Minoso did what he needed to get on base, setting a league record by being hit by pitches 189 times. He led the league in triples in 1954 and doubles in 1957. This was the sort of playing that helped bring about the "Go-Go Sox" era, though he wasn't there for the AL championship or World Series in 1959. In a curious trade, Bill Veeck traded Minoso and infielder Fred Hatfield to the Indians in 1957 for pitcher Early Wynn and outfielder Al Smith. But Minnie was back in Chicago by the 1960 season, marking his territory with a grand slam in the fifth inning of an April 19 game against Kansas City. With a 9–9 tie in the bottom of the ninth, Minnie sent a homer into the stands to win the game. Despite this sort of talent, in 1961 Minoso found himself traded to the St. Louis Cardinals. While there he suffered a number of injuries, including a fractured skull and broken wrist from running into an outfield wall while chasing a triple, and a broken left forearm after being struck by a pitch. Three years later, he retired from baseball after time with the Cardinals, the Senators, and active duty as a White Sox pinch hitter. Interestingly Veeck, the man who seemed so willingly to get rid of him, brought Minoso back from retirement for a game in 1976. While Minoso went hit-less in the game against the Angels, he did join the elite group of players who played the game in four decades. When he went to bat in a 1980 game, he became one of two major league players to play in five decades. Prior to that, he spent 1976–1978 as a White Sox coach.

In 1980, he again went into retirement, his number "9" retired in 1983 as the White Sox club president named him "Mr. White Sox." And yet, he couldn't stay away. In 1991, sixty-eight-year-old Minoso tried to go for a sixth-decade appearance, scheduled to appear in an April 13 game for the independent team Miami Miracle of the Class A Florida State League against the Ft. Lauderdale Yankees. Baseball commissioner Fay Vincent denied him the chance, however, refusing to allow him in for even one game. This didn't stop Minoso. At seventy, in 1993, Minoso played one at-bat as a designated hitter (DH) for the St. Paul Saints in an independent Northern League game against Thunder Bay. Seven times an American League All-Star, Minoso was elected to the Chicago Sports Hall of Fame in 1984 and inducted into the Shrine of Eternals in 2002. In 2003, he became the first player to play seven decades when he played as a DH for the St. Paul Saints as part of the team's Negro League tribute. He walked the first inning.

10. NORTH SIDE/SOUTH SIDE

You'd think Chicago would gratefully accept any championship. Ask a Sox fan, however, how he feels about a Cubs' victory and you'll get the same answer as if you asked a Cubs fan about a Sox victory: a sneer of disgust. Loathing doesn't begin to describe the relations between the North Side and the South Side. They hate each other's leagues, they hate each other's teams, and they hate each other's ballparks. The rivalry is very much a regional thing. Chicago is a city of neighborhoods made up of distinct cultures. Ethnicity, economics, and race often distinguish and divide these neighborhoods. To the Cubs fans, the South Side Sox and their fans are rough edged, blue-collar joes. To Sox fans, North Siders are little more than uppity yuppies with an overrated ballpark. Can the two sides ever put their differences aside? Probably not, for even if both teams were to end up best in their leagues, they'd then have to square off against each other. They did once, in the infancy of their teams. Back in 1906, they played in the first crosstown World Series. The Cubs led the league in batting, pitching, and defense, finishing twenty games ahead of the New York Giants. The 1906 Sox had been dubbed the "Hitless Wonders" with the lowest team batting average in the American League and won the pennant by a mere three games. Heck, the Cubs even won the coin toss deciding home field advantage. The Sox seemed up against it, until that first game. They won 2–1. The next three games brought the race neck and neck, Cubs, then Sox, then Cubs again. Then came game five and a Sox victory, followed by an 8–5 victory in Game Six. The Hitless Wonders had the last laugh, one of only a few they'd have in the team's history. Perhaps the seeds of hatred started in that series. No matter how much the fans of each team dislike each other during the season, it's only if another crosstown series should occur that the fireworks would really begin.

The Cubs

Oh, stop laughing. There was a time when the Chicago Cubs were a team to be reckoned with.

1. THE CUBS

It seems almost blasphemous but at one time the Chicago Cubs were known as the White Sox, or more accurately, the White Stockings, the name given to them when founded in the early 1870s by William A. Hubbert, a local businessman. The team was suffering from continued losses and baseball itself was becoming infested with scandals and poor play so in 1876 Hubbert met with the owners of other pro teams and convinced them to form the National League (NL). It was this year that the White Stockings captured the very first NL pennant. Hubbert had a strict code of conduct for his players and with the excellent skill of pitcher and team manager Albert Spalding (who later went on to form Spalding Sporting Goods Company), the Stockings had turned themselves around. In 1907, the team changed its name to the Cubs (a nickname given to them by sportswriters because of the youthful players on the team) and in 1907 and 1908 found themselves in the World Series against the Detroit Tigers, winning both championships. Over the next twenty years, they managed a few pennants but went no further. In fact, it seemed to get worse year after year. The 1984 season was

A hopeful Cubs fan at beloved Wrigley Field during the
team's ill-fated 2003 run for the pennant.

a heartbreaker for every Cub fan, because it was a stunner
compared to recent performances. The team was favored to
win when they entered the NL championship against the San
Diego Padres. It wasn't to be. Hearts were broken again in
2003 when, after another great season, the Cubs found
themselves close to the NL championship only to lose it
to the Florida Marlins. As in 1984, fans went home disappointed and spent the winter contemplating just what it
meant to be a Cubs fan. But on opening day, just as in 1985,
they will flock back to the bleachers because that's what it
means to be a Cubs fan. You ignore the odds and back them
anyway, hoping that this year, they'll turn it all around.

2. **MR. CUB**

"Mr. Cub," Ernie Banks, played nineteen years for the team.
Beloved by the fans, he walked onto the field with an infec-

tious optimism, helping make the losses that much easier to take. Born in 1931 in Texas, Ernie entered a poor but close family. His parents' philosophy of hard work rubbed off on Ernie who helped out by picking cotton, shining shoes, and carrying garbage. Though extremely shy, Banks became a star footballer, played basketball, and was exceptional at track and high jump. After graduation, Banks joined the Kansas City Monarchs, a semipro team in the black league, barnstorming across major cities like Chicago. After a two-year stint in the Army, Banks came home to offers from the Brooklyn Dodgers and Cleveland Indians, but found himself on his way to Chicago, the first black player to wear a Cubs uniform. Banks brought to the game a new style of hitting. His bat was lighter than bats of old, but using wrist action and arm speed gave the hit a lot more impact. He was the rare shortstop known for hitting power as well. In 1954, his first full season, he drove in seventy-nine runs and walloped nineteen homers. The following season he posted a .295 batting average with 44 homers; he drove in 117 runs. After a sluggish season in '56, some questioned his ability. His arm had weakened, threatening his abilities as a shortstop, and the knee he injured during his military years began to act up. By the next season, though, his batting average rose to .313 and he led the league in home runs and RBIs, winning the NL MVP in the process. While he retired in 1971 (after being voted Chicagoan of the year in 1969 and 1970), he remained connected to the team and the town. He was a frequent member of the broadcast booth and remained with the team as director of community relations. He also served on the boards of numerous charity organizations including Jackson Park Hospital, the Glenwood Home for Boys, the Chicago Rehabilitation Institute, and Big Brothers.

3. **THE FRIENDLY CONFINES**

William Wrigley Jr. knew nothing about running a ball club. Son of a soap maker who turned a keen business sense into gold, Wrigley hired William Veeck Sr. to manage the team.

One thing both Wrigley and Veeck knew was that baseball was an experience beyond the playing field. Over the years they created a ballpark where people could go to watch baseball, commiserate with friends, or just enjoy the sunshine. Wrigley Field is the second oldest ballpark in the country and remains a favorite. Designed by Zachary Taylor Davies, it was built in 1914 and went by the named Whales Park, Weeghman Park, and Cubs Park, before finally being named Wrigley Field after Wrigley bought the club. Wrigley deserved to have a park named after him. He may not have known a lot about managing a ball club, but he certainly understood the need to treat his players with respect. There was no major complaining over salary because Wrigley made generous offers to his players. In 1918, when the Cubs obtained pitcher Grover Cleveland "Pete" Alexander in a trade, Wrigley paid his wife a stipend while her husband was at war.

The "Friendly Confines," as it's known today, was notable for the first concession stand in baseball and for exquisite sight lines. At the time of construction, it was considered more spacious and cleaner than most parks. The improvements made along the way were subtle enough not to disturb the comfortable atmosphere of the park. Aside from parking problems, Wrigley Field has blended in nicely with its surrounding community. When lights came to Wrigley Field purists protested, but the team was in a rough spot. Now owned by the Tribune Company, they found themselves in a sport that was increasing its night games. Philip K. Wrigley had actually planned to install lights in 1941 but because of the war, chose to donate them instead to a shipyard the day after Pearl Harbor. Decades later, the league itself was growing impatient. This wasn't the first time a lightless Wrigley had affected the team. In 1938, the Cubs played the Pittsburgh Pirates in a game tied in the ninth inning. It was getting dark and the umpires decided that the game would be called if no one scored in the ninth. In the dusky haze, Cubs player Gabby Hartnett stepped to the plate and swung at what he could only hope was the ball. History would remember that chance swing as "the Homer in the Gloaming," which helped the Cubs win the pennant. Fifty years later, permission for lights was finally granted, and the first lighted game at Wrigley was played on August 8, 1988, the Cubs beating the Mets 6–4. The world kept spinning. The oceans never boiled over. Life continued on as normal. Most importantly, the vines kept growing on the outfield wall of Wrigley Field.

4. HEY HEY/HOLY COW

Most ball announcers have signatures, and Jack Brickhouse's "Hey! Hey!" assured the fans at home that hope still remained. The son of a Tennessee vaudeville promoter, Brickhouse was born in Peoria, Illinois, in 1916. He began his career as a sort of roving reporter for WMBD in Peoria before eventually joining WGN in Chicago in 1940. Aside from a few quick defections to other stations, and a two-year stint as a Marine during World War II, Brickhouse spent the majority of his broadcast career at WGN, announcing not only ball games, but also college football, wrestling, world championship boxing matches, college and pro basketball, and conventions for both Democrats and Republicans. But in Chicago, the name Brickhouse will always be synonymous with Cubs baseball. Listening to Jack do color for one of the Cubs games was like attending the game with your dad. With that special touch of optimism in his voice, he was able to make the almost certain loss somehow easier to take.

Harry Caray was a totally different breed of announcer. Animus Festivus—Party Animal. He was the "Holy Cow!" guy, his style of broadcasting often sounding more like an exuberant fan who's gotten into the announcer's booth. And in fact, Harry once said that his philosophy was to broadcast the way a fan would. To Harry, baseball was about atmosphere, not wins or losses, and he made the atmosphere fun. Sure he'd give you stats, but then he'd throw in the pronunciation of a name spelled backward. Why? No one knows. Because he could. In the seventh inning stretch he'd lean out the booth window and lead the fans in a chorus of "Take Me Out to the Ballgame." It was as if he yearned to be sitting among them, sipping a Budweiser, and yelling cheers of encouragement to the players. If Jack Brickhouse was like your father, Harry was like your crazy uncle who took you to a ball game and said, "Watch this," before doing some wacky little stunt. Make no mistake, Caray was a professional. At age nineteen, Caray started his career working at radio stations in Joliet, Illinois, then Kalamazoo, Michigan. He then returned to broadcast in St. Louis, the city of his birth. Born Harry Caraboni in 1914, he played semipro baseball before beginning a radio career. It was in St. Louis, broadcasting for the Cardinals, that he began his "Take Me Out to the Ballgame" tradition. In 1970, he did TV and radio games for the Oakland A's before taking the act to Chicago a year later. He did radio and TV color for the Chicago White Sox, then moved across town in 1982 to call games for the Chicago Cubs. He remained a "Bud man and a Cub fan" until his death on February 18, 1998, of complications from a heart attack. The fans loved him because he was one of them. More than any other announcer, he spoke directly to the heart of the average fan.

5. BALL HAWKS

As sun warms center field, they flock to Kenmore and Waveland Avenues, eyes scoping the sky, every nerve at the ready for any ball to come soaring over the outfield wall of Wrigley Field. They're known as "ball hawks," scores of people who stand on the streets, gloves at the ready, to catch the homers slammed over the wall. Most are from the neighborhood, some having started their hawking as children, catching the balls from batting practice. Some spend the game on their feet, anxious for any chance at a ball. Others, old pros at hawking, set up folding chairs and sit patiently until the time is right to join the action. Big action came the day of September 13, 1998, when Slammin' Sammy Sosa sent his #62 flying over the left-field wall. Outside Wrigley, the street was packed with hawking hopefuls itching for a chance to catch the record-breaking ball. When that chance came, it seemed as if it would be old pro "Moe" Mullins who would get the ball. Moe had been a regular on Waveland for what seemed like forever and he had trunks full of balls to attest to his skill at hawking. But it was Brendan Cunningham, a suburban mortgage broker, who ended up with the ball. He was quickly hustled into a van to get him away from the pursuing crowd. It was a free-for-all as people clawed at anyone who had the ball. When all was said and done, Moe insisted that he had actually had the magic ball before a group of people converged upon him, shoving and even biting him before the ball was pried from his hand. Witnesses backed up his claim, which bolstered the lawsuit he filed to get the ball back. Unfortunately, the judge ordered him to post a $50,000 bond to carry on the suit. A figure far out of his ballpark, it was one reason the case was settled out of court. Who ended up with the ball? Sammy Sosa.

6. DANGEROUS GROUPIES

Violet Popovich, a pretty dancer/singer, was in love with Cubs shortstop Billy Jurges. It's uncertain whether or not the feeling was mutual or if the two ever had relations at all (as Popovich later claimed). A fellow teammate had introduced him to the girl who had been lingering at the clubhouse after the games, but where it went from there is hazy. Lost in her obsession, however, Popovich found herself in the lobby of the Carlos Hotel on the morning of July 6, 1932, leaving three messages begging Jurges to see her. At last he relented, calling her up to his room, where Popovich brandished a .25-caliber handgun and threatened to kill herself. Within her purse was a suicide note to her ex-husband in which she asks, ". . . why should I leave this earth alone?" Three shots later, with a bullet going through one hand and another entering his side, Jurges was able to disarm her. As Violet was taken to be booked, Billy was taken to Illinois Masonic Hospital. He refused to prosecute the case, though. Popovich moved out of his life and out of the history books. Due to his injuries, Jurges missed the remainder of the 1932 season and that year's World Series against the New York Yankees (which the Cubs lost).

For another player, the drama repeated itself on June 14, 1949, after former Chicago Cubs first baseman Eddie Waitkus unknowingly stole the heart of another troubled fan. Ruth Steinhagen, a tall nineteen-year-old, had fallen in love with Waitkus in 1946 when he still played for the Cubs. Waitkus was traded to the Phillies in 1948, but Ruth's affection followed him to Philadelphia. From her rooming house on Lincoln Avenue, Ruth kept track of her idol's comings and goings. She even set up a private altar to him. Trips to a psychiatrist were of little help. Ruth bought hit records from 1936 to honor Waitkus's number 36. She ate baked beans in honor of Waitkus's hometown of Cambridge, Massachusetts. On June 14, Ruth checked in to the swank Edgewater Beach Hotel, where Waitkus and his Phillies teammates were staying for the Cubs/Phillies game at Wrigley.

After attending the game with a friend, Ruth took the .22-caliber rifle she had purchased at a pawnshop and went to the hotel. Fortifying herself with a few drinks, Ruth gave a bellboy a note to give to Waitkus and waited. Introducing herself in the note, she kept her intentions mysterious by simply asking Waitkus to join her in her room. Hormones in gear, Waitkus was only too glad to comply. That night, after letting Waitkus in and offering him a seat, Ruth reached into the closet, withdrew a rifle, and shot Waitkus. The bullet entered Waitkus's chest, went through his lungs, and lodged in his back near his spine. Stunned, the young first-baseman crawled toward the door in an effort to escape. Oddly composed, Ruth called the front desk for a house detective who found her sitting on a bench near the elevator, the still-bleeding Waitkus on the hotel floor. Recovery was slow for Eddie Waitkus, who suffered through five operations, but by 1950, he was named "Comeback Player of the Year" and helped the Phillies win the pennant. Long after, however, he was still nervous about meeting new people. Ruth wound up in the Kankakee State Hospital still obsessed with #36. Decades later, the story served as the inspiration for *The Natural*.

7. MERKLE'S BONER

The Cubs have actually won some pennants and even a few World Series, but one victory that led to a pennant remains controversial. It was September 23, 1908: Cubs vs. New York Giants, bottom of the ninth, game tied 1–1. With men on first and third, and two outs, Giants batter Al Bridwell hit a line drive to the outfield. Figuring that the game was won with the man on third heading home, Giant Fred Merkle, the man on first, confidently headed to the clubhouse as the field filled up with cheering fans who assumed the same thing. According to umpire Bob Emslie, Cub Joe Tinker came forward and told him that Merkle had never run the hit out to second. When the ball was hit, Emslie fell to the ground to avoid being hit by it so he hadn't seen the play. But fellow ump Hank O'Day seemed to support the story. According to a rule never enforced before, each base runner must proceed to the next base if there is a force. Previously, umpires ignored other base runners when a winning run scored. With Merkle's status technically an out, the winning run from third didn't count.

The Cubs had found themselves in similar circumstances at the end of their September 4 game against the Pittsburgh Pirates. In that case, it was Warren Gill breaking for the clubhouse without advancing to second after the winning hit had been struck. Johnny Evers, second baseman for the Cubs, claimed a force out on that play but Hank O'Day, umping that day as well, didn't buy the force-out story and the score remained 1–0 Pirates. A protest was filed with the league office, and while the Pittsburgh victory was allowed to stand, it was acknowledged that the protest had merit, and the rule was enforced from then on. The September 23 game against New York had a few extra problems. First, it was growing late and growing dark. There was little likelihood that the game could continue even if so ordered. Also, according to Johnny Evers, he called to center fielder Fred Hofman to throw the ball to him, but by that time the crowd was swarming onto the field. In the confusion, the throw went over Evers's head, hitting shortstop Joe Tinker on the back before being lost in the crowd. Realizing Merkle's error, New York coach Joe McGinnity ran after the ball in an effort to keep it from the Cubs, and managed to throw it into the crowd around the shortstop position while Tinker was trying to take it away from him. The ball got back to Evers after pitcher Floyd Kroh (who hadn't participated in the game) knocked the ball away from a spectator. Kroh walked it over to Evers who shouted out to umpire Hank O'Day and lifted the ball above the heads of the crowd to show him he had possession and affirm that he was on the second base bag. It was Merkle's misfortune that he hadn't paid closer attention to rulings from the league or he might have known which direction to move that night. He chose to advance to the clubhouse and ended up forcing the game to end in a tie. After that, the Cubs and Giants ran neck and neck in the standings and, but for the lack of one Giants win (or one Cubs loss), the Giants would have won the pennant. To his credit, Merkle continued playing that season despite the negative reaction of fans and newspapers. His mistake was dubbed "Merkle's Boner" and he was hissed and jeered when he stepped out on the field. As for the Cubs, they went on to beat Detroit in the World Series—the last World Series they've won, so far.

8. **CHARLES WEEGHMAN**

Charles Weeghman owned the Cubs for only two years but made a mark on baseball nonetheless, one of his major additions being the beautiful Wrigley Field, once known as Weeghman Park. Born in Indiana in 1874, after high school Weeghman wound up in Chicago in 1892, lured, like so many, by the potential of the 1893 World's Columbian Exposition. By the beginning of the twentieth century, he was the owner of a string of highly successful lunch counters throughout the city. A grand figure, exuberant and friendly, unafraid to spend money, his foray into baseball began with the "outlaw" Federal League, which had declared itself a major league in 1914. Weeghman took over the Chicago team, the Whales, and hired Zachary Taylor Davies to supervise the building of the team's home, Weeghman Park. The Federal League, however, eventually folded in 1915. As part of a peace agreement between the Federal League and its major league sisters, Weeghman was allowed to buy the Chicago Cubs. His ten-man syndicate, which included William Wrigley Jr., raised the necessary capital and purchased the team for $500,000, with Weeghman named president. His philosophy was highly fan-friendly, a philosophy that Wrigley would continue when he took over. After receiving complaints that strolling vendors blocked the view of fans, he installed what would be the first permanent concession stands in any park. Early baseball policy was to demand the return of any ball caught by a fan in the stands. It wasn't unusual for fans to be harassed by park police, searched, and even ejected from parks for what was considered stealing club property. Weeghman put a stop to that in his park, becoming the first baseball team owner to let the fans keep the balls they caught in the bleachers. His attitude would eventually inspire later owners and presidents who saw the need to keep the fans happy and coming back to the game. By 1918, financial problems led him to sell the club to Wrigley and his time as a baseball team owner came to an end. The Wrigley name went on to own the club until 1981. As for Charles Weeghman, he died in 1938 at the age of sixty-four, in the town that had meant so much to him: Chicago.

9. CHUCK CONNORS

Before he was *The Rifleman*, he was a Cub. That's right. Before he played Lucas McCain in the popular TV series *The Rifleman*, Chuck Connors played for the Chicago Cubs— briefly, and not very memorably by all accounts. In his seventy games with the team, his batting average was .233. Prior to the Cubs, he played for the Brooklyn Dodgers and before that he played basketball with the Boston Celtics. Success for Connors, however, seemed to lie on the silver screen, not the sports arena. From the Cubs he was sent to the Los Angeles Angels, a Chicago farm team, and it was while he was doing cartwheels while rounding the bases that he caught the eye of a Hollywood director. Connors was hired to play a highway patrolman in 1952's *Pat and Mike* starring Spencer Tracy and Kathryn Hepburn. He had one line. Connors left the baseball diamond in favor of acting and landed small parts on TV and in movies like 1957's *Designing Women* and 1958's *The Big Country*. His big break came in 1958 when he was cast in TV's *The Rifleman* as a rancher/ widower trying to raise a son in the untamed west. During the show's five-year run he also starred in movies like *Geronimo* and as Porter Ricks in 1963's *Flipper,* but after *The Rifleman* left the air, three more attempts at series were unsuccessful. He turned instead to making guest appearances on TV shows and in movies and even revived his Lucas McCain character for a cameo in Kenny Rogers's star-studded, made-for-TV movie *The Gambler Returns: The Luck of the Draw*. A short time after, that Connors passed away at the age of seventy-one from lung cancer.

10. THE GOAT'S CURSE

Okay, I'm not testifying to the validity of this, I'm just telling you what I heard. William Sianis, owner of the Billy Goat Tavern on Lower Michigan Avenue—yeah, the "cheezeboiga, cheezeboiga" guy—well, Sianis had this goat. Nice enough animal, mascot of the bar, and Sianis, a huge Cubs fan, brought the goat to Wrigley Field (actually, Sianis used to love smuggling the goat into all sorts of places like wrestling matches, conventions, and such). Keep in mind that this was 1940s, back in the days when you could do that sort of stuff. Anyway, in 1945, when the Cubs were playing the Tigers in the World Series, Sianis decided to take his goat to Wrigley

Field for game three but was stopped at the gate. Turns out the management didn't want the goat in there anymore. Sianis, steamed, put a curse on the team, sending a telegram to P. K. Wrigley for added effect: The Cubs won't win a series until they apologize to the goat. William Sianis passed away in 1970. Sam Sianis, nephew of William and owner of the billy goat, has tried to do away with the curse. He's even tried taking the goat back to Wrigley, but they wouldn't let him in until 1984. The Cubs won the division, but lost the playoffs to the Padres. In 1994, the goat returned after twelve home games were lost, and the Cubs won their next game, but the season was cut short by a players' strike. The Cubs haven't won a championship since Sianis put the curse on them in 1945. Maybe it's not just about letting the goat into Wrigley. Maybe they ought to come out and apologize to the goat.

The Bears

B ear down, Chicago Bears. This is meat and potatoes sports.

1. **DA BEARS**

In 1920, George Halas coaxed A.E. Staley, a Decatur starch manufacturer, to start a company football team. Staley already had a company baseball team, which was doing well. Why not a football team? Halas, who was working in the company mill house and playing on the company baseball team, set up a meeting with twelve other clubs to discuss forming a league. They met in Canton, Ohio, and formed the American Professional Football Association, which later became the National Football League (NFL). Halas coached and played for the Decatur Staleys who posted a 10–1–2 record that first year. Money concerns caused Staley to ax his teams, but rather than disband the football team, he sold it to Halas and partner Edward "Dutch" Sternaman for $200 in 1921. Halas and Sternaman decided to move the team to Chicago. Staley even gave them $5,000 to cover the first year's expenses with one stipulation: For their first year the team had to be called the Chicago Staleys. The Chicago Staleys played their first game on October 16, 1921, and they went on to win the league title that year. With a league championship under their belts, in 1922, they became the Chicago

Bears, a playful nod to Chicago's other sports team, the Cubs, and appropriate since they played in Wrigley Field. The team's colors of blue and orange were those of Halas's old alma mater, the University of Illinois. The Bears became the first team to buy a player from another team in 1922, paying $100 to bring Ed Healy from Rock Island to Chicago. They were the first team to play an indoor game (the 1932 championship against the Portsmouth Spartans held in the Chicago Stadium due to bad weather). And in 1933, they won the first NFL championship by defeating the New York Giants. One of their most legendary games was the 1940 championship when they shut out the Washington Redskins 73–0. The "Monsters of the Midway" went on to win three more championships, then suffered a seventeen-year drought until winning the title again in 1963. Known for ferocious defense, that year they met the New York Giants in eight-degree weather at Wrigley Field and walked away with the title by winning 14–10. In 1970, the Bears played their final season in Wrigley, moving on to Soldier Field. That same year, George Halas was elected president of the National Football Conference (NFC), when the NFL and the American Football League (AFL) merged. This was in the midst of another dry spell for the Bears, who didn't make the playoffs again until 1977. In the '80s, however, the team became contenders again as they made their way to an unbelievable 1985 season. After winning Super Bowl XX in 1986, the Bears slowed, but managed to make the playoffs in '90 and '91. The team that had been so strong in the mid-1980s began to break up, as players were traded or retired. Fans are still waiting eagerly for a Bears team as powerful and aggressive as the team of the early '40s or '63 and '85. In the meantime, they can appreciate their team's impressive history. One of two charter members of the National Football League, the Bears boast nine championships, one Super Bowl, six NFC Division championships, ten NFL Western Division Championships, most players inducted into the NFL Hall of Fame, and they were the first franchise in history to win 600 games. Not exactly a record to sneeze at. Even in eight-degree Bear weather.

2. **PAPA BEAR**

Papa Bear Halas was, for decades, the heart of the Chicago Bears. Born in Chicago in 1895, Halas played for University of Illinois and on the Great Lakes Naval Training Station team before becoming a player/coach for the Decatur Staleys, eventually buying the team in 1921 with his partner Dutch Sternaman. He played as hard as the rest of the team, even outracing Jim Thorpe in a rainstorm during a 1923 game to take a fumble for ninety-eight yards. Halas continued as a player and coach until 1929, retiring as a player and hiring Ralph Jones as coach. During the Depression, he chose to save money by returning to coaching. His on-again, off-again coaching would continue until he permanently retired after the 1967 season. A hard disciplinarian as a coach, he was a mass of contradictions, perhaps due to his hardscrabble beginnings with the team. The first season, the team came up short by $71.63. Sternaman pumped gas and Halas sold cars to keep going. In 1932, the Bears lost $18,000, forcing Halas to pay his players in promissory notes. His decisions were very often misguided attempts to keep the team going during years when all of football was struggling to gain popularity. During the 1940s, he held back a percentage of every player's salary so they'd have something for the off-season, yet the players never saw the interest earned on that money. Later, when the knee problems of Dick Butkus, one of his biggest draws, forced the star to retire early, Halas went to court rather than pay Butkus his salary.

He took one of his best yet underpaid coaches, George Allen, to court to keep Allen from taking a job as head coach of the Los Angeles Rams. Even though Halas won the case, he immediately gave Allen permission to go to Los Angeles. He was stingy and dictatorial, yet he loved his team and was highly innovative when it came to football. Hiring players like

Red Grange, Bronco Nagurski, Dick Butkus, and Gale Sayers were brilliant moves. During the 1920s, after colleges
complained of pro teams luring away students, he insisted
that no player could be signed until completing college. In
1940, he introduced the T-formation, which helped the play
of many teams. Halas helped write the first NFL rulebook
and created a league office to measure the consistency of
field officials. The Bears were the first team to film and study
their games and were the first to practice every day. In 1963,
Halas became a charter member of the Football Hall of
Fame. In 1982, after years of poor coaching, he named former Bear Mike Ditka as coach, and in 1986, the Bears won
the Super Bowl. Unfortunately, Papa Bear George Halas died
at the age of eighty-eight, three years shy of watching the
team he worked so hard for win the Super Bowl.

3. **SWEETNESS**

"Sweetness" fit Walter Payton to a T. Grace on the field, Payton was an all-around player who even played quarterback
in one game after all the quarterbacks had been injured. But
he was known for the runs that led him to break Jim Brown's
record on October 7, 1984. The Bears wanted a break in the
game for a short ceremony commemorating this feat, but
true to his nature, Payton turned the attention down. By the
end of his career he had rushed for 16,726 yards. Payton was
born in Michigan in 1954, and his parents raised him with a
determination that showed in the intense personal training
program he developed in high school. He played baseball,
basketball, and ran track, becoming a state champion long
jumper. In high school he was named all-state his senior year
before entering college, where his record of never missing
a game began. Graduating with a bachelor's of science in
education, six months sooner than most students, he was
drafted by the Bears in 1975 and Chicago fell in love with
him, as his grace on and off the field endeared him to fans.
Shy with the media, he had a wicked sense of humor and
enjoyed a good time. He loved setting off M-80 firecrackers

during the night in preseason and it wasn't unusual for him to fill in for the Bear's receptionist, fooling callers with his high-pitched voice. Payton even cohosted *Saturday Night Live*, using that soft voice of his to do a wicked imitation of a very buff Michael Jackson. Payton was a hit with the fans of other teams as well, and it wasn't unusual for him to receive standing ovations in Lambeau Field by, of all people, Packer fans. From the start, Payton was a team player unafraid to rush into tackles if it meant getting the ball further. By his third season, at twenty-three, he became the youngest player to be named NFL's Most Valuable Player. But he was vexed by a team that just couldn't take it all the way, until 1985, when the Bears found themselves on the road to Super Bowl XX. Unfortunately, he was unable to score a touchdown in the Super Bowl he worked so hard to get to, but the fans didn't care. It was a magical end to an incredible season. Payton was named Player of the Year in 1985, but the magic didn't last and the Bears were unable to repeat. Payton retired in 1988, entering the nightclub and restaurant business, often visiting Walter Payton's Roundhouse in Aurora, Illinois, with a huge greeting for the staff before going out to meet the customers.

Loved by the staff, at one Christmas party he even played bartender for the employees. In 1989, with the family of George Halas, he started the George Halas/Walter Payton Foundation (the name was eventually changed to simply The Walter Payton Foundation in 1998). Providing motivational support for youngsters, the Wishes for Santa program also handed out Christmas gifts to abused and neglected children. Then came the news in 1998. Walter Payton was suffering from primary sclerosing cholangitis, a rare liver disease. As he awaited a new liver, he was eventually diagnosed with bile duct cancer, which would make a new liver useless. On November 1, 1999, the man they called "Sweetness" passed away. The next day, flags at Soldier Field flew at half mast. Four days later, 20,000 fans came to Soldier Field to listen to current and former Bears, NFL officials, and coaches pay tribute to a gentle Bear with a playful soul.

4. BEARS VS. PACKERS

The Bears vs. Packers rivalry is Shakespearean in scope. Deep-seated and venomous, snowballs and cheeseballs are thrown between fans in the stands. Fights break out in parking lots and stadium restrooms. Sportswriters for both cities continually lob insults at each other. And the teams themselves? There's a focused intensity noticeable to anyone in the immediate vicinity of the players that takes over the practice sessions the week before a Bears/Packers showdown. But why? Is it the difference between the two cities? Packers see Chicago as a hard and tough town looking down on her northern sister. Chicago views Green Bay as the goofy "cheesehead" capital. The antagonism could stem from their first showdown. November 27, 1921, 7,000 people watched the Bears (then known as the Decatur Staleys) whip the Packers 20–0. Established in 1919, the Packers are the older team and they've won twelve championships, the highest in the league, while the Bears are second with nine. When they met again on October 14, 1923, in Green Bay's Bellevue Park, the Bears won 3–0.

Perhaps the root of this hatred lies within the animosity between two players who faced off against each other in that November 27 game, George Halas and Earl "Curly" Lambeau. These two continued the battle as coaches, each rallying their troops to mow down the opposition and each playing on the ticket-selling intercity rivalry. They refused to speak to each other before a game, refused to shake hands after a game, and had very little good to say about each other outside the game. Curiously, these two adversaries were capable of showing unexpected courtesy toward each other. In 1932, Lambeau made sure the Packers accepted Halas's IOU to cover a guarantee for a game at Wrigley. In 1961, on the eve of a sold out Bears/Packers game, Halas stated that Lambeau, who didn't have a ticket, would have a seat even if it meant a spot for him on the bench. Whatever the reason, the Bears/Packers rivalry has been a little bit of sports theater and will probably remain so for years to come.

5. IRON MIKE

Born in 1939 in Pennsylvania, Mike Ditka was instrumental in two Bears championships. He's one of only two men to have Super Bowl wins as a player, assistant coach, and head coach. He became an All-American in his senior year at the University of Pittsburgh, playing defensive end, linebacker, and tight end, and was considered one of the nation's top punters. In 1961, he became a Monster of the Midway, catching fifty-six passes and being named rookie of the year. During five seasons with the Bears, he earned a trip to the Pro Bowl each year and helped win a championship in 1963. In 1967, he was traded to the Philadelphia Eagles, then moved on to the Dallas Cowboys in 1969, where he later gained his first Super Bowl ring when the Cowboys beat the Miami Dolphins in Super Bowl VI. As an assistant coach for the Cowboys he was there, too, when the Cowboys won the Super Bowl again after the 1977 season. In the 1982 season, he signed on as head coach for the Bears, and he helped turn their play around. A colorful figure, at press conferences Ditka sparred with reporters whom he once compared to a three-week-old puppy (the difference being that the puppy will stop whining in six weeks). He roamed the sidelines, blustery, cursing the unfair calls of officials and snarling at the players. He referred to his team and himself as "Grabow-skis," hardworking guys just trying to get the job done. And they got the job done. In 1986, he was in the Super Bowl for a third time, watching the Bears beat the New England Patri-ots. He was named coach of the year by *The Sporting News* and the *Pro Football Writers Association* for that 15–1 sea-son, an honor he received again in 1988. While the heart was there, ensuing seasons weren't nearly as special and in 1992, he was let go by the Bears. Mike Ditka showed just what the Grabowskis could do and he will forever be a part of Chicago.

6. THE SUPER BOWL SHUFFLE

On January 26, 1986, the Chicago Bears rolled over the New England Patriots for a 46–10 Super Bowl XX win in the New

Orleans Superdome. It was an incredible ending to an incredible year for a victory-hungry town. Not since the 1963 Bears won the championship had the town seen the unstoppable force that was the 1985 Chicago Bears. What was it about this team? The aggressive, unpredictable defense was led by "Samurai" Mike Singletary, whose intense gaze warned opponents to stay clear, and the surprisingly agile William "The Refrigerator" Perry, who may have been the largest mammal to play the game at that time. The defense was a joy to behold, as opposing teams slammed into a brick Bear wall. The blitzes were staggering and when snow came to Soldier Field, it was Bear weather. Then there was the barking by the "The Junkyard Dogs" that, once it caught on, filled venues across the city and later the country with the echoed "woof woofs" of happy fans. This was not only great football, it was great entertainment, packing the stadiums and pulling people to their TV sets every Sunday.

They marked their territory the first game of the season, mowing down the Buffalo Bills for a 45–14 win. This team was willing to do anything to win. In their eleventh game, playing the Dallas Cowboys, William Perry picked up Walter Payton near the Bear's goal line and threw him into the endzone. The Bears clinched the NFC Central Division with that 44–0 game, sending the Cowboys back to the bunkhouse. The Bears were entertaining off the field as well, their attitude perfect for the video-driven 1980s. Jim McMahon became the "Punky QB" because of a mistake while cutting his own hair. Walter Payton was as sweet-looking standing still as he was running across the field. Okay, the day after their December 2 loss to the Dolphins, many of the Bears went off to record the single and video for "The Super Bowl Shuffle." Maybe they should have been studying the previous day's game footage, but it was for a good cause and these guys were fearless. What followed in the playoffs wasn't pretty. January 5, 1986, they mauled the New York Giants 21–0. The next week, they feasted on Los Angeles Rams 24–0. The Patriots never had a chance because the Bears were still hungry and only a Super Bowl trophy would satisfy them. And when they came back to Chicago after mauling the New England Patriots, they came back to a ticker-tape parade from a very proud city.

7. **THE GALLOPING GHOST**

Many considered Red Grange, nicknamed the "Galloping Ghost," to be the greatest football player who ever lived. Born in 1903, he played the game when headgear was pretty much a leather cap. His family moved from Pennsylvania to Wheaton, Illinois, and Grange, under six feet tall and only 170 pounds, enrolled in the University of Illinois, never expecting to play football. Yet he went on to be named All-American in 1923, 1924, and 1925. His four touchdowns in twelve minutes during the October 18, 1924, Illinois/Michigan game made him a college football star. Inspired by newsreels of his dashes across the field, people flocked to the games to watch him run. Believing amateur sports were meant to be played for sport, not money, purists criticized Grange's decision to sign on with George Halas's Chicago Bears for $25,000 in 1925. Grange admitted he simply needed the money. He did help breathe life into pro football. Thirty-six thousand fans spent Thanksgiving watching Red Grange's debut game for the Bears against the Chicago Cardinals, which, unfortunately, ended in a 0–0 tie, Grange gaining only thirty-six yards. Three days later, though, he showed Bears fans just what Halas was paying for. Playing the Columbus Tigers, Grange gained 140 yards and led the Bears to a 14–13 victory. Packing stadiums all over, Grange and his agent cashed in on his popularity by endorsing Red Grange dolls, clothes, ginger ale, even meat loaf. He even played himself in 1929's *The Galloping Ghost*. In 1926, when Halas balked at a demand for a five-figure salary and one-third ownership of the team, Grange left the team and joined his agent in establishing the American Football League. Grange went from the Chicago Bulls AFL team to the New York Yankees AFL team, but the league was unsuccessful and soon folded, the Yankees merging into the NFL. During a game against his old team, Grange suffered a severe knee injury that knocked him out of the 1928 season. Halas invited him back to the Bears after the Yankees folded in 1929, but his knee injury made it difficult for him to resume his running-back career, so he switched to defensive back and played until 1934. He stayed on as assistant coach until retiring completely in 1937. Grange became a sportscaster for TV and radio in the 1940s and '50s and was eventually inducted into the Football Hall of Fame in 1963. In 1991, the Galloping Ghost died from pneumonia at the age of eighty-seven.

8. NEVER GIVE UP

In 1970, pro football writers voted Gale Sayers "the most courageous player." His is one of the most inspiring stories in football. Born into a poor Kansas family in 1943, he was imbued with the belief that determination would lead to success. He played baseball and ran track, but football was Sayers's favorite sport. He was a superb high school athlete, developing his own workout regime, and even winning a race barefoot when his shoes kept sliding off. Named an All-American, after college Sayers joined the Bears where he finished the season with a record twenty-two touchdowns. Dubbed "the Kansas City Comet," Sayers ran with a gazelle-like speed and agility on the field and was named Rookie of the Year in 1966, after leading the league in yardage. In 1967, he was assigned to room with Brian Piccolo on the road. The relationship was contentious at first, but eventually they forged an unbreakable bond. After Sayers injured his knee during a 1968 game against San Francisco, Piccolo offered him encouragement during the recuperation. Sportswriters questioned whether or not Sayers would ever play again, and his uncertain play at the beginning of the '69 season seemed to warrant the doubt. But he went on to average 100 yards per game, and his 1,032 yards at the end of the year beat all in the league. Piccolo's diagnosis of incurable cancer, how-

ever, was a major blow and Sayers, still grieving over the
death of his friend, injured his left leg during a preseason
game in 1970. After three operations, Gale Sayers, who had
been named NFL All-Star Game MVP in 1967, '68, and '70,
officially retired in 1972. He went on to join the University of
Kansas as an assistant football coach in 1973, and became
the Southern Illinois University athletic director in 1976, also
serving on the boards of many children's charities. On July
30, 1977, at the age of thirty-four, Gale Sayers became the
youngest player inducted into the Football Hall of Fame.

9. THE TANK

Many called him the strongest man ever to play football. This
was a guy who plowed fields without a horse. At six feet, two
inches and 235 pounds, Bronko Nagurski was a formidable
addition to the 1930 Bears. Born Bronislaw Nagurski in Ontario in 1908, he was raised in Minnesota playing football in
high school. In 1926, he became the star of the University of
Minnesota team and in 1929 was the only player in football
history named All-American in two positions—tackle and
fullback. A year later he was one of the early superstars playing for the Chicago Bears, helping to turn the team into the
"Monsters of the Midway." During his nine seasons with the
team, he gained more than 4,031 yards, made All-Pro three
times, and led the Bears in rushing in 1933 and 1936. Arthri-
tis hit him hard in 1937 and he was forced to retire at age
twenty-nine. But in 1943, with so many young men off to
war, Nagurski was coaxed back to the field, playing one season with his old team as tackle. On December 26, during the
last quarter of the NFL title game against the Washington
Redskins, he scored the last touchdown of his career. The
Bears won 41–21. Afterward, he retired permanently and
turned to farming with a brief stint as a backfield coach at
UCLA. In 1945, he took his massive strength and focused it
on pro wrestling. In 1960, he turned from wrestling to refere-
eeing, and three years later was inducted as a charter mem-

ber of the Football Hall of Fame. He died in Minnesota in 1990 at the age of eighty-one.

10. THE CHICAGO CARDINALS

Founded in 1898 by a pack of South Side toughs as an amateur athletic team called the Morgan Athletic Club, in 1901, painting and decorating contractor Chris O'Brien turned the bunch into what would become pro football's oldest franchise. Their home was at Normal Park in Racine, so they became known as the Normals, then the Racine Cardinals before deciding on the Chicago Cardinals in 1922, the same year they joined the NFL. In 1925, the Cardinals won their first NFL championship based on having the best record. When World War II took many of the young players, the Cardinals combined with the Pittsburgh Steelers in 1944 to play as the Card-Pitt. In 1947, together again, the Cardinals won another NFL championship, this time by defeating the Philadelphia Eagles 28–21 in a title game. The team passed from Chris O'Brien in 1929 to Dr. David Jones, who then sold it to Charles W. Bidwell Sr., a vice president of the Chicago Bears, for $50,000. A football fanatic, Bidwell was free with money and yearned to make his new team a winner, even though still having deep affection for the Bears, a team he'd hoped to buy before the Cardinals came along. The Cardinals ended up losing more money than they made as other Chicago franchises such as the Tigers and the Rockets competed for Bear leftovers. Tragically, Bidwell died in 1947 before he could see his team win the title. The team was controlled by his wife, Violet, for the next fifteen years until the Bidwell family gave up on Chicago and took the Cardinals to St. Louis in 1960. They roosted there until 1988, then moved to Arizona, taking the name the Phoenix Cardinals before deciding, finally, upon the name Arizona Cardinals.

The Bulls

The Chicago Bulls had a mostly dreary history, but in the 1990s this team rebounded into greatness.

1. **THE BULLS**

The Chicago Bulls ruled the NBA in the 1990s and charged away with six championships. This was a hungry team and they gorged themselves on victory for a decade. Basketball has been around for over a century, but prior to the 1940s it wasn't a very popular sport. By 1961, Chicago's chances for a successful franchise seemed dim. The Chicago Stags had been a charter member of the NBA, but the team eventually folded in 1950. A new team, the Chicago Packers, gave it a try in 1961, but had the worst record in the league and could barely fill the Chicago Amphitheatre. Chicago businessman Dick Klein, having to pass on buying the Packers franchise, was able to find the money to back the Chicago Bulls, and Chicago was the tenth team in the NBA for the 1966–1967 season. Johnny "Red" Kerr, a former basketball star at the University of Illinois, became the team's first coach and played on the team. Like all good Chicago teams, they charged out of the gate their first regular season, beating the St. Louis Hawks 104–97. Their first game at the Amphitheatre, they beat the Warriors 119–116. Their record for the year was 33–48 and though they lost the Western Conference semifinals, Red Kerr was named NBA Coach of the Year. But as with all good Chicago teams, the worm turned. Often, playing in their new home, the Chicago Stadium, they played before crowds of less than a hundred. Annoyed with Klein's handling of the team, Kerr eventually left and was replaced by Dick Motta from Weber State in Utah. Things did not get much better. New GM Pat Williams's promotions brought more fans to the stadium, and in the 1970–1971 season, the team saw the fifty-win mark for the first time. Motta was named Coach of the Year. But the club was never able to get past the second round of playoffs. In 1974–1975, they missed the playoffs altogether. Eight coaches in eight years followed, and plagued by injuries and poor team chemistry, their standing sunk to league worst. That all changed in 1984 when Air Jordan touched down. By this time, the team had been sold to Jerry Reinsdorf, who searched for players like Charles Oakley, John Paxson, Scottie Pippen, and Horace Grant. These were the sort of names up to par with Jordan's. The 1990s would become the decade of the Bulls, as they brought an enthusiasm for the game that Chicago had never experienced before. Interestingly, the enthusiasm remains even though the team's stats are nowhere near what they were. Still, the Bulls have been counted out before. No one expected an Air Jordan and no one can tell what the future will bring.

2. HIS ROYAL AIRNESS

To understand what Michael Jordan brought to Chicago basketball, you'd have to first consider that the Bulls were a team incapable of filling a stadium. Jordan was born in 1963 in New York, but the family settled in North Carolina where his parents taught him to make things happen, as opposed to waiting for them to happen. As a boy, his favorite sport was baseball and in high school he was a pitcher and center-fielder on the baseball team. Amazingly, the first time he tried out for the varsity basketball squad he didn't make the team. This only motivated him to try harder and before long he was averaging twenty points a game on the junior varsity squad. By the end of high school, he'd been named to the All-America team and was receiving scholarship offers from all over. Accepting a full ride to the University of North Carolina, he was named Player of the Year in 1983 and 1984 and won a gold medal on the U.S. Olympic team.

In his first season as a Chicago Bull, Jordan found himself on a demoralized team that had finished the previous season with a record of 27–55. It wasn't long, however, before His Royal Airness began to emerge. By season end, he was named to the NBA All-Star Team and won Rookie of the Year. The Bulls finished the season 38–44, making the playoffs for the first time in four years. There was something graceful about the way Jordan seemed to hang in midair that made those few seconds seem to last forever. Attendance at Bulls games began to grow along with the Bulls' reputation (it nearly doubled during Jordan's rookie season). It was suddenly hip to watch basketball. And everyone wanted to be like Mike. His own demeanor—focused on court, humble yet sly off, only endeared him to the city. In his time on the Bulls he led his team to six championships, two three-peats in a row. This is Chicago. That kind of thing just doesn't happen. Suddenly, Chicago wasn't just a contender, it was the town to beat.

3. **SPIRITUAL HANGTIME**

Born in Montana in 1945, Phil Jackson fell in love with basketball in North Dakota, where his family eventually settled. Jackson brought a philosophical edge to the game, studying the coaches and learning the intricacies of the game. By the end of high school, with a state tournament under his belt, Jackson decided to attend the University of North Dakota, where he studied psychology and religion. Phil Jackson originally planned on becoming a minister but turned to a basketball career instead, becoming two-time Division II All-American. From North Dakota, he went to play for the New York Knicks in 1967, where he was drawn to coach Red Holzman's leadership style. Holzman's highly team-oriented style of play would influence Jackson's coaching style. Though a back injury kept Jackson out of the Knicks' 1969–1970 championship season, he was there when they won again in the 1972–1973 season. In 1978, he was traded to the New Jersey Nets where he was a player and assistant coach for two years. Sensing his playing career nearing its end, he decided he'd like to try coaching. There was one drawback. Few people wanted to take a chance on this young man who, with his beard and blue jeans, looked more like a hippie than an NBA coach. In 1987, though, Jerry Krause hired him as assistant coach for the Bulls. Having gained experience coaching for the Continental Basketball Association's Albany Patroons (and leading them to the league championship in 1984), he would now be working with Coach Doug Collins to lead the Bulls. By 1989, Collins was gone and Jackson was named head coach. His unconventional style proved an asset to the club. He stressed teamwork over hot-dogging. Encouraging Jordan to trust his teammates, he encouraged the rest of the team to trust themselves. Instituting Tex Winter's triangle offense, he inspired the team by using Buddhist teachings and Native American spirituality, and practiced a calm style of coaching from the sidelines. He trusted his players and let them know it, guiding them to six championships in the 1990s. But storm clouds darkened when tension between management and Jackson grew, and he decided to part ways with the Bulls after nine seasons, six championships, and 545 wins over 193 losses. He proved that he had been an integral part of the Bull's dynasty when he joined the Los Angeles Lakers for the 1999–2000 season and led the team (which hadn't won a title since 1988) to an NBA championship in his first season. To prove it wasn't a fluke, the team did it again the next year.

4.   THE KID WHO LOVED BASKETBALL

Scottie Pippen was one of the big guns in the 1990s Bulls' dynasty, though it would be hard to imagine watching him play back in college. In fact, there was a question about whether he would have a basketball career at all. He was born Maurice Scotty Pippen in 1965 in Arkansas, where he developed a love of basketball at age eleven. There was nothing flashy in his play. One hindrance was his height. Even by college he was only six feet, one inch. There also didn't seem to be much drive. Yet, he was considered a consistent player, if not fantastic. In fact, it was a call from his high school coach to Don Dyer, head coach of the University of Central Arkansas, that convinced Pippen to join the UCA team in 1983 as a student manager and player. As time passed, Pippen honed his skill and his height shot up to six feet, seven inches, and his talent began to show. One asset to his slow growth was that he retained the ability to handle the ball like a smaller guy, which made for a much more coordinated player. In his sophomore year, he averaged 18.5 points and 9.2 rebounds per game. That average rose to 23.6 his senior year.

He had an all-around talent which, on the Bulls, was second only to Michael Jordan's. He joined the Bulls during 1987 and averaged 7.9 points, 3.8 rebounds per game. Seeing his all-around talent, Jackson made him small forward in the 1989–1990 season. He averaged 16.5 points per game, was third in the league in steals, and best of all, he was named to the NBA All-Star Game. By 1990, he was second on the team (behind Jordan) in steals and scoring. In 1992, he joined Jordan on the Olympic Dream Team. When Jordan retired in 1993, Pippen found himself the leader of the team and averaged twenty-two points per game. While the Bulls lost to the Knicks in the playoffs, the Bulls finished the season with a 55–27 record. When Jordan came back at the end of the 1994–1995 season, the team was again complete, but Pippen had shown his talent as an all-around player. After the last championship, Jackson announced that he was leaving the Bulls, and Jordan announced that he was leaving basketball. And for some strange reason, in 1999 Chicago decided to trade one of their prime players, sending Pippen to the Houston Rockets in an effort to infuse new blood into the Bulls. Uncomfortable with his new team, he was soon traded to Portland where he racked up his 2,000th steal, his 5,000th assist, and 17,000th point. Who would have imagined, back in Arkansas, that the kid who loved basketball, but wasn't that spectacular, would one day go to the All-Star Game seven times, win two Olympic gold medals, win six NBA championships, and be voted one of the fifty greatest players in NBA history?

5. **THREE-PEAT TIMES TWO**

After the team acquired players capable of backing up Jordan, the team began to pull away from the herd. In 1985, John Paxson joined the team, and in 1987, the team gained a major player when Scottie Pippen joined the Bulls. Then in 1989–1990, Phil Jackson came along and allowed assistant coach Tex Winter to institute his "triangle offense" and Chicago finished 55–27. Later would come B.J. Armstrong, Ron Harper, Toni Kukoc, Luc Longley, Dennis Rodman, and others. In 1990–1991, they finished 61–21 and for the first time in the history of the Bulls, they walked away with a championship, winning over the Los Angeles Lakers. In 1991–1992, their record rose to sixty-seven wins. Best of all, they beat the Trailblazers for their second NBA championship. They went down a bit the next season, ending with 57–25, but they three-peated, stealing their third trophy from the Phoenix Suns. Then Jordan dropped his baseball bombshell. Stunned by Jordan's retirement the team soldiered on, Pippen taking on leadership of the team, with B.J. Armstrong and Horace Grant backing him up. Steve Kerr was signed, as were Longley and Kukoc, from Croatia, who proved himself invaluable to the team even after Jordan's return. That Jordanless season, though spotty, was generally successful for the team, finishing with a 55–27 record. They even made the playoffs but lost to the Knicks in the end. Despite the team's impressive show during the 1993–1994 season, the town couldn't help but breathe a sigh of relief when His Royal Airness returned. He was rusty, though. They lost the playoffs to the Orlando Magic. Fans hoped for the best but feared the worst. Then in 1995–1996, Jordan and the Bulls silenced all naysayers. In an interesting move Dennis Rodman, once of the hated Pistons, joined the team as its first dominant rebounder. Initially, it wasn't a smooth fit, but under the guidance of Jackson and Jordan, Rodman learned to become a team player. The team not only ended the season with a record-breaking 72–10 record, they beat the Supersonics for their fourth championship trophy of the decade. Three-peat number two was well on the way. The 1996–1997 season became the Drive for Five, but wasn't quite as easy as the previous year. Fighting Karl Malone and the Utah Jazz, Jordan was also fighting stomach flu in game five of the title series and home court advantage bounced around between the two cities. But game six, the deciding game, was decided in the Bulls' favor. Chicago won their fifth title and Jordan won his fifth MVP. They met the Jazz again the following year and it was a stunning series, but the second three-peat became complete when the Bulls won their sixth championship after a heart-stopping game in Utah.

6. **THE SHOT**

It could have been the ending to a Disney movie. Hero, with seconds to spare, makes the shot that keeps the hopes and dreams of his team alive. Our hero in this case was Steve Kerr, and while he didn't make the game-winning shot with seconds to spare, he saved game six of the NBA finals by making the shot that broke the 86–86 tie and gave the Bulls the chance to win against Utah 90–86. Jordan, harassed by Jazz flocking around him, passed the ball to Kerr and in a perfect arc, Kerr shot the ball twenty feet to swish into the basket. Steve Kerr joined the Bulls as a free agent after bouncing around a number of teams. He led the league in three-point field goals in the 1989–1990 season with the Cavaliers, but they eventually traded him to Orlando during the 1992–1993 season. When he discovered that John Paxson was going to retire, he signed on with Chicago. With Jordan having retired, Kerr saw more action than he otherwise might have, but even when Jordan came back he'd made a name for himself on the team and proved to be a valuable member of the second three-peat run.

7. THE ∏AIL-BITER

The battle for the sixth trophy was an example of the amazing talent shown by both the Bulls and the Utah Jazz who, after losing the championship to the Bulls the year before, had no intention of letting it slip from their grasp in 1997–1998. It was a weakened team the Jazz met in the playoffs. For one thing, the Bulls started off slow thanks in part to Scottie Pippen missing the first thirty-five games of the season recuperating from foot surgery. Once Pippen got up to speed, and thanks to incredible backup from Toni Kukoc and Dennis Rodman, the Bulls still ended the season with a record of 62–20. The Jazz had home court advantage when they met in the playoffs and managed to win game one of the series. The Bulls won game two, then in Chicago walked away with game three, and squeaked to a win in game four. The Jazz weren't finished yet, though, winning game five and forcing the series back to Salt Lake. People questioned whether the Bulls had the stamina to see this contest through, but game six proved to be the fairy-tale ending for the team, the tough road to victory perhaps making it that much sweeter. Toni Kukoc was in top form that night, helping to pick up the slack for an injured Pippen by scoring fifteen points in some remarkable plays. But it was Jordan who silenced questions as to whether his age was holding him back. He'd been working hard throughout the whole game to keep the Bulls on top, but by the fourth quarter, his shots were coming up short. When the going gets tough, though, Jordan gets going. With 41.9 seconds remaining, Jordan whittled the Jazz's three-point lead down to one. Trying to extend the lead, Karl Malone got control of the ball only to have it stolen from his hands by Jordan who proceeded to hit the winning basket. Bulls won 87–86, taking the sixth trophy home to Chicago where the city waited to congratulate them.

8. IT AIN'T OVER TILL IT'S OVER

Chicago teams have a way of surprising the fan. By the end of the 1975–1976 season, the Bulls had ended with a record of 24–58, and lost a coach. Dick Motta resigned after a terrible season, and Ed Badger took over. In the 1976–1977 season, they sank to a 24–34 record and few saw much hope for a winning season. But a funny thing happened on the night of February 22. The Bulls began a seven-game winning streak by trampling Golden State 118–102. Buffalo took some of the wind out of their sails, but after that defeat they bounced back with an eight-game streak. They followed the previous season's dismal record with a respectable 44–38 record and best of all, made it into the playoffs. Portland won game one, 96–83, but the Bulls won game two 107–104. Unfortunately, the Trail Blazers proved themselves the better team by winning game three, 106–98, but Chicago proved something that year: you can count the Bulls down, but you shouldn't assume them out.

9. THE RIVALRY

While Bulls' fans cheer extra loudly when the Lakers or Knicks are defeated, it's Detroit that gets their blood heated the most, especially in the late 1980s and early '90s when both teams were coming into their own as major players in the NBA. But where the Bulls, coached by Phil Jackson and led by Michael Jordan, relied on talent to climb their way up the ranks, the Pistons resorted to nasty tactics on the court to elbow their way past their opponents. In 1987–1988, the Pistons finished with a record of 54–28, four games ahead of the Bulls. The teams faced each other in the playoffs and the Bulls spent the very close playoffs concerned about being blindsided by the Pistons. The Pistons developed the "Jordan Rules," double- and triple-teaming Michael Jordan, and weren't above knocking him down. The Pistons won the contest and the rivalry had begun. They met again the following season, and the Pistons won again, still playing dirty, but showing signs that they would be the dominant of the two teams. However, 1990–1991 would tell a different story. Meeting in the Eastern Conference Finals, Detroit unsuccessfully tried whatever they could to keep the Bulls down. The Bulls swept the series and moved on to the NBA finals. In sore loser fashion, the Pistons left the court without a second look at the Bulls. When the media recorded the team's snubbing of the customary congratulatory handshake, the Pistons' reputation only darkened. But perhaps their bad mood was understandable. The two teams had spent the past few years battling for dominance, the Pistons usually on top. As the 1990s progressed, one would pull ahead of the other and the Bulls did so, without elbows in the face.

10. SWEET GEORGIA BROWN

There was another basketball team from Chicago that might have given even Jordan and his Bulls a run for their money if they had ever met on a court. They were the Harlem Globetrotters, a team of African American basketball players from the South Side managed by Abe Saperstein, a twenty-four-year-old Jewish merchant from the North Side. Many of the big dance halls of the day scheduled basketball games to bring in people whom owners hoped would stay for the dancing. In 1927, a team of athletes from Wendell Phillips High School, then known as the American Legion Big Five, became the Savoy Big Five and played at the Savoy Ballroom. Along with coaching, Saperstein was promoter and traveling secretary, even filling in for injured players when necessary. When the Savoy let the team go, the Big Five went on the road, changing their name to the Harlem Globetrotters (Harlem since it was considered the center of black culture, and Globetrotters to give it a well-traveled feel). The team barnstormed the Midwest, often having to sleep in the car when racism turned them away from nicer lodging. Teams like the Globetrotters and the Harlem Renaissance were changing the slow pace of basketball, resorting to heavy defense and quick passing to win the games. In 1939, the Globetrotters made their first pro-basketball playoff, though they lost to the more experienced Harlem Renaissance. Few other teams, however, were a match for the Trotters. Scores like 112–5 were hardly unusual and the Trotters began to have a hard time finding teams willing to play them. To make games more exciting for themselves and the audience, the Trotters began clowning around on the court. The crowd ate it up. Since there were only five members on the team, the antics, such as the extended dribbling of Trotter great Marques Haynes, and continuous passing, enabled those not involved to get a breather. Saperstein wanted a serious pro team and he got it, the Trotters winning the World Professional Basketball Tournament in the 1940s and beating the Minneapolis Lakers in Chicago Stadium in 1948.

By the early 1950s, they were considered one of the best teams in the world. But the world may forever remember them for that extra zing they added to the game; the strains of their theme song, "Sweet Georgia Brown" as they warmed up in the "Magic Circle," passing the ball to each other with amazing speed and finesse; and the laughs brought on by players like Reece "Goose" Tatum, Meadowlark Lemon, and Curly Neal, gifted athletes and comedians. Many of the moves they started for fun can be seen in pro games today, such as spinning the ball on the finger, and Goose Tatum's move of holding the ball above his head in one hand when passing or shooting a hook shot. They were also able to make baskets by bouncing balls off their heads and even drop-kicking the balls into the net. Because they were un-conventional, the Trotters were also able to be the first team to sign a one-armed basketball player, Boid Buie, who joined the Trotters in 1945 and averaged eighteen points per game. In 1950, Nathaniel "Sweetwater" Clifton, a former Trotter, became the first African American to play in the NBA. A year later, the Globetrotters played in Berlin to 75,000 people, the largest crowd ever to see a basketball game, when they appeared in Berlin's Olympia Stadium. They played in a special audience for the Pope. In international tours, and dressed in their trademark red, white, and blue uniforms, they helped bring basketball to Africa and Asia. In 1982, the Globetrotters became the first and only sports team to be honored with a star on the Hollywood Walk of Fame. In 1985, Lynette Woodard became the first woman to play professionally for an all-male team when she joined the Trotters. She left in 1987 to play professionally in Italy and Japan. And let's not forget, the Trotters were the first basketball team to be marooned on Gilligan's Island. Well, let's forget that one. But they did inspire a cartoon and were a favorite in the 1970s on *ABC's Wide World of Sports.*

The Blackhawks

C hicago hockey has to compete with two well-established baseball teams, a football team, and a basketball team. In recent years the popularity of the Blackhawks has declined to the point where they've had to search for a TV station willing to run the games. While throughout its history the popularity of hockey has ebbed and flowed, success can simply be a matter of riding out the fickleness of the fans.

1. THE MIGHTY BLACKHAWKS

In the 1960s and early '70s, with players like Stan Mikita and Bobby Hull burning up the ice, the Hawks skated into the hearts of the town, but it took decades for the love affair to develop. At the team's debut on November 17, 1926, at the Chicago Coliseum, most of the 9,000 fans in attendance had never seen a hockey match. The Blackhawks, one of only ten teams in the NHL, were backed by a syndicate of over a hundred friends, headed by Major Frederick McLaughlin. The Manor House coffee tycoon bought the Portland Rosebuds franchise for $12,000 and moved them to Chicago. "Rosebuds" was hardly a name fitting the Windy City, so he chose another. There are two stories about the origin of the name. Either McLaughlin named the team in honor of the 333rd Machine Gun Battalion of the Eighty-Fifth (Blackhawk) Division of which he served as a commander during

World War I, or he named it after a restaurant he owned. Perhaps it was a little of both. Whatever the origins, the Chicago Blackhawks became the name of the team and McLaughlin's wife, famed dancer Irene Castle, designed the uniforms. While that opening game scored a team win, that first season the Hawks finished third. The disappointing season led McLaughlin to fire coach Pete Muldoon, the first of fourteen coaches he would fire in the next thirteen years. Retooling the team as well, he acquired greats like Charlie Gardiner, Doc Romnes, and Johnny Gottselig. The team improved which led to two Stanley Cup wins in 1933 and 1938, but the golden years soon tarnished. The 1940s saw a weaker team made worse by McLaughlin's death in 1944. The Major, inducted into the Hockey Hall of Fame in 1963, was definitely the spirit behind the franchise.

It wasn't until ownership passed to James Norris and Arthur Wirtz that the team started crawling back into prominence in the early 1950s. Creating a player development system incorporating junior and minor league teams, new general manager Tommy Ivan harvested players like Stan Mikita, Bobby and Dennis Hull, and Elmer "Moose" Vasko. It also led to winning the Stanley Cup in 1961. Most importantly it helped build fan enthusiasm. The loss of Bobby Hull in 1972 when he left for the Winnipeg Jets had a definite impact on that decade. Not only was the play off, but the team lost one of its biggest draws. The 1980s saw a bit more cohesion and a lot of color, which made Hawks tickets very hard to come by. The team reached the playoffs every year during that decade and the stadium rocked with rowdy fans. But then Chicago developed a new love affair with basketball. At a time when even baseball, Chicago's first sports love, felt slighted, the Blackhawks found themselves, once again, edged out of the Chicago psyche. If the team can follow the Bulls' lead and bring home consecutive Stanley Cups, perhaps they can stoke a jaded town's enthusiasm, which has dimmed the past few decades.

2. **THE GOLDEN JET**

Pure excitement on the ice, Bobby Hull thrilled hockey fans not only with a slap shot once clocked at 120 miles per hour but with his power and agility. Skating at thirty miles per hour, it wasn't unusual for The Golden Jet to attempt rink-length rushes for the goal. The fans loved his sense of humor, charisma, and affection for them. He was legendary for holding up team buses to sign autographs. Born in 1939, Bobby Hull grew up in Ontario and sped through the minor hockey system before joining the Blackhawks in 1957. His second year with the team he led the league with thirty-nine goals and eighty-one points. Winning the Art Ross Trophy, he made the NHL All-Star team twelve times. His curved hockey stick, developed with teammate Stan Mikita, provided the shooter with a faster shot that often acted more like a curve ball. With Mikita, the excitement of Hull's play brought excitement back to a comatose franchise, brought fans back into the stadium, and led to a Stanley Cup.

Trophies and records continued, including leading the league in goals for a record seven seasons, garnering three Art Ross Trophies for scoring. But where Stan Mikita ended up playing twenty-two seasons with the club, Hull found his time with the Hawks shortened by a fluke. When re-signing time came along, he demanded $250,000, a figure amazingly low considering what he gave the team. It was a price the Hawks were reluctant to pay, but one WHA team, the Winnipeg Jets, apparently weren't. After repeated entreaties from the Jets, Hull told his manager to demand $250,000, up front, for five years, in the hopes of shooing Winnipeg away. On the contrary, the Jets readily agreed. It was an offer too good to refuse. In 1972, he joined the Winnipeg Jets, leaving a hole in the heart of Chicago. Much like Ernie Banks and Walter Payton, however, Bobby Hull remained a favorite of the city even long after he left. His number 9 was eventually retired by the Hawks and he was inducted into the Hockey Hall of Fame in 1983.

3. A CHANGE OF TUNE

A legend in the story of the Hawks, Stan Mikita was quick to anger on the ice, dishing it out as much as he took it. Born in Czechoslovakia in 1940, as a boy he immigrated to Canada, where he lived with an aunt and uncle. It was here that he learned the sport of hockey and became quite famous locally. Catching the Hawks' eye, he signed on in 1956, starting with their junior affiliate, before joining the Hawks themselves in 1958, a year after Bobby Hull joined the team. Together, their play helped reignite interest in the franchise. Leading in scoring in the 1961 playoffs, he helped the Hawks win their third Stanley Cup. Quick-witted, with a vibrant personality, his aggressiveness as a player was just as notable. A hundred penalty minutes per season were logged in four of his first six seasons. After he became a family man, however, he began to rethink his way of playing. It was, in fact, his daughter who inspired him to change his ways, after she began to question his methods. His 1966–1967 season he registered only six minor penalties. Recognized for his change of heart, he won, in one season, the Art Ross Trophy for scoring, the Heart Memorial Trophy for MVP, and the Lady Byng Memorial Trophy for, of all things, sportsmanship. It was a new Stan Mikita. He pioneered the use of the curved stick blade, and designed a helmet popular with many players after he suffered a concussion. His talent was still evident as he racked up the records. He holds the records for seasons played, 22; for assists, 926; and for points, 1,467. He also acquired an interest in serving the community, helping to create the American Hearing Impaired Hockey Association where young players could participate in the game despite their handicap. When Mikita retired in 1980, his number, 21, was the first to be retired by the team after his induction into the Hockey Hall of Fame in 1983.

4. THE MADHOUSE ON MADISON

The old Chicago Stadium was like a member of the team. Visiting teams often felt off-kilter playing in the "Madhouse on Madison" because the acoustics could make the roar of the crowd sound like a jet taking off. It was built by Patrick T. "Paddy" Harmon, who'd been trying to buy the Blackhawks club until Frederick McLaughlin beat him to the team. Harmon decided instead to be a part of the team by building it a stadium, using $2.5 million of his own money and borrowing the rest from friends. On March 28, 1929, the Chicago Stadium at 1800 W. Madison Street was inaugurated by a boxing match between Tommy Loughran and Mickey Walker. The $187,000 gate set a new record for indoor receipts. The Hawks themselves had their first game there on December 15, 1929, beating the Pittsburgh Pirates 3–1 before a crowd of 14,212. That's when they realized just how valuable their new home was. "Remember the Roar" became the motto. With a 37,000-square-foot main floor, the stadium had over 16,600 seats, 8,000 more than Madison Square Garden. Architecturally state of the art, its innovative ventilation system delivered 600,000 cubic feet of fresh air to the building every minute.

The Chicago Stadium hosted events beyond hockey. Both Republicans and Democrats held conventions there. Muhammad Ali won the 1960 light-heavyweight Golden Gloves there when he was still Cassius Clay. Sinatra, Elvis, the Rolling Stones, and Kiss all performed there as well as the Chicago Opera, the rodeo, the ice show, and roller derby. It was even used for Anton J. Cermak's funeral in 1933. If the roar of the crowd wasn't enough to consternate the opposing team, in the mid-eighties the stadium acquired a foghorn to be blown every time a Blackhawk scored a goal. The Chicago Stadium was also home to the championship Chicago Bulls. Unfortunately, the man who built the grand stadium never lived to see how much the town would enjoy it. On July 22, 1930, Paddy Harmon's new Packard sedan flipped over and he was killed. His last wish was granted. He was laid out in his stadium as hundreds of people came to pay their respects. The Chicago Stadium has gone the way of the wrecking ball, the land now a parking lot for the United Center across the street. Three times the size of the old stadium, it still has a lot of living to do to acquire the character of the Madhouse on Madison.

5. NFL AT THE NHL

The Chicago Stadium played host to many varied events, but it was a strange sight indeed to see the first championship in NFL history played inside the Madhouse on Madison. It was December 18, 1932. Without an official home, the Chicago Bears used Wrigley Field for home games. But as helpful as snow can be to a Bears game, the blizzard that raged through Illinois that month, followed by freezing temperatures, made it impossible to play in the snowbound Wrigley. The stadium seemed the only alternative, so the game was moved there. With rinkside seats pushed back several inches, trucks dumped layers of dirt on the previously iced-over floor. Once tramped down, the lines were marked and painted. Despite the size of the stadium, the field was still only eighty yards long, so every time a team crossed midfield, it was sent back twenty yards. As games go, it left something to be desired. Playing the Ohio Portsmouth Spartans, a passing play between legends Bronko Nagurski and Red Grange scored the game's only touchdown. The Bears won the day 9–0, and later in their career the Spartans eventually moved to Detroit where their name was changed to the Lions.

6. MULDOON'S CURSE

The Cubs aren't the only team in Chicago said to be plagued by a curse. The Blackhawks were supposedly cursed as well. Time has revealed the truth, however, and truth is that Pete Muldoon's curse on the Blackhawks was born from a reporter's need to fill space and meet a deadline. The story goes like this: In 1926, Pete Muldoon became the Blackhawks' first coach and did what he could with what he had, guiding the Hawks, who scored 115 goals, more than any NHL club, to a third-place finish in the American Division. Not good enough, insisted owner Frederick McLaughlin, who felt the

Hawks could have ended the season in first place if the coaching had been up to par. So out goes Muldoon, in comes Barney Stanley. Muldoon didn't go quietly, though. Calling McLaughlin an "SOB" he placed an "Irish Curse" on the team that would keep them out of first place forever. In light of Stanley Cup wins in '34, '38, and '61, it's possible that the curse could have been laughed off. But, considering all the sour seasons and forty years without a win, it wasn't unusual for journalists and broadcasters to contemplate Muldoon's curse as a cause. The thing is, the story of Muldoon's curse is just that, a story, concocted by Canadian sportswriter James Coleman who worked for the *Toronto Globe and Mail*. Many decades after that first shaky season, Jim Coleman admitted that it was a rush to meet the deadline for his column that led to the story. A drinking man, as many journalists were back then, Coleman found himself with the deadline looming, and a story short. So, to meet his obligation, he wrote the story, even inventing the exchange between Muldoon and McLaughlin as a way to explain the Hawks' poor record. In some respects, in the 1926 season, it's amazing they reached third considering that they won only nineteen out of forty-four games, losing twenty-two and tying three. Coleman himself never suspected that the story of Muldoon's curse would take on the legendary status it has over the years, yet some people are easily led. And who knows? Perhaps when McLaughlin died in 1944, it gave him peace of mind to think that it was the supernatural keeping his team from the number-one spot so often.

7. **THEIR OWN WORST ENEMY**

Few team sports are more prone to violence than hockey. Brawls on the ice are practically expected as testosterone gets out of hand and molehills turn into mountains. In March 1933, that molehill turned out to be what Chicago manager Tommy Gorman created when he felt a goal light was flashed before the goal went over the line. The Boston Bruins and Blackhawks were playing overtime in a 2–2 game. In the third minute of the extra period (back then a full ten minutes was played before a winner was declared) that goal by Boston put the Bruins in the lead. So furious was Gorman by what he thought was a preemptive goal decision, that, cursing, he grabbed referee Bill Stewart by the jersey as he skated past the Hawks' bench. Stewart's snarled response only poured gas on Gorman's already lit fuse. He attacked Stewart, who managed to get a few punches in before Gorman pulled off his jersey. When the referee broke free and ordered Gorman off the ice, Gorman refused to leave. As police escorted the ejected manager off, his loyal team followed, arguing with police who threatened jail time if the team didn't settle down. The Hawks were given one minute to return to the ice. Thanks to their stubborn refusal to comply, Stewart called the game in the Bruins' favor. Never before had a game been forfeited in such a manner. Later, Gorman would claim that Stewart struck first. To his credit, Stewart said little except to explain that the action the Hawks chose was a breach of the rules resulting in the loss of two points. A fine was assessed at $1,000. Ironically, four years later, Bill Stewart would be hired as coach of the very team he had fined, and would take them to a Stanley Cup championship.

8.   GO FIGURE

They won only fourteen of their forty-eight regular season games and finished barely two points ahead of the last-place Detroit. They had the weakest offense in the NHL, scoring only 97 goals, while their defense gave up 139 goals. Their coach had been an NHL ref, but had never played the game nor coached a hockey team in his life. The team owner was so sure that they'd lose a late-season lead that he sent the team's extra equipment back home before they'd played their last three road games. And yet, to the astonishment of many, the 1938 Chicago Blackhawks won the Stanley Cup. Even player Alex Levinsky, expecting not to see the playoffs, emptied his apartment, sending his wife back to Canada where he promised to join her in a few days. A month later, he was living out of his car. As is often the case, the team's standing depended not only on how they played, but how other teams played. For example, the Hawks did end up losing their last three games, but the Detroit Red Wings, losing two of their last three games, gave Chicago the chance to get back into the playoffs. Ironically, Bill Stewart, the same man who, as a referee, kicked former Hawks coach Tommy Gorman off the ice for fighting with him five years earlier, came to blows with the president and general manager of the Toronto Maple Leafs before game one of the playoffs. Whatever magical influence overcame the team that year, the 1938 team came away from the season as champions, and in Chicago, that's good enough.

9. THE ROVING SCOTSMAN

Only one goaltender has had his name appear on the Stanley Cup as the captain of a winning team. His name was Charlie Gardiner and he was willing to do whatever it took to keep that puck out of the net. Born in Edinburgh, Scotland, in 1904, he became known as the "Roving Scotsman" because of his aggressive style of goaltending. Rather than wait for the puck to come to him, he rushed out to meet it, intimidating anyone making a run for the goal. In his 316 regular season games, only 664 pucks slipped past his stick. Many still consider him one of the best goaltenders of all times. His energy also made him the driving force behind the Blackhawks' 1933–1934 Stanley Cup season when he was named captain of the team. By that season, he'd already been named to three NHL All-Star teams, and had won the Vezina Trophy (for lowest goals-against average) for the 1931–1932 season (a win he would repeat in 1933–1934). He suffered bouts of illness during that season but wouldn't let this keep the team from a winning season. In fact, it was after game three of the playoffs against the Detroit Red Wings that he spent the night in the hospital after becoming ill. A scuffle between Gardiner and fellow Hawk Johnny Gottselig over the lost game led owner Frederick McLaughlin to toss both players into a cold shower to cool them off. Later that night Gardiner took ill, but he insisted on playing the fourth game at the Chicago Stadium, which turned out to be an exciting match that remained scoreless the first sixty minutes. The winning goal was scored by Mush March after thirty minutes of overtime. Gardiner gained his second Vezina Trophy and a trip around the Loop in a wheelbarrow. Fellow Hawk Roger Jenkins had so little faith in the team's chances that he vowed he would wheel Charlie around the Loop in a barrow if they beat the Red Wings. Detroit went down and Gardiner went for a spin downtown pushed by a chagrined yet jubilant Jenkins. The young goalie seemed to have a great future ahead of him, but sadly, it wasn't to be. Two months after the Stanley Cup win, Charlie Gardiner was dead, felled by a brain hemorrhage while visiting his home in Winnipeg at the age of twenty-nine. Despite a shortened career, Gardiner will always be remembered as one of the best goaltenders in the sport, the Roving Scotsman rushing out to meet the puck.

10. THE LOUDEST MEMBER OF THE TEAM

It was once boasted that the organ at the Chicago Stadium was the largest in the world. There were 883 stops, 9 tiers, 6 rows of keys, 4,000 pipes, and it required twenty-four railroad cars to transport its pieces from its birthplace in Oshkosh, Wisconsin, to the Chicago Stadium. At full volume, it could simulate the sound of twenty-five brass bands. And in the driver's seat was Al Melgard, offering background music to underscore the action on the ice. Referees might be teased with the song "Three Blind Mice" (until the NHL ordered him to stop). A need to perk up enthusiasm from the crowd would bring forth the familiar salvo "Charge!"—the fans responding with a deafening roar. So powerful was this organ that one night, in an effort to break up a riot that was brewing in the stands, Melgard pounded the keys with a force that shattered windows in the stadium. The desired effect was accomplished as the fans cooled down. The son of a blacksmith,

Melgard learned about wind pressure at his father's bellows and paid a young female organist seventy-five cents a lesson to teach him how to play. Melgard was already an established musician by 1929 when he was hired to play the huge organ at the Chicago Stadium. Over the years he recorded a number of albums using the stadium organ, and his skill and sense of humor made him a favorite of visitors to the home of the Hawks. In October of 1974, Al retired to Las Vegas, leaving the huge Barton organ to his apprentice, Ron Bogde. After the stadium closed in 1994, the organ was hauled in seven semis to the Lyons, Illinois, nightclub of Bob Roppolo, who had purchased it from the stadium. From there, he moved it to Arizona but sold the console to Phil Maloof after the pipes were destroyed in a fire. Maloof had the organ restored and installed in his family's Fiesta Casino Hotel in Las Vegas.

Infamous Females

Naughty women prowled the streets of Chicago. Here are a few.

1. THE WOMAN IN RED

Promised $58,000 and dropped deportation proceedings, Anna Sage handed John Dillinger over to the FBI. An illegal immigrant from Romania, she arrived in the country in 1919 and came to East Chicago, Indiana, where local cop Martin Zarkovich protected her brothel from the law in exchange for a little kickback. In June 1934, she started business at 2420 N. Halsted in Chicago and met Dillinger, offering him prostitute Polly Hamilton to give him solace after his plastic surgery. Feeling slighted, Martin Zarkovich decided to tell G-man Melvin Purvis about Dillinger's cozy arrangement and Purvis drew Sage into his scheme to catch Dillinger by holding deportation over her head. On the steamy night of July 22, 1934, Dillinger, Sage, and Hamilton exited the Biograph after seeing *Manhattan Melodrama*. The red (actually more of an orange) dress Sage wore helped feds pinpoint Public Enemy Number One. As Dillinger passed by, Purvis signaled to his men. Sensing a setup near the alley, Dillinger whirled around and was hit by four shots. He collapsed with a bullet in the back of his neck and two in his left side. People dipped their handkerchiefs in Dillinger's blood, and he was sent to

Alexian Brothers Hospital, pronounced dead, then sent to the morgue. Just as Anna Sage betrayed Dillinger, she was betrayed by the government. Denied the $58,000, she was sent back to Europe as an undesirable in 1936. Little is known about her after that, though it seems she tried to make the best of the situation by traveling around Europe and the Middle East under assumed names.

2. **EVERLY YOURS**

Ada and Minna Lesters' grandmother ended her letters, "Everly Yours," so the Lesters became the Everleighs and became known for owning the best little whorehouse in Chicago. Opening in 1900, the Everleigh Club on South Dearborn Street was far from your average whorehouse. An upscale affair, clients were charged for superior service. Fifty dollars got you dinner and an evening with a lady in a sumptuously appointed parlor—fourteen were even soundproof. The Gold Room, for example, was trimmed in gold and featured a miniature grand piano. Others were styled in themes like Rose, Green, Chinese, and Egyptian, and there were also a library, an art gallery, silk curtains, mahogany staircases, and oil paintings. Those unable to pay were encouraged not to return. This was, after all, a very lucrative business, not only for the sisters and their ladies, but also for the Levee police and aldermen paid to look away. Seemingly sweet and unassuming, these little southern belles escaped unhappy marriages to tour the country as actresses. Migrating to Chicago after running a profitable brothel in Omaha, they opened up their pleasure palace in a fifty-room mansion. Sadly, though, all good things must come to an end, and the Everleigh Club was no exception. Perhaps their biggest mistake was publishing a brochure advertising their club. Mayor Carter Harrison II, bowing to pressure to clean up vice, ordered the club closed. On October 25, 1911, the doors were closed for good. After taking a six-month vacation in Italy on their $1 million in savings, the sisters returned to Chicago, but were unable to open another club. Minna died in 1948. Ada died at the age of ninety-three. As close as they were in life, they remain so in death, buried next to each other near Roanoke, Virginia.

3. RAZZLE DAZZLE

On March 11, 1924, an auto salesman named Walter Law was found dead in his car of a gunshot wound to the head. The case inspired the recent hit musical *Chicago*, based on two true murder cases. Your honor, I give you defendant number one—Belva Gaertner, a twice-divorced cabaret singer who by the end of 1923 was thirty-eight and having an affair with Walter Law. Found at her apartment with bloody clothes on the floor, Belva fully admitted to bar-hopping jazz clubs with Law the night of his death, but details were sketchy. Positive she didn't kill him, her theory was that he might have committed suicide. A man with a wife and child having an affair might be eaten up with guilt. A coworker of Law's testified at the trial that an obsessive Belva had threatened him with a knife when he tried to leave her. Indeed, Maurine Watkins, the reporter for the *Chicago Tribune* following the case, uncovered juicy details about one of Gaertner's marriages that was so troubled Belva and her husband often hired private eyes to follow each other. And it was Belva who was caught with her pants not only down, but off. When the Law case went to trial, Gaertner faced life in prison or death by hanging for the murder. There was no singing or dancing in the courtroom but there was plenty of razzle dazzle as Gaertner's defense team followed W.W. O'Brien's successful strategy from another notorious case and played up Gaertner's classy, very feminine demeanor (she was even called the "most stylish" woman on Murderess Row). The elegant act paid off and the all-male jury acquitted Gaertner of Law's murder. Gaertner remarried her second husband and traveled off to Europe, eventually disappearing into her freedom.

4. HULA BEULAH

Less than a month after Belva Gaertner was arrested for murder, another glamorous defendant came to Murderess Row.

Beulah Annan, a typical young housewife, shot her lover after he attacked her when she told him she was ending the affair. At least, that was her story, and she stuck to it, or tried to. Of course, that Beulah then spent the next two hours drinking and repeatedly listening to the same record, "Hula Lou," while her lover, Harvey Kalstedt, slowly bled to death, seemed suspicious. Only after Kalstedt died did she think to call her husband. In her confession to police, she claimed the gun had been in the bed when each reached for it, and it went off. Interestingly, Annan made at least three confessions, Kalstedt morphing from an acquaintance trying to rape her, to a lover enraged over an ended affair, to a bedmate shot in the back by a misfired gun. Belva and Beulah were both attractive and witty, and Beulah scored sympathy points when she announced her pregnancy. Like Gaertner, Annan was acquitted of the crime thanks in large part to the tactics of mob lawyer W. W. O'Brien, who used Annan's beauty to influence the all-male jury and manipulated the press to influence public opinion. Surprise, surprise, she never did give birth, but hers was not a happy ending. After divorcing her cuckolded husband, she married another, finding out later that he was already married. Suffering a breakdown, she was institutionalized and died in 1928 of undisclosed causes. Her life would later be fictionalized by *Tribune* reporter Maurine Watkins and became a hit play, a movie with Ginger Rogers, a hit musical directed by Bob Fosse, and a hit musical movie, starring Richard Gere, Renee Zellweger, and Catherine Zeta-Jones.

5. THE BLONDE TIGRESS

Dubbed "The Blonde Tigress," on August 8, 1940, Eleanor Jarman escaped over the wall of the Illinois State Women's Prison in Dwight, Illinois. You wouldn't have suspected it from her five foot, five inch, 110-pound frame, but there was a hellcat locked inside her, and on the afternoon of August 4, 1933, she let that fury go on Gustav Hoeh, a haberdasher. According to reports, that afternoon two men and a woman burst out of Hoeh's on Division Street. The seventy-one-year-old Hoeh put up a valiant fight, but the woman clawed and scratched at him, beating him to the pavement. After a shot rang out, the woman and the other man jumped into a car and fled. When Eleanor Jarman and her boyfriend, George Dale, were picked up less than a week later, along with Hoeh's murder they were implicated in forty-eight armed robberies. Jarman's weapon du jour was a blackjack, which she used to smack victims around. Witnesses claimed she used the blackjack on Hoeh before Dale shot him. Dale was sentenced to death for Hoeh's murder, while Jarman received 199 years in prison. She spent seven years in prison before making her escape. The ten-foot fence with barbed wire at the top never deterred her. She went over the fence and switched her prison attire for a dress stolen from staff headquarters. The FBI set one of the biggest dragnets in U.S. history, and Chicago police labeled her "the most dangerous woman alive." If she were still alive today, she'd be nearly 100 years old—far too old to cause any harm. But then again, you never know about hellcats.

6. **THE GOLD DIGGER**

Underworld kingpin Mike McDonald was a pro at manipulation and violence. He fell hard for Dora Feldman when he saw her dancing in a vaudeville show. His wealth influenced Dora, who eloped with McDonald immediately after her divorce from her former husband was made final. Mike had a troubled marital past himself. His first wife cheated on him with a priest in a special private chapel that she had asked Mike to build for her. But Mike and his second wife were happy initially. Then Dora began pursuing Webster S. Guerin, a youth living across the street from them, and the two carried on an affair for several years before she began to question his commitment. In a suite at the Omaha Building, when Guerin's brother brought his young fiancée along, Dora became obsessed with the idea that the fiancée would make a successful play for her lover. At last, on February 21, 1907,

Dora confronted Guerin, and after a brief quarrel, fatally shot the young man in the neck. Bursting into the suite, tenants found her covered in blood, screaming that he had shot himself. Still in love, Mike McDonald did whatever he could to help her. The defense cooked up stories about Dora's fragile state of mind, implying that the young man was a stalker. Succumbing to his embarrassed grief in St. Anthony's Hospital, even in death McDonald protected his unfaithful wife, leaving money to finance her defense. Feigning madness, she attempted suicide twice, carrying the act on long after her trial began in January 1908. Unable to prove who the stalker was and who the victim was, in the end the jury acquitted her and Dora was instantly cured of her hysteria. Free from jail and from Mike McDonald, she went on with her life.

7. THE TORSO MURDER

It begins in 1934 with a love triangle between a mother, a daughter, and the daughter's husband. Blanche Dunkel was not a smart woman, but she managed to keep a roof over the heads of herself, her daughter Mallie Lang, and son-in-law Ervin Lang. But living under the same roof was vexing Blanche since she was beginning to fall in love with her son-in-law. Mother and daughter fought over this, but Mom refused to let go. Ervin and Blanche engaged in an affair that lasted for months, but after a frail Mallie died from grief, Blanche's guilt turned into hatred for her son-in-law. Not helping matters was the fact that he quickly found a new lover to warm his bed. Blanche's sister put her in touch with Evelyn Smith, who had come to America from Germany at a young age. Evelyn's father had died of pneumonia, her younger sister was killed in a bonfire accident, and her mother had died from the grief. Evelyn rode the rails until she landed in Chicago, in 1932, and married Harry Jung, who had established a chain of laundries with his brothers. Suggesting murder, Smith offered the services of her husband. Using $100 of Lang's own money as a down payment on the hit, Blanche gave Smith the go-ahead. Lured to

Smith's apartment, Lang was dosed with sedative-laced booze, and, after dismissing Blanche, Smith administered ether, tied the victim up, and choked him to death in the closet. Once her husband arrived on the scene with a saw, Evelyn went to work dismembering the body. The remains, placed inside a trunk, were taken to a swamp near Hammond, Indiana. Four days later, the torso was discovered near Wolf Lake, the legs in a roadside ditch near Munster. Smith had already taken to the road again, but she was caught in New York within two days of the discovery. Blanche's sister had gone to the police about the whole affair. In a twisted insult to her own daughter, when Blanche was taken to view the remains in Indiana, she admitted to her part in the death, stating that Lang had been her common-law husband. Evelyn and Blanche were both sentenced to 180 years and ordered to spend the anniversary every year of the death in solitary confinement.

8. THEY MEANT WELL

Despite their good intentions, the work of the temperance workers paved the way for the violence of the 1920s, and organized crime might not have become the giant it did were it not for those lucrative days of Prohibition. The temperance worker had only good intentions in her heart. Survival was a tenuous thing in the poverty-laden ghettos of cities that grew too fast for their own good. For many, drink softened the edges of a hard existence. Women who saw their own families affected by alcohol abuse joined temperance leagues in the hopes of keeping other women from suffering their fate. They felt the nation would be stronger if its citizens put down the glass. They appealed to the saloonkeeper to stop selling the liquor, equating it with sin and playing on the fear of eternal damnation. Sometimes their efforts were successful, while sometimes they were scorned. The greatest hope of the temperance movement was realized when the Volstead Act took effect in 1920 and many people stopped drinking. But many more started because it is a well-known fact of human nature that something taken away is craved the most. Drinking went underground, joining the other vices, and feeding the world of crime. The temperance worker pictured a drink-free utopia and worked tirelessly to make this a better world. But outlawing an addiction won't take it away, and, in this case, it only made things worse.

9. FIELDS OF GOLD

Few prospects outside of marriage existed for women in the nineteenth century. Those who didn't marry often found themselves earning their daily bread in the brothels on the Levee. Some became madams, gaining a power almost as potent as the politicians who came to frequent their establishments. Vina Fields, a large African American woman, ran a respectable establishment and treated her girls well. She offered black girls for white clientele, running the biggest brothel in town, which often housed more than forty boarders and employed over seventy prostitutes. It did twice as much business during the 1893 World's Fair. Fields was a stickler for rules and never bribed a policeman, yet her brothel was never raided. There was no drunkenness allowed in her place, no nudity outside the bedrooms, no hustling from windows. Hers was a classy place and anyone unable to follow the rules was banished. Fields could afford to ride around town in a white carriage with bright yellow wheels. It was said that she even had a higher tax bracket than some members of the board of trade. And this money enabled her to raise her daughter (who knew nothing of where the money came from) in a convent school, as well as support the families of her southern sisters. During the panic of 1893, she offered food to help the destitute. It was interesting that Fields, the madam of a brothel, would have a daughter in a convent school. But then this unwed mother running a whorehouse believed that the problem with society was that women had forgotten that their highest ambition in life should be raising a family. A clear-cut case of "Do as I say, not as I do."

10. **WHITE SLAVER**

Not every madam was as genteel as the Everleighs or Vina Fields. White slavers were everywhere in Chicago, kidnapping teenaged girls and forcing them to work as prostitutes. The girls were drugged, broken in by being raped, and then sold to a brothel. Here they would ply their trade, addicted to drugs, with little future in sight. Mary Hastings ran such a place. She herself had seen her share of brothels in Europe, Canada, and the northwestern United States, before arriving in Chicago in 1888 and opening her own place. Interestingly, she became something of a Norma Rae for prostitutes' rights by complaining that the bribes Chicago police demanded of her were too high. Without the bribes, a cop was not above pulling out one of the generic warrants they carried, enabling them to arrest anyone whose actions seemed guilty of the crimes on the warrants. Hastings sued, claiming that the warrants were illegal, and a high court upheld her argument. This did little for the girls who worked for her. She assured her clients that whatever horrible act they desired, her girls would perform. Many of the girls in her establishment, some as young as thirteen, had been lured in and "broken in" to join the ranks of her prostitutes. These were hardworking girls, working from noon to 5 A.M., usually spending the day sipping absinthe or drinking other liquor, sitting in the windows to tempt whatever customers they could. Johns came in, paying the $5 fee (an incredible amount for the time) to literally have their way with the girls. The customers themselves weren't above being abused, either, often leaving with a wallet much lighter than when they came in. A little justice served cold.

Landmarks

Whether statues, buildings, or streets, landmarks abound in this historic city, bringing with them reminders of that history.

1. THE PICASSO

It's a bird, it's a plane. The age-old question has been, "What the heck is that thing that Picasso gave to Chicago?" It's been said to represent the head of a woman with long flowing hair. Others have seen in it the head of a horse. Whatever it is, seeing a picture of it makes you instantly think, "Oh yeah, that's that thing in Chicago." At fifty feet high and weighing 162 tons, the creature stands in Daley Plaza at 50 W. Washington Street, its plates and rods of self-weathering corrosive tensile steel impervious to high winds and winter snowfalls. It was William Harmann, a senior partner of Skidmore, Owings and Merrill, who visited Pablo Picasso in the south of France and persuaded him to design the piece that the eighty-two-year-old artist graciously donated to the city. Dedicated on August 15, 1967, in some respects it is a perfect representation of Chicago. There's an ungainly charm to it that grows on you—like the city itself.

2. BUCKINGHAM FOUNTAIN

At a cost of $750,000 the fountain, at one time the largest in the world, was presented to the city by Kate Sturges Buck-

What is that thing? Picasso's curious work of art looms
over an outdoor festival in Daley Plaza.

Betty Schmidt of J.T. Schmidt and Associates, Inc. (Crystal Lake, Ill.)

Grant Park's Buckingham Fountain, completed in 1927,
is one of Chicago's most-recognized landmarks.
In the background, the Amoco Building towers above the park.

ingham, who also endowed $300,000 for operating expenses. A band led by John Philip Sousa played "Stars and Stripes Forever" as the fountain was unveiled on August 26, 1927, in honor of Kate's brother, Clarence, a trustee and benefactor of the Art Institute. Architects Bennett, Parsons and Frost, of Chicago, following Buckingham's wishes, designing a fountain inspired by, but almost twice the size, of the Latona Basin in Louis XIV's gardens at Versailles. The fountain handles a million and a half gallons of water and recirculates at the rate of 15,000 gallons a minute. The computer-programmed water displays and special flood-lights create nightly colored arrays of lights in green, amber, blue, red, and white, that dance upon the water sprays. Three circular basins chiseled from Georgia pink marble sit one atop the other, decorated with carved sea creatures. Four twenty-foot-long bronze "sea horses" stand facing the basins in quadrant positions and spit water back at it. The whole work stands in a base pool that is 280 feet in diameter. This stunning fountain is a fixture of the city, always a favorite with tourists and a backdrop for wedding party pictures. Kate Buckingham would be proud that her gift has given the city such pleasure.

3. THE OLD CHICAGO WATER TOWER

It looks like a mini-castle. The Old Chicago Water Tower on North Michigan Avenue was designed by architect W. W. Boyington, who used a tall tower to house a 138-foot stand-pipe that equalized the pressure of the water pumped from the Pumping Station. Visiting Chicago in 1882, Oscar Wilde referred to it as a "castellated monstrosity with pepper boxes stuck all over it." And indeed, the miniature Gothic battle-ments do seem a bit of overkill. But it's a relic of a time when such embellishments represented strength. While it might seem very much out of style now, it still stands as a monu-ment, beloved by the citizens of Chicago, of a city that still stands strong. The Water Tower, now serving as a tourist in-formation center, is one of the buildings that escaped de-struction in the Great Fire of 1871. It stands tall and bright, as striking as the city itself.

4. THE FLAMINGO

Artist Alexander Calder named this piece "Flamingo" be-cause it had the look of one from the work's vermilion color and its graceful lines. From a certain angle, though, it looks more like a giant orange bug terrorizing Federal Plaza on Dearborn. Three steel plates sit on their points while two huge soaring arches spring from them, bringing the piece's height up to fifty-three feet. Unveiled in 1974, the piece cost $250,000, but unlike many public sculptures this is an interactive one as pedestrians can walk under and through it, getting to know the bug on a more intimate level.

5. **THE WRIGLEY BUILDING**

Not only a fine example of early Chicago architecture, the gleaming white terra-cotta of the Wrigley Building has become a landmark of Chicago. One glimpse of that eleven-story clock tower and you know where you are. Standing at the north end of the Michigan Avenue Bridge, it was designed by Graham Anderson of Anderson Probst and White, and remains the headquarters of the Wrigley Company. The South Tower was built in 1919 and completed in 1922, while the North Tower was started in 1924 and finished the next year. The towers are connected at the lobby level and by an upper-level skywalk. The Wrigley Plaza at the base of the building was designed in 1957, and contains plantings and a fountain scaled to fit the narrow area. The Wrigley Building has been seen in a number of movies and TV shows set in Chicago and was the scene of a risky publicity stunt by silent-film star Harold Lloyd back in the 1920s. Lloyd's 1923 comedy *Safety Last* has a nail-biting scene of Lloyd hanging from the hands of a clock outside a tall building. Lloyd, the Jackie Chan of his day, was going to promote the movie by breaking a bottle of champagne on the clock tower of the Wrigley Building. As 10,000 fans watched, Lloyd was seen heading up to the top of the building. At the very top, however, a double for Lloyd waited to be lowered to the clock face and complete the stunt. But the winds were so fierce around the clock tower that Lloyd's double decided that he didn't need the money that badly and backed out. Lloyd, himself, also exhibited common sense when he refused to do the stunt. Those in the crowd below, however, were good sports about the whole thing when told the truth and the stunt, even truncated, garnered the movie great publicity anyway.

6. **ART INSTITUTE LIONS**

They stand on guard at the west entrance of the Art Institute of Chicago. Cast in bronze, the two huge male lions have stood there since the building opened as the institute's permanent home. Prior to that, they'd been simply plaster models on display at the Jackson Park fairgrounds during the World's Columbian Exposition. They were designed by Edward Kemeys, a noted animal sculptor who also achieved distinction for being self-taught. Others of Kemeys's bronze creations prowl Central Park in New York. After the exposition, the lions were cast in bronze and were presented to the institute by Mrs. Henry Field. Eternally vigilant, they nonetheless seem unfazed by the many pats and pets given them by admiring institute visitors over the years. And they even suffered the huge football helmets put on their heads during the Bears' incredible 1985 season. They'll stand on guard over the institute and their city for as long as the city will have them.

7. **MERCHANDISE MART HEADS**

In some respects, there's a gothic feel to this row of heads on spikes facing the Merchandise Mart. Known as the Merchandise Mart Hall of Fame, it's an homage to capitalism brought to us by Joseph P. Kennedy (yes, that Kennedy family), who purchased the massive Merchandise Mart from Marshall Field in 1945. Lining the embankment of the Chicago River, the bronze busts, four times larger than life and mounted on tall marble pillars, honor eight merchants who helped build this country: Marshall Field (King of Chicago), George Hungtington Hartford (founder of the Great Atlantic & Pacific Tea Co.), John R. Wanamaker (founder of John Wanamaker Inc.), Frank Winfield Woolworth (founder of F.W. Woolworth Company), Edward Filene (president of Wilbur Filene and Sons), Julius Rosenwald (president and chairman of the board of Sears, Roebuck and Company), General Robert E. Wood (a later president and board chairman of Sears), and Aaron Montgomery Ward (founder of Montgomery Ward and Company). Several artists from across the country were commissioned to create the busts which were dedicated on June 30, 1953, members of the Kennedy clan on hand, including future president John F.

8. TOTEM POLE

Surrounded by an iron fence, the Lincoln Park Totem Pole, also known as Kwa-Ma-Rolas, rises forty feet into the air and adds a touch of whimsy to the surroundings. The founder of Kraft, Inc., James L. Kraft, gave the pole to the Chicago Park District in 1929, after obtaining it in 1926 during a collecting trip to Alaska and the Pacific Northwest. Dedicated by Kraft to the schoolchildren of the city, the pole had been carved from a single log by Kwakiutl Indians at Alert Bay, Vancouver Island, British Columbia. Several tribes of the forested regions along the Pacific Ocean were known to carve totem poles to celebrate births, deaths, and other auspicious occasions. The colorful Lincoln Park Pole has the image of a sea monster at its base, which supports an upside down baleen whale with a man riding the back of it. At the top, perched on the whale's tail, is a member of the Thunderbird family known as a "kulos."

9. ETERNAL SILENCE

On the grave of Dexter Graves, a hotel owner and businessman who came to Chicago in the early 1800s, there stands a figure, hooded and draped in a flowing robe, one arm raised and partially obscuring its face. This is Eternal Silence. Housed in the southeastern section of Graceland Cemetery, the bronze figure, eight feet high, has a face darkened and shadowed by its hood. Created by Loredo Taft, its enigmatic aura encourages the viewer to ponder the meaning of life and death. In fact, one of the haunting legends surrounding it claims that those who look into the face of the statue may get a vision of their final fate. It was also believed that any picture taken of it would never turn out, but countless pictures of the figure have proven this legend false. Graceland Cemetery is known for many elaborate tomb statues and monuments. The notable aspect of Eternal Silence is its stark simplicity.

10.   THE CANYON

They call it the "Canyon," that section of La Salle Street that runs right into the Chicago Board of Trade facing it on Jackson Boulevard. Not so much a landmark, but a landmark area, it's been featured in a number of films, including *The Untouchables*, *Mad Dog and Glory*, and *Hoodlum*. They call it the "Canyon" because at first glance the skyscrapers lining each side and the Board of Trade at the end of it resemble a dead end in a canyon until you realize that there is a cross street (Jackson Blvd.). It has a slightly claustrophobic courtyard feel to it, the art deco buildings competing with each other for superiority, towering over the pedestrians walking through it. It is that other side of Chicago, the steel-and-concrete side, desperate for space, with little choice but to build up and practically on top of itself.

Radio

The various entertainment industries found homes in Chicago and radio was no exception. Chicago has been the home to some heavy hitters in the history of radio.

1. STEVE DAHL

In California, radio personalities like Bob Crane and Lohman and Barkley inspired young Steve Dahl to explore radio's potential to entertain. Dropping out of the tenth grade, he hosted a morning show in Southern California before moving on to Detroit where his personality came out and he began doing bits, adding voices provided by him. By the time station bosses were aware of the direction his show was taking, it was a hit. Radio listeners hadn't heard anything like it before. What set Dahl apart from others that would follow was his sincerity. He was speaking his mind, not merely saying things for effect. In later years, when he provided fetus updates before the birth of his first son, both the joy and the anxiety were clear in his voice. He shared his personal life, the ups and the downs, and gained an intimate relationship with his audience. His judgment wasn't always impeccable; some bits were questionable, but Dahl was more often than not the first one criticizing his decision. By the time the late WDAI in Chicago lured him away in 1978, Dahl had the number one AM and FM show in Detroit. He came to town with his cast of characters, and listeners were treated to the sort of radio not heard for decades. After disco invaded DAI, Dahl landed at rock station WLUP where he formed a successful partnership with Garry Meier that lasted for many years and many radio stations. Their battles with management were legendary, usually stemming from the programmers' desire to control the show. From WLUP to WLS and eventually to WCKG, they became one of the most influential teams on radio. Broadcasts from Hawaii became an annual event, and they staged remotes and concerts. Their performance of *A Christmas Carol* at the Broadcast Museum remains a classic as they and a cast of local news, sports, and TV stars strayed constantly and hilariously from the script. Steve and Garry won many awards, including an Emmy for their TV special "Greetings from Graceland" but in 1993, Meier suddenly called it quits, citing irreconcilable differences with Steve. It was not only a blow to fans, but to Dahl as well. Both moved on, however, Dahl remaining at CKG, trying out a number of sidekicks before hitting upon three who worked. He remains top dog, though, still a force to be reckoned with in Chicago radio, celebrating twenty-five years with the city in 2003.

2. **WMAQ**

On August 1, 2000, Chicago's oldest radio station ended its broadcast day for the last time. WMAQ had been home to some of the most successful shows of old-time radio and was a powerhouse in local radio, but in the end it lost out to a fledgling sports radio station. It all started in 1922 when the *Chicago Daily News* joined the Fair Department Store to create WMAQ, or "We Must Ask Questions" radio. Purchasing the department store's share in 1923, the *Daily News* moved the station's broadcast to the LaSalle Hotel and in 1920 to the *Daily News* Building. WMAQ aired programs devoted to the household, children's programming, educational, and, of course, music. They were also pioneers in sports broadcasting when, in 1925, station program director Judith Waller worked out a deal with William Wrigley to broadcast Cubs games from Wrigley Field (eventually, WGN would become the home of Cubs baseball). As the years went by, the station would air games from all major teams in town as well as college football and basketball. In 1931, WMAQ became a network affiliate when it was purchased by NBC, and the station's operations were moved to the ninetheenth floor of the Merchandise Mart where NBC's early TV broadcasts also originated, eventually becoming WMAQ-TV. In the 1960s, WMAQ switched to music, changing from rock to country during the 1970s and 1980s, then in 1985 turning to a talk format. Among its hosts was the raucous Morton Downey Jr. When NBC was bought by General Electric, new ownership laws dictated that NBC had to make a choice between keeping TV stations or radio stations. It sold its radio stations to Group W–Westinghouse, who brought in a news format, and the station joined WMAQ-TV in the new NBC tower in 1990. When Group W merged with CBS, which already had a news radio station, WBBM, the company owned too many stations. They decided it was time to give their new sports station, WSCR, a shot by handing WMAQ's frequency to the Score. And with that, a piece of radio history was silenced.

3. WGN

The powerhouse of Chicago radio was started by the Tribune Company in 1924 that modestly chose call letters that stood for "World's Greatest Newspaper." As the popularity of radio increased, the Tribune Company applied for a license and debuted from the Edgewater Beach Hotel (moving later to the Drake Hotel) as WGN on March 28, 1924, with a broadcast that included Mayor William Dever, an opera star, and jazz by the Oriole Orchestra. Like the publishing company, 'GN's reach spread far and wide, and that first five-hour broadcast could be heard into Australia. It remains a Chicago institution, though its audiences closely resemble the demographic of the *Trib*'s readers: conservative, suburban, and fiercely Republican. By the 1950s, the station was broad-casting from a four-story building north of Tribune Tower that contained the company's television studios as well. Wally Phillips joined the station in 1956, doing a show with Bob Bell, who would later play the title clown on *Bozo's Circus*. Phillips hosted a celebrity interview program along with *Tribune* columnist Herb Lyon as well as a music and dance show called *Club 9*. Later, he'd host The Hi Fi Club in 1959 before settling into his morning drive show, which he held from 1965 to 1986. Unfazed by the popularity of rock stations or the increasing number of up-and-coming radio personalities landing on other stations, Wally continued to leisurely enter-tain the housewives of the Midwest with his casual, gently witty style. There would be other stars on the station, but none seemed to have a hold on the listeners the way Phillips did. His retirement from broadcasting in 1998 stunned the city, but the station went on and still goes strong today.

4. **JACK L. COOPER**

Jack L. Cooper was the first black deejay to become a true radio personality. He was Chicago's first black radio sports-caster and its first black radio executive, all after dropping out of the fifth grade. Born in 1888 in Tennessee, after leav-ing school he wandered in a number of directions. He was a racetrack gofer in the Midwest and the South, then turned to boxing in Cincinnati and fought 160 amateur fights, winning a number of championships including the Negro welter-weight crown of Ohio before playing second base for a semi-pro baseball team. Slowly, he began to find his way into the entertainment field, managing theaters in Florida and Arkan-sas, and starring in minstrel shows before eventually starting his own theater troupe in the early 1920s called The Cooper and Lamar Music Co. A journalist at heart, he wrote for sev-eral black newspapers including Chicago's *Defender*, writing with the desire to see his race triumph above racial oppres-sion and the economic realities they faced. In Washington, D.C., Cooper joined the cast of a local musical variety radio program, most of his performances using accents since blacks were not allowed to work on white stations. He returned to Chicago in 1926 and created *The All Negro Hour*, which debuted in 1929 on WSBC. A live one-hour variety show, it featured local and national guests. Cooper aired a gospel and spiritual concert and soon produced a mystery drama serial called *Nitemare*. His popularity grew, and it was estimated that by the late 1940s he had forty hours of airtime on four different stations. To get his shows on the air, he found himself buying airtime on any station he could. In 1938, he began a program known as *Search for Missing Persons* in conjunction with the Chicago Police Department. His one constant in life was to help African Americans and he did so by offering news of the community and advice on employment and rights. He even ran a news discussion show called *Listen Chicago*. With decades of service under his belt, Cooper finally retired in 1961. Nine years later, he was dead at the age of eighty-one. Cooper's story is inspirational not only for African Americans, but for Americans of all races who need to be reminded what one person can do once he finds his sense of direction.

5. **JACK BENNY**

Every Sunday night, the combined viewing audiences of the *Academy Awards* and the *Super Bowl* tuned in to *The Jack Benny Show*. On radio and later TV, he was the biggest star around. He started life as Benjamin Kubelsky, a kid from Waukegan, a town north of Chicago, and his parents hoped he'd be a concert violinist. But while the violin he practiced daily never left the act, as he got older he took a different direction with it. It was said Jack Benny (as he'd later call himself) could have been a very talented violinist, but Jack felt his talent lay more with the comedy his playing wrought. He went into vaudeville, his popularity growing, and while in vaudeville he met Sadie Marx, a cousin to the Marx Brothers, who eventually changed her name to Mary Livingstone. Mary played Jack's girlfriend on his radio show, and married him in real life. Able to elicit laughter just through his pauses, Benny surrounded himself with equally funny people and was content to give them the funniest lines. In a time when movie studios were guarded about allowing their stars to appear on radio and TV, they couldn't keep stars like Jimmy Stewart, Humphrey Bogart, and George Raft from appearing with Benny. From jokes cast members told about him, Benny gained his famous miserly persona, but in real life Jack was well known for a charitable nature equaling his good humor. Performing in various charity shows with symphonies worldwide, he raised over $6 million dollars. After being on radio and TV for thirty-three years, Benny retired in 1965, continuing his charity work well into his seventies. But pancreatic cancer took him in 1974, still well loved, at the age of "39."

6. THE BREAKFAST CLUB

From 1933 to 1968, America ate breakfast listening to radio's longest-running show, *The Breakfast Club*. Hosted by Don McNeill, there were comedy, music, and interviews with some of the biggest names in show business who were happy to stop by when in town. The show also had a cast of supporting players, including Fran Allison who played the gossipy Aunt Fanny and Sid Ellstrom as Grandpa Putterball. It was radio's first successful morning show, but McNeill was far from a shock jock. With the sort of Midwestern charm of a David Letterman, he broadcast his show from the NBC studio in Chicago without a script. Radical for the time, the live audience was an idea of McNeill's after a sick Marine asked to have a tour behind the scenes. McNeill had the ability to connect with his audience both in studio and in the home. His popularity was such that in 1945, when giving a talk in Madison Square Garden, 17,000 people turned out to see the man they woke up to every morning. When *The Breakfast Club* went off the air, it was two years shy of the twenty-year contract McNeill signed in 1950 with ABC, the network the show had moved to. The contract was revolutionary for the time and might have been fulfilled if ABC hadn't decided to change format to follow the times. McNeill himself died in 1996 at the age of eighty-eight, a legend in radio history.

7. *AMOS 'N' ANDY*

Was *Amos 'n' Andy* a show founded on racism or was it a satire of human nature, as its creators insisted? The question of racism may never be answered, but the show, broadcast from Chicago, was a powerhouse of radio. In fact, during its height *Amos 'n' Andy* was more popular with blacks than whites. The creators of the show, Freeman Gosden and Charles Correll, broadcasting from WGN, originally called their characters *Sam 'n' Henry*. When WGN, not wanting to lose control of the show, refused to allow the show to be recorded and distributed nationally, the pair jumped ship to WMAQ, which allowed the broadcasts to be recorded. Since WGN still owned the rights to *Sam 'n' Henry*, Gosden and Correll renamed it, and by late 1929, *Amos 'n' Andy* was heard nationally, broadcast six nights a week. The show continued on radio until 1960, and Correll and Gosden even appeared in two movies in blackface. When casting the television show, it was decided African American actors would better play the characters and, ironically, the show became the first network with an all-black cast. But even as early as 1931, *Amos 'n' Andy* had flak from its critics, especially black professionals who protested that the show stereotyped black Americans. During the civil rights movement, America had no time for *Amos 'n' Andy*, which had become an anachronism. Correll died in Chicago in 1972 at the age of eighty-two. Gosden died in Los Angeles ten years later at the age of eighty-three.

8. **WHAT'S IN THE CLOSET?**

Inviting the audience into their theater of the mind, Jim and Marian Jordan created one of the most successful and enduring classic radio shows of all time. The roots of *Fibber McGee and Molly* go back to a show that aired on WMAQ from 1931 to 1935. Written by the Jordans and Don Quinn,

Smackout began as a local show, then went national in 1933. Along with low-key comedy there were musical numbers with the couple singing duets while Marian played piano. On *Smackout*, two of the characters the couple played were Uncle Luke, the windy owner of a country store, and Teeny, who believed very little of what Luke told her. By 1935, *Smackout* had become *Fibber McGee and Molly* with Luke and Teeny transforming into the title characters. At the height of its popularity, it was the most-listened-to show on the radio. Forty million listeners tuned in to hear what would fall out of Fibber's closet when he opened it. A larger production than *Smackout*, *Fibber McGee and Molly* boasted an orchestra, singers, and a cast of actors entertaining a studio audience. The last *Fibber McGee and Molly* aired in 1959. Marian Jordan died in 1961 of cancer; Jim died in 1988.

q. THE MUSEUM OF BROADCAST COMMUNICATIONS

Located in the Chicago Cultural Center, the museum is dedicated to the history of radio and television and their impact on society. Over 70,000 hours of radio and television performances are archived in the museum and available for the public to enjoy in private booths. Exhibits include Edgar Bergen's puppets, Charlie McCarthy, Effie Klinker, and Mortimer Snerd; Burr Tilstrom's Kukla and Ollie; a replica of Fibber McGee's closet; and Jack Benny's vault. There's even a television station where visitors can anchor their own newscast (and purchase a copy of the tape), and the Play by Play Press Box where they can announce a baseball game. The Museum of Broadcast Communications helps people connect to that special time when people gathered around the radio and let their imaginations run wild.

10. ONE ADAM 12

We take police radios for granted today, but imagine the days when automobiles were new and radio even newer. Prior to 1881, policemen walked a beat alone. Calling for backup meant running back to the precinct and literally calling for help. Quite a run in a city the size of Chicago. In 1881, the Police Patrol and Signal Service set up booths around the city with telephones hooked up to stations. When a call came in, patrol wagons waiting at the precinct rolled on any incoming calls. This didn't do much for the rolling police cruisers that came about after the proliferation of squad cars. In 1929, the World's Greatest Newspaper answered that problem when, in agreement with the police department, five squad cars were equipped with one-way radio transmitters by the *Chicago Tribune*. With this equipment, squad cars were able to receive reports broadcast over the *Tribune*'s WGN radio. Because of the success of the experiment, a year later the department created its own radio broadcasting system. The program grew, and by 1942, two-way radios were installed in all squad cars.

Museums

S o many things to do. So many things to see.

1. THE FIELD MUSEUM

Where does one of the largest T. Rexes ever discovered live? Well, anywhere it wants to if it were alive. But the skeleton of Sue, the largest, most complete Tyrannosaurus Rex fossil ever discovered, can be found in the Field Museum. The museum began as a continuation of anthropological collections acquired for the World's Columbian Exposition. For a while, it was established as the Columbian Museum of Chicago in September 1893. The name was changed in 1905 to honor Marshall Field, the museum's biggest benefactor, and in 1921, it was moved from Jackson Park to join its sister institutions: the John G. Shedd Aquarium and the Adler Planetarium on Lake Shore Drive. The museum has been a leader in the research of evolution, biology, paleontology, and archaeology. Specimens have grown to over twenty million. One of the most popular and enduring exhibits is "Inside Ancient Egypt" where visitors can see pieces from two excavated Egyptian tombs brought to the museum in the early 1900s. "Underground Adventure" is a reproduction of the world belowground with giant robotic earwigs, centipedes, spiders, and more. And along with Sue, you can see bull elephants in mid-battle, a stuffed gorilla named Bushman, and the two man-eating lions of Tsavo, famed for killing and eating almost 140 railway workers in East Africa in 1898.

2. A WORK OF ART

Located on Michigan Avenue, the Art Institute is both a museum and a school, most of its 300,000 works of art collected through gifts. Many Old Masters and modern European works are there thanks to the estate of Mr. and Mrs. Martin A. Ryerson. "The Helen Birch Collection," presented by Frederic Clay Bartlett, was the first group of postimpressionist paintings to be installed in an American museum. And the grand lady of Chicago, Bertha Honoré Palmer, is not only responsible for much of the impressionist collection (it, along with paintings from the romantics and the Barbizon School, were presented to the museum after her death), she was also responsible for introducing impressionist art to America.

In the early history of the city, influential Chicagoans strove to instill more culture into the city. In 1879, a group of private citizens funded the Chicago Academy of Fine Arts, which replaced the Academy of Design founded in 1866. Three years later, the academy was renamed the Art Institute of Chicago and the museum moved into the new building constructed during the 1893 World's Fair. Since then, the Art Institute has continually added new wings and changed inner rooms as if a work in progress itself. Inside, you'll find small galleries geared to give you a more intimate experience. In them you can see European and American contemporary art, George Seurat's masterpiece "Sunday Afternoon on the Island of La Grande Jatte," archaic jades and Japanese prints, and an almost-complete history of photography. In 1922, the Department of Oriental Art was established and 1958 brought the Department of African Art. The year 1981 saw the establishment of the Department of Architecture, with an architectural library, which benefited from money left to the institute by Daniel Burnham in 1912.

3. HANDS ON

When Julius Rosenwald, chairman of Sears, Roebuck and Company, took his son to visit the Deutsches Museum in Munich, Germany, he was so impressed by the hands-on atmosphere that he wanted to bring that sort of interactive experience to Chicago. Shortly after returning, he donated $7 million toward refurbishing the Palace of Fine Arts building left over from the Columbian Expo and turning it into the Museum of Science and Industry. Opened in 1933 (in time for the Century of Progress World's Fair), it has since become one of the most popular institutions in Chicago, and one of the most popular in the country. The oldest and largest museum of its kind, the museum's goal is to make science and technology more accessible to the public. Within its 650,000-square-foot building, it houses more than 200 exhibits in more than seventy-five fields. Some of the treasures you'll find in the museum are a full-scale replica of a coal mine; a German submarine captured during World War II; the world's largest model railroad; a collection of vintage automobiles, racing cars, airplanes, and trains; and the toy house of Colleen Moore, a flapper who hit it big when she married a wealthy stockbroker. At nine square feet, the $500,000 dollhouse took 700 workers over nine years to complete. Its highest tower stands twelve feet high. Then there is the Omnimax Theater, a domed screen, five feet high, seventy-five feet in diameter, that surrounds the audience, giving them a feeling of being there as the super 70 mm projector runs movies like *The Dream Is Alive*—you can feel like you're aboard the space shuttle or in the Grand Canyon, where you feel like you're riding the rapids.

4. THE CORAL REEF

Like so many of the museums on Lake Shore Drive, the Shedd Aquarium was founded by a notable Chicago name hoping to give his town a new experience. Chicago businessman John G. Shedd donated $3 million to its establishment.

Opened in 1930, one million visitors a year tour what is the world's largest aquarium. There is a 60,000-gallon penguin habitat and a 1,000-seat amphitheater were people can view the natural behaviors of marine mammals. The popular "Coral Reef" is composed of a 90,000-gallon tank home to forty-five species of fish, all swimming among corals, sea fans, sponges, and sea whips. One hundred and ninety exhibit tanks are set up for various aquatic systems, both salt and fresh water. In 1991, a $43 million oceanarium, the Pacific Northwest Coastal Habitats House, was built. Within the 170,000-square-foot exhibit, the largest marine mammal pavilion in the world, are false killer whales, Pacific white-sided dolphins, harbor seals, and Alaskan sea otters. There are also Beluga whales, the acquisition of which caused quite a stir among animal rights activist. The museum was sensitive to the issue and the size of the habitat exceeds federal regulations. The Shedd Aquarium is a pioneer in the study of aquatic environments and has created a unique chance for the people of Chicago to experience them as well.

5. **STAR BRIGHT**

Step into this place and you'll see stars. Founded in 1930 by Max Adler, a Sears, Roebuck and Company vice-president, the Adler Planetarium was the first planetarium in the western hemisphere. Seven hundred thousand people a year visit the planetarium to use the observatory telescope, view live video feed of outer space from a hookup with an observing telescope in New Mexico, and enjoy sky shows, Friday shows projecting a live picture of planets, galaxies, and nebulae onto an eighteen-by-twenty-four-foot area of the sky theater dome in the Doane Observatory. The StarRider Theater offers a virtual reality tour through the Milky Way and into deep space thanks to a computer-generated 3-D graphic projection system. Among some of the features, there's also a 5,000-volume library, an Earth globe six feet in diameter, a scale that gives you an idea of what you'd weigh on other planets, and the largest astronomical instrument collections in the world. And if you're wondering what time it is, check the Henry Moore sundial located outside. At twelve feet high, it accurately shows the time of day.

6. THE RECORD KEEPER

Located on Walton Street, the Newberry Library has been recognized internationally as a top research library, one of only fourteen in the United States. Founded in 1887, using the money of Walter Loomis Newberry, an early settler and partner of William B. Odgen whose fortune was rooted in real estate, the library was completed in 1893 with a ten-story (two stories underground) addition in 1982. In his will, Walter Newberry left $2 million to the establishment of a free public library. After his death in 1868, by the time his will had been settled, the city had already started another library, which would be supported by public taxes, so Newberry's library became a noncirculating research library. Its materials, which date back to the Middle Ages, are worth over $300 million. Dealing primarily with history and historical documents, the library is a treasure trove of maps, rare books, and volumes of ancient historical text on subjects as varied as calligraphy, the English Renaissance, railroad history, cartography, and local family genealogy. A first edition of the King James Bible resides among the collection, as does a letter written by Michelangelo; a first edition of *The Whale*, the first American novel; and 500 atlases printed before 1820. Like many local libraries, the Newberry Library also sponsors public events and adult education seminars.

7. ARK IN THE PARK

In 1868, a pair of swans were presented to the city by the Central Park Zoo in New York, the donation laying the cornerstone for what would become the Lincoln Park Zoo, a taste of the exotic in the heart of the city. The second-oldest zoo in the United States, it has one of the largest collections in the world, over 2,000 exotic and endangered animals. Operated by the Chicago Park District with the help of the Lincoln Park Zoological Society, the zoo covers over thirty-five acres. It's one of the first zoos to be built within a city, attracting 4 million people annually who tour the zoo and note the naturalistic habitats. From 1970 to 1992, more great apes were born in this zoo than any other zoo, thanks to the wise stewardship of Dr. Lester Fisher, one of the city's most beloved names. Of course, two apes made headlines for taking strolls outside their cages. Bushman, the famous 550-pound great ape, decided to take an unexpected stroll but was scared back to his cage by an eighteen-inch garter snake. The second ape, Sinbad, weighing in at 530, needed to be tranquilized to be captured. Every so often, you just need to stretch your legs.

8. THE JUNGLE NEXT DOOR

Located in Brookfield, about fourteen miles from downtown Chicago, the Chicago Zoological Park, better known as Brookfield Zoo, is one of the most respected zoos in the country. Opened in 1934, it was one of the first zoos to present animals in naturalistic settings. Brookfield Zoo started with a contribution of 143 animals, 123 birds, and 4 reptiles. Since then, it's grown considerably, 216 acres offering the 200 million annual zoogoers a glimpse of 2,700 specimens. Among the more rare specimens are black rhinos, Father David's deer (extinct in the wild), and snow leopards. The zoo has made great strides in the breeding and conservation of endangered animals. One of its most famous residents was the late Olga the Walrus, acquired by the zoo in 1962. Known for her playful nature and for teasing people by spitting water at them, Olga died in 1988 at the age of twenty-seven. She was the oldest walrus in captivity, and a bronze statue stands near the Seven Seas Panorama in her honor. Bushman and Sinbad of the Lincoln Park Zoo weren't the only animals to get out and investigate their surroundings. At Brookfield, after a ninety-minute storm clogged the drains in the polar bear's moat, two polar bears were able to swim free. They raided a concession stand and even tried saying hello to the grizzlies next door before the grizzlies chased them away. Eventually, the animals were herded back to their habitat. The zoo offers a number of interesting and fun exhibits. In the Seven Seas Panorama, Atlantic bottle-nosed dolphins swim in their habitat and perform shows in the 2,000-seat viewing area. Below this is a viewing gallery with eight-by-eight-foot windows for an underwater and close-up view of these frisky creatures. A particularly impressive exhibit is Tropic World, the largest indoor zoo exhibit. Ever wonder what a rain forest looks like? Well a step inside will reveal three. Each area features animals native to that particular forest. Exotic birds fly overhead and rainstorms thunder through three times a day. And, of course, apes cavort in their natural environments. Gorillas, orangutans, chimpanzees, and monkeys are just some of what you'll find in these jungles. There's also the Australia House, giving the visitor a chance to go on a walkabout in the Australian Outback, and the Swamp, recreating a southern cypress swamp.

9.   THE TEMPLE OF LEARNING

Opened in 1991, this 756,000-square-foot building is the largest library in the world, housing, among other things, 2 million volumes of books. Neoclassical in design, the Harold Washington Library Center is named after the city's late mayor. Sculptures of owls on the roof keep watch over the ten-story structure, a square boxlike affair with five-story arched windows on sides of the redbrick building. From the lobby, the second floor walkway is visible, and mosaic murals on the wall portray the events in the life of Harold Washington as well as artwork honoring Jean Baptiste Du Sable, Chicago's first settler. Artwork adorns every floor. The seventh floor has the Chicago Author's Room, a lecture and meeting room. The eighth floor, devoted to the visual performing arts, has six individual piano practice rooms and a chamber music rehearsal room. Floor number nine has the lovely Winter Garden, a large public space available for special events with olive trees and a skylight 100 feet above. Also on the ninth floor are exhibits on architecture, the two world's fairs, the Chicago Theater, and the library's namesake, Harold Washington, among others. Back on the lower level, you'll find a 385-seat auditorium, an exhibition hall, a video theater, and meeting rooms.

10. GIVE PEACE A CHANCE

Not as glamorous, huge, or historical as some of the other museums, but just as important, the Peace Museum is the only one in the country dedicated to peace. The museum presents four exhibits a year, focusing on the culture of war and peace, and uses educational programs to further the cause of peace. Inside you will find exhibits, artifacts, and symbols of the struggle for peace including artwork from survivors of Hiroshima and Nagasaki, toys that promote peace, John Lennon's guitar, photos from the civil rights movement, and more. The museum was founded in 1981 by artist-activist Mark Rogouin and U.S. ambassador to UNICEF Marjorie Craig Benton, and the exhibit of drawings by the survivors of Hiroshima and Nagasaki inspired U2 to name one of their albums *The Unforgettable Fire.*

Names You Should Know

The following are names that may not be well known, but have, in their own ways, left an impact, whether socially, politically, religiously, or entertainment-wise, on the city of Chicago.

1. MUSIC MAD

He referred to himself as "music mad." He played the flute, the fiddle, the Scottish Lowland pipes and the Scottish Highland pipes. Francis O'Neill chose a career in law enforcement, but his heart was in music and thanks to him, Irish culture has been spared the loss of countless pieces of Irish music. Born in County Cork, Ireland, in 1848, at the age of sixteen he signed on as a cabin boy on an English merchant vessel, before finding his way to Chicago in 1873 and joining the police force. His first month he was shot during the apprehension of an armed burglar, and the bullet remained lodged near his spine for the rest of his life. In 1901, he was named chief of the Chicago police department, where he worked at trying to reduce corruption within it. A favorite among his men and considered one of the best officers on the force, Irish music was his passion. With an anthropological zeal, he collected tunes from Irish immigrants and musicians, listening to snatches of songs whistled or hummed, then playing them back for his sergeant James O'Neill (no

275

relation) to write down since he couldn't read music. Once, his concerned men went looking for him and found him at the apartment of a fiddler friend where they were playing music in the man's living room. Back on the old sod, Irish music had been suppressed by the church that looked upon it as pagan, and by the conquering English who viewed it as simply too Irish. Because of this, those traditional pieces that weren't lost altogether went underground and had to be unearthed by people like O'Neill. Most of the eight books he published were completed after his retirement in 1905. The most definitive reference source for those interested in Irish folklore, the 3,500 traditional Irish tunes that he collected helped keep alive both Irish music and Irish culture. O'Neill himself kept his passion for music up to his death in 1936 at the age of eighty-six, giving Chicago an important place in the history of Irish music.

2. PINKERTON, P.I.

Chicago's first police detective and America's first private eye, Allen Pinkerton was also a wanted man. Born in Glasgow, Scotland, in 1819, Pinkerton was the son of a police sergeant. Pinkerton himself took up the trade of barrel making, and was a staunch supporter of equal rights for all. It was this that put him at odds with the British Crown who, he was warned on the day of his wedding, was preparing to arrest him as a conspirator. The couple fled to North America, their ship wrecking on a shoal off the coast of Halifax, and from there they took a boat to Detroit. In 1842, the honeymooners landed in Chicago, where Pinkerton took up coopering at a local brewery, eventually opening up his own shop in the settlement of Dundee, about forty miles northwest of Chicago. One day, he was searching an island in the Fox River for material for barrel hoops and found the remnants of a burned $5 bill. His instinct as a detective came forth and he deduced that the island must be a meeting place for counterfeiters. He presented the Kane County sheriff with his theory, and the counterfeiters were caught. He opened his first agency in 1850. The original purpose of the Pinkerton National Detective Agency was to help runaway slaves escape to Canada, his shop serving as one of the stops on the underground railroad (by 1860, he was a prominent abolitionist). But soon, lawmen began consulting him on cases they were unable to solve. He also investigated mail robberies as a special agent for the post office. At last convinced to return to Chicago, he was appointed a deputy sheriff of Cook County in 1852. Pinkerton's agency was a perfect middleman between the police, underpaid and overworked, and the public, who were distrustful of a centralized police force. The one surprise in his character was his view of unions. This man, who'd been chased out of his home for his support of rights for the common laborer, looked upon unions as rife with anarchists.

A master of disguise, he caught an embezzler by posing as a ticket agent. He became a country bumpkin to catch a swindler. And through a friend of Abraham Lincoln, he became his bodyguard during the presidential campaign. During the Civil War he was chosen to head the United States Secret Service, even helping to foil a plot to assassinate the president in Baltimore in 1861. It was a Pinkerton detective who hunted Butch Cassidy and the Sundance Kid and their "Hole in the Wall" Gang. Gunman, army scout, and former Indian fighter Tom Horn was a Pinkerton, as was author Dashiel Hammett. Pinkertons pursued the James brothers, the Youngers, and the Daltons; the motto of the agency was "We never sleep." It was their representation of this symbol—a wide-open eye—that gave birth to the term "private eye." In 1875, in response to the sensationalistic dime novels he felt belittled his profession, he wrote *The Expressman and the Detective,* which sold 15,000 copies in sixty days. He went on to publish sixteen detective books, told from the perspective of the experts. In 1869, Pinkerton suffered a small stroke and left the agency to his two sons to run. He died in 1884 after a long and colorful career helping to make the world a little safer.

3. **THE GATE CRASHER**

There was actually an Andy Frain who started Andy Frain Services in 1924. Back then, gate crashing was a problem, especially at Chicago Stadium hockey games. Frain organized a small group of ushers who were able to prove to promoters how valuable they could be at crowd control. When the organization moved to Wrigley Field, William Wrigley was so impressed that he outfitted the men in the blue-and-gold uniform that became their attire. Born in Canaryville in 1904, Frain was one of seventeen children, which must have inspired his passion for crowd control. At age twelve, he was renting seat cushions at Comiskey Park and began to see a role for ushers in the stands. His first big indoor job was in 1929, at opening night for the Chicago Stadium during the Tommy Loughran/Mickey Walker fight. His organization went on to service horse races, concerts, trade shows, and even the Kentucky Derby. Introducing himself to Colonel Matt Winn, operator of Churchill Downs, by crashing the gate, when he was thrown out he crashed it again and entered Winn's private box. The demonstration convinced Winn of the need for the Frains at Churchill Downs. In true Chicago fashion, Frain was instrumental in the vice presidential decision during the 1944 Democratic convention in Chicago. By his fourth term, Franklin D. Roosevelt was in the market for a new vice president. When supporters of Vice President Henry A. Wallace got wind of this, they intended to load the galleries with Wallace supporters. Mayor Edward J. Kelly, who backed Roosevelt's decision to change VPs, turned to Frain to orchestrate a coup. That night, the seating arrangements were manipulated so that Wallace's supporters were scattered around the huge arena instead of in one large block. Any furor they created would lose its impact. Meanwhile, Kelly was able to stack the crowd with Truman supporters. The rest is history and Andy Frain, who died in 1964 at the age of sixty, was part of that history.

4. OPENING MINDS

Practicing Pagan (or Native) faiths openly can mean ridicule, discrimination, or possibly worse. For centuries, Christianity has vilified all things Pagan through a campaign of misinformation and scare tactics. What isn't portrayed as evil is painted simply as wacky. Ed Hubbard and Don Lewis have spent over a decade trying to reverse this misconception. As a child growing up in Chicago, Hubbard was very involved in the Southern Baptist church of his family. But by the 1980s, he started on a path of soul-searching to find the faith that truly spoke to him. In 1990, at a metaphysical fair, he met Don Lewis High-Correll and the two struck up a friendship. Following a matriarchal pattern, the High-Correll heritage is of Scots-Cherokee, and as a third-degree Wiccan priest, Lewis comes from a long line of Wiccans and practices a brand of Wiccanism that has been a part of his family for generations. What both realized was that while one of Paganism's greatest strengths is its philosophical freedom, this could also be one of its greatest weaknesses because it keeps the community from the sort of unity that the monotheistic religions have. To address this issue, Hubbard decided to hold a conference for Pagans that would address this, among other issues facing Chicago's large Pagan community. The inspiration for the event came while Hubbard was volunteering at the Parliament of World Religions held in Chicago in 1993. Funded mostly by the Pagan Interfaith Embassy, the organization started by Hubbard and Lewis, the first Pagan Leadership Conference was held. Structured much like the Parliament of World Religions, this event proved quite successful, leading to a better understanding of the part each person plays in the outside world's perception of their faith. The two have made numerous TV and radio appearances, even on the Christian Broadcasting Network's *Community Perspectives*, and both have written and published a variety of articles and books. After attending the third Parliament of World Religions, held in South Africa, Hubbard was inspired by the need to strengthen respect for the followers of black South African native traditions, which have come under heavy attack. As officers of the Pagan Interfaith Embassy, both have made it their mission to foster greater understanding and communication between Pagans and Judeo/Christians, and to help Pagans understand their potential for the sort of charitable works found in more traditional faiths.

5. BUSHMAN THE GORILLA

He came from Cameroon, Africa. He was said to be the first one to appear west of the Potomac River. He appeared in newsreels, was the focus of paparazzi, and on the day he was thought to be dying, over 120,000 people lined up for a last glimpse. He had his temperamental moments, and wasn't above hurling feces at those who displeased him. This was Bushman the gorilla, quite possibly the most famous gorilla in the nation at the time. Orphaned as an infant, Bushman was sold to Lincoln Park Zoo in 1930 by a Presbyterian missionary and an animal trader. The zoo paid $3,500 for the lowland gorilla and ended up with a gigantic publicity generator. He was an instant favorite. Thumping around in his iron cage, he either terrified or fascinated people, but they came to see him in droves. Remember, gorillas were a rare sight in zoos back then, and can be pretty intimidating even today. And Bushman was a bruiser, the largest gorilla in captivity at the time. Yet, on a day in October 1950, when he escaped from his cage and roamed through a kitchen, it was a garter snake that frightened him back to his cage three hours later. Hey, we all have our phobias. It was on New Year's Day 1951 that the big guy finally took his last breath. Mourners passed by his cage for weeks after and he had become such a symbol for the zoo, and such a part of Chicago, that he was stuffed and put on display at the Field Museum where he remains to this day, greeting all who pay their respect, but without the feces throwing.

6. THE LADY AND THE PUPPETS

Created by Burr Tillstrom, the popular children's show *Kukla, Fran and Ollie* premiered in 1947 in Chicago and aired almost every weeknight, going national by 1951. Before its debut, it was decided that Tillstrom needed a human presence for the puppets of his Kuklapolitan Players, and Fran Allison became the perfect presence. Born in 1907 in Iowa, forced to become caregiver to her sickly parents, she went to college, majoring in music and education, but the financial difficulties due to her parents' conditions led her to leave college after two years. After a series of jobs, her singing career began to take off in 1932 when her brother, Lynn, asked her to sing with his band on a radio show. During the 1930s, she revealed a true talent for improvisation. In 1933, however, an auto accident left her close to death for a few weeks. After her recovery, she was left with facial scars that made her self-conscious. She did go back to the radio, and gained an even stronger following. A 1937 invite to audition for NBC in Chicago sealed her future in the Windy City. She performed bit parts and commercials and displayed her improvisational expertise on Don McNeill's *Breakfast Club*, which pioneered the concept of an unscripted format. After a series of reconstructive facial surgeries, she felt confident enough to make personal appearances. Toward the end of World War II, she met Burr Tillstrom during a performance of his puppets outside the Wrigley Building. Watching with the crowd, she was drawn into a conversation with the puppet Kukla and the chemistry was obvious. What made *Kukla, Fran and Ollie* such a hit, even with such notable names as Orson Welles, Arturo Toscanini, and John Steinbeck, was Allison's talent for bestowing believability on the puppets she interacted with. There were no scripts, just a rough plan for each show's theme, Tillstrom and Allison improvising the rest. When the network decided to cancel the show in 1957, they were besieged by mail and telegrams. The show was canceled anyway, but the cast was brought back in the 1960s and '70s in specials and reruns and appearances. One notable series was the *Children's Film Festival* running from 1967 to 1979, which showcased international films concerning children. The series was hosted by Kukla, Fran and Ollie. Eventually, Allison and her husband settled in California in 1976, though, unfortunately, her husband died two years later. She continued into the 1980s with appearances and charities. In 1985, stricken with leukemia, Allison died at the age of seventy-six.

7. **SHE STOOD ACCUSED**

Mrs. O'Leary was the city's scapegoat for a terrible event. For decades, the Great Fire of 1871 was attributed to Mrs. O'Leary's cow kicking over a lantern when the woman was milking it late one night. The facts, however, seem to point to a neighbor, Pegleg Sullivan, sneaking into the O'Leary barn to steal a bit of milk. At the time, however, anti-Irish sentiment ruled and it was a simple thing for the news media to build a legend based on lies. For example, a *Chicago Times* report intimated that Catherine O'Leary set the fire in retaliation for being cut off the dole. Catherine O'Leary, however, was intensely proud of the fact that her family was not on the dole. They owned their own home and barn, with five cows, a calf, a horse, and the house in front of theirs that they rented to another family. Thirty-six years old when the fire started, she already had a successful milk route in the neighborhood, getting up early every day to milk the cows. The night of the fire, O'Leary, her husband, Patrick, a Civil War veteran, and their three children were in bed when the blaze broke out. They were awakened by a neighbor who spotted the fire burning their backyard barn. Another thing that played against the O'Leary family in the legend was that they didn't lose their home in the fire. After the fire, Catherine testified before a number of hearings about her role in the fire and insisted she had no idea how the blaze broke out. She was hounded by reporters every year on the anniversary of the event, and because the woman remained silent, reporters decided to invent statements, usually not in O'Leary's favor. Sensational pictures of women milking cows appeared in the papers, along with a variety of theories usually negative to the O'Learys in general, and the Irish as a whole. After the O'Learys moved from De Koven Street, Catherine became a recluse, leaving her house only for church or to run errands. In 1900, a reporter, Michael Ahern, admitted to a fellow reporter that he and two other reporters, James Haynie and John English, made up the cow and lamp story after finding a kerosene lamp in the wreckage. Their readers never questioned why O'Leary, a woman up delivering milk early in the morning, would be out at approximately 8:30 P.M. (the fire started at 8:40) the night before milking cows. They disregarded witness reports of seeing a man exit the barn at 9:15 P.M. They disregarded neighbors' reports of waking the O'Leary family shortly after noticing the blaze. Citizens only saw the devastation and blamed it on an industrious Irish family. Unfortunately, Ahern's confession came five years too late for Catherine O'Leary. She passed away in 1895, still haunted by the lies of that tragic night.

8. FAN DANCER

She changed her name to Sally because it would fit on a marquee. Cecil B. DeMille came up with her last name from the Rand McNally atlas he was looking at. She was Sally Rand, queen of the fan dancers. Born Helen Could Beck in 1904 in Missouri, she dreamed of dancing from the age of six. When she arrived in Chicago at age fifteen, she paid for her ballet classes in Chicago by modeling nude at Art Institute modeling classes. After appearing in a Ziegfeld-inspired revue a year later, she caught the eye of director Max Sennet when the revue appeared in Los Angeles. From there, she appeared in films for Cecil B. DeMille. Unfortunately, while her acting may have been suited for the silents, her voice was not, and at twenty-eight she found herself back in Chicago. It was while she was dressing for her number in a North Side speakeasy that the famous fans first appeared. She'd obtained them in a costume shop in New York, huge plumes of ostrich feathers lying on the floor.

Borrowing $200 from friends, she ordered a pair of the white, seven-pound fans and they arrived the very day of her new job. Planning to use a chiffon nightgown for her act, she was naked when her music started, so she grabbed her fans and the rest is fan-dancing history. In 1933, when the World's Fair was set to open, she was promised a job by a Chicago politician whose only request was that she play Lady Godiva at a benefit for one of the fair's exhibits. Renting a horse, and clad only in false blonde tresses added to her hair, she appeared on the lakefront and assured herself a place in the World's Fair. Sterner minds were not quite taken with this risqué act. She was arrested four times her first day. Her exposure, however, was an illusion, for beneath the fans she wore a flesh-colored body suit. The act, dancing suggestively behind the fans for six minutes to Debussy's "Clare de Lune" or Chopin's "Waltz in C Sharp Minor," rarely differed but always delighted. The publicity from the arrests, however, only helped her career and before long she was pulling down $3,000 a week, becoming the hottest attraction at the fair. Along with her seven shows at the Streets of Paris in the fair, she was doing seven shows at a Loop Theater and two at a North Side nightclub. When the fair was over, Rand tried to donate her fans to the Chicago Historical Society but was turned down. So she took her show on the road, and continued doing the act well into her seventies—not because she had to, but because she liked it. It helped her put her six brothers through college and she herself at the age of fifty-two entered the University of California, earning a diploma with a ninety-five-point average. Not bad for a girl who never finished high school. She died in California, a year after her last appearance at a benefit for the Historic Kansas City Foundation.

9. THE WOMAN BEHIND THE MAN

Back in the heyday of jazz, there was another Armstrong on the scene, and some say she was instrumental in the fame

that Louis Armstrong would later receive. Her name was Lil-
ian Hardin Armstrong, but she made a name for herself as
Lil Hardin long before she met her future husband Louis. She
was born near the turn of the century (possibly 1898) in
Memphis, Tennessee. Lil showed musical talent even as a
toddler and was encouraged by her mother, who sent her for
piano lessons in first grade. She attended the Hooks School
of Music and later studied piano at Fisk University before the
family moved to Chicago. Her first big gig was playing sheet
music for people to sample at a music store. It was here,
through fellow musicians, that she learned more about the
new sensation, jazz. When she gained an audition with the
New Orleans Creole Jazz Band, she was hired. In 1921, after
playing around Chicago in the New Orleans Creole Jazz
Band, she joined King Oliver's band. It was a unique situation: a woman, traveling the country with a male band, playing music that the more socially conscious considered
degenerate. It led to friction in her family, her mother and
grandmother frowning upon her choice of career.

In 1922, when Louis Armstrong joined the band, Lil and
Louis fell in love. Two years later, they were married and her
career would begin to take a backseat to his as she encouraged him to go out on his own and be a star. She inspired
him with her professionalism as well as the dedication
learned through formal training. She continued her own education, eventually obtaining a degree from the Chicago College of Music and a postgraduate degree from the New York
College of Music in 1929. Judging by her court fight with
Louis over copyright of certain songs, it's possible she wrote
some of his material. As the 1930s approached, there was
trouble in the marriage, and by 1931, they were separated.
Seven years later, they divorced. Lil formed a number of
bands, some all women, some all men, and continued to
compose music. While financial success never came, she
kept a hand in the music scene, becoming a house pianist
for the Decca Recording Company, performing at area clubs,
and even touring Europe in 1952. She also owned a restau-

rant and put out a line of clothes. In the 1960s, she also taught piano and French. It was in 1971, while performing a musical tribute to ex-husband Louis, who had died a month earlier, that Lil herself suffered a massive heart attack while playing the piano. As touching as this end is, it's also somehow fitting for a woman who kept playing no matter where the road took her.

10. THE PRODIGY

She was a pianist and composer but in a different vein than Lil Armstrong. Margaret Bonds was born in 1913 to a Chicago family heavily influenced by the arts, especially the genre of black musicians and writers emerging at the time. Writer Langston Hughes, soprano Abbie Mitchell, and other notable names visited the Bonds house regularly. Her mother, an organist at the Baptist church, encouraged her daughter by teaching her piano at an early age. By the time she was five, the young pianist had composed "Marquette Road Blues," and received the first of a number of scholarships to various schools, including the Chicago Musical College. Through organizations like the National Association of Negro Musicians and the Chicago Music Association (founded by her mother in 1919), she continued to have contact with artists who would help spur her career along, often accompanying them in concerts held at black churches. Through more scholarships she was able to attend Northwestern University in 1929, though, since African American students were not allowed to stay in campus housing she was forced to commute by train from her home on the South Side to the Evanston campus. She received her bachelor's degree in music in 1933 and eventually received a master's in 1934. An important event in Bonds's life, as well as a significant part of African American history, took place in 1933 when she became the first black soloist to perform with the Chicago Symphony Orchestra. Performed at the Auditorium Theater as a part of the American Series for the Century of Progress Exposition, the concert was also the first time an orchestra had performed music composed by an African American woman. She went on to perform as a guest artist at the Michigan Gardens Music Festival and to establish the Allied Arts Academy, serving as both director and teacher. Moving to New York in 1939, she continued her musical studies and later formed the Margaret Bonds Chamber Society. She performed on radio, taught at the American Theater Wing, and during the 1960s became director of music at the Inner City Repertory Theater in California. In 1972, Margaret Bonds died in California at age fifty-nine.

Live from Chicago

Who would have thought the cow town would turn out to be a major theater town? When Chicago did things it did them in a big way. Plunging into the world of the theater was no exception.

1. THE LAUGH MAESTROS

In 1959, three college friends got together and created what would become a Mecca for improvisational theater. Paul Sills, Howard Alk, and Bernard Sahlins originally planned to open a coffee shop. Finding two adjacent storefronts on Wells Street, they converted them into a small nightclub inspired by European-style cabarets. The name came from an article in the *New Yorker* magazine entitled "The Second City" by A. J. Liebling. He unflatteringly dubbed Chicago "the second city." Turning a negative into a positive, the name Second City is now synonymous with great improvisation. The first show, entitled "Excelsior and Other Outcries" was a hit, running for eight weeks (now the shows are likely to run for six months). The show wasn't all improv. The players performed a scripted revue of short comic scenes featuring a variety of characters with blackouts, musical numbers, and parodies. Afterward, they returned to the stage and took suggestions from the audiences, performing improv based on those suggestions. The improv served as a development tool for future revues, which would feature many of the bits that sprang from it. Later, the troupe moved to a permanent home at 1616 N. Wells Street and spawned a Canadian troupe. Its big fame came later in the 1970s when Second City alumni John Belushi, Dan Aykroyd, Bill Murray, and Gilda Radner joined the cast of *Saturday Night Live* and brought their background training to light. Later, the brilliant syndicated skit show *SCTV* would feature the talents of Second City alums Harold Ramis and John Candy.

2. THE KING OF RAZZLE DAZZLE

His routines were distinctly urban, a sexuality rooted in jazz. Considered the king of razzle dazzle, Bob Fosse was born in Chicago in 1927, and by thirteen had formed his own dance act in nightclubs. Touring in productions during his naval stint in the Pacific, he spent two years in the chorus of *Call Me Mister*, before landing on Broadway in the revue *Dance Me a Song*. Fosse become an MGM contract player in the 1950s and got the chance to choreograph 1955's *My Sister Ellen* and 1958's *Damn Yankees*. In between, he won a Tony for his first Broadway show, *The Pajama Game*. His first feature directorial debut, 1969's *Sweet Charity*, was a box office disaster, making him a Hollywood pariah for years. 1972's *Cabaret* came to him only after several other directors had turned it down. An unsentimental musical, *Cabaret* was innovative in its brash energy, but hardly pretty. The movie made stars out of Liza Minelli and Joel Grey and won eight Oscars. Awards came fast and furious, but while editing the biopic *Lenny* and conducting rehearsals for his Broadway musical *Chicago*, Fosse suffered a near-fatal heart attack. Five years later, the autobiographical movie *All That Jazz*, inspired by that heady year, won four Academy Awards. In an ending worthy of one of his musicals, Fosse had a fatal heart attack in a Washington, D.C., hospital moments after the opening of the 1987 revival of *Sweet Charity*.

3. **THE GREAT ZIEGFELD**

The ultimate showman, Florenz Ziegfeld made his Follies a household name. Springing from musical roots, Ziegfeld was born in Chicago in 1869, his father the founder of the Chicago Academy of Music. Active in amateur theater, Ziegfeld went to Europe to gather acts for the 1893 World's Fair. While his German band, Russian singers and dancers, Hungarian string orchestra, and English singer unfortunately were failures, the popularity of his "Perfect Man" Eugene Sandow proved that he could tap into the public's appetite for perfection. Three years later he was in New York, producing costly musical revues. Three flops later, Ziegfeld, who financed the shows himself, was on the verge of financial ruin and nervous collapse. Resting in Europe, he was inspired by France's Folies Bergére and came back home to present his 1907 Ziegfeld Follies, a revue featuring singers, dancers, comedians, and the famous elaborately costumed glamour-girl chorus lines. Claiming that certain gowns could glorify certain women, Ziegfeld became known as the "glorifier" of the American woman. The Follies were held annually and launched the careers of W.C. Fields, Sophie Tucker, Eddie Cantor, and Fannie Brice. Critics considered the Follies old-fashioned, but Ziegfeld wasn't trying to impress the critics, rather to please the audiences who streamed to his shows. Other shows he produced went on to gross millions. Sadly, the Great Ziegfeld didn't live to see it. In 1932, weakened from the effects of pneumonia, he suffered a fatal heart attack.

4. **FIREPROOF**

It was beautiful. White marble walls, large mirrors framed in gold leaf and stone, two uncarpeted marble staircases that led to the upper balconies. The outside of the four-story theater had a Greek temple facade with a high stone archway. Most important, the management of the Iroquois Theater assured the public that Chicago's newest theater was "absolutely fireproof." With twenty-five exits and an asbestos curtain that could be quickly lowered to protect an audience should a fire break out, it seemed the theater might live up to the boast. What wasn't pointed out was that the seats were wooden and stuffed with hemp, there was no fire alarm or fire alarm box outside, and some of the safety equipment promised had not been installed at all. On a freezing cold December 30, 1903, the matinee performance of *Mr. Blue-beard* was playing to a crowd of 1,600 in the seats and 200 people standing four-deep in aisles. Around 3:20 P.M., a hot stage light started one of the velvet curtains burning, with falling debris from the curtain and burning scenery causing the fire to spread. Ironically, the so-called asbestos fire cur-tain, which got stuck before it reached the full down position to protect the audience, ended up being consumed by fire as well. Soon the aisles leading from the auditorium gallery and upper balconies became choked with panicked people. The twenty-five exits either opened inward or were barred to keep out freeloaders.

The auditorium filled with heat and poisonous fumes, and families died clutching each other by the exits or crying out for each other in the dark. When theater employees backstage opened a rear set of huge double doors, it sent a powerful wind tunnel inside, sucking in huge sheets of fire. A second gust of wind sent a fireball out over the audience in their seats, incinerating them instantly. In the gallery and upper balconies, firefighters found 200 bodies stacked ten high. In fact, bodies stacked up against the doors made it difficult to enter the auditorium. Bodies brought out of the building were lined up on the sidewalk or taken to temporary morgues set up in area stores. All told, 572 lost their lives, among them 212 children, and 250 were injured, many dying in the weeks to come. New Year's Eve celebrations were banned, and January 1, 1904, became an official day of mourning. While there were 272 civil lawsuits filed, the Iroquois Theater Company filed bankruptcy so the money was never collected. The tragedy led to improvements in the fire code, including requiring outward-opening exit doors that were to remain unlocked and fitted with panic hardware. And theaters are now expected to include visible exit lights, automatic sprinklers, fire alarms systems, and flame-resistant scenery, props, and curtains.

5. TREAD THE BOARDS

The award-winning Steppenwolf Theater Company has been in existence since 1974 when it was started by Terry Kinney, Jeff Perry, and Gary Sinise in a Highland Park church basement. From those humble beginnings, the theater has become an internationally respected organization, boasting a company of thirty-five theater artists skilled in a variety of talents. Past Steppenwolf performers include Joan Allen, Gary Cole, Laurie Metcalf, and Glenne Headly. And occasionally, even the biggest names among the alumni can be found indulging their passion for live theater on the Steppenwolf stage. The company has performed over 200 works including Sam Shepard's *True West*, Lyle Kessler's *Orphans*, and an adaptation of Ken Kesey's *One Flew Over the Cuckoo's Nest*. Influenced by great ensemble theaters such as the Royal Shakespeare Company, the quality of the productions presented has helped make Steppenwolf one of the most enduring American theater ensembles. In 1985, the theater won a Tony award for regional theater excellence, and it was the only arts organization to be presented a 1998 National Medal of Arts by President Clinton. Not too shabby for a little three-man operation that got started in a church basement.

6. CLASSICAL GAS

In 1905, Orchestra Hall, the home of the Chicago Symphony Orchestra (CSO), was dedicated. Sadly, Maestro Theodore Thomas didn't live to see it, having died three weeks earlier. In 1891, Chicago businessman Norman Fay turned to musical pioneer Theodore Thomas, the nation's top conductor, to start a symphony orchestra. Thomas wished to provide Chicago with a symphony orchestra of the highest quality, and led the orchestra for thirteen years until his death. His successor was his assistant conductor, Frederick Stock, who'd started in the viola section in 1895. At thirty-seven years old, his would be the symphony's longest musical tenure. Hoping to inspire a love for classical music in the young, he organized the first subscription concerts specifically for children, encouraged youth auditions, and founded the Civic Orchestra of Chicago, a training orchestra affiliated with the CSO that was the first of its kind in the country. During the 1950s, the CSO, under the direction of Fritz Reiner, recorded what many consider to be some of the finest recordings of a symphony orchestra. But it was the symphony's eighth conductor who may be its most famous. Born in Budapest, Hungary, in 1912, Sir George Solti had an award-winning career as a pianist and conductor before joining the CSO in 1969. He was even an assistant to Arturo Toscanini during the summers of 1936 and 1937. After World War II, he became musical director of the Munich Opera, then moved on to the Frankfurt Opera. The Los Angeles Philharmonic Orchestra tapped him as musical director in 1961, but eight years later he came to Chicago, remaining until 1991. Under his direction, in 1971 the CSO embarked on its first international tour and a later tour took it to Europe, Japan, and Australia, where it was extremely well received. Prior to Solti, the CSO was never considered an equal to its rivals in New York or Philadelphia. Feeling the orchestra was a bit too provincial, he decided it needed more attention and managed to bring the orchestra a new national success. Chicago's pride in its orchestra grew and after the 1971 tour, the CSO was given a ticker-tape parade down State Street on its return. Since those early days, it has amassed over 900 recordings. It's won fifty-six Grammys, including several for Classical Album of the Year, and Best Performance in the orchestral, choral, instrumental and vocal soloist, and engineering categories.

7. **SALOME**

Born in Aberdeen, Scotland, in 1877, Mary Garden emigrated with her family to Chicago in 1888. Thanks to a wealthy benefactor, she was able to go to Paris, where she debuted in the Opera Comique. Performing as a stand-in during the third act of Charpentier's *Louise*, she was an immediate hit, continuing with the production and eventually filling major opera houses. With the financial backing of Harold F. McCormick of the International Harvester Company and Charles Gates Dawes, vice president of the United States, the new Chicago Grand Opera Company's season began in 1910. Mary Garden made her debut in *Pelleas et Melisande*, but it was her sensual portrayal of Salome in the opera of the same name that proved too risqué for the public. After two sold-out shows it was closed by protest from the Chicago Law and Order League. Despite great support from opera enthusiasts, the Chicago Grand Opera Company still finished the 1913–1914 season $250,000 in the hole. A restructuring created the Chicago Opera Association in 1915. Six years later, Mary Garden became the first woman to head up an opera company. As feisty a director as she was a performer, her decision to bring in famous, expensive talent almost bankrupted the company, while her quarrels with staff led to several resignations. Yet, she wasn't above going to the Chicago Stock Exchange to fund performances of charitable operas, and many critics considered her first season to be the most brilliant in the city's history. Tiring of the contentiousness, she stepped down to return to singing, continuing to wow audiences until her retirement at age forty-three, at the top of her career.

8. RAISIN

In 1965, cancer took the life of one of Chicago's most gifted playwrights, Lorraine Hansberry. Her classic *A Raisin in the Sun* became the first play written by a black woman to be produced on Broadway. She was also the first African American and the youngest American playwright to win the New York Drama Critics Circle Award for best play. The 1956 play, inspired by a Langston Hughes poem, was also inspired by personal experience. When her family moved into the white neighborhood of Washington Park, a 1938 decision by the Illinois courts evicted the family on the grounds of racial housing codes. After two years, appeals by her father—a U.S. marshal and later a real-estate broker and banker—led the U.S. Supreme Court to prohibit racially restrictive housing ordinances. Hansberry studied at the Art Institute of Chicago and attended the University of Wisconsin and the University of Guadalajara in Mexico. In 1950, she moved to New York and joined the staff of Paul Robeson's political magazine *Freedom*. Six years later, she wrote *A Raisin in the Sun*. Debuting in Chicago in 1959 to critical acclaim, it went onto Broadway the following month and in 1961 was adapted to the screen. Her second play, *The Sign in Sidney Brustein's Window,* met with mixed reviews, many of her peers criticizing her for writing the play from a white male perspective. The play concentrated on a young Jewish intellectual in Greenwich Village. Her next play debuted at New York's Cherry Lane Theater, on January 2, 1969, presented by her husband after her death. *To Be Young, Gifted and Black* incorporated work from shorter plays, letters, and a novel. Hansberry broke new ground in her thirty-four years, presenting pictures of black and white society that were at times pleasant and at times difficult to watch.

9. **THE TEMPLE OF SOUND**

Completed in 1889, the Auditorium Theater was the first major commission of Dankmar Adler and Louis Sullivan and a testament to their skills as architects and engineers. Seating 4,300, its acoustics were considered the best in the world and at the time it was Chicago's tallest building. Groundbreaking began in 1887, and building continued uninterrupted even by the Republican Party's national convention held in the not-yet-completed theater in July of 1888. In fact, the sounds of construction could be heard even amid the shouting of delegates. Planning a building that was truly Chicago, Sullivan was also dealing with cost-conscious financial backers organized by Ferdinand W. Peck who felt it was time for Chicago to have a temple of music to rival that of New York's Metropolitan Opera House. The Auditorium was practical, the theater itself enclosed in a multiuse building that also housed rental offices and a 400-room hotel. Illustrating Sullivan's thoughts on symbiotic design, non-supporting elliptical arches work with Adler's acoustical plan, as well as with the mundane issues of heat and ventilation. There was a glorious lobby with gold leaf columns, the colors organically dynamic. A magnificent staircase rose up through a monumental arch and into a second floor parlor. On the tenth floor was a huge dining room that ran the length of Michigan Avenue. A banquet hall and ballroom rested over the theater, with a barroom on the first floor as well as a café. The acoustics were such that conversational tones onstage could be heard well into the upper balconies half a block away. Hydraulic mechanics enabled the stage to rock with wavelike effect as well as to raise or even disappear. Seating capacity for the theater could be decreased by half with the use of movable floors while charity balls, political conventions, and such could be held thanks to a stage that pulled out to form a massive floor, increasing capacity to 8,000. The theater's cooling system, using dehumidified air over blocks of ice that were sprayed with water, was the first of its kind in a building of that size. It seemed as if most of Chicago turned out the morning of October 2, 1889, when the Auditorium was officially opened after an ancient Masonic ritual was performed and the building consecrated by the lodge's grand master. In the audience were the governor, mayor, and even President Benjamin Harrison and Vice President Levi Morton. The building of this grand theater marked a change in attitude when it came to the arts. Inspired by it, libraries, museums, and concert halls were soon to follow, adding a new dimension to the city.

10. SHAKESPEARE ON NAVY PIER

It's not Stratford-on-Avon but rather Chicago-on-Michigan. Some of the finest Shakespearean performers in the country have appeared with the Chicago Shakespeare Theater, which was founded in 1986 as Shakespeare Repertory and has become critically acclaimed for its productions. In 1999, they moved into a new home on Navy Pier: a seven-story theater with 510 seats on three levels that wrap around the main stage, making it possible for the most distant seat to be no further away from the stage than nine rows. Also in the building are a teacher's resource, an English pub, a Shakespeare-geared bookstall, and a theater upstairs where non-Shakespeare plays are performed. To encourage a love for the Bard from a young age, the company sponsors Team Shakespeare, which offers student matinees of the full-length main stage plays throughout the school year. The main stage itself hosts three plays a year. Pretty classy for a city that was at one time more interested in pork packing than stage direction.

The Gangsters

No matter where you go in the world, mention Al Capone and people instantly think Chicago. It's a sad fact that this city, where corruption was part of doing business, was ripe for the underworld.

1. SCARFACE

It was once said of Al Capone that he could have made a formidable legitimate businessman. In Al's mind, that's exactly what he was, running the mob like a corporation and supplying a desired product to consumers.

Al Capone came to Chicago by way of Frankie Yale, a Brooklyn boss who called his one-time partner, Johnny Torrio, and asked him to give his young employee a job. Born in 1899, Capone was a first-generation Italian from Brooklyn, New York, who started running with the wrong element as a kid. He became a bouncer in a bar owned by Frankie Yale and started his foray into the underworld. His famous scar came from an incident in a bar when he told a woman, whose brother was sitting right by her, that she had a beautiful rear end. Her brother, a small-time hoodlum, pulled out a knife and slashed the left side of Capone's face. He was forever ashamed of the scar. When Capone moved to Chicago in 1919 to avoid retribution for beating a member of the notorious White Hand gang, he arrived at the perfect time. Prohibition was on the way. Capone started as a driver for Torrio and as bouncer and barkeep at Torrio's Four Deuces. Perhaps seeing in Capone something of himself, Torrio soon made him his lieutenant and for his part, Capone called his chief "Johnny Papa." Capone stood by Torrio when the time came to deal with Big Jim Colosimo, whose decision not to get into bootlegging risked Torrio and Capone's money-making plans. After Colisimo was gunned down, Torrio took the reins, handing the second-in-command position to his young protégé. Flamboyant and liberal with money, Al Capone commanded attention, hoping to be seen as a gentleman about town. When Torrio brokered a peace agreement among the local mobsters in which everyone got a cut of the action, it was the start of bootlegging as business. The organization took in an estimated $122 million a year from liquor, prostitution, and gambling. The peace didn't last long, though. In 1923, the beer wars began, mob-on-mob violence escalating between September and December, and again after the Torrio/Capone–arranged hit on North Side mob leader Dean O'Banion.

Shots were exchanged between the North and South Side mobs, convincing a wounded Torrio to retire and pass control of the Chicago mob to Capone, who became the king of the underworld. With massive security, secret tunnels and a seven-ton, $20,000 armor-plated car, he was untouchable by fellow gangsters. Using intimidation and bribery, he was able to keep the police force under control as well. So bold was he that when accused of a crime, he often called a press conference, once bringing along a photographer as he surrendered at various precincts only to be told that no one would arrest him. The king of the underworld often meted out brutal justice. When one-time boss Frankie Yale, the man Capone turned to for hits on enemies, was discovered stealing East Coast booze shipments in 1928, Capone had him whacked. The same fate awaited John Scalise and Albert Anselmi, the two behind the O'Banion killing, when Capone found out they planned to cross him. In a particularly vicious act of retribution, the two were invited to a dinner at a roadhouse in Indiana. After dinner, the doors were locked and the two were beaten to death by Capone and his men. It became apparent that Capone felt his safest bet was to begin to eliminate the competition. The last straw came when Bugs Moran started hijacking whiskey shipments. In 1929, while Capone was vacationing in his fourteen-room Miami mansion (the perfect alibi), several of Moran's men were mowed down in the worst case of mob violence to that point. Waking up to the pictures of bullet-ridden bodies in the paper the next day, the public was horrified by the St. Valentine's Day Massacre. This was the beginning of the end for Capone. Declared public enemy number 1 by the Chicago Crime Commission, Capone tried to repair his image by opening soup kitchens, but a five-year investigation came to fruition when a Capone bookkeeper presented the feds with evidence of income tax fraud. This well-dressed gangster who frequented the ritziest nightclubs, owned a large home in Chicago and a mansion in Miami, and drove around in a $20,000 Cadillac, filed "no income" on his tax returns. In 1931, Al Capone was indicted on twenty-two counts of income tax evasion. It was not a hard sell by U.S. attorney George E.Q. Johnson to convince a jury that Capone should be jailed for not paying over $250,000 in back taxes. Capone tried to put a hit out on Johnson and when that failed, tried to plea bargain. When that too failed, he attempted to buy the jury off, but a clever judge switched juries moments before the trial began.

Found guilty, Capone was sent to Alcatraz but in 1938, after entering a much tougher prison, he was diagnosed with syphilis. His mind was going. Eventually, he was released from prison and in 1940 sent to live out his days at his Florida mansion where he was often seen in a bathrobe, fishing on the pier. Seven years later, Capone died of heart failure at forty-eight and his body was laid to rest in Chicago. Prohibition died long before Capone, and the mob had discovered new ways to make money, but while he ruled for less than a decade, Al Capone will always be considered the king of all mobsters.

2. JOHNNY PAPA

The smartest move Johnny Torrio ever made was making Al Capone his protégé. Big Jim Colosimo, however, probably should have reconsidered importing his nephew Johnny from New York. Born in 1882, Torrio came to this country with his family when he was two, soon running with leading street gangs. Looked upon as cold, cruel, and calculating, he took a job as a bouncer at a tough Manhattan bar, and turned his energy to the bars and brothels in the Brooklyn dockyards. Ambitious and clever, he envisioned turning organized crime into a big business. When his uncle, Big Jim Colosimo, took him on board to manage his Chicago operations, under Torrio's direction the brothels and gambling dens in Colosimo's empires flourished, allowing Big Jim to step back and enjoy life. It was Colosimo's biggest mistake. Blood may be thicker than water, but in some families, money outweighs them both. Torrio and Capone had an idea.

Prohibition was on the way. Expand the operation. But Colosimo was content and didn't want the hassle. This put a crimp in Torrio's dreams of citywide control. Uncle Jim had to go. Torrio and Capone turned to New York buddy Frankie Yale, who visited Chicago one day to pay a fatal call on Colosimo. With Big Jim out of the way, the field was clear for Torrio to take over. The organization that Torrio and Capone created played on the strengths of Chicago's ethnic diversity. Prior to this, gangs were very centralized, with territories based on ethnicity. The Torrio gang didn't care who was running the rum as long as they got their cut. The Chicago mob would control everyone by embracing everyone, but make no mistake, there'd be only one leader and that leader was Torrio. Torrio worked at uniting the various mobs, each paying a tribute to Torrio for the sole rights to their territory and most gangs agreed, knowing Torrio's mob had the strength to enforce this plan anyway. But O'Banion's North Side gang had to do things the hard way. After O'Banion led him into a federal trap, Torrio arranged to have his New York pals Frankie Yale, Albert Anselmi, and John Scalise pay O'Banion a little visit. O'Banion's death stunned but didn't stop the North Side mob. Hymie Weiss took the reins, then he and Bugs Moran struck back, ambushing Torrio twice and scoring points on their second attempt in 1925. Wounded in the stomach, arm, and chest, Torrio's condition remained uncertain for over a week, but he rallied. Then he made probably the smartest decision in his life. He decided to retire. At forty-three and a millionaire, he would still have tribute flowing in. Handing the organization over to his trusted lieutenant, he moved back to Brooklyn and in a very uncharacteristic move for a Prohibition mobster, lived until he was seventy-five years old.

3. **AN OFFER HE SHOULDN'T HAVE REFUSED**

Before Capone, before Torrio, Big Jim Colosimo was Vice King of Chicago. He started out as Giancomo Colosimo, arriving here from the south of Italy with his father in the mid-1890s. Like many immigrants, he survived in the Levee by turning to crime. Working his way up from picking pockets to precinct captain (thanks to his ability to guarantee votes for the favored candidates of Bathhouse John and Hinky Dink), his career really took off after he married Levee madam Victoria Moresco. Their holdings went from her brothel to a number of bordellos and saloons, and Colosimo cornered the market on white slavery. Soon, the little pickpocket from the Levee was making $50,000 a month, his house filled with fancy artwork and fancier servants, and he was being driven around in chauffeured motorcars. He was also the "Padrone" to new Italian immigrants, helping them get their start with jobs and housing, and gaining their devotion from it. The thugs of the Levee swore loyalty to Colosimo on a Bible during a ceremony in his office at Colosimo's Café, a nightclub on Wabash that was the hot spot for celebrities and a favorite spot for the criminal elite. Johnny Torrio, one of the lieutenants swearing allegiance to Colosimo, brought into the fold a kid from Brooklyn named Capone.

On the cusp of Prohibition, these two tried to convince Colosimo to expand the bootlegging operations, but comfortable with the prostitution, gambling, and small-time bootlegging, he wasn't interested. Then came May 11, 1920. Torrio phoned and alerted Colosimo to a shipment of bootleg whiskey that was to be dropped off at the café that afternoon. Jim went to the café to accept the shipment and was later found dead in the lobby, shot behind the ear. The murder was filed away as unsolved, but word was that a stranger in the café that day looked a lot like Frankie Yale. Whoever did the deed, it cleared the way for Torrio and Capone to expand the operation with bootlegging and to create one of the most notorious crime organizations ever.

4. **THE FLORIST**

Born in 1892 and raised in Chicago's Little Hell, Dean O'Banion would become the major stone in the shoe of the Torrio/Capone empire. He was into everything when young, peddling papers, jack-rolling drunks, and snatching purses. After joining the Market Street Gang, which roamed the streets of the Forty-Second and Forty-Third Wards, he turned his hand to burglary, then hired on with the *Tribune* beating up newsstand vendors unwilling to sell the paper. Later, he was hired by the *Herald* and *Examiner* for the same purpose. He became ruler of the Forty-Second and Forty-Third Wards, delivering votes through ballot box theft and brutal intimidation, and he did it with a charm that the people loved. Like most other gangsters of the time, he saw the financial potential inherent in the coming Prohibition. By 1922, he had established a $2-million-a-year Lake Shore bootlegging territory. Curiously, he worked as a floral designer in Schofield's florist shop, an establishment he had bought half interest in. He liked the work since it gave him a chance to relax after a hard night's brutality. A teetotaler, he was dapper, expecting his gang to dress as nicely as he did.

O'Banion's problems with Torrio/Capone seemed to stem from the Gennas, a band of six brothers working for Mike Merlo and the Unione Siciliana, sneaking into the North Shore territory and selling their booze at a cut-rate price compared to O'Banion's expensive Canadian whiskey. O'Banion complained to Torrio who told him there was little he could do since the Gennas answered to Merlo. So, O'Banion retaliated by hijacking a shipment of Genna whiskey. The Gennas wanted blood, but Merlo suggested negotiations. Catching wind of the Genna vote, O'Banion decided it was time to retire to the West. Still, there was time for one more dig at Torrio. He tricked Torrio into attending a raid at a brewery knowing that once captured, Torrio risked jail time. Of course, key witnesses suddenly contracted amnesia so none of the gangsters were found guilty, but the seeds had been sown. Capone suggested destroying the markers Angelo Genna owed at an O'Banion establishment, but O'Banion only upped the payment schedule. This was the last straw. When Mike Merlo succumbed to cancer on November 8, it was O'Banion who worked on the various funeral wreaths and flowers ordered for the gangster. Three men entered the shop and O'Banion extended a hand to them. The one in the middle clasped O'Banion's arm and held it tightly as the other two men started firing. As O'Banion fell to the floor, the killers ran from the shop and disappeared into waiting cars down the street. It was clean. Quick. And Dean O'Banion was buried the day after Mike Merlo.

5. **A CLOSE CALL**

When Hymie Weiss fell to Capone-gang bullets, George "Bugs" Moran grabbed hold of the North Side mob. Bugs Moran was born in 1893, the son of Irish and Polish immigrants. He grew up on the North Side of Chicago, ran with a number of gangs, and eventually joined the North Side mob. O'Banion liked his new recruit, enjoying his dark sense of humor. Moran was able to charm the press as well, which only helped with the gang's good reputation in the neighborhood. But he could be brutal when he wanted to. He and Hymie Weiss hunted Torrio and Capone after the murder of Dean O'Banion, and were successful in driving Torrio into retirement. And he headed up the caravan that drove past the Hawthorn Inn the day 1,000 bullets missed Capone. That could be another reason he so disliked "The Beast" as he called Capone—Big Al always managed to get away unharmed. Moran accepted gestures of peace from Capone and would agree to a truce, only to break it shortly after by hijacking one of the Chicago mob's shipments of whiskey. Moran's hijinks were wearing on Capone, who never felt safe with him around. Capone knew that he'd have to deal with Moran before he could have any true peace. So, the elaborate St. Valentine's Day Massacre was set up. Moran's late arrival saved his life that day, but Capone's brutality left Moran shaken. Even after his arch nemesis went to prison, Moran's power in the North Side mob began to wane. He eventually left, moving to Ohio where he reverted to petty crimes. In July 1946, he was arrested for stealing $10,000 from a bank manager. After serving ten years, he was released, but was soon arrested again and sentenced to another ten years in Leavenworth for an earlier bank raid. In 1957, he succumbed to cancer and was buried in a wooden casket in the potter's field outside the prison.

6. THE ENFORCER

For a man known as "The Enforcer," Frank Nitti's ending was rather anticlimactic. Born Frecesco Raffele Nitto in 1889, he emigrated from Sicily to the United States in 1892. He worked as a barber in Brooklyn, as well as a fence for stolen goods, but came to Chicago to become a gunman for Torrio and Capone. As an enforcer, he "coaxed" illegal speakeasies to buy the Outfit's hooch. A small, unassuming but very forceful man, you didn't say "no" to "The Enforcer." He was Al's second in command as well as the moneyman for the Outfit, and when Big Al went to prison, Nitti took over the Chicago mob (though there's speculation that Paul Ricca was really in charge). Having campaigned on a pledge of ridding Chicago of its gangsters, on December 9, 1932, Mayor Anton Cermak sent two tough, corrupt cops to Nitti's office. They were bagmen who collected protection money from organized crime for the mayor. Without a gun, Nitti was helpless. While a third detective held him by the wrists, another shot him in the back and once in the neck. The detective then went into the next room and shot himself in the hand, claiming to newspapermen that Nitti had shot him first. Nitti survived and beat the rap, managing to rule smoothly until the famous Hollywood Extortion case, a racket involving major motion picture studios that went sour. Faced with reprisals from Paul Ricca and sentenced to prison, on March 9, 1943, an inebriated Nitti took a walk along the railroad tracks around his Riverside home and shot himself. The Enforcer was gone.

7. VENDETTA

When Torrio and Capone rubbed out Dean O'Banion, they picked up two more stones for their shoes: Bugs Moran and Hymie Weiss. Weiss had been Dean O'Banion's number-two man in the North Side and took over when the boss was slain. He also quickly retaliated for his boss's murder. Born Earl Wajciechowski in 1898, he changed his name to Weiss and became known as the only man Al Capone ever feared. Weiss was brutal, credited with inventing the phrase "one-way ride." After O'Banion's death, a note of condolence from Big Al was sent to the North Side mob, but Weiss saw through it. In 1925, Hymie and Bugs went gunning for Capone and Torrio. They missed Capone but Weiss attempted to have Capone killed three more times, the most spectacular attempt being in 1926, when Weiss staged a raid on a restaurant Capone and his bodyguard were in. A few cars drove by and opened fire at the building, but realizing that something wasn't right Capone's bodyguard held the gangster down as the rest of the ten-car caravan drove by. The first cars had been firing blanks hoping to rouse Capone into position to be sprayed by the live ammo fired by the rest of the cars. Finally, a gunman got out and stood in the doorway, destroying the restaurant in ten minutes with a spray of 1,000 bullets. Capone saw the writing on the wall. Weiss's desire to kill didn't stem from business. It was personal. He would never stop until the man who ordered the hit on Dean O'Banion was dead. On October 11, 1926, Hymie Weiss was gunned down walking across the street from Weiss/Moran headquarters. Capone's men had rented a room that overlooked the headquarters and from the window opened fire, killing Weiss and his driver, Sam Peller, and wounding three of his men.

8. BIG TUNA

By the time Tony "Big Tuna" Acardo took over, the days of easy bootlegging money were long gone. The Chicago Mob was a major player in the world of national organized crime, but the juice that had gotten it there was now legally obtainable. The Mob turned its attention to nastier things, including narcotics. Acardo, the son of an immigrant shoemaker, played with the big boys of Prohibition, ruling the rackets in town and coming to the attention of Capone and his mob. His closest friend was Paul "The Wailer" Ricca, who took over when Nitti checked out. Acardo started out as a bodyguard and enforcer and there was speculation that he swung a bat at the last dinner party Albert Anselmi and John Scalise would ever attend. Acardo became Ricca's second in command and soon controlled more than 10,000 gambling dens in Chicago. Refusing to touch narcotics, he still gained unfavorable publicity in the 1960s thanks to prosecutions on labor racketeering and income tax evasion. Ricca suggested, for the good of the organization, that Acardo allow Sam "Momo" Giancana to handle things for a while. The starstruck Giancana, however, ended up bringing more publicity to the mob than Acardo. After Giancana agreed to a selfimposed exile, Acardo resumed control of the mob and showed that he could be stern in his dealings with those who crossed him. When a burglary crew operating outside the

Outfit hit his home on Ashland Avenue, he sent a hit squad after them who dealt with them brutally, including castrating one and disemboweling another. Acardo was repeatedly hauled in front of U.S. Senate subcommittees and grand juries as the government tried whatever they could to break him and the mob, yet he never spent a night in jail. When he passed away in 1992, frail and riddled with cancer, a part of Chicago history passed away with him as well. That cohesiveness that started in the Prohibition era began to unravel.

9. **STAR COLLECTOR**

After becoming a liability to his mob pals, Sam "Momo" Giancana met his end, shot with seven bullets to the head, as he cooked a midnight snack of sausages in his basement kitchen. Born in 1908 in a Chicago Italian ghetto known as the "Patch," Giancana became a member of the Forty-Second Gang that ran on Chicago's West Side and did his first jail term, one month for car theft, at seventeen. In 1931, after serving a three-year prison term for burglary, he returned to his pals in the Forty-Second Gang who were working for Capone's organization. He found himself in prison again in 1939 after a raid on a still he and his buddies were using, and while there learned of the money to be made by nickel-per-bet "policy" games. After his release, he hooked up with a bail bondsman and gambler named William Skidmore who introduced him to Acardo. Now the boss of the Outfit, Acardo liked Giancana's ideas on the "policy racket," and made him his driver. He also gave Giancana the green light to move in on a policy racket of his own. The money garnered from this racket earned Giancana a position on "the board" and from there he took control of gambling, loan sharking, prostitution, and labor racketeering. When Acardo went into semiretirement, Giancana took the reins with Acardo always prepared to step back in if necessary. Giancana made a mistake, though. He became starstruck. He loved the good life and flaunted the fact that he could afford it. While he dated many dancers and singers, his most famous romance was with Phyllis McGuire of the McGuire Sisters singing group. When the Outfit moved into Vegas in the 1950s, it only whetted his appetite. He was treated like royalty in Vegas and he palled around with the Rat Pack, becoming a good friend to Frank Sinatra. He got caught up in politics, too, conducting deals with Joseph P. Kennedy to help get John F. in the White House by raising money for the West Virginia primary and giving him key Chicago wards. There was even talk of helping to win back Cuba after Castro took over. The Kennedys turned on him, though, when J. Edgar Hoover revealed what he knew of their connection to the mobster. Robert Kennedy went after forty mobsters, Sam the number one priority. Tony Acardo's hope that Giancana would lead with a low profile was dashed. When he was hauled before a grand jury in 1963, Giancana was informed that he had been given immunity from any prosecution that might result from his testimony. It was a brilliant move by the FBI. Prevented from using his Fifth Amendment right, Giancana spent a year in jail for refusing to speak to the grand jury.

Once freed when the grand jury ended, he hightailed it to Mexico in 1966 to avoid further governmental tricks. Using Mexico as a base for ten years, he went on a world tour, living the high life in the Bahamas, Beirut, Switzerland, and other countries. When bribes no longer kept him from extradition, he was sent back to the United States, but his return spelled trouble for Acardo, who had taken control again. When he was ordered before another grand jury, Giancana was again given immunity, this time voluntarily accepting, yet trying to give away as little as possible. But Giancana had embroiled himself in a nest of controversy, criminally and politically, and anything he said would bring unwanted publicity to the Outfit. On June 18, 1975, in his small Oak Park home, Sam Giancana, the mobster who ran with the stars and helped create presidents, was gunned down as he cooked his sausage. An inauspicious ending, but not necessarily an unusual one, for one of Chicago's gangsters.

10.   **"BIG JIM" O'LEARY:**

Poor Mrs. O'Leary. Carrying the blame for the Chicago Fire, she also had to face the fact that her son, Jim O'Leary, was one of Chicago's first gangsters. He even succeeded Michael McDonald as king of the Chicago gambling world, running the South Side as part of the most influential gambling syndicates in town. What's a mother to do? Under the threat of reform in Chicago, O'Leary took his operation into Indiana where betting parlors were run freely. Indiana tried to shut him down, but he claimed he had rights and surrounded his barn with a stockade of logs eighteen feet high, ordering men stationed to shoot anyone trying to forcibly enter. Back in Illinois, he opened a huge bookie joint that was protected by spiked fences and packs of watchdogs. Cashing in on the action, the Santa Fe Railway ran three "Gamblers Special" trains out to O'Leary's while Western Union supplied the wire service until the furious attorney general demanded that both Santa Fe and Western Union cut ties with O'Leary. The loss in business caused Big Jim to close his doors. O'Leary peppered his two-story stronghold on Halsted Street with false partitions, tunnels, hidden passageways, and reinforced doors, and, thanks to tips he received from bribed police officers, was able to clear the place completely when raids were conducted. Gamblers escaped through various routes and mingled among the patrons of his legitimate businesses on Halsted Street, which included a Turkish bath, bowling alley and billiard parlor, barbershop, and restaurant. His hands were in a number of pies and partnerships, but he wasn't above a bit of backstabbing, either. Provided no one tried to gain the upper hand, handbooking was allowed during the summer racing seasons, but in 1902, O'Leary violated an agreement the syndicates had made the year before by trying to move his operation into the city and racetracks. In 1905, he was a partner in a gambling ship on Lake Michigan, the first of its kind in American history. With a $40,000 investment by the syndicate, the thirty-six-year-old steamer named the *City of Traverse* set sail from the Illinois Central Slip, its maiden voyage carrying hundreds of "sporting men" onboard who were given the green light to gamble once outside the jurisdiction of Illinois. Several decades later, to get around dry land antigambling laws, casino boats would obtain licenses to conduct their business on the river. Jim O'Leary and his syndicate proved to be ahead of their time.

Clubbing Then and Now

C hicago is, without a doubt, a party town. Always has been, always will be.

1. THE SAUGANASH HOTEL

It was Chicago's first swinging night spot, owned and operated by a part-French, part-Indian father of twenty-three and grandfather of fifty-three. In 1826, twenty-six-year-old Mark Beaubien traveled to Chicago to visit his brother. There was no town as yet—really just fourteen or so houses and around a hundred citizens. Beaubien liked what he saw, though, and sent for his family. Purchasing a house from John Kinzie, and building an addition, he opened a hotel and tavern known as the Sauganash Hotel. It was a white, two-story building with bright blue shutters and music pouring from it thanks to Beaubien's love of his fiddle. A congenial man, Beaubien made everyone feel welcome and the place soon became popular. White women drank liquor straight from the bottle right next to men, as Indian braves danced with the wives of fort officers. Conservative easterners, already shocked by the goings on, might have been startled even further by the family of John Kinzie, who would don feathered headdresses and rush into the crowded tavern with war whoops simply for shock value. Eventually Chicago grew, and that wild world changed. Beaubien sold the hotel, and by 1836, it was renamed the United States Hotel. Mark Beaubien went on to live as a Chicago lighthouse keeper and manager of a tavern. In 1881, he died at the Kankakee house of one of his daughters.

2. METRO

Metro is the place to go for alternative rock. Not known for its ambiance, it's where the big acts play when they're in town. Located in an old auditorium near Wrigley Field, the club has played host to bands like Nirvana, REM, Pearl Jam, and Smashing Pumpkins along with lesser and local acts. The best place to be if you want to watch the performance is at one of the tables in the balcony. For dancers, there's a dance floor on the main floor though that can get pretty crowded. If you're just in the mood to dance, you can go downstairs to the Smart Bar where mixes are played seven nights a week. It has the atmosphere of its subterranean location and is a perfect place to lose yourself in movement and music. And some of the acts have been known to head down there after their show.

3. THE GREEN MILL

The history of the Green Mill is rooted in the heady days of Prohibition. One of Al Capone's speakeasies, it was a hangout for big names of the day. Charlie Chaplin, Mary Pickford, and Douglas Fairbanks could be seen hoisting a few after a day's filming at Essanay Studios. Established in 1907, the Green Mill also holds the distinction of being the oldest jazz club in the United States. It was here that comedian Joe E. Lewis got his throat slashed from ear to ear when he accepted a better offer that Jack "Machine Gun" McGurn advised against. *The Joker Is Wild*, a movie starring Frank Sinatra, is based on Lewis's story. Located in Uptown, it was and still is the place to hear some of the best jazz in town. Back in the day, the Green Mill was an entire block long, with a restaurant, beer garden, and cocktail lounge. Men wore tuxedos and ladies evening gowns as they listened to Billie

Holiday sing or jumped to the jive of Benny Goodman. World famous, it was even profiled on *60 Minutes*. But the area changed in the 1970s and '80s, going downhill. A cleanup of the area in the 1990s, along with current owner Dave Jemilo's hard work at restoring the club, has brought it back to its former glory. It's still the place to hear the best jazz as well as swing, big bands, blues, and even poetry slams with the Uptown Poetry Slam. Belly up to the bar and thumb through the scrapbook of days gone by. Or better yet, take a seat in the red velvet booth and savor the speakeasy flavor that still exists in the historic hot spot.

4. ELBO ROOM

You may think you've entered a corner bar. Dark and full of tables, there's a game room and a bar and hosts of people sitting around. They're waiting, however, for the show to begin downstairs, and from the TV monitors upstairs they can view the preparations going on down there. Elbo Room plays host to an eclectic mix of bands from alternative rock to rock-a-billy, hip-hop, soul, funk, goth, and more, and a diverse crowd fills up the bar. For a (usually) low cover charge, you can head downstairs and savor the sounds of acts both local and national. There aren't a lot of places to sit, but most of the acts get you in the mood to move around. And when you're dry, you can head over to the bar in the back for a refill. Its lack of pretentiousness is important to the club's atmosphere. It has a low-key comfort that makes anyone feel at home.

5. BUDDY GUY'S LEGENDS

A legendary name in the world of blues music, Buddy Guy's nightclub has been called the best blues club in town. Near the South Loop, it's a hot spot for famous names in blues and beyond. Mick Jagger, a friend of Guy's, has been known to jam there. The club is comfortable, the walls decorated with blues paraphernalia and photos, and yuppies mix with fans in baseball caps and sweats. The food served pays homage to the cuisine of the Mississippi Delta and the calendar is chock full of live music with free acoustic sets every Friday and Saturday. And if you're lucky, you may even come on a night when Buddy himself is jamming onstage.

6. ARAGON BALLROOM

The Aragon Ballroom has seen better days. Built in 1926, this was the premier place to go to see a live band or dance the night away on the maple floor. Floorwalkers wore tuxedos, while men and women were both expected to wear formal attire. Brothers Andrew and William Karzas were going for an air of respectability during the unbridled 1920s. Dance halls were often ripe with vice. The Karzas's early club, the Trianon, had been a hit with the more conservative minded, and the brothers hoped to duplicate this success by making the Aragon as elegant as the Trianon. The strict policies on alcohol and smoking also made it possible to admit middle-class youths. A carpeted grand staircase led up to the dance floor on the second level. Once inside, you were transported to a different land. Surrounded by an architectural facade of balconies and entranceways, the dance floor was beneath a ceiling lit with small lights that twinkled like stars, leaving the dancer to imagine dancing in a Spanish courtyard. At some point, WGN radio conducted remotes from the ballroom six nights a week. The death of swing, and the rise of television, left the Aragon in the dust. After the 1960s, it hosted various events from wrestling matches to roller derby. Now, it serves as a venue for rock concerts, its elegance gone in favor of mosh pit brawls and overpriced drinks in plastic cups. But its size lends itself to larger acts, and it remains a place where people go to hear their favorite music. It's just not quite as classy.

7. THE PUMP ROOM

Sixty years and you still know you've arrived when you're enjoying a meal in Booth One of the Pump Room. Located in the Ambassador East Hotel, the Pump Room has been the place to hobnob with socialites and celebrities since it opened in 1938. Booth One celebrated the wedding of Bogie and Bacall, played host to sports greats like Muhammad Ali, Michael Jordan, and Walter Payton, and the Chairman of the Board Frank Sinatra held meetings of the cool crowd there. The Pump Room was an instant success when it opened on October 1, 1938, with a black-tie charity event where the waiters were dressed in scarlet tailcoats with feathered head-dresses. The Ambassador East itself, located in the Gold Coast area, opened in October 1926 and still has some suites named after movie stars or authors. The photos of celebrities cover the walls leading to the Pump Room, which still plays host to the in crowd when they're in town. Take a seat in Booth One, and maybe you'll be seen in the next morning's papers.

8. THE BABY DOLL POLKA CLUB

If you like to polka, this is the place for it. Located across from Midway Airport, it's beer-hall-meets-airport, with air-plane accents such as photos of vintage planes and four bi-planes made from beer cans hanging from the rafters. There's even a windsock on the roof. Formerly a house, it's a perfect place to sit and watch, through the picture window, the takeoffs and landings going on at Midway, but it's also a haven for polka enthusiasts who flock to the club to listen to the cream of the polka crop. The club takes its name from a 1948 hit polka "The Baby Doll Polka," put out by owner Eddie Korosa Sr. Open since 1955, the club was started by Eddie and his wife, Irene, but is now run by Eddie Jr. in the location they've called home since 1981. Eddie Jr.'s band, Eddie Korosa Jr. and His Boys from Illinois, are often on-stage, and the jukebox is loaded with Tommy Dorsey, Hank Williams, and Peggy Lee. With its carpeted bar and mirrored walls, the Baby Doll Polka Club will take you back to a time when people polkaed till they dropped.

9. FUNKY BUDDHA LOUNGE

Cover-charge-wise, this is a steep one. Located in the River North district, it's also one of the hottest nightspots in town. The Buddha statue on the front door welcomes you into an industrialized and eclectic world, atmospheric with low lighting from the antique light fixtures that used to illuminate a church, and plenty of candles to lead you on. There's a large dance floor where you can dance to a techno mix of salsa, Brazilian, hip-hop, and soul.

Or you can lounge on the black leather and fake-leopard-skin couches, or enjoy a martini at the tables or booths that surround the bar.

10. THE CHECKERBOARD LOUNGE

One of the premier blues clubs, the Rolling Stones and Led Zeppelin have taken to its small stage. But then, most importantly, so have Buddy Guy, Muddy Waters, Junior Wells, and Koko Taylor. Located on the South Side, you'll find some of the best new blues artists performing at the Checkerboard. It has a friendly, no-frills atmosphere and reasonable drink prices, and the walls are covered with photos of blues legends.

Cameos

The following films use Chicago, not just as a backdrop, but more like a costar, embracing her scenery, her history, or her people to tell the story.

1. *THE BLUES BROTHERS*

The Blues Brothers didn't just embrace Chicago, they made love to it, albeit violently. Joliet Jake and Elwood Blues first hit the scene as a bit on *Saturday Night Live*. John Belushi and Dan Ackroyd took their characters to the big screen in 1984, telling the story of two slightly shady, out-of-work blues musicians "on a mission from God" to help save an orphanage from the Cook County tax assessor. Tearing up the town in search of their bandmates, the brothers are hounded by state troopers, a jilted lover, a pissed-off country-and-western band, and an equally agitated pack of Illinois Nazis. Directed by John Landis, this rampaging taste of Chicago also showcased the talents of the Blues Brothers band and featured musical cameos by Aretha Franklin, James Brown, Ray Charles, John Lee Hooker, and a stunning performance as Minnie the Moocher by the late Cab Calloway (who played the brothers' mentor in the film). Mayor Jane Byrne lifted Mayor Daley's ban on filming in town and the production took full advantage of streets, landmarks, and hundreds of actual law enforcement personnel. We get to see

Maxwell Street as it once was—suburban streets, inner-city neighborhoods, and everything in between. A breathless chase sequence occurs on lower Wacker Drive as the brothers make their way to Daley Plaza chased by everything that can roll, trot, or swim. The grand finale has Daley Plaza choked with cop cars, trucks, and even tanks. SWAT-team members rappel down the sides of the Cook County Courthouse, and hundreds of security personnel stream inside. There's even a cameo by a young Stephen Spielberg. You don't ask questions when you watch the Blues Brothers. You just enjoy the ride.

2. *MEDIUM COOL*

Channel surfing reveals how ahead of its time the question at the core of *Medium Cool* was. Ridiculous reality shows where ridiculous people do ridiculous things for a ridiculous prize (considering the dignity they sacrifice) infest TV, and who is responsible for these shows—the networks that shove them down our throats or the public for swallowing willingly? This question comes up in a cocktail party during the movie as partygoers bemoan the violence on TV, and others remind them that violence is on TV because it sells. The journalists in *Medium Cool* are constantly confronted by situations that ask them how much they are willing to swallow to keep their objectivity. The opening scene involves a cameraman played by Robert Forrester and a soundman played by Peter Bonerez, standing on the expressway getting film and sound of an accident for that night's news telecast. It's only after they've gotten their footage that they radio the accident in. They are, after all, journalists. They have to remain on the outside for the sake of the story. But this is Chicago, 1968. As the Democratic National Convention drew closer, everyone's objectivity would be put to the test. The makers of this film had serendipity on their side. The actual riot in Grant Park is used as a backdrop for the story of a young mother searching the city for her son who's picked an inconvenient time to run away. Dressed in a light yellow dress, she's a standout against the violence of the day. This is what makes the film truly remarkable, its use of the riot as a backdrop to tell its story. Those are real troops marching down the street, and real blood pouring out of real wounds. And like the journalists in their films, the filmmakers of *Medium Cool* find themselves in the position of recording events without interfering.

3.   *CALL NORTHSIDE 777*

For the reporter, it begins as a human-interest story. An ad in the classifieds, asking for any information on a murder, was placed by an old Polish scrubber woman who's been washing floors for eleven years to save enough money to offer a reward for information. Her son has been in prison for a murder he didn't commit. Or so he claims. Talking to the convicted murderer, the originally skeptical reporter begins to consider the possibility that the man has been railroaded. And so begins the hunt to solve a mystery. The 1948 film *Call Northside 777* is based on a true story that started in the City News Bureau. In real life, it was two reporters sent to crack the case. In the film, the two reporters are made into a composite played by James Stewart. More than just filmed on location (in the "Back of the Yards" area . . . a rough district near stockyards), the movie uses the city's reputation. It uses Chicago's bootlegging past, speakeasies, and hints of corruption and clusters of immigrants, average people trying to survive, crossing into the gray areas of the law and becoming embroiled in much more than they bargained for. The film is notable for its dark and gritty portrayal of a reporter trying to right a criminal injustice. The reporter runs up against well-meaning police trying to defend the reputation of their force, uncooperative eyewitnesses, doctored evidence, and a governor who would prefer that the matter just go away. As in real life, the fictional reporter's efforts pay off, helping to gain a pardon for the man.

4. *ONLY THE LONELY*

John Candy plays Chicago cop Danny Muldoon, nearing forty, single, and living with his mom, Rose, played by Maureen O'Hara. A comfortable routine permeates the situation and eases any urges he may have for change. That is, until he meets Teresa Luna, played by Ally Sheedy, a young woman whom Rose disapproves of because she's Sicilian, because she works in her father's funeral home, and mainly because Mom is old-school Irish and in her book, in matters of love you consort with your own kind. It's for the same reasons that she rejects the advances of her neighbor "Nick the Greek" played by Anthony Quinn, though deep down she is very interested. Directed by Chris Columbus, this wonderfully romantic 1991 tale celebrates the old Chicago neighborhoods, with the blocks of houses with pubs or grocery stores on the corners, and elevated tracks running through the neighborhoods. There were people you lived next to for decades, saying hello as you passed by. The romance of the setting underscores the romance of the two people. Using connections, Danny makes the first date a nighttime picnic on the pitcher's mound of the old Comiskey Park (it was scheduled for demolition shortly after the filming), complete with scoreboard and fireworks. The montage on their second date has the city lit up at night, blending into a morning skyline as they walk along the lake. But Rose, in her loneliness, has a hold on Danny that may prevent him from the best thing that's ever happened to him. She's a woman who tells it like it is and often drives people away in doing so. This is a time of change for the characters, and as with neighborhoods themselves, change is usually unstoppable.

5. *THE UNTOUCHABLES*

Despite the glaring historical (and often hilarious) errors (Frank Nitti did not fall to his death after being pushed off the Federal Building by Elliot Ness), Brian De Palma's 1987 *The Untouchables* was an ambitious retelling of how a unit of federal agents formed to smash the illegal liquor industry and bring down Al Capone. As with the TV show by the same name, the movie buys into the mythology brought forth in Elliot Ness's autobiography where the Untouchables are given a bit more credit than they deserve for the fall of Capone. The tale told by Ness is heavily mythologized, and the sweeping musical score by Ennio Morricone underscores that mythology. And why not? This was a time of war, a war on crime, and war has a tendency to be mythologized when it's retold. Starring Kevin Costner as Ness, Sean Connery as Ness's fictional mentor, and Robert De Niro as Al Capone, the shooting of the film was aided by the old-time architecture of Chicago. Many areas still have the look and feel of that era.

6. *A Raisin in the Sun*

Walter Lee is tired of being a chauffer. If he can just convince his mother to invest in the liquor store his friends are considering, then maybe he can make a better life for his family. But Momma has other plans for the $10,000 insurance check she's been waiting on since her husband's death. She's been watching her family living on top of each other in that small, South Side apartment for too long. She went out and bought a house where five people would have room to breathe and she could have a little garden to putter in. The problem, aside from Walter Lee's frustration-fueled temper, was that Momma bought the house in a white neighborhood, and in 1950s Chicago, whites were very particular about who moved into their neighborhood. Based on the award-winning play by Chicagoan Lorraine Hansberry, the 1961 film *A Raisin in the Sun* starred Sidney Poitier and Claudia McNeil and is another example of a movie that utilizes the social reality of Chicago to tell a story. The Younger family's story could have been that of any number of African American, South Side families of the time trying to better their lives only to run into financial reality, racism, con men, or self-destructive pride. The movie has the Youngers prevailing as many families did. A number of families, however, were unable to make it beyond those walls, carrying on the cycle.

7. *EIGHT MEN OUT*

This 1988 movie tells the story of the 1919 White Sox, who were dubbed the Black Sox after a conspiracy to throw the World Series was revealed. Considering how rare it is for Chicago to even get into playoffs of any sport, throwing a championship that most people then and now believed could have been won leaves a particularly sore spot. Interestingly enough, the movie wasn't filmed in Chicago, but it does star a few Chicago actors like John Cusack as Bucky Weaver and *Frasier*'s John Mahoney. And in a clever twist, Chicago writer Studs Terkel plays the sportswriter who breaks the story in print. But the real star in *Eight Men Out* is Chicago's eternal love of baseball. The story of the child telling Shoeless Joe Jackson "Say it ain't so, Joe!" is a fabrication, but it speaks to the pain all Chicagoans felt during that terrible scandal. They put their hopes and dreams on the team and felt the sting of betrayal. The film uses that emotion to tell its story.

8. *THE FUGITIVE*

This 1993 remake of an old TV show—which itself was inspired by the true-life murder case of Dr. Sam Sheperd—begins with a news report showing Dr. Richard Kimble being led away from his home by the Area 6 police. The reporter's voice is unmistakably that of John Drummond, a Chicago television journalist. Drummond (one of a number of actual Chicago news reporters used in the film) refers to the policemen as Area 6 detectives and Kimble's residence as his "near North Side home." These are details you'd expect to hear in a Chicago newscast and they add color to a film set in Chicago. Kimble is a vascular surgeon at the fictional Chicago Memorial Hospital. He claims that he returned home to find his wife fatally injured by a one-armed intruder and after battling with the intruder, the man got away. The state doesn't buy it and Kimble is sent to prison for the murder of his wife. It's en route to custody that a bus crash enables him to make his escape back to Chicago, hounded by FBI agent Tommy Lee Jones and his team. In Chicago he discovers the conspiracy behind his wife's death. As with *Call Northside 777*, *The Fugitive* uses an old murder mystery to tell a compelling story. Director Andrew Davis, born and bred on Chicago's South Side, tries to film in Chicago whenever he gets the chance. Sights like the elevated train tracks, Daley Plaza, the St. Patrick's Day Parade, and Cook County Hospital (where Kimble begins his search for the one-armed man) are all used to full effect.

9. *FERRIS BUELLER'S DAY OFF*

In high school, everyone wanted to be like Ferris Bueller. Ferris sets up an elaborate plan to arrange a day off for himself, his girlfriend, and his best friend, Cameron, who would love to let loose but spends most of his time waiting for the other shoe to drop. Their objective: a day in downtown Chicago. This 1986 movie illustrates what every suburban highschooler knows: Chicago is where you go when you cut school. You catch a ball game at Wrigley, you tour the Art Institute, have a nice meal at a fancy restaurant, and maybe even find yourself marching in a parade. Well, Ferris Bueller might be the only one capable of finagling his way onto the float of an ethnic parade, wowing the crowd by lip-synching "Twist and Shout." Directed by John Hughes (who films in Chicago regularly) and starring Mathew Broderick as Ferris, the film is a lighthearted romp with an underlying point. Even at seventeen, life's too short. Sometimes you need to take the chance and enjoy life. And there's no better city in which to do so than Chicago.

10. *THE BEGINNING OF THE END*

I couldn't resist including this 1957 movie where a shot of bugs crawling on a picture of the Wrigley Building is considered a special effect. Radioactively enlarged grasshoppers chewing up Illinois (though judging by the mountainous terrain early on in the film, Illinois was nowhere in the vicinity of the production) converge upon the Windy City and it's up to Peter Graves to stop them. In a fabulous fit of cinematic fantasy, the stately Wrigley Building is besieged by the giant bugs. Only, it's not the Wrigley Building or even a carefully constructed model. It's a photo, flat and quite obvious as the six-legged marauders begin to step off the building and into the sky. Cut to the concerned face of Peter Graves as he desperately works on a plan to save the world. His plan: Send a boat out onto Lake Michigan with a recording of a horny bug to coax the hungry hoppers to their watery deaths.

Television

1. CHICAGO SCHOOL OF TELEVISION

The term was first used in a 1951 *Look Magazine* article describing the relaxed, intimate style of Chicago television productions. With its improvisational nature, Chicago jerry-rigged the new medium of television to fit the town's sensibilities. This was a town that knew how to fly by the seat of its pants. Without the big names from Broadway that New York had, or the stars from movies like Hollywood had, Chicago had to rely on the strength of the ensemble. Burr Tillstrom and Fran Allison, for example, worked sans script on *Kukla, Fran and Ollie. Stud's Place, Zoo Parade* and *Garroway at Large* were unscripted and immediate. Camera work was fluid and daring, not fixed like many East Coast productions. It was an artist's tool to enhance the show, not merely record it. The stars were quick on their feet, able to work without a net and willing to experiment to find out just where the medium could be taken. It was that unpredictable element that kept the viewer coming back. The relaxed style made a comeback with the news in late 1960s and into the 1970s. Inaccurately known as "Happy Talk" news, it was more a presentation of the news in the relaxed and intimate way that Chicago TV was so proficient at. Newspeople were allowed to bring a little more humor to the newscast, presenting lighter stories in a lighter way than the usual stiff way of most news readers. One of the most popular of the news teams was the Channel 7 Eyewitness News with Fahey Flynn and Joel Daly, sportscaster Bill Frink, and John Coleman as the weatherman. Coleman, especially, became a local favorite with his oftentimes hilarious weather forecasts. Coleman later became a founding member of the Weather Channel.

2. THUMBS UP

Gene Siskel and Roger Ebert became household names nationwide thanks to their 1975 *Sneak Previews*, which began on WTTW, the local PBS station. Together, Siskel and Ebert critiqued the week's films hoping to either turn the viewer on to a worthy offering, or save the viewer the cost of admission. The main appeal was the dynamic between the two. Gene Siskel from the *Chicago Tribune* and Roger Ebert from the rival *Chicago Sun-Times* were like oil and water, and their verbal boxing matches could get pretty heated. But the discussion on films they agreed on could be just as lively, mainly because they had in common a love of film and a clever way of presenting that affection. In 1975, Ebert became the first film critic to win a Pulitzer Prize. Siskel was a Yale graduate who enjoyed *Wayne's World* as much as he did *Fargo*. They weren't above spoofing themselves, either, their senses of humor making them favorites on talk shows like *Late Night with David Lettermen*, or guest-star voices on Fox's *The Critic*. Eventually, the show became *Siskel & Ebert* and went national. Sadly, in 1999, Gene Siskel died from a brain tumor, a loss not only to Chicago but to the film world. Many stars and directors paid tribute to him, and the Film Center at the Art Institute was renamed the Gene Siskel Film Center in his honor. Ebert decided to keep the show going, working with a series of guest hosts until choosing fellow *Sun-Times* columnist Richard Roeper to sit across the aisle from him. Still, one can't help but get nostalgic for the days when a Siskel and Ebert disagreement made you wonder if that would be the night that they came to blows.

3. CHILDREN'S TV

When it comes to children's TV in Chicago, two names deserve more mention than they get: Ray Raynor and Bill "B.J." Jackson. A generation of kids woke up with Ray and lunched with B.J. and Dirty Dragon. The *Ray Raynor and Friends* show ran weekday mornings from 7:00 to 8:30 on WGN. His jumpsuit covered in notes that would direct him on what was coming up next, Ray joked between cartoons on a low-maintenance set with whatever props were handy. He might march about to band music in a band uniform and baton, the cameraman doing what, for the time, were pretty clever camera tricks. Perhaps he'd go visit Cuddly Duddly, a stuffed dog puppet that lived in a doghouse on an astroturf hill who teased Ray good-naturedly during their discussion. Then there was Chelvaston the duck, a real and really nasty white duck that demanded food and was none too polite when taking it. Ray didn't talk down to kids. He had fun doing his skits and trusted the kids to find the humor. And then there were the crafts, suggestions sent in by viewers that never looked the same when Ray tried his hand at them. Of course, Ray was intrepid. This was a man who, as a young soldier, had been shot down over Germany and wound up in a POW camp (the one that *The Great Escape* was based on).

The other big local station at the time, WFLD, had B.J. Jackson, a little more sedate than Raynor, but still someone who enjoyed creating on camera. He started out with a show called *Clown Alley* where characters such as Dirty Dragon and the Blob were born. Dressed in suit and bowler hat, in 1968 he went on to *Cartoon Town*, becoming mayor of a fictional town populated by his special puppets. Postmaster general was the dragon named Dirty Dragon who blew fire and yelled "Fiiiii!" when upset, which seemed to be often. Then there was the old Professor, Mother Plumtree, The Lemon Joke Kid (who, from an airplane, dropped lemons with jokes printed on them that were so bad the reader's mouth instantly puckered). And let's not forgot the Blob, the blob of gray clay on a pedestal that communicated with moans, grunts, and whines. A talented artist, B.J. would sculpt Blob into whatever form the blob of clay desired that day. A wrong move would elicit a disgruntled moan from the clay while the end result would leave Blob grunting with happiness. In front of a large easel, B.J. would draw pictures from letters or numbers that had been printed on the paper. The bit might take five minutes but kids at home would munch on their sandwiches and watch transfixed, anxious to see what he came up with. In 1973, the show was changed to *BJ and Dirty Dragon Show* and moved to WGN. Along with the show, Jackson took his puppets on the road, making public appearances at malls and fests, which were always huge draws as kids lined up to meet their favorite characters. In 1975, Jackson took his puppets and checked into the *Gigglesnort Hotel* at WLS, where as manager he tried to keep control over the crazy inhabitants of the hotel. Ray and B.J. produced magical shows that were among the cream of local children's television.

4. A NEW EXPLORER

Along with his coanchor, Walter Jacobson, Bill Kurtis helped bring WBBM Channel 2 news to the forefront during the 1970s. Though he made a solid anchor, he wasn't strapped to the desk, more than willing to do field reporting and reporting from such tumultuous locations as war-torn Vietnam (two weeks before the fall of Saigon) and Northern Ireland. He came to Chicago from Kansas where he earned a bachelor's degree in journalism and a juris doctorate. After a stint in Wichita news, he came to Chicago in the late 1960s just in time to cover the riots of 1968 and the Chicago Seven conspiracy trials. He also covered stories beyond Chicago, like the Charles Manson trial. Teamed with Walter Jacobson in 1973, Kurtis continued as an investigative journalist, developing a unit, which led to his work exposing the story on

Agent Orange and the effect it was having on soldiers exposed to it. Nine years later, New York called and Kurtis joined the team of *The CBS Morning News* in 1982. He hosted a number of documentaries for *CBS Reports* also. He grew weary of network politics, however, and three years later returned to Chicago, rejoining WBBM and developing hourlong documentaries for the station. Soon, he formed Kurtis Productions, run out of Chicago, producing documentaries that he was able to sell to the developing cable industry. His work is shown regularly on A&E and has won many journalism awards. His love of exploring inspired the series *The New Explorers*, which has won the George Foster Peabody award as well as several Emmys. Kurtis Productions remains headquartered out of Chicago.

5. **TUNE IN TOMORROW**

The mother of daytime soaps, Irna Phillips was born in Chicago in 1901. Hired to provide voices for WGN radio, she was given the project of creating a daily program and her *Painted Dreams* is usually considered radio's first soap opera. An ownership dispute at WGN led to her departure and she went on to create *Today's Children* for WMAQ, which aired for seven years followed by 1937's *Guiding Light*, 1938's *Road of Life*, and 1939's *The Right to Happiness*. Selling the shows to national networks, in 1943 she had five programs on the air. The first to use organ music to connect scenes, Phillips was also the first to keep audiences returning with cliff-hanger endings. She developed the slow pace of the soap opera story lines so that housewives needn't be glued to the set every second. While productions for her shows were based on the coasts, she remained in Chicago. In the 1950s, Phillips's association with the Proctor and Gamble company brought her shows to television. Her most famous, *As the World Turns*, debuted in 1956, and at its peak in the '60s was viewed by 50 percent of the daytime audience. At thirty minutes (most serials were fifteen), *As*

the World Turns was also the first soap to introduce a schem-
ing female character while her 1964 *Another World* (the first
sixty-minute soap) was the first to deal with the subject of
abortion. In 1965, she created *Days of Our Lives*, another
long-lasting soap. Phillips was never afraid to broach sensi-
tive subjects, but by the '70s, her simpler stories couldn't
compete with the more sensational plot lines audiences were
craving. Eventually in 1973, Proctor and Gamble fired her
and in December of that year, she passed away.

6. *STUDS' PLACE*

This ensemble was a perfect example of the Chicago School
of Television. Studs Terkel used his experience in his mother's boardinghouse to play the owner of a greasy-spoon-type
establishment containing its share of colorful characters.
The show first aired at the tail end of 1949 as a segment on
Saturday Night Square, a variety show. Then it was set in a
tavern. When it returned on its own in April 1950, the setting
was changed to the restaurant. Working without a script,
Studs and the cast would be given a rough outline of the
show's plot at rehearsal and then improvise their lines on
the air. Along with Studs and Beverly Younger, who played the
waitress, there was Phil Lord, who played an old-time actor,
jazz pianist Chet Roble playing himself, and guitarist and folk
singer Win Stracke who also played himself. The absence of
script meant the absence of camera marks, so cameramen
were put through their paces trying to anticipate which actor
would speak next. *Studs' Place* was an ambitious attempt to
do a free-form style of television, much in keeping with
Studs's affinity for jazz. The problem was finding a sponsor
for it. It went off the air in August 1950, and returned the
following year on ABC backed by local sponsors like Manor
House Coffee in Chicago. It remained a tough sell, though,
and soon left the air. Despite its short life, it remains a fascinating glimpse into work being done in the early years of the
medium.

7. *HILL STREET BLUES*

Chicago is written all over this television series and yet it's
never once mentioned in the show. In fact, the city protected
by Hill Street's finest remains unnamed throughout the series, but the feel of the Windy City permeates the entire production, from the opening credit shot filmed at Maxwell
Street Police Station to the bitter winter weather. Even the
uniforms have the blue-and-black colors of the Chicago police and the characters have that gritty, down-to-earth feel to
them. Add to the cast Chicagoans like Betty Thomas or Dennis Franz with that unmistakable accent and there's no escaping the connection. *Hill Street Blues* was a landmark
television series: a police drama with continuing story lines
where the characters were drawn with shades of gray. The
ratings for the award-winning series were so low originally
that it might not have survived the first few airings had Bran-
don Tartikoff not seen the show's potential and decided to
stick with it. It left the air one of the most popular and highly
respected shows ever. It also helped further the careers of
Thomas, who went on to direct movies, and Franz, a star of
the critically acclaimed *NYPD Blue*.

8. *THE UNTOUCHABLES*

Recently, the TV show *The Sopranos* caused the community
to protest that the show was portraying Italians in a bad light.
The show was in a bad position. Based on a Mafia family, it
would be hard not to have the characters be of Italian descent. Back in 1959, long before Italians were up in arms
over their race portrayal on the HBO show *The Sopranos*,
there was another show that made the community see red.
Its name was *The Untouchables*.

Based on the memories of Elliot Ness, *The Untouchables*
began as *The Scarface Mob*, a two-part movie on CBS's
Desilu Playhouse (the company started by one-time husband-
and-wife team Desi Arnaz and Lucille Ball). The series,
which was a consistent hit and ran from 1959 to 1963, was

based on the battle between Elliot Ness and his Untouchables, and kingpin crime boss Al Capone and his syndicate.
The TV show, like Ness's memories, was often loose with the
facts, but the stories concerned the legendary fight between
good and evil. Every week people tuned in to hear the na-
sally Walter Winchell narrate the show and watch the com-
manding presence of Robert Stack as Elliot Ness. The
problem, of course, was that a good portion of the gangsters
running the streets of Chicago in the 1920s, the show's time
frame, were of Italian descent. Like *The Sopranos*, another
show dealing with mobsters, *The Untouchables* was handicapped by that fact. True, Chicago crime in the '20s was as
varied ethnically as the city itself, and a Dean O'Banion or
Hymie Weiss character did make their way into episodes.
But the majority of gangsters, with names like Frank Nitti,
John Scalise, and Big Al Capone, were of Italian descent.

q. CAROL'S EXPERIMENT

In 1997, after twenty years, Carol Marin resigned as coanchor of WMAQ/Channel 5 news in protest of the station
hiring tabloid TV host Jerry Springer to do commentaries on
the 10 P.M. newscast. The possibility of Springer's arrival was
the last straw for well-respected coanchor Ron Magers as
well, who resigned and went on to join the Channel 7 news.
Marin tried something slightly different. The dismal ratings of
WBBM/Channel 2 news led network bosses to agree to an
experiment of Marin's. A two-time Peabody Award winner,
Marin was known in Chicago as one of the finest investigative
journalists in the business. Concerned over the dumbing
down of TV news, she hoped to put the focus back on hard
news. Gone would be the fluff. Shortened would be sports
and weather. Marin and her team of exceptional television
reporters including Mike Parker, Mike Flannery, and Pulitzer
Prize–winning Pam Zekman would give Chicago a newscast
that would concentrate on real news. Assured of a year to
make a dent, they pulled the plug after nine months. *The 10
O'Clock News Reported by Carol Marin* had strong ratings

and good reviews, locally and nationally, in February 2000. But by summer the ratings dipped lower than they had been for past newscasts. Running scared, however, the network axed the show on October 30, 2000, bringing in two new anchors and returning to the old format. If the newscast had been given a chance to grow, to be tweaked here and there, had it been given the full year promised for the audience to warm to it, it's possible the experiment would have been successful. Despite how it turned out, it was a worthwhile experiment in what could be done with local news.

10. THE NUMBERS

Ever wonder why your favorite show got axed from the schedule? It just didn't have the numbers. The numbers tell a network how many people are watching a TV show and, consequently, seeing the commercials sponsoring the show. The ratings tell if that show will survive another six shows, and give the network an idea of how much to charge sponsors. It's not hard to imagine how much a company pays for a spot during the Super Bowl, one of the most watched events of the year. The numbers begin with the Neilsen ratings. This large family is all hooked up to ratings boxes giving the A.C. Neilsen Company an idea of what the public likes to watch. Born in Chicago in 1897, Arthur Charles Nielsen started out as an engineer before establishing a firm that surveyed the performance and production of industrial equipment. The year was 1923. By 1933, the Nielsen Food and Drug Index was created. It monitored and reported regularly on the volume and price of packaged goods. Before long, the A.C. Nielsen Company dominated marketing research. Eventually, the firm found its way to measuring radio audiences, which were on the rise during the Depression of the 1930s. During the time, a recorder had been invented at MIT that could be attached to the tuning mechanism of a radio receiver and monitor the stations the listener chose. Nielsen snatched up the audiometer (as it was known) and the rights to it and, by 1943, was conducting audience surveys with the device. In the early 1960s, however, the reliability of the surveys came into question. A.C. Nielsen turned from radio to the still relatively new television industry and began a rating system for that, which would become highly influential on what shows stayed on the air.

Rare Gems

The special places and people that help make Chicago so fun.

1. V. I. WARSHAWSKI

It may sound like a truck driver, but it's actually the name of a female private investigator in a series of popular mysteries based in Chicago. In 1982, such a character was revolutionary when author Sara Paretsky's first Warshawski novel *Indemnity Only* was published. She presented a strong, tough investigator capable of using her fists as well as her wits and wiles. Since then, nine more best-selling Warshawski novels have been published and Paretsky's books have been published in twenty-four languages. There was even a film based on the series starring Kathleen Turner. Originally from Kansas, Paretsky came to Chicago to help out with community service programs organized by Martin Luther King. Deciding to stay, she has since used the city for the settings of her novels. Paretsky was named woman of the year in 1988 by *Ms.* magazine for helping found Sisters in Crime, an organization lending support to women mystery writers. She's been a visiting scholar at Oxford in England where she's also received the 2002 Cartier Diamond Dagger for lifetime achievement from the British Crime Writer's Association.

She's been a visiting professor at Northwestern University and has earned three honorary doctorates.

2. MEIGS FIELD

In the wee hours of March 30, 2003, backhoes made their way to the small airstrip on the lake and tore huge X's into the runway. Mayor Daley's covert operation left the runways damaged, a dozen planes stranded, and their stunned pilots fuming. Built on Northerly Island, a landfill originally created in 1932 to house the Century of Progress Exposition, Meigs Field opened in 1948 serving as a runway for small aircraft visiting Chicago, as well as a place for hospital planes to land when bringing organs to downtown hospitals. Positioned in the heart of downtown, it was prized by people wanting to avoid the long travel times from O'Hare or Midway. With Mayor Daley eyeing the piece of land, suggesting in 1995 that the field be closed and turned into a park, groups such as Friends of Meigs Field had been fighting to block him, which was why they cast a suspicious eye on the March 30 destruction. Daley claimed that 9/11 illustrated how, even barring terrorism, a legitimately flown plane could accidentally fly into a skyscraper. The suspicious, however, suggested that the destruction took place before dawn to prevent the filing of restraining orders against such action. Whatever the reason, the city lost a unique little airport in a major city, and you don't see many of those around.

3. THE LASALLE THEATER

In 1972, in the basement of what is now the Talman Bank on Irving Park Road, Radio Hall of Famer Chuck Schaden began showing old movie classics that hadn't seen the silver screen for decades. It turned out to be quite a success. A few years later, the bank decided to build a 298-seat theater above it. Unlike theaters such as the Music Box, which show the old flicks but also foreign and modern movie productions, the LaSalle Theater has been the only one to show those old movies that are rarely on TV and hardly ever available on video. For $5, or $3 for seniors (the majority of the audience), moviegoers can sit in a clean theater and watch a short, a cartoon or two, and a main movie, and get a taste of the old-time moviegoing experience. Occasionally there are double features. Rarely is a film produced after 1940 shown, and each series goes by a different theme. There was a series devoted to crime films, for example, and one featuring rare American films. One of the most enjoyable aspects of the theater occurs in front of the screen, as scores of Saturday night regulars, many who saw the movies when they were first released, discuss with excitement the prospect of that night's show. It's a wonderful chance for seniors in the neighborhood to enjoy a trip down memory lane, or for younger audiences to connect with long-lost classics.

4. OLD TOWN SCHOOL OF FOLK MUSIC

Now located in the Lincoln Square area in an art deco building known as the Hild Library, Old Town School of Folk Music opened in 1957, enjoying a swell from the emerging folk movement that would become so prevalent in the 1960s. Guitar and banjo classes were offered along with folk dances and family sing-alongs. Names like Big Bill Broonzy, Mahalia Jackson, and Pete Seeger performed live at the school while Roger McGuinn, John Prine, and the late Steve Goodman are just a few of the names who got their start there. By the 1970s, the concert schedule became larger, instruction in instruments became more varied, and enrollment peaked at 650. Changing attitudes in music, however, led to a decline in enrollment, and by the 1980s, the school was ready to close. But thanks to an emphasis on fund-raising and opening the school up to international ethnic and traditional forms, it made a comeback. What hasn't changed with the school is its commitment to helping students find their own voices. The dedication of the new building on Lincoln Avenue in 1998, acquired after an upsurge in popularity, saw a concert by Joni Mitchell and Peter Yarrow. Today, enrollment is around 6,000 students per week, and 50,000 people attend the concerts annually.

5. COWS ON PARADE

According to legend, it was a cow and a lantern setting the town ablaze in 1871. In the summer of 1999, the cows ruled again. Cows on Parade was an interactive art exhibit that spanned the city as full-size fiberglass cows were decorated by local artists and sprinkled on streets throughout downtown Chicago. The exhibit was inspired by an event known as "Cow Parade" gracing the streets of Zurich, Switzerland. Chicago businessman Peter Hanig approached the Greater North Michigan Avenue Business Association and suggested a similar event. In conjunction with Chicago's Department of Cultural Affairs, corporations, museums, ad agencies, stores, not-for-profit groups, and even individuals were corralled in to sponsor the cows. The organization sponsoring a cow could take a hand in decorating it, or turn to Chicago's Public Art Office for an artist to use. No advertising, political slogans, gang symbols, religious messages, or inappropriate art were allowed. The medium was up to the artist: paint, mosaics, plaster. The unveiling was June 15, 1999, with a ceremony in Daley Plaza that included the mayor, the cultural commissioner, the businessmen who helped back the idea, sponsors, and the Swiss Consul. Then the cows, ranging from elaborate to whimsical, were placed around the city. A ladybug cow could be seen climbing up the building at 20 E. Delaware. One cow was painted as Uncle Sam and another encased in an astronaut suit. "Cowch Potato" could be seen on an astro-turf couch watching TV, while "Muddy Holly and Peggy Sue" were gathered around a piano. There was even a yellow duck-billed cow hatching from an egg. Cows on Parade proved a roaring, or rather, mooing success, drawing a million visitors and $200 million. When it ended, sixty-five cows were sold at a charity "cattle" auction at the Chicago Theater in November. There were posters, catalogs, books, and other items. Some of the cows themselves were reproduced in miniature and sold in area gift shops.

6. CHRISTMAS AT MARSHALL FIELDS

Christmas on State Street remains a magical experience. Trees sparkle with fairy lights, storefronts gleam with Yuletide spirit. No one does it bigger or better than Marshall Fields. For almost a century, people have crowded around the store's windows to see what enchanting Christmas display has been dreamed up. In the early 1900s, toys were placed in the window and wound up every hour to present a movable display. In the 1940s, they created displays in each window that told a story. In 1944 and '45, a visual retelling of Clement C. Moore's *'Twas the Night before Christmas* appeared. In 1948, Uncle Mistletoe, one of Marshall Fields's most endearing concepts, was introduced. Billed as one of Santa's helpers, the little figure dressed in a tall black hat trimmed with mistletoe and a long red coat first appeared in the display for *A Christmas Dream*, a poem written by Helen McKenner, a Marshall Fields copywriter. Uncle Mistletoe became an instant Chicago celebrity. People would wait in lines for up to two hours in Marshall Fields to visit with Santa and Uncle Mistletoe and his wife Aunt Holly. The character became so popular that Marshall Fields developed *The Adventures of Uncle Mistletoe*, a television show that debuted on November 15, 1948, shown twice a week, and lasting four seasons. Fields continues to feature dazzling displays in the windows, recently adding characters from the *Harry Potter* series in 2000. And people continue to crowd around the windows at Christmastime to see what Fields has dreamed up now.

7. BUDDIES

Located on Clark in the heart of Chicago's gay community, this corner bar offers a relaxing alternative to the sometimes high-pressure world of nighttime clubbing. Owners Marty (whose father owned a neighborhood bar) and George (a former schoolteacher), both inductees into the gay and lesbian hall of fame, have created an atmosphere comfortable for everyone. The bar area is cozy as is the restaurant section where, depending on the time of day, you can enjoy breakfast, dinner, late-night snacks, or lunch. Don't let the fun southwestern decor fool you, the food can please almost every palate. Sunday brunch is particularly tasty with specialties like crab cake benedict. Perfect for those out late partying the night before.

And in summer, patrons can enjoy a drink or something more in the outside café section with hanging flowerpots to add color. There's even a selection of homemade desserts (some made by Marty himself). But it's not all about eating. Open till 2 A.M., the bar gets humming come evening time and is a great place for those late-nighters looking for one more cocktail before heading home. The staff is friendly and enthusiastic, dancing along with the crowd to the eclectic music played there. Disco, '80s club mixes, country tunes, even old standards. Ask the bartender what the latest drink creation is, or choose from the more than ten giant Long Island iced teas. There are many fun events held there as well. You can imagine the excitement on the day of the gay pride parade, too.

8. PAULINA MEAT MARKET

It was simply a neighborhood butcher store. So what happened? Gentrification happened. The neighborhood, Germantown as it was called, had been going downhill a bit until a few years ago when yuppies started taking advantage of the great and affordable houses in the area. When they discovered the neighborhood, the Paulina Meat Market, located around Lincoln and Addison, became the hottest little butcher shop in town, featured in tour books and on local news shows. *Chicago Magazine* voted it best in town. And why not? Twelve butchers and four sausage makers are on site to make the more than 100 varieties of homemade sausage that season the air with savory scents. When Sigmund

Lekan bought the butcher shop he'd been working in after returning from the war, he used old-world recipes and traditions to create tempting specials like apple pork sausage, landjaeger, and bratwurst.

The air is sweet with the scent of these smoked delicacies. There's also a small selection of frozen specialty meats like ostrich and venison. Chicago has a rich tradition of corner butcher shops and the Paulina Meat Market carries on that tradition in a tasty way.

9. GOOSE ISLAND BEER COMPANY

After reading an article in an in-flight magazine on the increasing popularity of brewpubs, John Hall decided to give it a go. In 1988, he established Goose Island Brewpub on Clybourne, one of only sixteen in the United States at the time. Tapping into Chicago's history of beer making (the Clybourne pub was a brewery supply company before Prohibition), Goose Island gave people the chance to witness the brewing process as well as taste the final result. Soon, it was named a top-ten brewery in the world by the Beverage Testing Institute. A second brewery and bottling plant were opened on West Fulton in 1995, having 37,000 square feet devoted to the art of brewing with stainless steel kettles and fermenting tanks. In 1999, Goose Island Wrigleyville opened with ten deluxe party rooms, custom menus, and a beer buffet. Since the beer isn't pasteurized and doesn't contain preservatives, eight states seem to be the best traveling distance for distribution. But Goose Island isn't just about beer. It also offers soft drinks like orange cream soda and of course, root beer, made from an old family recipe. With John's son, Greg Hall, serving as brewmaster over a staff of former students of the United States Brewers Academy at the Siebel Institute of Technology in Chicago, Goose Island prides itself on quality, originality, and local roots. Not to mention its tasty ales like Hex Nut Brown Ale, Christmas Ale, Oatmeal Stout, and Oktoberfest.

10. **POLK BROS.**

In 1992, Polk Bros. stunned Chicago by announcing that it was closing its doors. For six decades, Polk Bros. had been the place Chicagoans went to find the best deals on major appliances and electronics, and it was the first to start many of the selling techniques that would be adopted by the industry. In 1935, eighteen-year-old Sol Pokevitz started a small, no-frills appliance outlet store in Northwest Chicago and soon brought his brothers and sister in, offering quality goods and services at low prices. By 1945, they were recognized by the national press as a Chicago institution. So popular was Polk Bros. in the community that in 1955, the family held "The World's Largest Birthday Party" to celebrate the twentieth anniversary of the store. Anyone presenting a Polk Bros. receipt got a free ticket to the party at the Chicago Stadium where Ed Sullivan's *Toast of the Town* planned a live remote followed by a performance of the Ice Capades of 1955. Twenty thousand people showed up that night to celebrate.

Thanks to the marketing savvy of Sol Polk, and the closeness of the family itself, they continued to run the business as a family business. After 1955, along with the North Central Avenue store, and one on Cottage Grove Avenue (with a parking lot capable of holding 4,000 cars and a main floor the size of a football field), five more would be added by 1960. Polk utilized promotions to draw customers. A summer ice-skating rink covered by a circus tent was created in the parking lot of the Central Park Avenue store, where the Blackhawks ran practice games and drew spectators. Shopping at Polk Bros. was like going to a carnival, with giveaways, clowns entertaining the customers, and the constant noise of appliances being tested. Polk Bros. was the first retailer in history that sold on Sunday. They were the first to sell color TVs and microwave ovens. For that matter, they were one of the first major retailers to mix selling appliances and electronics together. But the key to the Polk Bros. success was in the relationship the store had with the community. With an army of clever yet personable supersalesmen in the store, Polk remained the giant super store with the mom and pop feel. A couple bought furniture for their new apartment, went back a few years later to buy fixings for the baby's room, purchased their first color TV and washing machines from them, and directed their children to the store when it came time for the children to furnish their nests. This was why the company's announcement in 1992 felt like a death in the family to so many people in Chicago. Suddenly, the company the *Saturday Evening Post* named the "King of the Discounters" in 1963 would be gone. It was the end of an era. But the Polk Bros. family gave Chicago one last gift before saying good-bye. They donated the entire $220 million the company was worth to the Polk Bros. Foundation, a charitable organization. Now that's a way to go out with style.

Food

C hicago is one of the tastiest towns around. If there's one idea a tourist brings home, it's that in Chicago there's always something good to eat.

1. ETHNIC DIVERSITY

Chicago is the food capital of the world. No, make that the United States. No, make that the world (and it's possible that it outdraws a few planets as well). Chicago has something to please everyone and the reason for the richness has to be the ethnic diversity. As polarizing as the ethnic enclaves could be historically, they also made it a stronger city. As in a stew, each culture added a particular spice. Drive down the main streets and Korean neighborhoods change into Indian, which change into Latin, German, Jewish, and so forth, each with some of the best ethnic local eateries in town. Soul food may be only a few blocks away from Lebanese fare. There are tons to choose from, even for the meat and potatoes fan. Add to that the upscale sections of town where some of the finest restaurants serve some of the finest, often most daring food, and a Chicago palate never gets bored.

2. A MEAL

You'll wonder why you even bothered with that thin stuff once you've dived into this luscious experience. Big and sloppy and bursting with flavor, this is true-blue comfort food that'll stick with you while you work through the pain. Of course, even if you're the happiest person on earth, a bite of this will make you happier. The creators of this gastronomic delight are assured a place in culinary heaven. When Ike Sewell and Ric Riccardo opened a restaurant on the corner of Ohio Street and Wabash, they wanted to serve pizza that was more of a meal than the thin crust variety being served by so many of the Little Italy restaurants. What they created to serve at their Pizzeria Uno was the Chicago Style Pizza. It's not so much made as constructed. Resting in a pie dish, first comes a thin layer of crust, then a splash of tomato sauce, maybe some olive oil, followed by cheese and lots of it, then any other ingredients, and finally another thin layer of crust, smeared with more sauce. Construction may vary with the restaurant. Some may bury the additional ingredients with the cheese. Some place them on top. That's all incidental. The key ingredient of this masterpiece is the core of artery-blocking cheese. Sure you tempt fate with this dish, but that's the only way to dine in Chicago.

3. THE KING OF THE SCENE

The king of Chicago's restaurant scene, Rich Melman, is a founder, chairman, and CEO of the Lettuce Entertain You Enterprises, a comestible empire that steers the destinies of almost seventy-five restaurants nationwide. He worked in fast food and selling restaurant supplies as a teenager, but when his father shot down the idea of him becoming partner in the family-owned restaurant, Melman and partner, Jerry A. Orzoff, opened R.J. Grunts in 1971 (R for Rich, J for Jerry and Grunts for the sound a pig makes eating). The hip burger joint was the forerunner of what would soon become a trend where dining out would become an experience beyond the food. It was about atmosphere, energy, and entertainment. The empire's genius is its variety. Each restaurant differs in style, price, and menu. R.J. Grunts, the burger joint; Maggiano's for Italian cuisine; Shaw's Crab House for seafood;

Nacional 27 for Latin American food. Sadly, the partnership with Orzoff, who had showed a tremendous amount of faith in Melman, would last only ten years due to Orzoff's death in 1981. But the corporation continued and the empire kept growing, expanding into Vegas, Arizona, and Minnesota; it has even jumped across the ocean into Japan, giving jobs to over 5,000 people.

4. ELI'S CHEESECAKE

It takes more than four million pounds of cream, 500,000 pounds of eggs, and one million pounds of sugar just to make one cheesecake. Okay, that's an overestimate. Actually, that's how much Eli's goes through in a year producing its cheesecakes and other baked goods. But once you've taken a bite of an Eli's cheesecake you can't help but wonder just how much cream, eggs, and sugar *has* gone into it. It's a substantial staple of Chicago. The recipe was created by Eli Schulman to serve as a signature dessert for his restaurant Eli's Place for Steaks, which opened in the 1960s. The popularity of the cake went nationwide and now it can be seen in grocer's freezers in fifty states as well as parts of Europe and Asia. A proud, pound-packing portion of Chicago.

5. THE BERGHOFF

Herman Joseph Berghoff was a German immigrant who arrived in 1870. Starting in the beer business, he opened the Berghoff Café in 1898, serving free sandwiches with five-cent beer. When Prohibition hit town, the Berghoff Café became a full-service café, selling Bergo soda pop to replace the beer. Once Prohibition had been repealed, Herman Berghoff was the first person in America to receive a liquor license, issued as number 1. World famous for its American and German cuisine, the restaurant, still family owned and operated, remains a dining tradition in Chicago. It has a seventy-five-foot-long stand-up bar, which prohibited female patrons until feminists challenged this policy in 1969. Thanks to their dedication to preserving its turn-of-the-century architecture both inside and out, the Berghoff gives patrons a glimpse of the past. And custom-made beverages are still on hand. Enjoy the Berghoff beer, or the Berghoff's private stock of 90 or 107 proof bourbon that is aged ten years.

6. VIENNA HOT DOGS

The Chicago-style hot dog is a simple creation: A pure beef frankfurter in a steamed bun with mustard, bright green relish, chopped onion, tomato wedges, pickles, peppers, and a dash of celery salt. That and a ball game and you have summer. Make it a Vienna beef hot dog and you've found Nirvana. The Chicago-style hot dog was first served and became a sensation at the Columbian Exposition in 1893. Known as a hot dog sandwich, it soon became a national treat. Well over a century later, Vienna can be seen in restaurants and grocery stores, its line including Polish sausage, knockwurst, corned beef, roast beef, Italian beef, and pastrami among other deli delights, and the Vienna Sausage Manufacturing Company has sales nationwide as well as in Europe and Asia.

7. NOBODY DOES IT LIKE SARA LEE

In 1953, Charles Lubin developed a process to freeze baked goods that enabled the product to retain its delicious taste. He also developed foil baking pans, which allowed the company to bake, freeze, and distribute all in one go. Because of that, you can enjoy Sara Lee's delicious creamy cheesecake anytime. Named after Lubin's daughter, Sara Lee started as a small chain of neighborhood bakeries in Chicago. Lubin and his brother-in-law bought the Community Bake Shops in 1935 and later changed the name to Kitchens of Sara Lee, selling fresh-baked goods to grocery stores. By 1951, Sara Lee introduced the All Butter Pound Cake and All Butter Pecan Coffee Cake. It was a request in 1952 from a buyer from Texas who asked to have Sara Lee goods shipped to him that inspired Lubin's interest in the freezing process. Not wanting to miss an opportunity, Lubin discovered a way to freeze the products which retained its freshness, opened up the market nationwide, and lowered the cost of production and thereby the cost to consumers. By 1971, Sara Lee could be found in Australia, and by 1977, in the United Kingdom. And on July 4, 1976, Sara Lee presented the nation with a four-story bicentennial birthday cake that filled Freedom Hall in Philadelphia. Not bad for a little chain of Chicago bakeries named after an eight-year-old.

8. THE TASTE

For ten days in summer, you can eat yourself silly in Grant Park. This is the Taste of Chicago experience. Now, every town has its Taste Of . . . but the Taste of Chicago is the big one! Purchasing a pack of tickets, diners can sample the goods of over seventy restaurants. From specialties to everyday pizza, diners immerse themselves in the tasty choices Chicago has to offer. But wait! There's more. While stuffing their faces, 3.5 million happy eaters can digest to the sounds of live music playing on the several stages set up in the park. Ending the Fourth of July weekend, an Independence Day fireworks display is a perfect cap to the week's fun. In 2003, the Taste of Chicago celebrated twenty-three years of filling the town's tummy.

9. TASTY RECIPES FROM THE WINDY CITY

Have a hankering for Shrimp de Jonghe or Chicken Vesuvio? These two garlic-based extravaganzas were created in Chicago. Dreamt up in the 1920s, Al Capone may have enjoyed the delicious dish of shrimp smothered in butter, garlic, mustard, and wine, covered in bread crumbs and lemon and then broiled to perfection. Chicken Vesuvio is a little younger. A signature dish at Harry Caray's restaurant, chicken and potatoes are covered in garlic, olive oil, white wine, and oregano.

10. FANNIE MAY™

To top it off, how about a piece of chocolate? But this is not just any chocolate. It's Fannie May™ chocolate. For over eighty years the Fannie May™ chocolate company had been tempting Chicagoans with its delectable candy confections housed in sparkling white storefronts. Founded by real-estate broker H. Teller Archibald in 1920, the Archibald Candy Corporation is a family-owned business and still privately held. It owns three major brands, including Fanny Farmer™ and Laura Secord™, but it's Fannie May™ that had us licking our lips. The candy had been produced on West Madison Street since the late 1930s and sent for sale to one of the forty-seven shops in Illinois and neighboring states that existed by 1935. More than 250 stores in twelve states sold such delectable treats as toffees, Trinidads™, butter creams, and crunchy nut clusters. And let's not forget the Mint Meltaways™, mint chocolate coated by Fannie May's own milk chocolate or creamy pastel, which really do melt away in your mouth. Candies called Turtles were first created in Chicago. Fannie May has its own version known as Pixies™, a signature candy of crunchy pecans covered in rich caramel and then smothered in milk chocolate. H. Teller Archibald named his candies Fannie May because he thought the name sounded like that of a candy-maker. He was right. Sadly, 2004 saw the closing of the Chicago Fannie May stores. Lines formed 'round the block the last few days before closing as people hoped to get one more box of those delicious candies. The company has assured those with sweet tooths that the candies will be available in area grocery stores and online, but somehow it's just not the same as being able to walk into one of those white stores with the red-and-white awnings and feel your mouth water as you see all those luscious chocolates in the display case.

Infamous Males

There's an odd historic charm about gangsters, but the names of these guys elicit nothing but contempt.

1. BAD CLOWN

When John Wayne Gacy was executed on May 10, 1995, few people mourned his passing. He killed thirty-three young men in six years, giving emotionless confessions about them, even painting his victims as society's trash. Born in 1942, Gacy had a loving mother, but a brutal, drunken father. Even as a child, Gacy exhibited strange proclivities. At nineteen, he ran off, finding a job in a Las Vegas mortuary before returning to Chicago six months later and attending Northwestern Business School. In Springfield, Illinois, where he became manager of a shoe company, he married and had a child. In Iowa, his father-in-law gave him a job managing fried chicken outlets, and Gacy became active in the Jaycees, even being voted their state chaplain and man of the year in 1967. Then the other Gacy emerged. In 1968, he was sentenced to ten years for sodomizing two teenage boys. His wife divorced him. A model prisoner, Gacy even started a prison chapter of the Jaycees for which he was again named man of the year. In 1970, despite a prison psychiatrist's concerns about his psychopathic and sexually sadistic tendencies, Gacy was paroled and moved back to Chicago to care for his ailing mother. They moved into a house together, a house with a crawl space, and Gacy started his contracting business from his home. The neighborhood never had a clue. A well-respected businessman and neighbor, he became a local precinct captain, volunteered for charities, and was active in civic events. He posed for pictures with important people and entertained at charity functions as Pogo the Clown. He was also spotted frequently cruising downtown streets for young men, and he killed, for the first time in January 1972, when he picked up a young man from a bus terminal and took him home. The body was buried in the crawl space. He killed again in 1974, but in all that time, not his second wife, his stepchildren, or his mother ever knew what was in that crawl space.

After his divorce in 1976, the killing escalated as he prowled in his car, similar to an undercover cop car, flashing a badge at young men, ordering them into the car. Once they were brought home the tricks he showed them with handcuffs and ropes became deadly; once they were bound and helpless, he strangled them. Visitors to the house or people attending his backyard parties never realized that Gacy's barbecue rested over the body of one of his victims. It was the disappearance of Robert Piest in 1978 that led to the breaking of the case. Piest, an honor student and gymnast, went to talk to a man outside the store he worked at about a possible summer construction job and was never seen again. Discovering it was Gacy that Piest had been speaking to, police went to question him one night around 9 P.M. An arrogant Gacy told them that he would be happy to come to the station and talk more later and he showed up at 3 A.M., covered in mud. Unbeknownst to the cops, Gacy had just finished dumping Piest's body into the Des Plaines River. Obtaining a search warrant for Gacy's house, police found items that tied him to the young men who'd been reported missing the past few years. Some of these men were Gacy's employees. They even found a rope with a human hair attached to it. In the crawl space they found the floor covered in lime, but nothing else notable. A twenty-four-hour surveillance began after a photo receipt that had been in Piest's jacket was found in Gacy's garbage. Gacy's arrogance grew. He toyed with the cops, taking them on high speed chases at night, buying them dinner during the day, and bragging about all his connections. The pressure, however, finally got to Gacy. At last, he met with his attorneys and gave them a four-hour confession of the killings. Attorney/client privilege forced them to sit on the confession, but they persuaded the police to keep up their investigation. When Gacy was arrested the next day on drug charges for leaving a bag of marijuana at a gas station, the cops were able to obtain a second search warrant and this time do a thorough search of the house. That's when they found bodies in the crawl space. Gacy confessed and drew the police a detailed map of where the bodies where buried; for months after his arrest, bodies were excavated from the crawl space like ancient remains in an archaeological dig. Twenty-seven bodies were found in the crawl space. Two were found beneath his garage. Four others had been tossed into the Des Plaines River. Gacy, charged with the murders of the thirty-three young men in April 1979, was found guilty in 1980. The sentence was death by lethal injection. While his lawyers appealed the sentence for years, Gacy milked his celebrity, amazingly maintaining his innocence, joking crudely that the only thing he was guilty of was running a cemetery without a license. He began painting, creepy pictures of clowns and even what he called the "Hi Ho" series featuring Disney's Seven Dwarves. Yet the paintings garnered him thousands of dollars after he sold them through the mail. This bizarre entrepreneur was also able to set up a 900 phone line in 1993 that people could call to listen to him insist upon his innocence. But nothing he or his lawyers said could convince the appellate courts to grant him a stay of execution. He was put to death, his last words being that he was the thirty-fourth victim.

2. THE LANDLORD

As Jack the Ripper was slashing his way through Whitechapel, an ocean away, America's first interstate serial killer was making his way through the Midwest. Despite the pre-meditated depravity of his actions, Herman Webster Mudgett, or H. H. Holmes, as he was known, wasn't quite as well known. Mudgett was a psychopath, born in New Hampshire in 1860. In 1878, he found a wife, Clara Lovering, whose inheritance was helpful when the two moved to Michigan, where Mudgett began studying at the University of Michigan Medical School. He managed to hide the murder of his first son for several years, leaving a grieving Clara and traveling the Midwest as a con man before settling in Wilmette, Illinois. As H.H. Holmes, he met his second wife, Myrtle Belknap, who just happened to come from a wealthy family. Marrying Myrtle in 1887, he began an insurance fraud scheme that included slowly poisoning his wife's father, but it proved un-successful and Myrtle ended the marriage in 1889.

In the Chicago suburb of Englewood, Holmes was hired on at the apothecary of Mrs. E. S. Holden, who disappeared shortly after, Holmes claiming that she had sold him the store and gone west. The prospering drugstore enabled Holmes to take out a mortgage to build his dream house of horrors across the street. It was a castle, three stories high, shoddily designed with malicious intent, workmen changed with regularity so none would catch on. Upon completion, Holmes decided to rent rooms out to visitors to the Columbian Exposition. Many of those tourists never made it home. The year of the fair, Holmes became engaged to Minnie Williams, heir to a Texas real estate fortune who was working in town as a teacher. It's hard to imagine that Minnie wasn't a willing accomplice, and that's how police viewed her after Holmes was captured. His first accomplice was Ben Pitezel, who helped him carry out insurance fraud schemes until he became one of Holmes's victims. In 1894, Minnie acted as a witness to the wedding of Holmes and Georgiana Yoke. Minnie, perhaps under the assumption that Holmes's interest was purely in Georgiana's money, found herself expendable once they went to Texas and claimed property due Minnie.

It's believed that she had an acid bath. Through 1894, more people disappeared and more cons were committed, this time with Georgiana Yoke and his old accomplice Pitezel, who, under the name B.F. Perry, took a $10,000 insurance policy out on himself. Through a bait and switch with a corpse, they planned on bilking the insurance company, but upon identification the corpse turned out to actually be Pitezel. Traveling with Holmes and Georgiana, Carrie Pitezel expected to meet up with Ben in New York and continued east, leaving her three children in the care of the Holmeses. Holmes poisoned young Howard Pitezel and locked Pitezel's daughters, Alice and Nellie, in a truck, running a gas pipe into it. In the meantime, authorities were closing in. A previous horse swindle helped lead them to Holmes, and given the choice between hanging for the horse swindle or pleading guilty to insurance fraud, he chose insurance fraud and was sent back to Philadelphia to stand trial.

When police investigated Holmes's castle, what they found sickened even the strongest stomach. There were hidden rooms, secret staircases, concealed panels, trap doors, peepholes, drops, and air-tight rooms where people were sealed in and slowly gassed to death by a bowl of noxious poison. There were also greased chutes that sent the bodies downstairs to be dropped in vats of acid. In his basement "laboratory" torture devices and jars of poison were found, along with an incinerator that still contained ash and fragments of bone. Holmes later admitted to designing a torture rack to conduct stretching experiments on. After the chamber of horrors was discovered, Holmes confessed to killing twenty-seven people, though it's possible he killed many more. The embellishment of yellow journalism and Holmes's own desire to toy with the police make facts hard to pinpoint. Holmes was hanged for his crimes on May 7, 1896. As for the castle of death, it sat empty for a month before three explosions were heard through the neighborhood; in less than an hour, the structure burned to the ground.

3. **THE BUTCHER**

In the early morning of July 14, 1966, the bodies of eight student nurses were found strewn about their townhouse. The identity of the murderer might have remained a mystery had not one nurse, a young woman from the Philippines named Corazon Amurao, crawled under a bed during the carnage. Born in Monmouth, Illinois, in 1941, Richard Speck was often beaten by his alcoholic stepfather. The family moved to Dallas, Texas, where dropout Speck became a father himself at nineteen. By the age of twenty, with forty-two arrests for serious crimes to his record, he fled back to Chicago. He was shiftless and unpredictable, often violent, with an I.Q. of ninety making his job hunt unsuccessful. Searching for work as a merchant seaman, the union hall was right across from the townhouse where the nurses lived.

Speck did find work on a vessel, but was stricken with appendicitis and eventually returned to Chicago in mid-June 1966. The next three weeks were spent doing whatever odd jobs he could to get drinking money. Drinking heavily and ingesting narcotics, the darker forces finally got the better of him the night of July 13. Armed with a .22-caliber pistol, a hunting knife, and a pocketknife, he wandered off to one of the student dormitories that he'd been studying the past few weeks. When Corazon Amurao answered the knock at the door that night she was greeted by Speck, who forced his way in, insisting that he only intended to steal money. He ordered three nurses into a rear bedroom where two others were getting ready for bed. The nurses' wrists and ankles were bound and as more nurses came in from dates, they were brought into the back room at gunpoint. When the last two nurses had arrived and presented him with some resistance, he took them into another room and killed them, stabbing them repeatedly, and starting his butchery. Speck took the nurses from the back bedroom into various rooms of the house where he killed them. It was while he was out of the room that Amurao slipped under the bed, shivering as the other nurses were taken out to be slaughtered. After murdering eight nurses, Speck left. The mass murder sickened and terrified the city. Women didn't feel safe for years afterward, even in their own homes. Speck was found, lying in a pool of his own blood, behind a plywood partition (which served as a "room" for the transients paying ninety cents to stay the night) of the Starr Hotel, a flophouse on Madison Street. The blood was from a suicide attempt with a shard of glass. The jury took only forty-nine minutes to convict Speck and he was sentenced to die in the electric chair, but due to the U.S. Supreme Court's decision to abolish the death penalty in 1972, he was resentenced to 400 to 1,200 years. Speck died of a heart attack on December 5, 1991. He wasn't yet fifty.

4. THE LESS THAN PERFECT CRIME

Leopold and Loeb fancied themselves too clever for anyone's good and Bobby Franks paid dearly for their arrogance. Nathan Leopold's father made money in shipping and mining before owning a paper company. Richard Loeb's father was vice president of Sears. Both grew up in the privileged community of Kenwood. Both excelled academically, Loeb the youngest graduate of the University of Michigan and Leopold a nationally known ornithologist who taught bird classes regularly. Forming a bond when both were at the University of Michigan, each considered the other a superior human being and yearned to commit the perfect crime. What they committed became known as the "Crime of the Century." On May 21, 1924, the pair drove a rented car to the Harvard School for Boys and waited. The crime had been plotted meticulously for six months and they did a practice run of the kidnapping. A number of possible victims were considered, including Loeb's younger brother, Tommy. They chose fourteen-year-old Bobby Franks, a boy from the neighborhood who wouldn't refuse a ride from someone he knew. After he finished umpiring a baseball game, Franks began the walk home when the car pulled up and the pair offered him a ride. Once inside the car, Franks had a rag stuffed in his mouth while being bludgeoned with a chisel. Bobby Franks was killed around 5:30 P.M. and to keep with their schedule, the pair casually stopped for hot dogs with the body still wrapped in a robe on the floor of the car. Then, under cover of darkness, on the marshes of Wolf Lake they disrobed the body, poured hydrochloric acid over him, and stuffed Franks into a drainage pipe. After stopping to call Franks's parents with ransom demands, the killers returned home to burn the boy's clothes and scrub out the rental car. A pair of glasses found at the scene ultimately broke the case open. Leopold played it cool as reports of Franks's disappearance and the discovery of his body became known. Loeb, however, offered theories on the case to anyone who'd listen, even telling reporters that if he were going to murder anyone, he would murder just such a cocky little son of a bitch as Bobby Franks.

When the eyeglasses found next to Franks's body were traced back to Leopold, suspicion fell on the young men. More evidence came to light and ten days after the murder Richard Loeb confessed, pointing the finger at Leopold as the mastermind, while Leopold claimed Loeb was the brains. The trial turned into a circus as thousands tried to get into a courtroom that held a few hundred. State's Attorney Robert Crowe said he would seek the death penalty. Sixty-seven-year-old defense lawyer Clarence Darrow agreed to defend the young killers primarily to speak out against the death penalty. His defense, based on the testimony of a psychiatrist (then known as "alienists"), basically insisted that the two weren't responsible for their actions. His closing argument, an eloquent denouncement of capital punishment, lasted for over two days. The judge took three weeks to decide on the fitting punishment, and moved by Darrow's summation, he chose to sentence the pair to life imprisonment plus ninety-nine years for the crime of kidnapping. Once inside the Illinois State Penitentiary in Joliet, the two had little contact with each other but still managed to maintain a friendship. In 1925, Leopold was transferred to Statesville where he taught classes and organized the library while also working in the prison hospital. In 1931, Loeb joined him there and they became model prisoners, even organizing a school for other inmates. Loeb retained his darker side, though, and in 1936, he allegedly tried to force a prisoner to have sex. He was slashed violently by the other prisoner and rushed to the prison infirmary. Told of the attack, Leopold hurried to his friend's bedside and remained there as he died. After that, Leopold went even further in changing his image, volunteering for a project during World War II where he agreed to contract malaria to rate the effectiveness of anti-malaria drugs. The public seemed convinced that this fifty-year-old man was no longer a monster, and in 1958, he was released from prison. Hoping for a normal life, he avoided the press and went down to Puerto Rico where a job in a mission awaited him. On August 30, 1971, Nathan Leopold died of a heart attack.

5. THE LIPSTICK KILLER

Born in 1929, as a youth William Heirens enjoyed sneaking around other people's houses. At thirteen, his first arrest was for carrying a loaded gun and once caught, he confessed to a number of small burglaries. After a stint in a juvenile home, Heirens was arrested again in a hotel and sent to St. Bede's Academy in Peru, Illinois, for three years. Something about the youth impressed the academy and they encouraged him to enter the University of Chicago at sixteen. Education, however, held less fascination for him than crime and his theft spree continued. On June 5, 1943, Heirens entered the North Side apartment of Josephine Ross and her two daughters. When Josephine woke to find Heirens going through her belongings, he slashed her throat, wrapping her body in a dress before leaving the scene. Eerily, one of Ross's daughters, arriving home that morning, passed Heirens as he left the building. On December 11, 1945, a maid discovered the body of Frances Brown after noticing the woman's apartment door open and music playing inside. Shot twice in the head, Brown was dragged into the bathtub and wrapped in towels, the butcher knife used on her still protruding from her body. On the mirror, written in lipstick, was the now famous plea, "Stop me before I kill more. I can not control myself." Authorities began calling the perpetrator "the Lipstick Killer." On January 6, 1946, Jim and Helen Degnan awoke to find their six-year-old daughter, Suzanne, missing from their Chicago apartment. An upstairs neighbor reported hearing the child speaking to someone and Mrs. Degnan remembered thinking that the child had cried out during the night. A ransom note on the floor of the bedroom demanded $20,000 for the girl's safe return. But the girl did not return. In a secluded area, she had been killed, dissected, and the pieces stuffed through nearby sewer gratings. On the morning of January 7, witnesses recalled a man matching William Heirens's description walking around the area carrying a small shopping bag. That same evening, Suzanne's head was discovered after two police detectives noticed that a sewer grate was ajar. Her torso and legs were found in nearby sewers, her arms found weeks later.

Heirens himself was caught prowling another North Side apartment house. After a shootout with police, he was taken in for questioning and confessed under truth serum to the three homicides. Trying for an insanity plea, he blamed the actions on George Murman, another personality of his. Heirens was sentenced to three consecutive life terms without parole. And yet, over fifty years later, lawyers are raising the possibility that Heirens was railroaded. Small points such as the message on the mirror not matching Heirens's handwriting, and Josephine Ross giving a description of the man who passed her that didn't match Heirens, have been considered suspicious. But it's Heirens's confession that really poses the questions in the minds of those who doubt. When Heirens was escaping from the scene of his capture, he came across an off-duty policeman walking his dog who subdued him by hitting him on the head with a flowerpot. Unconscious, he was taken to Edgewater Hospital, then to Bridewell Hospital where he was subjected to a four-day grilling as doctors administered a spinal tap and injected him with sodium pentothal. Heirens was also wrong on certain facts such as locations, times, and events of the crimes. All told, supporters of this theory have counted twenty-nine inconsistencies in the case and have called for executive clemency. They say that the seventy-three-year-old Heirens, in ill health, would pose little threat to society and should be released considering the questionable investigation. Betty Degnan, sister to little Suzanne, has continued to lobby the parole board to keep him in prison.

6. THE LOVING HUSBAND

Around 9:00 on the night of June 1, 1920, neighbors in the vicinity of 4732 N. Campbell heard shots ring out. When one neighbor hit the vestibule lights of the apartment building, he saw Carl Wanderer fiercely beating a man with his army revolver. Already dead from three gunshot wounds, the man remained motionless. Bleeding to death nearby, Wanderer's wife, Ruth, moaned that her baby was dead. She died before help arrived. What Wanderer told police of that night was that he and his pregnant wife Ruth were returning home to their apartment from a movie when a voice from out of the darkness ordered them to throw up their hands. Wanderer, now a butcher, had seen his share of action as a lieutenant in World War I. He fought back but the assailant shot Ruth before Wanderer could take him down with his own gun. Next to the dead man was a gun that had fired two shots. The assailant's prints weren't on file, so the police worked on tracing his identity through the gun. In the meantime, Wanderer received the city's sympathy for the loss of his childhood sweetheart and their baby. A churchgoing man, Wanderer never drank and had a quiet humility about him. What police discovered when tracing the gun to a Chicago gun shop was that the gun had been sold six years earlier to a man named Hoffman who, in turn, explained that he sold it to a Fred Wanderer. Fred told police that the gun had been borrowed by his cousin, Carl, a day before the attack on the couple. Further investigation revealed a $1,500 withdrawal by Ruth from her bank account the day before the attack. It was also discovered that the now-grieving husband and future father had been writing love letters to a sixteen-year-old typist named Julia Schmidt. In his pathetic confession once he was confronted by the evidence, Carl Wanderer admitted to being sick of marriage even after only nine months. Yet, he loved his wife so much that he couldn't stand the thought of anyone else having her. Hiring a derelict, he instructed the man to play a robber. When the derelict carried out the performance, Wanderer, apparently quite a marksman, shot him with a gun in one hand, and his wife with the gun in the other hand. He then carried on with the drama while both Ruth and the bum lay dying. For the last job he would ever be hired for, the still unknown bum received $1. Carl Wanderer was sentenced to twenty-five years in prison for the murder of his wife but sentenced to hang for the murder of the derelict. His last words on September 30, 1921, were to sing a few stanzas of a song before the trap door opened and his body fell through.

7. THE SAUSAGE KING

So sure was defense attorney Lawrence Harmon that his client, Adolph Luetgert, was innocent, he devoted $2,000 and his sanity to finding Luetgert's missing wife, Louisa. He wound up in an insane asylum. Known as the Sausage King of the Northwest Side, Adolph Luetgert owned the A.L. Luetgert Sausage and Packing Co. He had a five-story factory and a residence on this site, the factory turning out to be the last resting place of Louisa Luetgert in what came to be known as the "Sausage Vat Murder." Adolph Luetgert came from Germany and began a successful sausage business on the North Side. His wife Louisa often had to suffer the local gossip concerning Adolph's various infidelities. His most scandalous affair was with her own niece, Mary Siemering, a servant in the Luetgert house. It was not unusual to hear the couple yelling at each other late into the night. One day, Louisa turned up missing. Luetgert claimed she had ridden north to visit an aunt in Wisconsin, but Louisa's younger brother, Dietrich Becknese, turned to the police who began an inquiry. The most damning story came from a hostler named Wilhelm Fulpeck who told them that, on the night of May 1, he'd seen Mrs. Luetgert go into the factory around 10:30 P.M. but he couldn't recall seeing her leave. And neighbors remembered seeing smoke coming out of the factory's smokestack late into the night. Led by Captain Herman Schuettler, known for his integrity but also brutality during interrogation, police investigated the factory, in particular the vat in the basement. In large furnaces used for smoking meat they discovered amongst the debris two gold rings. One bore the initials L.L.—for Louisa Luetgert, who, Schuettler surmised, had been strangled by Luetgert, boiled in acid, and sent into the smoke shaft. It turned out that despite the factory being closed for a couple of months, the day before his wife disappeared, Luetgert had obtained 378 pounds of potash and fifty pounds of arsenic. While there were no witnesses, the evidence was damning. On June 7, 1897, Luetgert was put on trial for the murder of Louisa Luetgert. While he was found guilty of the crime, the trial ended in a hung jury since the jury couldn't decide between the death penalty and life imprisonment. The verdict of the second trial on February 9, 1898, found him guilty and sentenced him to life at Joliet Penitentiary. In shock and denial, Luetgert was led from the courtroom insisting that Louisa would be back. He died in 1900, still believing that his wife would return.

8. THE HORSE MAFIA

The name is something out of a Dickens novel. Linked to two of the most sensational murders in Chicago's history, Silas Jayne was probably better known as the godfather of the "Horse Mafia," a band of men who dealt in fraudulent show-horse trading and insurance schemes. Their victims: the wealthy, elite equestrians of the North Shore. Their leaders:

Silas Jayne and his brothers, who were the most powerful members of the band of con men. Jaynesway Farms stables were well maintained and had an impressive list of wins at horse shows. But the real money came from taking a run-down horse, perking it up with drugs, and presenting the animal to someone unskilled in horseflesh. Insurance fraud was even less pretty. It required that a heavily insured horse die. Tommy "The Sandman" Byrnes was a specialist in this. His method was to electrocute the poor beast. But it was a barn fire that brings us to Silas and his connection with the Schuessler-Peterson murders. One Sunday, John and Anton Schuessler and Bobby Peterson left their North Side neighborhood to see a movie downtown. They never returned. Instead, their naked and bound bodies were found in the Robinson Woods Cemetery. They were last seen hitchhiking on Montrose, very likely on the way home.

The case remained open for decades, until a government informant, being questioned on the disappearance of candy heiress Helen Vorhees Brach, brought up instead the name of Kenneth Hansen in connection with the Schuessler-Peterson murders. Hansen was arrested in August 1994, based on the accusations of the informant and testimony from other men who claimed Hansen had bragged to them about the murders. According to prosecutors, Hansen, who in 1955 was a twenty-two-year-old stable hand for Silas Jayne, lured the boys into his car under the pretense of showing them some of Silas Jayne's prize horses. At the Jayne stables, he molested and killed the boys. Jayne burned the stables to destroy any lingering evidence and Hansen's brother dumped the boys' bodies in Robinson Woods. What could have been scandal for Jayne turned into a payday as he filed and collected on an insurance claim for the stables. Hansen was convicted of the murders in 1995.

Ultimately, it would be The Sandman who figured into solving the next big crime: the disappearance of Helen Vorhees Brach. It had plagued Chicago since February 17, 1977. That's when the candy heiress left the Mayo Clinic in

Minnesota with a clean bill of health and headed back to Chicago. She never arrived. Helen Vorhees Brach found her way into Chicago's equestrian world by way of Richard Baily, a former dance instructor who, unbeknownst to her, was earning his bread bilking rich old ladies. And Helen was the mother lode of rich old ladies. Originally from the coal mines of Ohio, she went to Miami to start a new life, working as a hatcheck girl. There she met Frank Brach, whose family owned Brach's Candies, one of the largest candy companies around. The couple married, and were very happy together, but Richard left her a widow in 1970. A $20 million widow. Enter the charming Mr. Baily. Taking lessons at the Jayne stable, he discovered the lucrative world of horse trading and was only too happy to get in on the con. When he met Brach in 1973, he realized that with her fortune he could milk her for a long time, and he did so, even down to selling her the same horse twice.

In 1976, Helen got suspicious when Baily and his pals tried to convince her to spend additional money training a horse recently purchased. Consulting an expert, she was told that the horse was worth nowhere near what she paid for it. She told a friend that she wanted to speak to the state's attorney after visiting the Mayo Clinic. Her delay would prove fatal. The investigators eventually turned to Baily, who claimed he'd been in Florida prior to her disappearance and had receipts to prove it. The case grew cold and eventually died leaving Chicagoans to wonder for a decade what happened to Helen Brach. Then one day, Tommy Byrnes ratted out the Horse Mafia and the case was opened again. This time, U.S. States Attorney Steve Miller went after Baily on racketeering and conspiracy to commit murder. Two key witnesses said they'd been approached by Baily on a warm day in February to kill the candy heiress, but Baily's lawyers claimed that a warm day in February in Chicago was unlikely. Weather statistics, however, indicated that there had been a few days of unseasonably warm temperatures in Chicago. The most damning evidence, however, was probably phone records discovered by the prosecution that indicated Baily's Florida alibi didn't hold water. He was in Chicago during the time of Brach's disappearance. On June 15, 1995, sixty-five-year-old Baily was convicted of conspiracy to kill Helen Brach and sentenced to thirty years in prison without parole. The whereabouts of Helen Brach remain a mystery. And Silas? A competitive feud between Silas and his half brother George came to a head in 1970 when Silas paid $30,000 to have George killed. Three years after George's death, Silas was finally convicted of the murder. He was paroled at age seventy-two in 1979 and died of leukemia in 1987.

9. OVER THE WALL

His is the face of nightmares. Cold, cruel, sharp featured, "Terrible" Tommy O'Connor was a tough customer. Unpredictable. With three known homicides on his record, including that of his best friend, Tommy ducked out on his date with the hangman, escaping from the old Cook County jail on December 11, 1921. He was never recaptured. Tommy O'Connor was born in 1890 in Ireland, and brought to Chicago at the age of two. His family lived in the "Bloody Maxwell" district, a breeding ground for murderers, robbers, and thieves. It was during a February 11, 1918, robbery of the Illinois Central railway station that he logged his first kill. Dennis E. Tierney, a retired policeman and railroad security officer, came upon O'Connor and his three pals in the midst of the robbery. Rather than run, O'Connor shot the man twice. Harold Emerson, a fellow bandit, was so upset by the cruel murder that he later confessed to the robbery and fingered O'Connor as the killer. Furious, and a fugitive, O'Connor got his boyhood pal, Jimmy Cherin, to visit Emerson at the Joliet pen and kill him, but Cherin backed out. Cherin's body was found in an abandoned car in Stickney, shot five times. Louis Miller, an eyewitness, pointed to O'Connor as the gunman. A massive dragnet went out for Terrible Tommy and they found him, hiding under his father's bed. Amazingly, despite Emerson's eyewitness testimony, he was acquitted of Tierney's murder. As for Cherin . . . Louis Miller, police star witness, suddenly disappeared. It turns out that Miller had been abducted by members of O'Connor's gang. With the guarantee of police protection, he agreed to testify, so a new warrant was issued for O'Connor's arrest. After receiving a report that O'Connor was hiding out at his brother-in-law's house Sgt. Patrick O'Neill, leading a squad of five detectives, was mortally wounded by O'Connor, who had opened fire as the policeman approached the house. O'Connor became the most infamous man in the country until the manhunt ended in July 1921, when authorities caught him in St. Paul railroad yards. O'Connor was found guilty and sentenced to death for the murder of Sgt. Patrick O'Neill, but hardly seemed repentant. In fact, he boasted that his attack on O'Neill had garnered him so much publicity that he could get a job as a movie star. His appointment with the gallows was for December 15, 1921, but he would never make it. Somehow, perhaps smuggled in by a visitor, O'Connor got hold of a gun and, accompanied by three other inmates, left four guards tied up as he walked out of the jail. Crawling over the twenty-foot fence, he jumped onto the running board of a passing car and ordered the driver to "Drive like hell!" After the car, driven by a nervous young law student with a gun in his face, skidded into a wall, O'Connor jumped off and rushed into a waiting car. Police investigating the crash alerted Cook County to O'Connor's escape but the jailers, assuming he was still locked up on death row, let an hour slip by before they checked. It was, apparently, all O'Connor needed. At one time the country's most wanted man, he was never heard from again.

10. **THE FATHER OF CHICAGO**

He's been called the father of Chicago. Even though Jean Baptiste Point Du Sable and others beat him to the area, John Kinzie was considered Chicago's first permanent white settler. He was a trapper, a trader, a pioneer, and a killer, though the facts of the fight with his one-time assistant, Jean

Lalime, that resulted in Lalime's death remain nebulous, weakened by time. Born in Quebec somewhere around 1763, John Kinzie was the son of a British army surgeon. A silversmith's apprentice, he had a restless spirit and soon began trapping and trading, developing a friendly relationship with the Indians. Learning their language and gaining their trust, he became a valuable asset to the community as a middleman between local natives and white settlers. Kinzie established business connections throughout the Midwest and became an Indian trader in Detroit before bringing his skill to Chicago in 1804, along with his wife and children. On friendly terms with the Potawatomi tribe, Kinzie's importance rose between 1804 and 1812. But John Kinzie could be a rogue as well. He owned slaves in Chicago—illegal under the Northwest Ordinance—and when one ran away to the South, Kinzie hunted him down. Luckily, the provisions of the Ordinance gave the slave his freedom.

Kinzie also wasn't above defying the orders from Fort Dearborn, selling liquor to the Indians despite the ban on such sales from Capt. John Whistler. Quick to anger, Kinzie held a grudge, and when he tired of Whistler's interference he used his influence to convince the War Department to relieve Whistler of his command. Jean Lalime had a taste of the Kinzie temper. Lalime was an educated man who acted as an interpreter at Fort Dearborn and was making a name for himself in the area. He'd also been Kinzie's assistant who in 1800 purchased Du Sable's property and sold it to Kinzie when the family arrived in 1804. It wasn't long, however, before their relationship grew contentious and their personal differences got the better of them. More than likely, Lalime felt Kinzie was stepping in on his territory and Kinzie had no desire for the competition. It's believed that the last straw occurred in an April 1812 attack on Kinzie by Lalime, who shot Kinzie in the shoulder. Not long after, Kinzie had just finalized business within Fort Dearborn one night, when he was warned to be on the lookout for Lalime who was angry and vowing to deal with Kinzie. Once outside the garrison,

Lalime attacked Kinzie with a knife, but Kinzie was able to wrestle the weapon away from him and stab his aggressor in the side. Wounded from a knife cut in his left hand, Kinzie ran to friendly Indians who helped him escape to Milwaukee. The father of Chicago feared that his reputation would not assure him the benefit of the doubt in a matter of self-defense. A military tribunal found him not guilty and Kinzie was accepted back in the village, a few months shy of the Fort Dearborn massacre. When instructions came on August 9, 1812, for Captain Nathan Heald to evacuate Fort Dearborn, Kinzie placed his family in a boat and sent them to safety while he remained with the party that was leaving the garrison for Fort Wayne. Kinzie survived the massacre of Fort Dearborn and fled with his family to Detroit, returning to Chicago in 1816, when the region had been stabilized and resuming his trading business. He remained there until his death in January 1828 at the age of sixty-five. He now resides in Graceland Cemetery.

Planes, Trains, and Automobiles

B y 1892, Chicago streets had become so congested with streetcars, horses and wagons, and pedestrians that getting to the city center from its limits by horse could take longer than it took to travel to Milwaukee by steam. Despite such little inconveniences, Chicago became a major hub for railroad and airport travel.

1. THE ORCHARD

The congestion of Midway Airport showed the need for a second major airport in Chicago. In 1942, the federal government bought 1,000 acres of surrounding orchard land (the airport's code is still ORD, for Orchard Place Airport) and established the Douglas Aircraft Company, which built C-54 transport planes for World War II. After the war, with the existing infrastructure of streets and railroads along with the open spaces around the land making it perfect for development, city engineer Ralph H. Burke devised a master plan for a commercial airport that would pay for itself. By 1949, the airport was christened O'Hare Airport, in honor of Edward H. "Butch" O'Hare, a World War II flying hero who lost his life over the Pacific in 1942. (An interesting note: O'Hare's father, Edward O'Hare, ran dog-racing tracks for the mob. Not wanting to tarnish his son's name when the younger O'Hare was entering Annapolis, he decided to serve as a government informant and helped bring down Capone on charges of tax evasion. Sadly, he was killed by the mob in reprisal.) By 1960, with parts of the airport still under construction, 13 million passengers passed through. By 1990, 59.9 million a year patronized it. O'Hare Airport has been the source of debate the past few years as Chicago has been battling with surrounding towns to obtain the right to expand the airport. It's uncertain if expansion will go through, but O'Hare will undoubtedly remain a strong player in the industry.

2.   SCHOOL HOUSE ROCK

In the 1920s, many little airports used for airmail service dotted the city. As the airplane industry evolved, the city saw the potential for a commercial airport and began searching for a viable site. They found a site at Sixty-Third and Cicero and the field was dedicated in 1926 as Municipal Airport. There was a slight problem. On land leased from the Chicago Board of Education, a hundred yards from two of the runways, the Nathan Hale School rocked to the sound of airplanes flying overhead. It was decided that when school was in session the two runways would be closed. Eventually, a new school was built elsewhere. By 1940, 700,000 passengers a year passed through Municipal Airport and 1 million four years later, despite wartime restrictions on civilian travel. In 1949, the name of the airport was changed to Midway, but it was having a hard time keeping up with the continuous evolution of commercial flight. The area surrounding it was becoming highly developed, making expansion of the airport difficult, and the larger planes had a harder time landing on the short runways. Then there was the young upstart O'Hare on the outskirts of the city, which was an airport more conducive to modern air travel. For nearly two decades, Midway primarily became a home for private plane traffic. Recent years have seen a revival for Midway as cheaper airfares offered by discount airlines since the 1970s helped bring commercial traffic back to the airport. And the debate over O'Hare expansion has had many people looking toward Sixty-Third and Cicero to help alleviate some of the overcrowding at O'Hare. Perhaps Midway can return to its former glory.

3. THE CABLE CZAR

Charles Yerkes built a fortune through questionable stock trades and political chicanery. He left his wife, the mother of his six children, for a younger woman, and soon created what was considered the world's greatest transportation system. So, nobody's perfect, right? Well, in the eyes of Chicago, Charles Tyson Yerkes was a villain who many would have liked to see run out of town on one of his cable cars. Known as the "Cable Czar of Chicago," he yearned for a mo-

Chicago Historical Society

A horrific traffic jam of streetcars and horse-drawn wagons
on Dearborn Street (looking south) at the intersection of
Randolph Street inside the Loop, circa 1900.

nopoly of the cable car system. Born in Pennsylvania in 1837, by the time he was twenty-five Yerkes opened his own banking house. A financial genius but morally bankrupt, after the recession of 1871 he went to prison for mishandling Philadelphia municipal funds. Pardoned seven months later, he resumed investing in Philadelphia railroads and transit companies and, arriving in Chicago in 1881, he saw opportunity in the city's inefficient streetcar system. From the city, he leased tunnels under the Chicago River that, once de-ratted, cleaned, and renovated, were lined with electric lights and white-glazed tiles. These tunnels avoided the delays of cable cars having to wait as the river swing-bridges opened for river traffic. Initially the electric trolleys made commuters nervous. The overhead wires were unsightly and many feared they would interfere with the work of firemen. For this reason, the trolley was not allowed downtown for years. Instead, commuters taking trolleys to the edge of the Loop paid an extra fare to take a horse car to work.

To ease downtown congestion, Yerkes constructed elevated rail-lines that went down the middle of streets rather than alleys. Initially ill received, the "el" encircling the Loop did ease transportation congestion, but citizens blamed Yerkes for poor service. His arrogant plan to grab what he could from Chicago and run back to his New York mansion didn't help. Joseph Medill of the *Tribune* and Victor Lawson of the *Daily News* went after him regularly, writing up the slightest violation on his cable cars. With the public favoring municipal control of transit lines, Yerkes worked on his monopoly by gaining control of a number of independent street car companies, flooding the city council with bribes to make an end run around various ordinances, and even controlling a block of councilmen whom he hoped would extend his traction franchises for another fifty years. Opposed by Mayor Carter Harrison II, and considered an upstart, he was snubbed by Chicago society. On the day of a critical vote, a mob marched on City Hall, inspiring the aldermen to vote forty to twenty-three against extending his franchise rights.

Fed up, Yerkes sold his traction franchises and ran off to London, becoming instrumental in the creation of its underground. He died in England, in 1905, almost penniless, no longer the Cable Czar of anywhere.

4. YOU DRIVE IT

The founder of Hertz rental car agency was fighting middleweights before he was fighting traffic concerns. Born in Austria in 1879, when John Hertz was five his family moved to Chicago's West Side. Quitting school, he sold newspapers to help support the family, then moved on to copy boy, sports reporter, and finally assistant sports editor. Unemployed when his paper merged with another, Hertz took up boxing, winning amateur tournaments and becoming a middleweight contender, until a friend convinced him that there was money to be made in the burgeoning auto industry. Hertz became a successful car salesman and soon he was co-owner of an automobile agency. In 1907, he turned used vehicles into taxicabs, cutting fares and making taxicab travel, at one time affordable only for the rich, available to the masses. Drivers were to be polite, taxis were to be kept clean, and he promised that the cabs would arrive punctually. In 1915, Hertz began the Yellow Cab Service consisting of seven limousine cars, and smaller yellow cars offered at cheaper rates. Eventually, he was able to establish his own manufacturing plant. In 1924, he began the Yellow Drive-it-Yourself Company after buying a rental firm in 1923. After a year he sold the rental company, along with his manufacturing plant, to General Motors, and in 1929, Yellow Cab was sold to Parmalee System, which was bought by Checker Cab. Decades later, in the early fifties, Hertz's Omnibus Corporation bought back Yellow Drive-it-Yourself and changed the name to Hertz Rent a Car. Hertz wore a number of hats in his life: director of the First National Bank of Chicago, director of Keeshin Transcontinental Freight Lines, and director of Paramount Pictures. He also served as a civilian expert with the Motor Transport Division of the U.S. Army in World

War I, and as assistant in charge of motor vehicles to Undersecretary of War Robert Patterson in World War II, for which he received the Presidential Medal of Merit. Retiring as chairman of the Hertz Corporation in 1955, Hertz died in California in 1961.

5. THE BUS FIRE

For many years, Chicago boasted the largest streetcar system in the country. Convenient, reliable, and affordable, streetcars also lacked maneuverability, something that would play a key role in the horror of May 25, 1950. At the helm of the Green Hornet Streetcar that day was forty-two-year-old Paul J. Manning, who had been involved in at least ten minor streetcar accidents. Chicago Transit Authority (CTA) flagmen were out detouring southbound trolleys away from a flooded viaduct. Driving recklessly fast for conditions, Manning ignored a flagman trying to warn him away from a switch in the track that would lead the trolley into oncoming traffic. Rather than stopping, the streetcar increased speed and kept going. Witnesses reported seeing him raise his arms over his face and scream as the Green Hornet, with thirty-three passengers aboard, sped through the intersection, straight into a tanker truck filled with 8,000 gallons of gasoline. The sparks, as the collision gouged open the steel, ignited the gasoline pouring out and the explosion rang through the entire neighborhood. Walls of buildings collapsed, others were set ablaze by the gasoline. It took two hours and thirty fire companies to bring the inferno under control. It was only then that the true horror was discovered. Bodies, fused together, were piled behind doors that hadn't opened. In the middle of the car was a red knob that, when pulled, opened the center doors enabling several to escape. The back doors didn't open so those who tried to escape from there were crushed. Another factor limiting escape through side windows were steel bars placed over them to keep the passengers from sticking their heads out the window. These bars were eventually ordered removed from streetcars and future CTA buses were equipped with window hatches for easier escape.

6. THE BARNSTORMER

Bessie Coleman wanted to learn to fly but in 1919, if you were black and a female, aviation schools were closed to you. She studied French and went to France to enroll in France's most famous flight school, *Ecole d'Aviation des Freres Caudron* at Le Crotoy. The following September she returned home with the first license ever issued to an African American. Bessie was born in Texas in 1896; her father abandoned the family so her mother worked as a cook and housekeeper while the children picked cotton and took in laundry. Upon arriving in Chicago, Bessie enrolled in beauty school, eventually acquiring a reputation as a manicurist. Her interest in flying came as she listened to the stories told by the World War I airplane pilots whose hands she manicured. Robert Abbott, publisher of the *Chicago Defender*, encouraged her to seek a flight school in France when she was repeatedly turned down in her home country. With the financial aid of African American philanthropist Jesse Binga, head of the Binga State Bank, in June of 1921 she received her pilot's license in France and sailed back a celebrity. Featured on the cover of most black weeklies, she was interviewed by reporters from the *Air Service News, Aerial Age Weekly,* and the *New York Tribune.* Using her savings, she purchased three Army surplus planes and began barnstorming to earn money to open a flying school. Crowds came out to watch the first black female pilot's stunt flying. In 1924, she cracked up in California, but despite a broken leg and minor cuts, she was back in the air as soon as possible. By 1926, with enough funds to open her schools, she decided to do one more show, a Labor Day air show in Jacksonville, Florida, sponsored by the Negro Welfare League. During a morning test run with her mechanic at the controls, she rose to an altitude of 3,500 feet, then proceeded to dive. At approximately 2,000 feet, the plane flipped and Coleman, who wasn't strapped in or wearing a parachute, was thrown to her death. Unable to recover in time, the mechanic was killed upon crash landing. Dead at thirty-two, Bessie Coleman left the world an inspiration to many who came after her.

7. THE 1911 AIRSHOW

In the early days of the century, many had the dream of manned flight, but chasing that dream was a pursuit for the rich. The Aero Club of Illinois, for example, consisted of rich aviation enthusiasts like the McCormick family whose influence helped promote aviation shows. For the Airshow of 1911, hundreds of thousands flocked to Grant Park to watch an international meet of airships and daredevils. It wasn't an overly safety-conscious event. Crowds gathered close to the runways, unattended kids ran around the planes. But all were anxious to get a look at the new planes, including early seaplanes, and the stunt flying. Fans watched amazed as Lincoln Beachey, with an aircraft made simply from a frame with a wing and a pusher engine, flew straight up, a little over two miles above ground, a record-breaker for the time, until his gas ran out and he glided back to earth. On hand were Orville and Wilbur Wright, who studied the planes with keen interest to make sure that none were breaking one of the many patents they had obtained during their work. With the brothers so passionately litigious, the Aero Club found it necessary to settle with them right before the show because every flyer at the show could be sued since the Wright Brothers owned the only patent covering an airplane.

8. THE EL

An elevated train was first proposed in 1869 but wasn't taken seriously until the 1880s, after it was estimated that two people per day were injured or killed on the street-level railroad tracks. In 1892, the city's only elevated railway was built as a freight line to serve the Armour and Company packing plant. The prospect of the following year's World's Fair, however, led to the construction of two elevated railways for

passengers' sake, and the plans for the system closely resembled the modern day el. There were fifty-four unpowered
trailers and eighteen motor cars that had enough power to
pull seven fully loaded trailers, but only four trailers were
used per motor car. Seven doors on each side allowed the
quick loading and unloading of passengers. The ten-cent fair
was a bit steep and acceptance was slow, but as the fair went
on, ridership increased to 27 percent of the fair's attendance.
Closed shortly after the exposition, it still showed how effec-
tively an el system could work. The Metropolitan West Side
Elevated Railway turned to electricity in 1895, but the problem for railway companies was where to build. In 1883, an
act had passed that required the consent of two-thirds of the
property owners along each mile of line before a line could
be opened. Rather than spend money bribing property owners as the cable car companies had done, many railways
bought alleyways or open land and ran the elevated through
that. For property in the Loop where there was no open
space, companies relied on their influence with the City
Council to acquire the street franchises. The more things
changed, the more they stayed the same.

9. UNION STATION

The Pennsylvania Railroad, the Burlington Route, the Alton
Railroad, and the Milwaukee Road all met in Union Station.
In fact that's where the station got its name, in honor of the
union of four major railroads. It was in Chicago, a major railroad hub, that cross-country travelers could transfer between trains without ever having to leave the station. The first
Union Station opened in 1881, but became obsolete as the
city's population and traffic grew. The Chicago Union Station
Company decided to build a new station and between 1914
and 1925 new Union Station was designed with efficiency
and aesthetics in mind. When Daniel Burnham died in mid-
planning process, the job was handed over to Graham, Anderson, Probst and White. World War I shortages hampered
construction and the final result ended up costing much

more than originally expected, but when it was completed it turned out to be one of the largest, most modern stations of the time. Filling ten city blocks, the station is highlighted by the grand-looking waiting room with its wooden benches, pink marble floors, and impressive skylighted ceiling ninety feet off the ground. Fully designed for comfort, there were restaurants, shoe-shine stands, even a police force and hospital. During World War II, in an effort to boost the morale of soldiers, the concourse was draped with war bond murals and the national flags of our allies. In 1969, that concourse was replaced by two office buildings and a modernized concourse. The entire station underwent a renovation during the 1990s, but Union Station's atmosphere has proven perfect for a number of movies like *The Sting*, *My Best Friend's Wedding*, and most notably *The Untouchables*. Even though train travel has dropped off in the past few decades Union Station still remains a vibrant transportation hub for the city.

10. THE SHOWPLACE

Held in McCormick Place, the annual Chicago Auto Show brings in almost 1 million visitors. Over a thousand vehicles, both domestic and foreign, are on display, giving attendees a taste of the past while offering them a glimpse of the future. The latest trends and the latest innovations are premiered at the show. And it's not only cars on display at the auto show. You can also see celebrities (mostly former) promoting their latest project, signing autographs for the thousands waiting in line. The first Chicago Auto Show was held March 23–30, 1901, in the Coliseum. Horseless carriages had been shown at the 1893 World's Fair but few people were interested in the new invention. By the 1901 show, there were between fifty and seventy exhibitors. There was even a makeshift racetrack that circled the area, though many spectators risked their lives crossing the tracks on their way through the show. A hit, the show grew in popularity and was eventually held in the International Amphitheater in 1936. There was a nine-year hold on the show from 1941 to 1950 due to World

War II but by 1953, the Chicago Auto Show was the largest show of its kind. While New York's auto show also began around the same time that Chicago's did, Chicago became the place dealers went to show off their wares. Even Detroit, at one time car capital of the world, was unable to draw the crowds that Chicago did.

Sayings Better Left Unsaid

C hicago has had its share of characters, and they had quite a lot to say on a lot of subjects. The only problem was that often, what they said made no sense at all.

1. LIKE FATHER, LIKE SON

The two Richard Daleys were alike in many ways. Most notably they shared a unique style of phrasing their thoughts. What follows is a bit of wisdom from the House of Daley:

Richard J.: "Gentlemen, let's get one thing straight once and for all. The policeman isn't there to create disorder—the policeman is there to preserve disorder.

"It's amazing what they will be able to do once they get the atom harassed."

"I resent the insinuendos."

"Together we must rise to ever higher and higher platitudes."

Richard M.: "Next year is going to be a very important day for us in Cook County."

"If a rat is on your sandwich, it would help to know it before."

"I'm a proponent of cities going bankrupt."

"No one likes negative. One thing I found out is that negative is negative, and it doesn't say anything positive about the individual."

Now you know why an aide to Richard J. Daley once plaintively commented that the press should "report what he means, not what he says."

2. THE CRACK IN THE WALL

In the wall of Wrigley Field, there's a legendary crack. It was put there by a tank of a man called Bronko Nagurski, a football player for the Chicago Bears. For the first fifty years of its history, the Bears used Wrigley Field as a home stadium. In one classic game, during an unbelievable touchdown run, Bronko Nagurski slammed into two opponents, knocking one out and breaking the shoulder of the other, bounced off a goalpost, then crashed into the wall. Nagurski, who was dazed, but barely, picked himself up and commented, "That last guy hit pretty hard."

3. HONESTY IS THE BEST POLICY

In 1885, Albert G. Spalding, manager of the Chicago White Stockings and a bit of a dictator, decided to have detectives follow a few players to help keep them on the straight and narrow. Responding to one of the detective's reports on him, White Stockings infielder King Kelly commented, "I have to offer only one amendment. In that place where the detective reports me as taking a lemonade at 3 A.M., he's off. It was straight whiskey; I never drank a lemonade at that hour in my life."

4. WORDS TO LIVE BY

Joseph "Pop" Panczko was one of four brothers who worked the wrong side of the law for four decades. They were also known to be four of the most inept thieves ever to brandish a lockpick. One of his pearls of wisdom was, "Never break into a building more than one story tall in case the cops start shooting 'cause if the bullets don't kill you, the fall will."

5. IT'S ALL IN A DAY'S WORK

Al Capone considered himself simply a businessman, no different than a banker or a merchant. After a summit among the various gangster factions, Capone explained the peace agreement made to a reporter by stating, "It's a hard and dangerous work, aside from any hate at all, and when a fellow works hard at any line of business he wants to go home and forget. He don't want to be afraid to sit near a window or open a door . . ."

6. THE VOTES ARE IN

First Ward alderman Michael "Hinky Dink" Kenna had a unique way of determining an election. "First we counted the voters, then we counted the votes." At times, aldermen weren't very cultured. When a suggestion had been made that six gondolas be bought for the Lincoln Park lagoon, Alderman "Little" Mike Ryan suggested, "Why waste the taxpayers' money? Get a pair of them, and let nature take its course."

7. REALISM 101

Jayne Byrne had a no-nonsense approach to life. "If we've got a lemon, I don't want to make lemonade. I'd rather just throw out the lemon."

8. IT'S AN ART

Bertha Honoré Palmer was largely responsible for bringing impressionist art to America. She collected numerous forms of art, and her collection of French Impressionist art was later donated to the Art Institute. In summing up her philosophy of art, she put it this way, "What is art? In my limited conception, it is the work of some genius graced with extraordinary proclivities not given to ordinary mortals. Speaking of art, my husband can spit over a freight car."

9. LOVE IS

The great writer Nelson Algren found affection in both the good and the bad of his city. He once described the feeling as, "Loving Chicago is like loving a woman with a broken nose."

10. **TOO MUCH TIME IN THE SUN**

Of course, baseball players aren't rocket scientists. When future Cub and future Rifleman Chuck Connors signed with the Dodgers in 1939, they gave him a check for $200. His response: "I don't want this. I want money." Cubs pitcher Dizzy Dean once commented, "It puzzles me how they know what corners are good for filling [gas] stations. Just how did these fellows know there was gas and oil under here?" And then there was Cubs pitcher, Guy "The Busher" Bush who explained a train trip he experienced. "I missed my first train because the porters said it was a Pullman, and I didn't know what a Pullman was and wasn't going to take a chance on finding out." Well, at least he could pitch a shutout.

Hauntings

With a town like Chicago, it seems only natural (or supernatural) that she'd have spirits as spirited as the town herself.

1. RESURRECTION MARY

The queen of ghostly legends, Resurrection Mary resides in the village of Justice's Resurrection Cemetery, though no one's really sure who she was or which grave is hers. The legend describes her as a young woman, fond of parties, who was struck by a car on her way to a dance. Since then her ghost, clad in a flowing dress, has walked Archer Avenue, hitching rides from unsuspecting male drivers who drop her off outside the cemetery gates as directed and watch in shock as she vanishes. Eyewitness accounts go back as far as the late 1930s when some young men reported actually dancing with the specter at area ballrooms. She would accept the rides home they offered her, instruct them to drive down Archer Avenue and often disappear from the moving car. She's also been spotted walking in front of cars whose horrified drivers stop to find that the victim has vanished. In the 1970s, Mary may have left a tangible calling card. One day a young woman was spotted behind the cemetery gates, clutching the bars. Police were alerted and what they found was a deserted cemetery and a gate with two bent bars with what appeared to be the impressions of a pair of female hands.

2. BACHELOR'S GROVE

The origin of its name is as mysterious as Bachelor's Grove itself. Settled by a group of bachelors (one possibility for its name) in 1833, over time it's functioned as a homestead, a cemetery, and a spooky sort of lovers' lane. Vandals have broken its tombstones, ripped down signs, and torn open gates. Eventually, authorities declared it off-limits, but vandalism has continued. Stepping into the grove brings about the sense of dread permeating many haunted places. An odd mist, invisible to the naked eye, shows up clearly on photographs. A phantom black car has been seen driving into the area despite a chain across the drive. Colored lights float above the ground and apparitions of dogs, humans, and even a two-headed-giant have been spotted. A phantom farmhouse wanders the grove as well, never reported in the same area twice, disappearing when it's approached. One theory for some of the haunting is that the pond near the grove was rumored to have been used as a victim dumping ground by the mob. Whatever the reason, many consider Bachelor's Grove the most haunted place in the Midwest.

3. ROBINSON WOODS

Andrew Robinson, the son of an Ottawa Indian woman and a Scottish trader, assumed the role of chief of the Potawatomi tribe upon the death of his father-in-law and helped foster peace between area Indians and settlers in the 1820s. In gratitude for his help, the United States gave Robinson a piece of the land obtained from the Potawatomi in the Treaty of Prairie, and he in turn signed away huge portions of land to the arriving settlers hoping to make the inevitable growth of Chicago a smooth one. A portion of the land around River Road and Lawrence Avenue remained in the family until 1955. In 1958, the land was annexed by Chicago to join O'Hare Airport to the rest of the city. The last Robinson descendant had been granted permission to be buried at his ancestral plot, but after his death in 1973 his wishes were denied by the city of Chicago, thanks to the insistence of sanitation officials. This could be the cause of the supernatural unrest. A ball of light can occasionally be seen darting around the lonely woods at night. Recording devices have captured the sounds of beating tom-toms, and people have claimed to hear voices whispering out of the air. There's also been reported the scent of flowers, even in winter. Photographs have captured what appear to be the shadowy visages of Native Americans in the background of the Robinson monument. Is Andrew Robinson trying to take back the land taken from his family?

4. THE ST. VALENTINE'S DAY MASSACRE

On February 14, 1929, gangster Al Capone delivered the notorious Valentine's Day message with brutal efficiency. No one was indicted for the hit, but as George "Bugs" Moran, the intended target, put it shortly after the massacre, "Only Capone kills like that." The SMC Cartage Company garage at 2122 North Clark Street also served as headquarters for Moran's gang. That fateful Valentine's Day a knock at the door surprised seven members of the gang, who thought it was a Chicago police raiding party. Unwittingly, they lined up against the wall, and were mowed down by machine guns. Gory pictures of the dead were splashed across papers nationwide, and the spot remained popular with gangster enthusiasts even after the building was torn down in 1967 to make way for a Chicago Housing Authority senior citizens development. The building may be gone, but the horror of that day seems to be lingering. The spot where the men were gunned down is situated in a yard on the south end of the building. People have reported that their dogs grow extremely agitated when they pass by. One of the slain gangsters had a pet German shepherd named Highball who witnessed the massacre and was so distraught afterward that he had to be put down. Could it be that Highball remains on the spot, his spirit seen only by canine senses? Moaning and sobbing can be heard also, while some who live in the complex have reported visitations by a shadowy figure that could easily be mistaken for a gangster of the 1920s. The psychic unrest seems to have permeated the very bricks of the old garage. When SMC was torn down, collectors who gathered bricks found that their fortunes changed for the worse. Health, financial, and marital problems suddenly struck their lives, leaving them wondering if the bricks they obtained as tokens of history were instead tokens of bad luck.

5. THE BIOGRAPH

On July 22, 1934, John Dillinger was gunned down in the alley of the Biograph Theater on the 2400 block of Lincoln Avenue after having been betrayed by the famous "woman in red," one of his two dates for the night. But was it really Dillinger? Decades later, there is still a creepy feeling about the alley that causes many people to avoid what could be a short cut from Halsted to Lincoln. Those who've experienced paranormal activity in the alley report cold spots, and some have witnessed the apparition of a man running down the alley, falling to the ground, then disappearing. A gangster being gunned down while fleeing the law could produce such a ghostly specter. Yet, according to an eerie theory posed by criminologist Jay Robert Nash, the man gunned down that night wasn't Dillinger but rather a doppelganger set up by the two women. The evidence is convincing. On the night of the shooting, a small-time criminal who bore an uncanny resemblance to Dillinger disappeared. According to the autopsy report, the slain man had brown eyes while Dillinger's were blue. Dillinger's naval records show a man whose heart was in perfect condition, while the corpse revealed a childhood rheumatic heart condition. Further, two scars on Dillinger's body were not on that of his supposed corpse, which was also much shorter and heavier than the gangster was known to be. So what exactly does haunt the place known as Dillinger's Alley: Public Enemy number 1 not willing to give up the ghost, or an unwitting pawn never suspecting he'd have to?

6. THE RED LION

Located on Lincoln Avenue across from the Biograph, the building housing the Red Lion Pub was built in 1882 and has housed, among other things, an illegal betting parlor and a country and western bar. In 1984, Red Lion owner John Cordwell renovated the building and placed a plaque commemorating his late father (who died in England) below the stained-glass window over a stairway. People passing by the window often sense a presence nearby, as if his father's spirit were there to check on his son's venture. Upstairs, bar patrons sometimes pick up the scent of lavender perfume and have reported feeling a tapping on their shoulders only to find no one there when they turn around. Occasionally, when no one is upstairs, there can be heard crashing and stomping. The oddest ghostly game begins when the spirit locks women in the upstairs bathroom. Unless the outside world can be roused to their plight, the women are stuck until the otherworldly allows them out. Also witnessed are the apparitions of a cowboy (possibly the violent former owner of the country and western bar that existed before the Red Lion), a blond man, and a bearded man with a black hat.

7. FLIGHT 191

The crash of American Airlines Flight 191 just outside of O'Hare Airport was considered the worst aviation disaster ever. Two hundred and seventy-one passengers and two people on the ground lost their lives when the Los Angeles–bound plane crashed near a mobile park in Des Plaines. Ghostly encounters have continued sporadically over the years since the crash, especially in the part of the mobile home park near the crash site. Mobile-home owners have reported hearing footsteps outside their houses, sometimes within the house, yet seeing no one there. A directed light appears outside their windows, and indentations sometimes appear in furniture as if someone was sitting beside them. There've also been reports of people answering knocks on doors to find a stranger standing there, inquiring after his luggage, then disappearing when he moves away from the door. What makes this a notable and poignant tale, though, is what started almost immediately after the crash. According to reports from a number of houses in the far northwest corners of the city, people were roused to their doors by footsteps, doorbells, and knocks only to find no one at the doors upon opening them. This went on for weeks. Were these visitors lost and confused souls torn suddenly and violently from life?

8. THE EASTLAND

The Eastland tragedy of 1914 left psychological and psychic scars on Chicago. Two places in particular are said to be supernaturally affected by the watery disaster. The *Eastland* docked at the Clark Street Bridge at Wacker where the hapless passengers boarded, expecting a day of picnicking fun. When it capsized in the Chicago River, there was only terror and death. Cross the bridge during the hot months, especially in July, and you may hear moans, screams, and wild splashing: a taste of the horror that erupted that day. And when you look into the river you may see the nebulous shapes of poor souls unable to find rest. The majority of the 844 bodies fished from the river were taken to the Second Regiment Illinois National Guard Armory on Randolph Street and Washington Boulevard. There, in light of the summer heat, they were immediately embalmed and laid in rows to be identified by the grieving relatives lined up outside. The old armory may have had a facelift inside and out to turn it into Oprah Winfrey's Harpo Studios, but according to reports, some energy may linger from the days when the spot was used as a makeshift morgue. Even after hours loud crashing, clinking glasses, laughing, running children, and doors opening and closing can be heard. There's also the scent of flowery perfume, while the ghostly apparition of a sobbing entity known as the "Grey Lady" was seen on security cameras, floating through the halls. She wears a long flowing dress with a large, fancy hat: the female dress for a 1914 picnic. Oprah herself admitted that she felt the building was haunted and wouldn't stay after hours. Is the Grey Lady a victim of the tragedy replaying the motions she went through before the ship capsized? Or is she, perhaps, a loved one who came to collect the dead, fated forever to wander the halls of Harpo Studios, reenacting one of the saddest duties a Chicagoan was ever forced to bear?

9. EXCALIBUR

Once the home of the Chicago Historical Society, nearly a century later the building at 632 N. Dearborn has become the home of the Excalibur Club, a linchpin in one of the city's most popular tourist areas. Across from the Hard Rock Cafe and near the Rock 'n' Roll McDonald's, the castlelike structure is built from granite that seems to change color, from gray to a deep brownish red, depending on the amount of light there is. The building began its nightclub career in 1985 as the Limelight and stories began circulating about strange phenomena taking place there. Glasses would fall, items would move, the sounds of dragging could be heard in the downstairs storage room, and, long after closing, employees would sometimes hear their names being called. In 1989, the Limelight became the Excalibur Club but the hauntings continued. Every day for a week after opening, one of the bars would be found strewn about, and a light-blue shape was once observed running up the stairs. The Chicago Historical Society's first home on the site was destroyed during the Great Chicago Fire in 1871. The fire's all-consuming nature made it difficult to keep records of fatalities during the fire. Is it possible that some unfortunates who perished in the historic blaze have remained?

10. INEZ CLARK

Sometimes, the allure of a haunting lies not in the facts we know but in the mystery that remains. Inez Clark is such a mystery. Graceland Cemetery is the home of some remarkable monuments to notable dead, but one of the most intriguing markers is that of little Inez Clark, a young girl buried there in 1880. Little is known about her life or death, and the cemetery has no information on how she really died. One story is that she was struck by lightning during a family picnic. In their love for their lost daughter, Inez's parents commissioned a life-size statue of the child to be sculpted for her grave. The child sits on a chair, holding a parasol, her elegant hat resting on her shoulder. To protect it, the statue has been encased in a glass box. Over the years, security guards and other witnesses have reported that, while making their rounds, they've noticed the Inez Clark statue missing from the glass case. Later, the statue would be back again. Some reports have the statue missing and the glass case filled with fog, even on nonhumid nights. One wonders if Inez is playing the sort of pranks she might have played if time had been on her side.

Bibliography

There's a wealth of information on this fascinating city. The Chicago Historical Society has a host of interesting records and photos. Also helpful were the following books:

Bernstein, Arnie. *Hollywood on Lake Michigan: 100 Years of Chicago and the Movies.* Chicago: Lake Claremont Press, 1998.

Bielski, Ursula. *Chicago Haunts: Ghostlore of the Windy City.* Chicago: Lake Claremont Press, 1998.

Bielski, Ursula and Hucke, Matt. *Graveyards of Chicago: The People, History, Art and Lore of Cook County Cemeteries.* Chicago: Lake Claremont Press, 1999.

Bolotin, Norm. *The World's Columbian Exposition.* Washington, D.C.: Preservation Press, 1992.

Chicago 1968 (videorecording). Boston: WGBH; Distributed by PBS Video, 1995.

DeBartolo, Joseph A. *The Original Chicago Trivia Book.* Chicago: Sasparilla, Ltd., 1985.

Dybwad, G. L. *Chicago Day at the World's Columbian Exposition.* Albuquerque: The Books Stop Here, 1997.

The Eastland Disaster (videorecording). Kenosh, WI: Southport Video, 1999.

Flammang, James M. and Frumkin, Mitchel J. *World's*

Greatest Auto Show: Celebrating a Century in Chicago. Iola, WI: Krause Publications, 1998.

Hill, Libby. *The Chicago River: A Natural and Unnatural History.* Chicago: Lake Claremont Press, 2003.

Johnson, Curt and Sautter, Craig R. *The Wicked City: Chicago from Kenna to Capone.* New York: De Capo Press, 1998.

Karamanski, Theodore J. *Maritime Chicago.* Chicago: Arcadia, 2002.

Spinney, Robert G. *City of Big Shoulders.* DeKalb: Northern Illinois University Press, 2000.

Kaczmarek, Dale. *Windy City Ghosts.* Alton, IL: Whitechapel Productions Press, 2000.

Klineberg, Eric. *Heat Wave: A Social Autopsy of Disaster in Chicago.* Chicago: University of Chicago Press, 2002.

Ledermann, Robert P. *Christmas on State Street: 1940's and Beyond.* Chicago: Arcadia, 2002.

Lindberg, Richard. *The Armchair Companion to Chicago Sports.* Nashville: Cumberland House; Kansas City, MO: Distributed to the trade by Andrews and McMeel, 1997.

Lindberg, Richard. *Chicago by Gaslight: A History of Chicago's Netherworld.* Chicago: Academy Chicago Publishers, 1996.

Lindberg, Richard. *Return Again to the Scene of the Crime.* Nashville, TN: Cumberland House, 2001.

Lindberg, Richard. *Return to the Scene of the Crime.* Nashville, TN: Cumberland House, 1999.

Mark, Norman. *Mayors, Madams and Madmen.* Chicago: Chicago Review Press, 1979.

McFarlane, Brian. *The Blackhawks.* Toronto: Stoddart, 2000.

Miller, Donald L. *City of the Century: The Epic of Chicago and the Making of America.* New York: Simon & Schuster, 1996.

Paden, Ann. *I Bought It at Polk Bros: The Story of an American Retailing Phenomenon.* Chicago: Bonus Books, 1996.

Platt, Harold L. *The Electric City: Energy and the Growth of the Chicago Area, 1880–1930*. Chicago: University of Chicago Press, 1991.

Sachare, Alex. *The Chicago Bulls Encyclopedia*. Lincolnwood, IL: Contemporary Books, 1999.

Sahlins, Bernard. *Days and Nights at the Second City*. Chicago: Ivan R. Dee, 2001.

Skilnik, Bob. *The History of Beer and Brewing in Chicago*. St. Paul, MN: Pogo Press, 1999.

Young, David M. *Chicago Aviation: An Illustrated History*. DeKalb: Northern Illinois Press, 2003.

Young, David M. *Chicago Maritime: an Illustrated History*. DeKalb: Northern Illinois Press, 2001.

Young, David. *Chicago Transit: An Illustrated History*. DeKalb: Northern Illinois Press, 1998.

Index

About the Author

Laura Enright works as an editorial assistant for the North Shore editions of Pioneer Press newspapers and in the circulation department of the Park Ridge Library. She lives in Park Ridge, Illinois.